The best of **Britain**

Northern Ireland

Mal Rogers

Contents

The Guide

Photo Essays

Introduction

Perched at the very edge of Europe, Northern Ireland is a land apart – British yet strikingly different from Britain; on the island of Ireland yet not Erin; Celtic certainly, but Calvinist and Catholic in almost equal measure.

A once troubled land border marks the western and southerly terrestrial limitation of the Six Counties; tumultuous oceans and great sea cliffs guard the northern and eastern maritime frontiers. The land is dotted with ancient stone remains – ever-present reminders that this is the seat of an age-old tradition, home to a once brilliant Celtic civilisation, and for centuries one of the most important ecclesiastical centres in Europe. The landscape of the North of Ireland – scarred by millions of years of belligerent weather – is home to Neolithic graves, cairns and dolmens some 5,000 years old; the Giant's Causeway, in Antrim, is arguably even older, going back to the time when banshees, monsters and giants roamed the earth.

Ireland, as an island, has always operated to its own distinctive pulse. The only part of Europe not to have fallen under the Roman yoke, it developed along different lines from the rest of the continent – the city of Armagh with its great monastery and learning centre was a model for early communities. It remains a hauntingly ancient place to visit. The distinction between Ireland and the rest of Europe lives on, seasoned now by influences which drifted over to this north-westerly outpost – Celts, Vikings, Normans, Scots, Huguenots, Quakers, Catholics – and whatever you're having yourself, as they say in the best pubs. Ulster was the last Gaelic stronghold of Ireland, the last part of Europe to remain largely free of outside influence – until about 400 years ago.

You'll soon spot the different pulse of life here if you pop in to a traditional music session in Belfast, go along to a hurling match deep in the rural fastness of Tyrone, or merely stop to ask the way in Fermanagh. Talk will run free, for here on the westerly fringes of Europe is one of the last strongholds of the art of conversation. Whether it's a pint at the local, or chatting with your B&B hosts, a major discourse is always in danger of breaking out. The area's romantic sight-seeing routes take their place alongside the most famous in the world: driving along the Causeway Coastal Route, walking through the Mountains of Mourne or cruising through Lough Neagh provide more eye-popping views than you could reasonably shake a camera at.

An alternative Northern Ireland exists too, a less well-known one, of hidden byways, secret gardens and mystical castles. Lady Dixon Park in Belfast, with the Lagan running broad and clear beside the rose gardens, or Castlewellan Forest Park with its ornamental lakes and haughty swans in the shadow of an outrageous faux castle – both offer days of languid serenity. But then it's easy to get a thrill from the natural things in life here. The National Trust administers some of the most strikingly beautiful – and least visited – stately homes and gardens in Britain or Ireland. This complex, volatile, beautiful, bombastic place comes with a delicious irony: if you want to experience old Ireland, Ireland as she used to be, don't bother with the Lakes of Killarney or the castles of Bunratty or Blarney. Instead, head for a land where tourists haven't ventured for over 40 years, a land of lavishly spectacular glens and mountains, quiet rural backwaters, and warm welcoming people – in other words the British part of Ireland, Northern Ireland, the Six Counties, Ulster. Whatever you're having yourself.

Northern Ireland has scenery, music, sport and culture, the equal of anywhere. But perhaps most important of all, people here still have time to bid you 'the length of yer days'. Deep in the bogland country of Tyrone locals will pull their car over to say, 'Grand ould day all the same', while in Belfast, asking the way can turn into a minor social occasion. One of the central paradoxes during the very darkest times of the Troubles, and one which international journalists would comment on regularly, was how two sets of people could

be so extraordinarily welcoming to outsiders, while being murderously uncivil to each other. Of course, as a concept, friendliness is difficult to quantify; it's something you instinctively sniff in the air. But if your definition of a holiday includes the words 'conviviality', 'cordiality' or 'craic' – then this corner of Europe has to be high on your list of destinations.

The North of Ireland's recent history has certainly put people off journeying across the Irish Sea, but it has one of the lowest crime rates in Europe. As for the full sweep of history – well, never mind too much about the recent past. The country's dolmens and Megalithic tombs will give you some 6,000 years of the stuff. The archaeological record left by the ancient forebears testifies to their superb eye for beautiful, often dramatic locations, and their subtle, indeed enigmatic, aptitude for engineering. These Neolithic monuments are as sophisticated as they are intriguing – and there's not a county without them. That's before you even consider the next few thousand years' worth of bloody history and the mark it made on the land.

As for scenery, the region has charms aplenty to cast a spell over you. Get yourself a set of waterproofs and hiking boots and get out there to experience a countryside as breathtaking and ancient as any in the world. Have the craic with locals and feast your eyes on a landscape so grand that to paraphrase the old song, it'll steal your heart away.

Unmissable highlights

01 Slieve Donard

Wander along the 4-mile long strand of Newcastle, County Down, dominated by Northern Ireland's highest peak. This is where 'the Mountains of Mourne sweep down to the sea', p. 266

02 Tyrone's standing stones

Stop off at the Creggan Visitor Centre and ask for directions to the 44 monuments 'of prehistoric significance' within a 5-mile radius of the centre. Neolithic tombs, cairns, and standing stones, p. 331

03 St Patrick's Grave

You get three saints for the price of one at St Patrick's Grave in Downpatrick. Ireland's other two patron saints, St Brigid and St Colmcille, according to legend, also lie here, p. 227

04 The Causeway Coastal Route

Also called the Antrim coast road – reckoned today to be one of the most spectacular routes in the world, it's regularly put in the same company as the San Bernardino Pass in the Alps or the Monterey-Carmel coast road, p. 97

05 The Ring of Gullion

A textbook example of an extinct volcanic ring-dyke system, the Slieve Gullion range was recently described by Laurence Llewelyn-Bowen as simply 'one of the most beautiful places in the world', p. 165

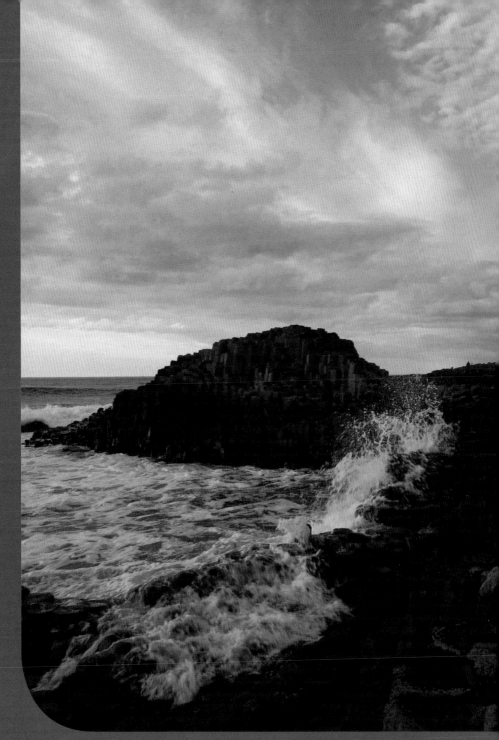

06 The Giant's Causeway

For centuries a geological wonder known only to kelp gatherers and shepherds, the 40,000 columns of basalt are today one of Ireland's three UNESCO World Heritage Sites, p. 96

Bobby Sands MP

07 Belfast murals

The republican murals in West Belfast have been 40 years in the making and are certainly impressive. In a spirit of even-handedness, see if you prefer the loyalist murals in East Belfast. But keep the verdict to yourself, p. 75

08 Devenish Island

This island in Lough Erne, some 4km from Enniskillen, has the most extensive remains in Northern Ireland of early Christian settlement, complete with round tower, monastery and shrines, p. 297

09 Bushmills Distillery

Whiskey is a Gaelic word, so no surprise about its long history in Ireland. Treat yourself to a dram in the world's oldest distillery in Bushmills, p. 101

10 The Walls of Derry

Enclosing the world's most northerly Roman Catholic city, the blood-stained history of this haunting city is etched in these old walls, among the most complete anywhere in Europe, p. 183

Secret
Northern Ireland
Local recommendations

01 The Hermitage
Tollymore Forest Park, County Down – The gothic follies of Tollymore stirred the muse in C S Lewis and Edward Lear, it could do the same for you, p.268

02 The Entries, Belfast
The Entries, a cluster of narrow alleyways or closes running off High Street and Ann Street, are all that remain of Belfast's oldest quarter. The pubs here are second to none for drinking, conversation or traditional music, p.73

03 Traill Monument
On leaving Bushmills Distillery, get your designated driver to stop at the nearby Traill Monument. Its stones appear to swell and contract before your very eyes. It's not the drink, only an obscure law of physics in action, p.102

04 Road bowling, County Armagh
The ancient sport of road bowling takes place in the quiet, leafy lanes of rural South Armagh. Heavy betting is not unknown at these events, you never know, you might underwrite the cost of your holiday, p.172

05 Pettigo

See how a town functions with an international border running through its centre. Pettigo straddles the border with the Irish Republic between Fermanagh and Donegal, p.307

06 Inch Abbey, County Down

Inch Abbey, a ruined Cistercian monastery, stands at a bend on the River Quoile. The Abbey was built with a view upwards toward Down Cathedral and St Patrick's Grave, p.231

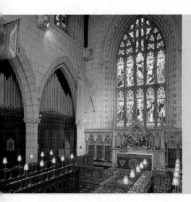

07 St Columb's Cathedral

Derry's oldest building, St Columb's Cathedral, was completed in 1633. The shell case that contained the encircling Catholic army's terms of capitulation in 1689 resides here; the riposte has echoed down the centuries, 'No surrender', p.186

08 Tayto Castle, Tandragee

County Armagh is the very home of flavoured potato crisps. Cheese 'n' onion crisps were first dreamed up by Tayto founder Joe Murphy (the original 'Spud' Murphy) more than 50 years ago, p.158

09 Peatlands Park

Tyrone is blanketed by bogland over much of the county, but at Peatlands Park you get a chance of walking through this unique, beautiful ecosystem on boardwalks, p.348

10 Shannon-Erne towpath

Walk, cycle or hire a pony to meander along the towpath of the Erne-Shannon waterway in County Fermanagh, p.297

Factfile

01 Bushmills is the oldest distillery in the world, still servicing the thirsty folk of Ireland after 400 years.

02 The world's most famous boat since Noah's Ark, the *Titanic*, was built in Belfast.

03 *Chronicles of Narnia* were written by Belfast man C S Lewis. Much of his inspiration came from places such as the Mountains of Mourne and Slieve Gullion.

04 A volcanic outcrop behind Belfast reputedly inspired the story of Gulliver in Lilliput. The author, Dublin man Jonathan Swift, regularly passed Cave Hill en route to his parish in Kilroot.

05 Belfast can claim one of the few airports in the world named after a footballer – the George Best International Airport.

06 Oscar Wilde went to school in Portora in Enniskillen, as did Samuel Beckett, while Seamus Heaney and Brian Friel went to school in Derry, and Katie Melua went to school in Belfast.

07 Ulster was the last Celtic stronghold anywhere in Europe. After Ulster fell in the 17th century, Gaelic-speaking peoples were steadily pushed to the westerly fringes of the continent, including Bretons, Galicians, Welsh, Manx, Cornish, Scottish Gaelic and Irish speakers.

08 Lough Neagh is the largest lake in Britain or Ireland, bordering five of the six counties.

09 The *'red sails in the sunset'* in the eponymous song written by Omagh man Jimmy Kennedy were actually white sails caught in the sunset off Portrush.

10 County Antrim is home to one of Ireland's three UNESCO World Heritage Sites, the Giant's Causeway.

THE FACTS

WHEN TO GO

One of Ireland's foremost meteorologists, the late Austin Bourke, noted: 'In Ireland we are spared disastrous weather extremes which plague other lands. We are not afflicted by hurricanes, tornadoes, duststorms, avalanches, torrential rains, or really disastrous floods, killing drought or fatal extremes of heat or cold. One could also add no snakes, no mosquitoes, no poison ivy. It is virtually unique to find a countryside in which one could walk so freely with so little menace from anything – other than man.'

The temperate maritime climate of Northern Ireland is marginally milder than most parts of Britain. Despite its northerly latitude, snow is uncommon except in the highest mountain areas such as the Mournes or Sperrins, while in summer temperatures are unlikely to top the mid twenties. In January, the average daytime maximum in Belfast is 6.5°C (43.7°F), just about the warmest place in the world on this latitude at this time of the year and 17.5°C, (63.5°F) in July.

Most of the Six Counties have significant rainfall – being hilly and close to that huge weather machine called the North Atlantic means that on average it is marginally wetter than Britain. It tends to be a bit damper in the west than the east, although cloud cover is persistent across the region. The western counties of Fermanagh and Tyrone can be particularly wet – in Fermanagh it can tip it down two days out of three; unfortunately you can't tell in advance which two. Rain is as likely in the middle of August as in the depths of winter. The damp climate, plus the extensive deforestation Ireland suffered in the 16th and 17th centuries – along with the fact that alone on this latitude the ground is not covered with snow in the winter months – has resulted in much of Northern Ireland being carpeted with lush green grassland. In other words – it doesn't get that green by accident.

The weather is unpredictable at all times of the year, and although the seasons are distinct, they are considerably less pronounced than in interior continental regions. Having said that, spring and summer are good times to visit Northern Ireland for one simple reason – daylight lasts much longer in these northerly latitudes than further south. In summer time Belfast officially has 'astronomical twilight' all night – which basically means it doesn't get properly dark till well after 10pm. In places such as Derry on the north coast it's even later: you could be playing football on the beach until gone 11. And if the rain sets in you could install yourself in a cosy pub, order up a few pints, and listen to the rain turning the landscape even greener.

GETTING THERE

By air

There are two international airports in Belfast and one in Derry. Dublin Airport is also a practical arrival point – coaches from Dublin to Belfast depart every half hour, run throughout the night, are cheap and comfortable and take just over two hours. The drive-time from Dublin Airport to the border is about an hour.

Both Belfast airports are well served by Ireland's two main airlines, Aer Lingus (www.aerlingus.com) and Ryanair (www.ryanair.com), as well as easyJet (www.easyjet.com), BMi (www.bmibaby.com), Flybe (www.flybe.com),

ManxAirlines(www.manxairlines.com),Jet2.com (www.jet2.com) and flyglobespan (www.flyglobespan.com). If you have deep pockets – or are just wantonly extravagant – Woodgate Executive Air Charter (☎ 028 9442 2478; www.woodair.com) will fly you and your family to any airport in the Six Counties.

Dublin Airport is similarly well served, with services to Britain every half hour or thereabouts – over 40 airlines land in Dublin; over 30 at the two Belfast airports and Derry Airport.

Flights depart from almost all main cities in Britain to Northern Ireland – but Heathrow, Gatwick, Stansted, Luton, Glasgow, Bristol, Edinburgh, Liverpool, Aberdeen, Manchester, East Midlands and West Midlands airports have daily, frequent flights.

It's worth noting that the George Best International Airport is within Belfast city limits; Belfast International Airport is some 18 miles north of the city. So if you are on a short break to Belfast city, try to opt for George Best International – if you are heading for the Derry or Antrim coasts, go for Belfast International or Derry Airport.

Several budget airlines serve Northern Ireland, including Ryanair, easyJet and Aer Lingus (the latter now regards itself as a no-frills carrier). As with all low-cost airlines, if you book early, avoid school holidays and travel any time except Fridays, Sunday nights or Monday you will get the best deals. Bearing that in mind it's possible to get a return flight from Britain to Belfast or Dublin anywhere from £25 to £40.

By ferry

Ferries ply the Irish Sea from Stranraer and Cairnryan to Belfast and Larne; from Liverpool and Birkenhead to Belfast, from Fleetwood to Larne, and from Troon to Larne. The shortest route is Cairnryan to Larne, taking just an hour.

Another alternative is the Holyhead to Dublin car ferry. Land at Dublin Port or Dun

---

CAR HIRE FROM NORTHERN IRELAND'S AIRPORTS

Several major British and European car hire firms are variously available at airports and city centre:

- **Budget Car Hire** – Belfast International Airport ☎ 028 9442 3332; Belfast City Airport ☎ 028 9045 1111.

- **Avis Car Hire** – Belfast International Airport ☎ 028 9442 2333; Belfast City Airport ☎ 028 9045 2017; Derry Airport ☎ 028 7181 1708.

- **Herz** – Derry Airport ☎ 028 7181 1994; other ☎ 0878 44 88 44.

- **National Car Hire** – Belfast International Airport ☎ 028 9073 9400; Belfast City Airport ☎ 028 9073 9400.

- **Europcar** – Belfast International Airport ☎ 028 9442 3444; Belfast City Airport ☎ 028 9045 0904; Derry Airport ☎ 028 7181 2773.

Laoghaire and drive time to Belfast is just over two hours. (Dublin Port, served by Irish Ferries, is closer to the North, as you don't have to cross the city.)

Some useful websites are:

- www.stenaline.co.uk
- www.norsemerchant.com
- www.irishferries.com
- www.poferries.com

Fares for car and one adult start around the £65 mark one way; for a return fare from one of the Scottish ports to Larne or Belfast with two adults and two children, fares begin at around £250. However, various cheaper deals (some including accommodation) are available.

GETTING AROUND

By car

In general, traffic conditions are very good. Even driving through Belfast (outside rush hour) is relatively painless, and parking near the centre is still a practical option. In rural areas you are unlikely to experience any traffic disruption, and parking is usually free (and easy) except in the very biggest towns such as Enniskillen or Ballymena.

The most iconically scenic routes are through the Mountains of Mourne and along the Causeway Coastal Route in County Antrim (which just edges into County Derry). Keep heading for Derry city via Castlerock and Downhill and you will pass some of the finest beaches on the island.

Any drive through rural Northern Ireland will take you through primeval, rugged landscape that inspired such disparate talents as Jonathan Swift, C S Lewis, Seamus Heaney, Van Morrison, Snow Patrol and Edward Lear. Rolling hills, heather-clad mountains and idyllic waterways are a feature throughout the region. Along the way you will come across ancient folklore, tall stories – and back-breaking history.

By public transport

Public transport in Northern Ireland (outside the main cities) is not terribly comprehensive or convenient. Northern Ireland Railways (www.nirailways.co.uk) only runs trains to Derry, Dublin (via Newry and/or Portadown), Coleraine and Portrush, Bangor and Larne. The whole of the region west of the Bann has no rail links.

Translink (www.translink.co.uk) runs an integrated rail and bus service on behalf of Ulsterbus and Northern Ireland Railways. Ulsterbus Tours coaches visit all of the North's tourist sites and destinations (☎ 028 9033 7004 or 028 9033 7004; www.translink.co.uk/ulsterbustours) or visit Ulsterbus Tours, The Travel Centre, Europa Bus Centre, Belfast BT12 5AH.

CROSSING THE BORDER TO THE IRISH REPUBLIC

Crossing the border to the Irish Republic – whether driving, walking, cycling or on horseback, requires no ID. The UK and Ireland together make up the Common Travel Area, so that legally you are not required to have paperwork or passport to cross the international frontier.

Further, Ireland and Britain are alone in Europe in that legally you don't have to prove who you are when stopped by the police. Not that you will be stopped anyway, because in practice there is no border. If you cross even county boundaries in England, there will be something saying 'Welcome to Surrey' or the like. In the border areas of the Six Counties all you get is a sign which says 'Speed limit in kph' if heading south (or west), and mph in the other direction.

Today, most of the people living along the border are Catholic. Many of those on the northern side are keen to show their allegiance with the South. When an American tourist visiting the borderlands asked how he would know if he was in Northern Ireland or the Republic of Ireland he was told: *'Watch for the flags – if you see lots of Irish tricolours, then you'll know you're back in the British part.'*

Although these areas were once a byword for civil strife and mayhem, today they are peaceful and, no matter what your accent, you will find nothing but friendliness. And you definitely won't need a passport or visa.

10... things and places to avoid

1 **You should avoid, at all costs, venturing up Shankill Road** – Belfast's Protestant heartland – wearing a Celtic top. This also apples to Irish tricolours and Palestinian flags – in this polarised community, every dispute has its sectarian bias. Thus Irish nationalists always support Palestine, and loyalists Israel.

2 **The opposite also applies to journeying up Falls Road in Belfast,** the main Catholic enclave. Things to avoid: Rangers top, Union Jack, Star of David flag.

3 **The university flatland area in Belfast, around University Street, Rugby Avenue, etc** – after closing time. Scenes of devastation will assail you. Long-term residents have now formed an association to force university authorities to clean up their act. Or at least the people under their nominal control.

4 **The Elim Christian Centre** – Alexandra Park Avenue, Tiger's Bay, Belfast. Situated in one of the grimmest areas of north Belfast, this is an area sorely challenged by the ravages of drugs, unemployment and poverty. Despite this, it has been described as a Protestant Lourdes, a place of astounding miracles – but it's actually more akin to US Christian television channels. Recently claimed the credit for bringing back to life a dead man, which, should it prove true, is impressive enough.

5 **Coleraine should be a lot more interesting than it actually is** – it was here (or just up the road) that the first prototype Irish people first arrived some 9,000 years ago. The prosperous town has therefore had plenty of time to come up with a bit of craic – but the reality is that after 6pm, the town is closed. Visitors are hard-pressed to find anywhere decent to eat and, far worse, anywhere decent to drink.

6 **BBC Radio Ulster of an afternoon** – after the illuminating Talkback programme (12–2pm) which you shouldn't miss if you want a handle on Northern Ireland affairs, it's wall to wall country and Irish music with the odd bit of oul' homespun craic. Excruciating stuff.

7 **A Gaelic football match** – hurling yes, a national treasure, and well worth the effort to see a game but Gaelic football is pretty dire, and more often than not merely consists of localities settling old scores.

8 **The Giant's Causeway during the height of the tourist season** – wait until a November Tuesday morning just after dawn.

9 **Craigavon** – Northern Ireland's effort at creating a new capital for the region, a sort of Ulster Brasilia if you will. It didn't work.

10 **Any golf course with 'Royal' in its title** – among the oldest and finest courses in the world. They're also among the most exacting and expensive.

ACCOMMODATION

Accommodation in Northern Ireland has, in many parts of the jurisdiction, not reached the same degree of sophistication as in the Republic. Indeed, the North is often described as being *'just like the Republic of Ireland, only unfurnished'*. Good hotels are available, however, and there are a handful of really special places to lay your head for the night.

A logical rule of thumb is – the greater the population, the more chance of imaginative digs. You won't find many boutique hotels in west Tyrone, where a 'good-sized town' will be anywhere with a population which struggles to top 500. However, you will almost always find a friendly **guesthouse or B&B**; you're never likely to be stuck. Note however, that your host or hostess is likely to know what time you left the pub at. *'Ach, I was there too,'* you will be told. *'I kept my eye on youse. And when you headed home I knew it was time for me to get home too, so I did. Sure didn't I have yer breakfast to make.'*

Belfast has a couple of five-star establishments where the manager won't be trying to gauge whether you are night birds or not; same goes for the several four-star hotels about the town, plus a handful of boutique hotels.

It's possible to stay in **castles**, **cottages**, **former gatehouses**, **crofts**, **lighthouses** and **clachans** – traditional farm settlements with cottages and farm buildings huddled together for shelter. Some, such as the clachan, that makes up accommodation at An Creágan, blend so beautifully with the landscape that you will not want to leave the close environs of the settlement for the rest of the holiday.

For **hotels**, www.centralr.com carries some first-class deals for Northern Irish hotels. www.lastminute.com is also good for Belfast hotels. Self-catering in Northern Ireland is a good option, with a wide range of **cottages** **and apartments** for rental throughout the Six Counties. Many of these that we've selected are situated near activities of particular interest to visitors – angling, hill-walking, watersports or equestrianism. All are geared to deal with inclement weather, and offer good value – particularly for families or groups of friends. Good websites to check for alternatives are:

- www.cottageguide.co.uk/Northern_Ireland
- www.4ni.co.uk/38538 × 569 × 6_rural-cottage-holidays-belfast.htm
- www.holidaycottages.cc/northern-ireland/

Camping and caravanning is well-developed. The Forestry Service has well-maintained sites, and there are several private sites throughout the region. For further information visit:

- www.forestserviceni.gov.uk/index/activities/caravanning-and-camping-in-northern-ireland-forests.htm
- www.discovernorthernireland.com/accomfinder/
- www.camping-ireland.ie/links.html
- www.caravancampingsites.co.uk/nireland/nireland.htm
- www.eurocampings.co.uk/en/europe/great-britain/northern-ireland/
- www.go4camp.co.uk

FOOD AND DRINK

Walter Raleigh is credited with having introduced the potato to Ireland in the 16th century, and soon **prátai** (**potatoes**) spread throughout the country. Still called praties in parts of the Six Counties, they are an ever-present guest at any dinner in the region. If you are self-catering and want to sample a local variety, you could scarcely do better than stop at one of the many farmers' stalls which line the roads advertising 'Ulster queens', 'Kerr's pinks' or 'Ulster chieftains'.

10... special self-catering cottages

1 Coole Cottage, Belleek, Fermanagh – a traditional cottage in the equally traditional village, p. 306

2 Enniskillen Townhouses & Apartments, Drumclay, Fermanagh – a great base for visiting Enniskillen, p. 292

3 Devenish Villa Holiday Homes, Garrison, Fermanagh – excellent base for fishing and canoeing. Also praying, as the holy island of Devenish, just nearby, has been welcoming pilgrims for centuries, p. 292

4 Sophie's Cottage, Derrylin, Fermanagh – luxurious cottage in a rural area which will be reliably languid and uneventful. Bleak chic at its best, p. 319

5 An Creagán, Creggan, Omagh, Tyrone – demurely beautiful rural cottages in the heart of old Tyrone; you won't want to go home, they'll have to evict you, p. 339

6 Gortin Accommodation Suite & Activity Centre, Gortin, Tyrone – the eponymous activities range from hill walking to orienteering, p. 339

7 Slieve Croob Inn, Castlewellan, Down – one of the finest sites to stay in the country, with stunning views of the Mourne Mountains, p. 277

8 Hanna's Close, Kilkeel, Down – a beautifully restored traditional 'clachan', or gathering of cottages and barns, p. 277

9 Black Gap Farm, Armagh – below the radar of most tourists, this is just the place for living at one with nature, p. 173

10 City Resorts – in the heart of Belfast's shopping and restaurant area, and within easy reach of the city centre, p. 88

The best... hotels and B&Bs

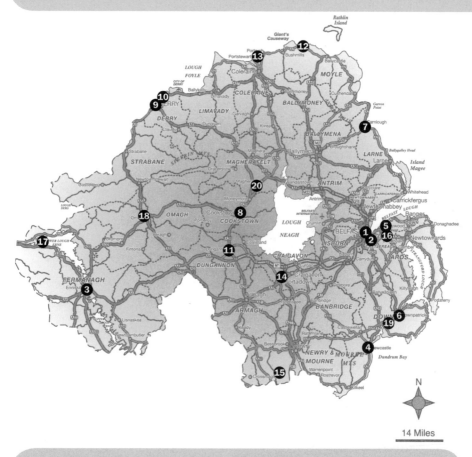

14 Miles

Hotels

1. The Malmaison – loaded with artistic merit and cutting-edge design, p. 69
2. The Europa – one of the most famous hotels in Europe, p. 69
3. Lough Erne Golf Resort boasts a Nick Faldo designed golf course, p. 290
4. Slieve Donard Resort & Spa – a wonderful old railway hotel, now a five star spa resort, p. 277
5. Culloden Estate and Spa – five-star luxury on the banks of Belfast Lough, p. 88
6. Denvir's Hotel – one of the oldest hotels a few hundred yards from the grave of St Patrick, p. 241
7. Londonderry Arms – a fine old hostelry overlooking Carnlough harbour, p. 118
8. The Tullylagan Country House Hotel – set in beautiful countryside, p. 353
9. Everglades – magnificent views of Derry from this ultra-modern hotel, p. 194
10. Tower Hotel – award-winning, stylish, four-star hotel located within Derry's walls, p. 194

B&Bs

11. Grange Lodge – full of character, you can even learn how to cook here, p. 353
12. Whitepark House – the landlord here has won the AA Landlady of the Year Award, p. 105
13. Maddybenny Farm House – Rosemary White's enormous breakfasts are legendary, p. 206
14. The Bleu Apple – award-winning guesthouse set in the midst of 2 acres of gardens, p. 147
15. Adrigole – excellent value B&B in the heart of South Armagh, p. 173
16. Beech Hill – gracious living for the price of a B&B, p. 194
17. Lusty Beg Island, Boa Island – on an island in a lough in Fermanagh, p. 306
18. Golden Hill Guest House – luxury B&B with panoramic views over four counties, p. 338
19. The Mill At Ballydugan – lovely old converted mill, p. 241
20. Brooke Lodge – 3-star guesthouse in the heart of Derry, p. 217

Berries, too, sold at the roadside, can be particularly succulent. When the Vikings first landed here blackberries sustained them; likewise the Scottish settlers. The latter, it is alleged, wouldn't eat potatoes as they're not mentioned in the Bible. So the Presbyterians turned to blackberries and blaeberries, which gave them blue noses. To this day Protestants are often referred to as Bluenoses, and Northern Ireland in general as 'the Wee Black North'.

Northern Ireland in general has never been held in particularly high esteem for its cuisine. Drink yes, dinner no. But in the last couple of decades standards have risen out of all recognition from the days when a salad might have been the cold chips left over from the night before, or an hors d'oeuvre would more than likely be a ham sandwich cut up into tiny pieces. Today, local produce – including the finest of **seafood and freshwater fish** – is served with panache and imagination, and without chips. Of course the great Northern standby, vernacular bread, is available everywhere – **potato farls**, **wheaten bread** and **soda bread** are a truly unique culinary experience, and different to and better then that available in the Republic. Oh, and those chips are still on the go actually, with Northern Ireland boasting some of the finest chippers on the planet.

The North of Ireland, because of its climate, grassland and the expertise of its farmers, produces some of the healthiest animals and tastiest meat in Europe. Beef, lamb and pork are of the very highest quality. The Northern Irish particularly love **bacon**, **sausages**, **black pudding** and **white pudding**. The latter two, made with state-of-the-art offal, are both mentioned in James Joyce's *Ulysses* – and surely no higher recommendation is possible. Perhaps because of this great liking of porcine products, sayings connected with pigs have a positive connotation – rather than negative – in Northern Ireland. To be 'on the pig's back' is to have been the recipient of good luck, while to be 'as happy as a pig in shite' is a wholly enviable situation to find yourself in.

There's even a traditional poem – which you will regularly hear recited – extolling the admirable nature of the pig:

Twas an evening in November
And I very well remember
I was walking down the street in drunken pride.
My feet were all a-flutter,
So I landed in the gutter
And a pig came up and lay down by my side.
Yes I lay there in the gutter
Thinking thoughts I could not utter
When a colleen passing by did softly say,
'Ye can tell a man who boozes
By the company he chooses'
At that the pig got up and walked away.

The pig, of course, has never been implicated in the distilling of illegal whiskey (note: Irish spelling is 'whiskey' not 'whisky'). The potato is the main culprit here. **Poitín** (also spelt poteen and potcheen) has been distilled from the root vegetable since time immemorial. Should you happen to catch out of the corner of your eye bottles of lemonade being sold at a farmers' market for anything between £5 and £10, well, you may be sure it's not lemonade.

Today the exquisite taste of Northern Ireland's local produce has been used as the basis of a culinary renaissance, and while most top restaurants are to be found in the cities, fine dining is possible in every county.

Cuisine may be at an innovative exciting stage of development. The ethos of drinking is similarly at an exciting stage, one that it has occupied for centuries. County Antrim is home to the oldest distillery in the world – **Bushmills** has been making the 'cratur' officially since 1608, unofficially much longer, and in the hillsides round about, even longer. Outlets for the silky, smooth drink are easy to find, including the likes of the Crown Liquor Saloon in Belfast, acknowledged as one of the world's great drinking establishments.

The best... Northern Ireland pubs

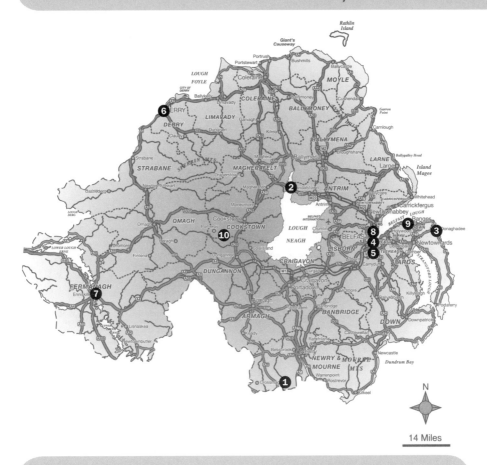

1. **Welcome Inn** – hosts one of the longest running traditional Irish music sessions anywhere, p. 174
2. **Crosskeys Pub** – a key venue for traditional music for over half a century, p. 129
3. **Grace Neill's Inn** – officially the oldest pub on the island of Ireland. Customers have included Franz Liszt (Brahms, disappointingly, couldn't make it), p. 235
4. **Crown Liquor Saloon** – undoubtedly one of the world's great pubs. Partly decorated by men building the Titanic – accounting for some strange marine artefacts, p. 73
5. **Kelly's Cellars** – one of the oldest pubs in Belfast, this was a meeting place for the United Irishmen in the 18th century, plotting to change the course of Irish history, p. 73
6. **Peadar O'Donnells** – one of the best places for traditional music in the north west, p. 193
7. **Blakes of the Hollow** – the exemplary author John McGahern described this as one of the happiest and most beautiful bars in the whole of Ireland. No further comment necessary, p. 295
8. **John Hewitt** – arguably among the finest bars in the whole of Great Britain and Northern Ireland, and probably nowhere better to argue about it than over a pint here in the heart of old Belfast, p. 71
9. **The Old Inn** – eponymously old indeed, with a history stretching back 400 years, p. 262
10. **Quinn's Corner** – a family-run pub in the heart of Tyrone, p. 351

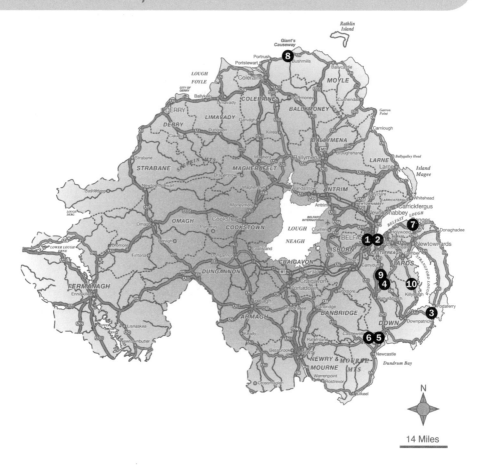

1 The Kitchen Bar – traditional Northern Irish cuisine, and the home of the paddy pizza, p. 72

2 Deane's – Northern Ireland's only Michelin-starred restaurant, p. 72

3 The Lobster Pot – serves the best seafood anywhere, with the eponymous lobster taking the starring role, p. 244

4 The Pheasant – traditional cuisine served with brio, p. 242

5 The Buck's Head Inn – highly regarded, imaginative restaurant, p. 279

6 The Mourne Seafood Bar – takeaway and sit-in, everything from seafood to freshwater salmon, p. 278

7 Coyle's, Bangor – innovative cooking on Northern Ireland's 'Gold Coast'

8 The Distillers Arms – in the shadow of the world's oldest distillery, the Arms is the perfect place to stop off for a meal – you can even stay for a day or two, p. 106

9 The Plough Bistro – serving the great and good in Northern Ireland's governing town

10 Balloo House – one of Northern Ireland's favourite restaurants, p. 243

Caffrey's Irish Ale, a robust cross between a stout and an ale, is brewed by the Thomas Caffrey Brewing Company (formerly Thomas Caffrey & Son, established in 1897). The perceived smoothness of Caffrey's is due to its low level of carbon dioxide. It's available throughout Ireland.

FESTIVALS AND ANNUAL EVENTS

Whether your interests lie in comedy, music, theatre, busking, drama, film, food – or merely getting quietly drunk – you will find a gathering to suit your taste. Warning: romance is a likely by-product of any festival visit in Ireland – after all, the ingredients are all there. Northern Ireland is a sexy country these days – it has the music, the scenery, the culture, the whiff of cordite – there are even those who find the slightly aggrieved accent very sexy: so it's a great place to meet people.

Northern Ireland boasts some truly esoteric festivals, such as the **Red Sails in the Sunset** bash, where you will hear more versions of Jimmy Kennedy's song than you could reasonably shake a conductor's baton at. Everything is on offer from opera to oysters and from gigs to gags. Festivals are frequent and all-encompassing – traditional music at the **West Belfast Festival** where you can join in, horse-trading (and much more) at the **Ould Lammas Fair** at Ballycastle. You are more than welcome to join in the horse-trading auctions – just remember though, that a nod in the wrong place could mean you trying to get a string of ponies on board your no-frills flight back home.

The **Belfast Festival** is one of the longest established festivals in these islands, while the **Halloween Festival** in Derry is reckoned to be the biggest in the world. Mind you they've had plenty of practice – Halloween has been celebrated in this neck of the woods since pre-Christian times. Halloween, or the Celtic new year, is a product of Ireland and Scotland.

The biggest social event in the farmer's year is the **Royal Agricultural Society Show** in May (held in Belfast) with demonstrations ranging from shearing a sheep to ploughing a straight furrow. The national ploughing championships are taken very seriously, with world championship qualifying events taking place. To show you how seriously it's taken – champion ploughmen now have their own photogenic WAGs whose photographs appear in the Ulster *Tatler*.

HALLOWEEN

Halloween has been taken very seriously in Ulster, and throughout Ireland, since the ancient Celts – and probably the people who came before them. A more-than-usually virulent dose of occult action could be expected round this time, with spirits a-visiting on Samhain Eve – for this was the appointed time when the souls of the dead returned to their old haunts.

The ancient Celtic year began at Samhain, now Halloween, when cattle had been brought in from their summer grazing; this was the time when spirits ran free between this world and the Otherworld. With the harvest in, Samhain Eve, the last day of the year, became a huge celebration. The great fire was kept burning and a feast was laid out so that the ghosts would find a welcome. It also seems that carousing, licentiousness and excessive behaviour played a part in proceedings.

With the arrival of the Christians, things were toned down a bit. 1 November became All Saints' Day, in honour of all saints, known and unknown, and Samhain was transformed into All Hallows Eve. However, pagan Celtic customs of Samhain lingered on, unchanged by Christianity (or commercialism) until well into the last century. Up until the 1960s, Halloween in Ireland – particularly in the north – was as big a celebration as Christmas, if not bigger. St Patrick's Day was barely celebrated at all, except as a Holy Day of Obligation. But craic? Forget about it.

Of course Halloween had a huge start on Christmas. Despite the Church's best efforts to stamp out the old pagan ways, the Celtic influence has managed to hang about for several thousand years. Halloween has proved to be as evergreen as those ancient Celtic holy trees – holly and ivy. Jack-o'-Lanterns, now a familiar sight once again in Ireland, come from a Celtic legend about Jack of the Lantern, a man who could enter neither heaven nor hell and was condemned to wander through the night with only a candle in a turnip for light – nowadays more likely a candlelit pumpkin. There's also a belief that candles which flicker on Halloween night have been touched by the spirits of dead ancestors.

All these customs headed to the USA from Ireland (and Scotland) in the 19th century – taken by emigrants – where they slowly took hold, gradually being reinvented for the American market. The commercialism of Halloween began to develop in the USA as early as the 1930s. Halloween was also helped on by another Irish influence in America. A civil servant from Dublin, Bram Stoker, wrote the most enduring horror story of all time – Dracula. The motifs from this novel now adorn Halloween – vampires, counts with capes, witches and undead spirits. And yet, according to many learned authorities, all that Bram Stoker was getting at was the semi-feudal order maintained by the Ascendancy in Ireland, both North and South, before reform came.

The Celts used to say that Fear is sharp sighted. It sees things in the dark that aren't even there. The Bible, on the other hand, cautions its followers to avoid things that go bump in the night. *'Have no fellowship with the unfruitful works of darkness, but rather reprove them,'* it says in Ephesians. The problem is, as any ancient Celt will tell you, lots of exciting things happen in the dark as well. Especially on this day, the one time of year when we give official recognition to death and the spirit world.

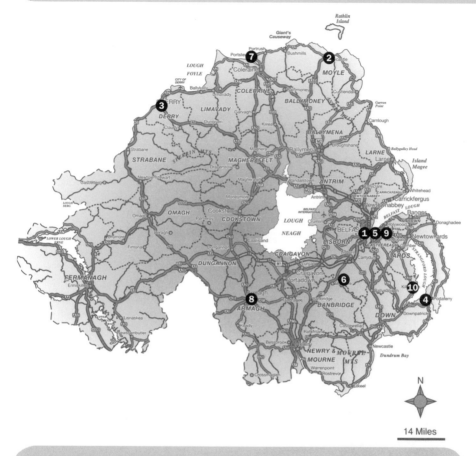

14 Miles

1 Féile an Phobail – also known as West Belfast Festival (centred round the Falls Road). Set in the heart of the nationalist area of Belfast, traditional music, dance and storytelling take their place alongside international artists, p. 89

2 Ould Lammas Fair – one of the oldest, most famous festivals on the island, with everything from horse-trading to Irish dancing, p. 117

3 Halloween Festival – Derry's Halloween festival is reckoned to be the biggest in the world, and lasts five Bacchanalian days, p. 191

4 Festival of Opera – just the place if you know your arias from your elbow, p. 224

5 Belfast Festival – highly respected, international festival, p. 67

6 Oyster Festival – the biggest bivalve binge outside Galway (the world leaders in oyster scoffing). Set in the lovely village of Hillsborough, this is where to see Northern Ireland's society at play, p. 258

7 Red Sails Festival – you will, of course, hear many versions of Jimmy Kennedy's biggie; but you will also get plenty of entertainment for children (and quite a bit for adults too), p. 204

8 The William Kennedy Piping Festival – one of the greatest gatherings of pipers you will come across – everything from the traditional (uillean) pipes through to the bombarde from Brittany, p. 159

9 12 July Orange marches – widespread but high concentration in Portadown and East Belfast. Lambeg drums, flute bands, accordion bands, pipe bands, lots of bowler-hatted (mostly) men marching up and down. It's a great day out, although you may find the politics a bit perplexing, p. 64

10 Killyleagh Magnus Barelegs Viking Festival – a festival celebrating this corner of Ireland's Viking, Danish and Norse influences, p. 240

TRAVELLING WITH CHILDREN

Coming to a rainy place might make you wary as regards travelling with children. But the very fact that inclement weather often threatens means that just about every town (if not village) has some organised provision for children's indoor entertainment. Aside from that, most accommodation – particularly self-catering cottages – has comprehensive drying facilities. As they say in Ireland – there's no such thing as bad weather – only bad clothes.

Watersports are well catered for – canoeing, boating, sailing, rafting, fishing – and for learning to ride a horse there can be few better places. Multi-activity centres throughout the region utilise the terrain of Northern Ireland for supervised rock-climbing, orienteering, paintballing, laser skirmishing, bouldering, mountain boarding, caving, etc.

The older children may also be bitten by the enormous bug that is Irish traditional music – either learning to play an instrument or dance like they do on *Riverdance*.

SPORTS AND ACTIVITIES

Horse riding

The two things which kept the cognoscenti coming to Northern Ireland from all over the world during the bleakest times of the Troubles were fishing and horses. The rich lime soil of Ireland produces some of the finest horses in the world, and the North is home to the oldest race course in Ireland – Downpatrick – with claims to being the oldest still in continual use.

Every type of equestrian sport is covered in Northern Ireland – from pony-trekking in the hillside to learning how to show-jump. Just about every town is within easy distance of an equestrian centre. People from ages 6 to 80 come to equestrian centres nestling between drumlins, or by the shores of the

Irish Sea to learn how to ride. The top sites for riding include the East and West Strand in Portrush, Portstewart Strand, Florence Court Forest Park in County Fermanagh, Greyabbey Estate in County Down, Murlough Nature Reserve and Newcastle Beach in County Down, Tollymore Forest Park in County Down and near enough anywhere in the Sperrins in Derry/Tyrone.

Recommended equestrian centres include:

* **Mount Pleasant** – ☎ 028 4377 8651; www.mountpleasantcentre.com
* **Peak Discovery Group** – ☎ 028 4372 3933; www.pd-group.eu
* **The Forest Stables** – ☎ 028 8952 1991

Fishing

Lough Erne, Lough Neagh, the River Bann plus myriad smaller loughs, rivers and streams – not to mention the Irish Sea and the Atlantic Ocean – are all available for every type of angling. For details of licences etc., visit www.dcal-fishingni.gov.uk.

Walking

In Ireland in days gone by walking was never regarded as a sport – it was something you did for want of a donkey. This has all changed now, of course. The Ulster Way, the best know trail, is 560 miles long and wends through the area's most iconic sites (www.geographia.com/northern-ireland).

Derry's mixture of beaches that go on forever and tranquil glens are ideal for everything from a saunter (or dander as they call it in these parts) to a bracing power walk. Tyrone's **Sperrins**, designated an Area of Outstanding Beauty, are threaded with mountainous valleys, streams, forests and shady glens, trails, tracks and quiet laneways. With its rich cultural heritage etched on the landscape, this is the perfect place to explore on foot. The Central Sperrins Way is way-marked for 30 miles.

Fermanagh is best known for its angling and watersports, but this magical and mystical

The best... things to do with children

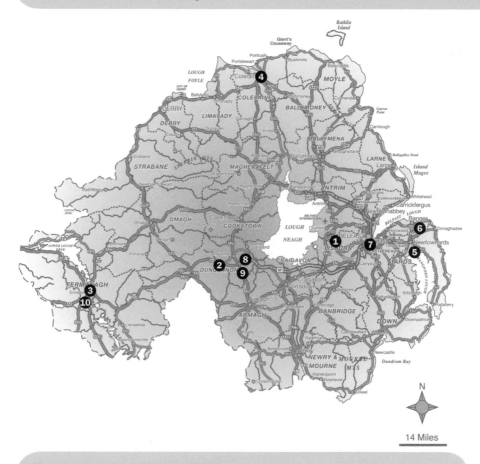

1. W5, Belfast – a vastly entertaining, interactive, scientific discovery centre, p. 86
2. Toddsleap – quad biking, paint-balling, archery, canoeing etc among 100 acres of picturesque countryside, p. 351
3. Corralea Activity Centre – water trampoline, windsurfing, dinghy sailing, canoeing, kayaking, banana skiing etc, p. 316
4. Benone Tourist Complex – situated on one of the finest strands in Ireland, the tourist complex includes paddling pool, various play areas, two outside heated pools (seasonal), adventure play area, p. 188
5. Ark Open Farm – a haven for rare and endangered species of domestic animals; children can come face to face with animals they're likely only to have glimpsed before, p. 257
6. Pickie Fun Park – just about Northern Ireland's favourite children's venue, featuring everything from go-karting to adventure playgrounds, p. 257
7. Auntie Sandra's Candy Factory – old-time sweetie-making at its best, p. 85
8. Armagh Planetarium – meet the stars using the world's most advanced digital projection system, p. 155
9. Loughgall Country Park – all sporting facilities, plus adventure trails and play areas, p. 143
10. The Lakeland Forum – the biggest leisure complex in the west of the Six Counties, with swimming pool, soft play areas, sports hall (badminton, squash) plus a variety of water sports, p. 290

area with its spectacular waterscapes is an enchanting place to stroll or hike. One of the finest places to walk is **Castle Archdale Country Park** (see p. 300). Armagh's prime walking area is better known by the world's geologists than by hikers. **Slieve Gullion** is a centre point of a former volcano torn apart by a massive explosion some 60 million years ago, leaving behind a textbook example of what's known as a ring-dyke system; however the turf-covered trail making up the **Ring of Gullion Way** twists its way through this spectacular volcanic landscape, and is prime walking territory.

Antrim offers a range of spectacular walks, along incomparable coastline scenery as well as fertile upland. The **Causeway Coast Way**, stretches from Portstewart (in County Derry) to Ballycastle; en route you pass through the Causeway Coast Area of Outstanding Natural Beauty, a World Heritage Site and several areas of Special Scientific Interest. County Down's walking areas can be summed up as summits and seas. The **Mountains of Mourne** make up one of Ireland's most spectacular hiking and climbing areas, and uniquely for a mountain range, most of the summits are grouped together in an expanse only 7 miles wide. The 26 mile **Mourne Way** is almost entirely off-road as it traverses the foothills of the Mournes from Newcastle on the Irish Sea to Rostrevor on Carlingford Lough. A spellbinding route.

Other outdoor activities

For **climbing** courses the Tollymore Mountain Centre (☎ 028 4372 2158; www.tollymore.com) provides qualified instructors who will have you scaling the craggy peaks of the Mournes – such as the Crooked Chimney on the Bernagh Slabs or the Pot of Legawherry just beyond the Blue Lake. The Peak Discovery Group covers various locations in Northern Ireland (☎ 028 4372 3933; www.pd-group.eu).

For action-packed holidays, including climbing, canoeing, orienteering and sailing, the region's multi-activity centres are an excellent way of sampling what the area has to offer. These include:

- **Action Outdoors** – ☎ 07789 754 565; www.actionoutdoors.info
- **Xplore Outdoors** – ☎ 07734 365 321; www.xploreoutdoors.co.uk
- **Corralea Activity Centre** – ☎ 028 6638 6123; www.activityireland.com
- **Share Holiday Village** – ☎ 028 6772 2122
- **The Outdoor Fox** – ☎ 028 7779 295 299
- **Activities Ireland** – ☎ 07971 087 480
- **Bluelough Adventure Centre** – ☎ 028 4377 0714

Specifically for **aquatic activities**, Craigavon Watersports Centre has superb facilities on Lough Neagh (☎ 028 3834 2669; www.craigavonactivity.com). For general information on activity holidays visit www.outdoorni.com. The Countryside Access & Activities Network (☎ 028 9030 3930; www.outdoorni.com) can organise everything from sky-diving to cycling.

Watching sport

For those interested in spectating, the North of Ireland can provide a handful of sports to be found in few other places: **hurling**, Gaelic football, court handball and road bowling. These are all promoted by the Gaelic Athletic Association (GAA) – its website (www.gaa.ie) will guide you to the prime events. President of Ireland Mary McAleese (originally from Belfast) recently attempted to describe hurling to an audience of foreign citizens thus: *'Imagine hockey played by maniacs.'* She went on to say that hurling is the fastest field sport in the world, adding that it is also the most skilful. Although stopping short of giving a quick demonstration, President McAleese's assessment of the 15-a-side game was fairly accurate.

Gaelic football is somewhat less exciting, being a hotch potch of rules which has resulted in a game that is a hybrid of rugby, soccer and American football. Partisanship levels at matches are high, and even if you are not particularly into sport, witnessing

The best... activity destinations

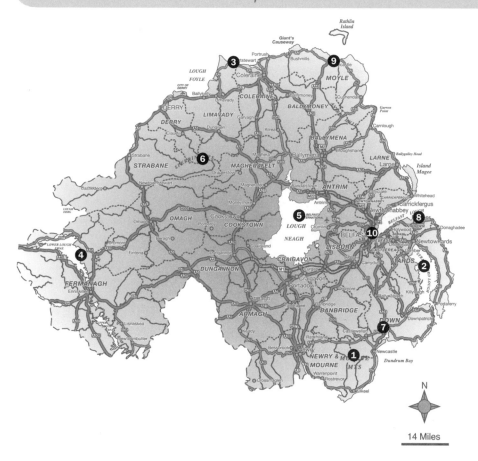

14 Miles

1 Mountains of Mourne – rock-climbing, hill-walking or prospecting for Mourne Diamonds (worthless in financial terms, priceless in the search for the dark smoky quartz) , p. 264

2 Benone Strand – now recognized as one of the finest surfing spots in Europe, p. 188

3 Strangford Lough – one of Europe's prime bird-watching spots, p. 231

4 Lower Lough Erne – a nirvana for anglers of all ages and abilities, p. 297

5 Lough Neagh – the biggest freshwater lake in Britain or Ireland, ideal for cruising, sailing and fishing, p. 347

6 Sperrin Mountains – hill-walking terrain with the added bonus of some of the oldest stone constructions in Europe, p. 211

7 Tullymurray – horse-riding in the superlative drumlin country of County Down, p. 275

8 Bangor – learn how to helm, crew or captain your own dinghy, p. 248

9 Ballycastle – Northern Ireland has some of the finest links courses in the world, including Ballycastle on the north coast, p. 112

10 Casement Park – the region's main Gaelic Athletic Ground; try to catch a grudge match such as Tyrone versus Armagh, p. 66

a local derby can be an exciting affair. The principal GAA stadium, Casement Park in Belfast, is home to senior Antrim Gaelic football and hurling teams. Named after one of the participants of the 1916 Easter Rising, Sir Roger Casement, the ground has a capacity of 32,600. For fixture information and tickets consult the GAA website.

Northern Ireland **football** isn't a particularly pretty sight and still tends to be somewhat riven with sectarian undertones. The main international ground is Windsor Park, also the home of club side Linfield. The ground just about manages to meet international standards as required by FIFA and UEFA. For fixtures visit (www.irishfa.com). **Ice hockey** draws support from both sides of the community – the Belfast Giants can be seen in action at the Odyssey (www.belfastgiants.com).

Rugby has always been the big sport within the Protestant community, although somewhat bucking all expectations, its top performers play in an all-Ireland international side – a united Ireland team. For years the Irish international side was made up from Ulster Protestants, Dublin public schoolboys and fanatical Limerick players. Today the game is more evenly spread out across both jurisdictions.

The Ulster side, former European champions, performs at Ravenhill Park in Belfast. For tickets and fixtures list visit www.ulsterrugby.ie.

FURTHER INFORMATION

Tourist information

The region's official tourist information organisation is Northern Ireland Tourism (www.discovernorthernireland.co).

Local media

Northern Ireland is served by several local radio stations. The most widely listened to is BBC Radio Ulster (FM94.5, AM1341 www.bbc.co.uk/radioulster) for weather, events and plane delays, etc. Radio Foyle (FM93.1, AM792) serves the Derry area, while Downtown Radio has several local stations including:

- FM96.4 (Causeway Coast)
- FM96.6 (Enniskillen)
- FM97.1 (Larne)
- FM103.4 (Newcastle, Down)
- FM102.3 (Ballymena)
- FM102.4 (North-west Northern Ireland)
- FM103.1 (Newry, Newry and Mourne)
- FM103.4 (South Down Coast)

The area is also served by all the main BBC stations (Radio 1, 2, 3, 4 and 5), as well as the main Republic of Ireland stations RTE1 and RTE2.

Northern Ireland has three main daily newspapers. The *Belfast Telegraph* is the main middle class unionist paper (although owned by a company in the Republic), and is read, to some extent, by both communities. It carries comprehensive theatre, cinema, concert and restaurant listings, as well as festival news. The *Irish News*, with a Catholic perspective, has similarly comprehensive listings, but concentrates on 'nationalist' activities – Irish dancing, ballad sessions, traditional music, ceilis, Irish language courses, Gaelic games etc. The *Belfast Newsletter*, the oldest English language general daily newspaper still in publication in the world, first rolled off the presses in 1737. Staunchly Protestant, its editorial stance has softened somewhat over the past decade. But this is the newspaper for details on Orange marches and Ulster Scots festivals, as well as more mainstream activities such as soccer and horse-racing.

All of the English dailies are widely available throughout the Six Counties. Some have a 'local' edition, with entertainment listings included. All the Irish papers are available in all nationalist areas and most mainstream newsagents. Only the *Irish Times* carries listings of events in Northern Ireland. Most areas have at least a couple of local newspapers – this being a divided community, each side tends to have its own newspaper.

THE BACKGROUND

HISTORY

Prehistory

The very first inhabitants of Ireland arrived some 9,000 years ago, fetching up somewhere near Coleraine. Immediately house prices went through the roof. Or so the locals like to joke ...

From these few hundred settlers – who almost certainly arrived from Scotland – the indigenous population grew. You can visit the site of their first landfall in Mount Sandel (p. 200), the bucolic scene today giving no hint of the back-breaking history which took place nearby: the running battle between Edward the Bruce of Scotland and the Red Earl of Ulster in 1315, the murderous insurrection involving the MacDonnells in 1584, or the massacre at Portna in 1641; events which are still controversial today.

However, the happy untroubled band of fledgling Ulster folk who landed in 7,000BC had a few thousand years of 'stone-age affluence' before their peace was shattered. At the time Ireland was almost completely wooded: a red squirrel could have watched the s un go down on Galway Bay before making his way comfortably from the west to watch the Mountains of Mourne sweeping down to the seas in the east – all without his little claws ever touching the ground. So the aboriginal Irish had plenty of game to eat (particularly if they liked stewed squirrel), had wood for shelter and fuel, and animal hides to keep them warm. They were hunters and fishers, without agriculture but with plenty to eat, and presumably happy with their lot in life.

Rudimentary farming began with the Neolithic era – the new Stone Age – when somebody, somewhere announced that there was work to be done. This spoilsport ensured that, indeed, work was done, and it didn't just stop at farming. Huge stone dolmens, court graves, standing stones and chambered vaults – with few contemporaneous competitors elsewhere in Europe – were built. The exact function of all these early rock groups is unknown, but we can assume some attempt to communicate with the we-know-not-what. They can be seen throughout the region but are particularly numerous in Tyrone and South Armagh.

The Celtic era

The Celtic era began around 500BC or 600BC, the exact origin of Celts being the subject of some academic debate, not to mention chit-chat at the local pub. After all, 600BC isn't that long ago in Northern Ireland terms. (One of the most innovative – albeit tongue-in-cheek – proposals by Peter Hain, former Secretary of State for Northern Ireland, was the proposed introduction of a 'date fine'. Any Northern Ireland politician, he argued, should be fined every time they mentioned an inflammatory date, e.g. 1690 for the Battle of the Boyne, 1969's Civil Rights March, 1014 – the defeat of the Danes by Brian Boru. The further back you went, argued Secretary Hain, the bigger the fine should be.)

The arrival of the Celts is a fraught subject. According to legend, the Gaels were the last tribe of Celts to appear in Ireland, Armagh their main sphere of activity. To this day the people of Armagh (or at least the Catholic variety) pride themselves on being the 'most Celtic' in all Ireland. The fact that the Armagh Gaelic football side is one of the strongest on the island only supports this belief (see p. 164).

Scholars and historians are coming increasingly to the conclusion that the Celtic civilization was not the creation of a separate race but a language, a culture, a way of life that spread from one people to another. Archaeological research shows little evidence of formidable invasion into Ireland during the period the Celts were reputed to have arrived en masse. Rather, a steady infiltration from Britain and Europe, plus an interchange of ideas, seems to be a more likely scenario. A constant melding of language, custom and beliefs took place, and the Gaelic civilisation – to survive independently in Ulster for the longest period of time – developed not just from the Celts but from the people who occupied Ireland from the earliest times.

The arrival of Patrick

'I am Patrick, a sinner, the simplest of country men ... was taken into captivity with ever so many thousands of people.' It is with these words, in Latin and found in the Book of Armagh, that written Irish history begins.

The monks of St Patrick's Church recorded not only the missionary work of their head man, but also the rivalry, not to say open warfare, among the various tribes now inhabiting Ulster. At that stage only the monks built capably with stone, their monasteries icons of eternity in the midst of a disposable world of mud and wattle housing. The monks' handiwork can still be seen throughout the island, especially notable in the tall graceful round towers built to withstand Viking raids that continued from the 9th to 10th centuries.

The Normans

Until 1169, Ulster belonged to the High Kingship of Ireland. Then Henry II, best known outside Ireland for his one-liner about a turbulent priest, decided he needed a powerbase to the west. When the Normans first arrived in Ireland they had little luck in subjugating the northern tribes and clans which made up Ulster. The area where the Anglo-Normans' writ ran was known as The Pale. Everything beyond that, more especially the Ulster 'savages', was 'beyond the Pale', a possible origin of the phrase.

The Vikings merely made a nuisance of themselves; the Normans changed the landscape forever. Today there are few counties on the entire island that don't boast a few Norman ruins, castles or keeps – probably the most striking north of the border is that in Carrickfergus (p. 124). It was the Normans who introduced the county system into Ireland. The GAA – which runs all their competitions on an inter-county basis – will be forever grateful (although it will continue to keep quiet about it!).

The early modern era

The 16th century dawned, and it was an auspicious century for Northern Ireland – which hadn't been invented yet. But for the first time it looked on the cards. Queen Elizabeth was becoming increasingly concerned about the threat of a Spanish attack on England via Ulster. Accordingly she attempted to subjugate Hugh O'Neill, Earl of Tyrone, and de facto boss of Gaelic Ulster. He was ably abetted by the Scottish Catholic MacDonnells, who had progressively entrenched themselves in County Antrim, consolidating the Scottish character of much of Ulster even before the Plantation.

James 1 succeeded Elizabeth and made a better job of bringing Ulster's Gaelic leaders to heel, eventually banishing them to the Continent in what was known as the Flight of the Earls. 'I will abandon all further attempts at extending my territory in the north, and undertake that my people adopt English laws and customs,' said Hugh O'Neill, agreeing in London to a ceasefire in hostilities in 1590, before finally abandoning Gaelic Ireland's last bastion.

Ulster was subsequently 'planted' with tens of thousands of Scottish settlers – plus

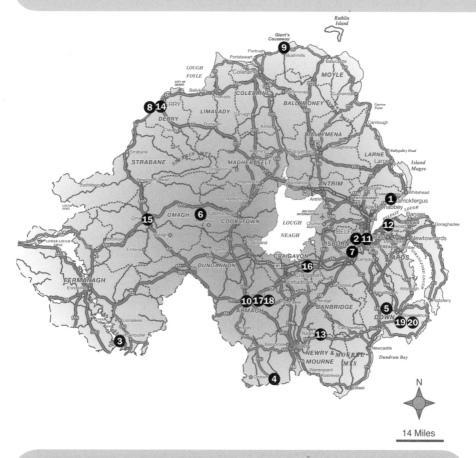

14 Miles

N

Historic sites

1. Carrickfergus Castle – this medieval castle is the very model of impregnability, p. 124
2. Parliament Buildings, Stormont – beautifully over-the-top, jack-the-lad building, p. 80
3. Crom Castle – a plantation stronghold built in 1611, p. 314
4. Kilnasaggart Standing Stone – the oldest Christian field monument in Ireland, p. 168
5. Legananny Dolmen – a 5,000-year-old megalithic burial site, p. 254
6. Creggandeveskey Court Tomb – a well-preserved court tomb dating back 3,000 years, p. 330
7. Milltown Cemetery, Belfast – the last resting place of some of the iconic names in Republican history, p. 79
8. Walls of Derry – some of the best preserved medieval walls in Europe, p. 183
9. Dunluce Castle – overlooks the Atlantic Ocean with operatic grandeur, p. 99
10. Armagh Observatory – they've been star-gazing in Armagh for over 1,500 years, p. 151

Museums

11. Ulster Museum – Ulster's history, culture and natural history examined in some detail, p. 62
12. Ulster Folk Museum – shows how Ulster developed socially, p. 247
13. Brontë Homeland Interpretative Centre – explores the Brontë link with County Down, p. 257
14. Tower Museum – traces Derry's history from the early days through to Bloody Sunday, p. 185
15. Ulster American Folk Park – documents the American connection with Ireland, p. 332
16. Museum of the Royal Enniskillen Fusiliers – an essential destination for anybody interested in military history, p. 288
17. Armagh Planetarium – state-of-art, astronomy central, p. 155
18. St Patrick's Trian – examines Armagh's ancient history, including St Patrick's influence, p. 156
19. Down County Museum – surveys Down's history, p. 237
20. The St Patrick Centre – the principal exhibition on the life and times of the Apostle of Ireland, p. 228

SOME COMMON ULSTER WORDS AND EXPRESSIONS

- **wee** – literally small, but its use is ubiquitous as a term of description; also 'Wee folk', the fairies
- **aye** – yes
- **craic** – a Middle English word which lasted longer in Northern Ireland than anywhere else. Originally spelt (and still pronounced) 'crack', it has been somewhat hijacked – with its spelling changed – by tourist boards, drinks manufacturers and theme pubs. But it's still going strong up north, and means free-wheeling fun, or merely 'What's happening?' as in 'What's the craic?'
- **weans (or wains)** – children
- **'bout ye'** – hello, especially in Belfast
- **farl** – a piece of bread, particularly soda farl or potato farl
- **'going for the messages'** – to go shopping. Dates from the time when the local post office would double as the main shop and your letters etc. would be there
- **champ** – mashed potatoes with scallions added (the Northern version of colcannon)
- **boxty** – potato pancakes
- **dulse** – edible seaweed
- **boreen** – lane, small road; **loanin** also used identically
- **poke** – ice cream
- **sheugh** – small ditch
- **thon** – that
- **dander** – walk or stroll
- **a lock** – a few ('a lock o' hens')
- **a clatter** – a lot
- **quare** – a variety of meanings, but usually meaning great. however 'the quare one' usually refers to one's spouse
- **reddin'** – as in 'reddin' the dishes up', cleaning
- **brave** – good, as in 'it's a brave day'
- **evening** – afternoon. In former times the day was divided into morning, evening and night. 'Afternoon' was a modern departure introduced by the British. The old system carries on in many rural areas, with evening being anytime after about 2pm

a few from the north of England – mostly Presbyterian, and mostly skilled farmers and craftsmen. They got the good land, the native Irish being pushed onto the poorer upland areas. It was this 'Plantation' that gave Northern Ireland a substantial part of its character.

The Plantation was followed by attempts to spread Anglicanism, with Catholics being barred from their own churches or official positions. This was no blueprint for good community relations; armed conflict soon flared. The 1641 Rising, the Siege of Derry, the Battle of the Boyne and the 1798 Uprising all duly followed, with the latter seeing Presbyterians siding with the Catholics against the established order. All were unsuccessful, but the 19th century eventually brought a calm of sorts, with Catholics obtaining some suffrage, and Protestants winning tenant rights and land security.

20th century Troubles

The 20th century dawned, and trouble across Europe loomed. During the First World War tensions continued to mount in Ireland. Eventually on Easter Monday, 1916, rebels in Dublin began an uprising against British rule. The rebellion itself proved futile, but the subsequent execution of the leaders turned out to be a propaganda coup for militant republicanism, and Sinn Féin's previously negligible popular support grew.

Republicans gained further support when the British government attempted to introduce conscription into Ireland in 1918. Sinn Féin was at the forefront of organising the campaign against it. When the veterans of the Great War, on both sides of the political divide, returned from the front, trouble was once again fomenting. In the general election of 1918, voting was along sectarian lines, and bother duly ensued. Guerrilla warfare raged across Ireland – in the north it involved the Irish Republican Army (IRA), the British Army and the Ulster Volunteer Force (UVF).

After a bloody war of independence an uneasy accommodation was eventually found. The Home Rule Bill (the Government of Ireland Act 1920) partitioned the island into Northern Ireland (six north-eastern counties) and 'Southern Ireland' (the remaining 26). The partition was governed by the religious majorities within each of the northern counties of Ulster – an overall Protestant majority had to be maintained, so eventually the counties of Donegal, Cavan and Monaghan (part of the ancient province of Ulster) were ceded to the South. Even today residents of these counties will quip: 'What's the three greatest things about Ulster? Cavan, Monaghan and Donegal!'

Funnily enough, for three days from midnight on 6 December 1922 Northern Ireland stopped being part of the UK, and became part of the newly created Irish Free State. The constitutional and legal ins and outs of this would require the rest of the book, so suffice to say, Northern Ireland came into being in 1922 and there followed decades of varying degrees of sectarian bitterness nourished by seemingly inexhaustible grievances. Civic disturbance and violence only ceased in the very closing years of the 20th century. The Troubles are now over, and the visitor to Northern Ireland is unlikely in the very extreme to be caught up in any sectarian bitterness. On the contrary, because the tourist industry is in many respects at a fledgling stage, locals are only too happy to welcome visitors.

The years of isolation that Northern Ireland suffered in the second half of the 20th century, however, have had one advantage. The place is utterly unspoiled; ironically here in the British part of the island you will find Old Ireland slumbering on, virtually unchanged.

GEOGRAPHY AND GEOLOGY

The ancient province of Ulster is bounded to the north and west by the Atlantic Ocean, and to the east by the Irish Sea. In the northern parts of counties Derry and Antrim a great ridge of basalt lies in the path of the Lower Bann River – the Upper and Lower Bann divide the country in two. After having flowed in stately fashion slowly from Lough Neagh, the river is funnelled between hills and cliffs to finally make its way out to the Atlantic. Half of the water draining off the surface of Ulster passes through here.

Geologically speaking, north-eastern Ireland is made up of five distinct areas, which accounts for such a diverse landscape in a relatively small area and for the likes of the Giant's Causeway and the Mountains of Mourne. To the south of the region, Slieve Gullion (p. 165) is a destination for geologists from around Europe, being a textbook example of an extinct volcanic ring-dyke system. In layman's terms this means you can stand on top of the central mountain, Slieve Gullion, and see an encircling ring of lesser peaks. Basically the volcanic lava plopped up like custard leaving this strange geological formation.

Should you be pining for the fjords, there's good news. The southerly borders of the region are bounded by Carlingford Lough, a typical fjord which stretched from Newry to Northern Ireland's most southerly extremity, Cranfield Point.

For further elucidation on Ireland's troubled history the following are regarded as seminal works:

• *The Troubles* by Tim Pat Coogan
• *A History of Ulster* by Jonathan Bardon
• *Ireland – A History* by Robert Kee

Brian Feeney's *Pocket History of the Troubles* is as good as its word, condensing the crucial points into an easily digestible book.

WHAT'S IN A NAME?

Ulster, the Six Counties, Northern Ireland, the North of Ireland, Occupied Ireland, the Fourth Green Field, the Black North: the north-eastern corner of the island of Ireland has many names, reflecting a history to which the word chequered barely does justice. Locals, wanting to avoid using either of the politically loaded designations 'Northern Ireland' or 'the North of Ireland' will often employ the light-hearted, phonetic 'Norn Iron', or the pet name 'the wee North'. (By the way, everything in Northern Ireland is 'wee'. In a shop you will be asked for your 'wee credit card number' with its 'wee security number', and you will frequently be given directions to the nearest wee village, wee shop or wee cathedral).

But back to the nomenclature of the North. Surely anywhere that can muster more than half a dozen names is worthy of further investigation. For the sake of clarity, and because the rest of the world knows it as Northern Ireland – unaware of the political undertones – we will tend towards that term throughout the book, although in situations where another name is considered more appropriate the context should hopefully make this clear. Northern Ireland's imbroglio has been some 800 years in the making, so nowhere will you be expected to grasp the many subtleties of this divided community. For historical accuracy, when the term Ulster is used in this book, usually the historic province – the nine counties – is being referred to.

Although the country is now at peace, in your travels throughout the region you could try to observe one courtesy: just as the locals tend to do, avoid referring to the place at all. After all, in the not very distant past how a local described his home land could, quite literally, be a matter of life or death. The *jurisdiction* (always a handy word if you want to avoid the politically loaded descriptions 'province',

'country' or 'statelet') had a Deputy First Minister who managed not to mention the place he was ministering to during his entire five-year tenure.

Prosaically, Northern Ireland is six of the nine counties of the ancient province of Ulster, or Uladh, an area that more than a million and a half people simply call home. The Six Counties remain British, although they are not in Britain – even the most dyed in the wool loyalist will correct you if you should erroneously refer to Northern Ireland as part of Britain or Great Britain – the collective term is very specifically, and legally, 'the United Kingdom of Great Britain and Northern Ireland'. The term 'British Isles' is also frowned upon by the majority of people living on the island of Ireland, as is the term 'mainland' referring to Britain – so we have tended to avoid both terms. You should probably do the same on your journeys through the area, although nobody will really take exception if you get it wrong.

Northern Ireland then falls under the jurisdiction of Her Majesty's Government – the Queen's writ runs as far west as the town of Belcoo in Fermanagh, where in summertime it's not dark till 11 in the evening, and as far south as the leafy, soporifically beautiful laneways of Armagh. Here they routinely refer to the Union Jack as 'the Butcher's Apron', and it is a place where few representatives of the British government could venture with any degree of safety until the 21st century. Today power has been devolved back to Stormont, and the loyalist, largely Protestant Democratic Unionist Party is now in uneasy coalition with the nationalist, largely Catholic party, Sinn Féin (Irish for 'Ourselves Alone'). But the very name of the area they govern is still a vexed issue. When it comes to politics here, it's probably best to take poet Seamus Heaney's advice: *'Whatever you say, say nothing.'*

The best... geographical features

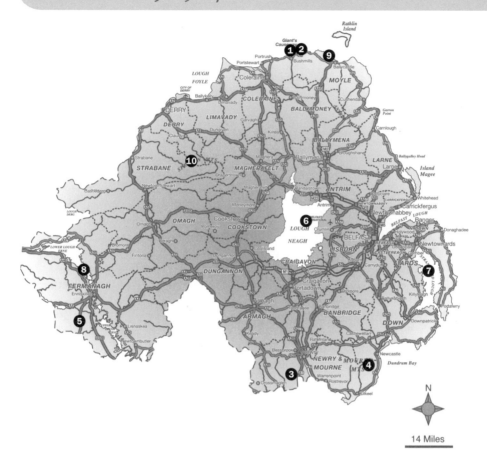

14 Miles

1 Giant's Causeway – one of the island of Ireland's three UNESCO World Heritage Sites, p. 96

2 Carrick Island and Carrick-a-Rede Rope Bridge – a precarious crossing to Carrick Island. Sure to set the adrenaline pumping, p. 98

3 Slieve Gullion – a classic ring-dyke system in geological speak, and a beautiful climb in layman's terms, p. 165

4 Slieve Donard – the province of Ulster's highest mountain, p. 266

5 Florence Court – site of the world's first Irish yew, p. 312

6 Lough Neagh – bordering five counties, this is one of the finest freshwater angling spots in Europe, p. 347

7 Strangford Lough – a birdwatcher's paradise, p. 231

8 Lough Erne – ideal for cruising, sailing, canoeing; or just staring at the sun as it sinks in the west, p. 297

9 Causeway Coastal Route – adjudged to be one of the dozen most spectacular roads in the world, p. 97

10 The Sperrin Mountains – has inspired everyone from Jimmy Kennedy ('Teddy bears' picnic' fame) to poet Seamus Heaney, p. 211

10... quotations about Northern Ireland

1 *'God what a bloody awful country. Get me a large Scotch'* – Reggie Maudling, after his first, fruitless visit to Northern Ireland in 1972, to the hostess on his aeroplane home

2 *'Our Irish ancestors believed in magic, prayers, trickery, browbeating and bullying. I think it would be fair to sum that list up as Irish politics'* – Tyrone man Flann O'Brien

3 *'I'm an Ulsterman of planter stock. I was born on the island of Ireland, so secondarily I'm an Irishman. I was born on the British archipelago and English is my native tongue, so I am British. The British archipelago consists of offshore islands to the continent of Europe, so I'm European. This is my hierarchy of values and so far as I am concerned, anyone who omits one step in the sequence of values is falsifying the situation'* – writer and poet John Hewitt

4 *'God made us Catholics, but the Armalite made us equal'* – graffiti in Belfast

5 *'L'Ulster est l'écosse de l'Irlande'* [Ulster is Scotland in Ireland] – Gustave de Beaumont, 1802–1866, French commentator and writer

6 *'They're like a couple of drunks walking out of a bar-room – when they get to the swinging doors they just turn around and go right back in.'* President Clinton in a speech in Canada talking about the warring factions 'in the land of his forebears' – he has family roots in County Fermanagh

7 *'I feel like an exile at heart – the call of the North is always there'* – President of Ireland, Mary McAleese, who comes from Belfast. Technically speaking, as President, she must ask the government for permission to go home for her tea

8 *'NOTE: In some of our copies the article The Power Of The Papacy described the Pope as His Satanic Majesty. This should have read The Roman Antichrist.'* – a correction in a 1969 edition of the *Protestant Telegraph*

9 *'A disorderly set of people whom no king can govern and no God can please'* – Boyle Roche MP (1743–1807)

10 *'So why is all this happening? The long answer involves the Normans landing in Ireland 800 years ago, and the short answer isn't much less tortuous.'* The *Guardian* on the extradition of Roísín McAliskey, daughter of Bernadette McAliskey, née Devlin

WILDLIFE AND HABITATS

On any holiday in Northern Ireland you could reasonably hope to see the largest organism ever to have lived, plus the world's fastest animal – respectively, the **blue whale**, the biggest animal to have graced planet Earth, so large that you could swim along its arteries, and the **peregrine falcon** which dive-bombs its prey, and if it's only doing 100mph it's dawdling along.

Of course, the presence of these two wildlife superstars doesn't mean that crossing the Irish Sea is going to be on a par with heading out on safari in the Serengeti. Quite simply the island of Ireland has nothing like the species count of Britain or continental Europe. For reasons that aren't fully understood, every time a sea divides a land mass from its continent, a dramatic decrease in the variety of wildlife results. Ireland, for instance, has about 300 species of native birds, Britain about 500, while in the continent of Europe the mildest of twitching anoraks could come up with some 1,000 different species. Nonetheless, Northern Ireland is a truly rewarding place for those wanting to let their inner David Attenborough free – all you will need is time and just a little insider knowledge.

Whales, dolphins and porpoises can be seen off all the coasts, although the northern headlands are the most promising. Whales annually migrate between the frozen Poles and tropics. Those seen off the north coast of Ireland are generally heading north to feed in rich Arctic waters, or heading south in the autumn to winter in tropical breeding grounds. The larger whales – including the blue whale with his heart the size of a family saloon car – use the European continental shelf to feed and rest up on their long migrations. And luckily enough the island of Ireland is Europe's closest land to this 'whale superhighway'.

Irish waters are home to at least 23 species of cetaceans (the zoological name for the whale and dolphin family), representing more than a third of the world's species. Aside from the blue whale, you could expect to see the fin whale, the humpback and the minke whale. Dolphins include the common, bottlenose, Atlantic white-sided and striped.

The whale may be the biggest mammal lurking round Ireland's shores, but if you want to see Ireland's largest land mammal, the **red deer**, you have to head for woodland areas such as Tollymore (p. 266). Ireland's other two native mammals which you might commonly see – on farmland, woodland and moorland – are the **stoat and the Irish hare**, which have both been on Irish soil far longer than man. A rarer sight is the **pine marten**, which looks somewhat like a stoat, and inhabits mountain areas from the Mournes

---

FIVE ANIMALS YOU CAN SEE ONLY IN IRELAND...

- **Irish jay** – *Garrulus glandarius hibernicus*
- **Irish dipper (bird)** – *Cinclus cinclus hibernicus*
- **Irish mountain hare** – *Lepus timidus hibernicus* (some authorities now regard the hare as a species on its own, *Lepus hibernicus)*
- **Dollaghan** – large migratory brown trout found in Lough Neagh and its tributary rivers
- **Gillaroo** – species of trout found in Lough Melvin (County Fermanagh and County Leitrim) and in County Mayo and parts of Scotland

... AND FIVE ANIMALS WHICH DON'T OCCUR NATURALLY IN IRELAND:

- Moles
- Toads
- Snakes
- Woodpeckers
- Weasels

to the Sperrins. In both areas it has shown a welcome increase in numbers. The **peregrine falcon** can be seen everywhere in Ireland, particularly in mountainous or cliff areas such as the Mournes or the Sperrins. The word peregrine, means 'pilgrim', presumably an allusion to the fact that these birds can, and do, travel great distances.

The peregrine falcon stands at the top of avian life. But ornithological treasures are all around. Larks sing matins on the moorlands of every county, while the sound of old Ireland is still alive in the western counties of Fermanagh and Tyrone where the **corncrake** lives on. **Swans** perform their elaborate courting ritual everywhere from Lough Neagh to the River Lagan in Belfast. With necks craned and entwined, dancing and embracing, these magnificent creatures bring grace to their moment of passion as only swans can do. A discreet veil will be drawn across the full proceedings – but it's safe to say a pair of swans look well satisfied after an event like this.

Ireland has such a long, indented coastline (the whole island has one of the longest in Europe), so the easiest birds to see are **waders**, **seabirds and coastal species**. The likes of **Strangford Lough** (p. 231) and **Lough Neagh** (p. 122) are among the world's premier wildfowl reserves – and you won't even need your binoculars. Just stand and gawp. Much of the entire world population of Brent and Greenland white-fronted geese stop off at these avian service stations to dine, and as they flock in groups of up to 500 its pretty hard to miss them. These are truly magnificent wildlife spots, where you can watch some of the world's great travellers as they journey from the New World to the Old. Remember – the birds knew the world was round before we did.

CULTURE

Music

Music fills the Northern Irish air, from rock to baroque, from contemporary to Celtic. It's one of the most evocative sounds in the country, second only to the words, 'Put your money away, the drinks are on the house.'

Ruby Murray, one of the most successful female singers of the 20th century – never mind her name being immortalised as Cockney rhyming slang for a curry – came from Belfast. Northern Ireland has always produced more than its fair share of pop acts and rock bands, not forgetting Ulster's contribution to the Eurovision Song Contest. Dana from Derry won the contest (for Ireland) in 1970, setting her on the road to a great political career. As Dana Rosemary Scallon she became MEP for Connacht-Ulster, with politics slightly to the right of Vlad the Impaler on a crotchety day.

The Six Counties have had a presence in three other Eurovision triumphs: 'Puppet on a string' by Derry man **Phil Coulter** who also co-wrote 'Congratulations' for Cliff Richard, second in 1968. **Clodagh Rogers** (from Newry) sang 'Jack in the box' for Great Britain and was fourth in 1971. Today's (avowedly non-Eurovision) superstars include **Van Morrison**, **Ash**, **Snow Patrol and Therapy**. Between them they almost match the output of Omagh man **Jimmy Kennedy** whose big numbers include 'Red sails in the sunset', the 'Teddy bears' picnic', and 'The hokey cokey' – the latter can perhaps be seen as the forerunner to Riverdance.

Despite this shaking it all about, traditional music – the jaunty jig or raucous reel – remains the defining soundtrack of the country. An extraordinarily relaxed atmosphere helped along by Irish fiddle tunes and uillean pipe music floating on the breeze pervades Ulster. Significantly, Ireland (the Republic) is the only nation in the world to have a musical instrument, the harp, as its national emblem; but the harp slunk over the border – even the (disbanded) Royal Ulster Constabulary used it as their emblem.

Although embedded in Ireland's DNA, the traditional music perceived today as quintessentially Irish only entered showbiz some three centuries or so ago. The first people to start tampering with native Celtic music were the Normans. They liked it so much that the English Parliament was soon passing laws to stop them becoming *'more Irish than the Irish themselves'*. By 1366 the 'degenerate English' were warned not to *'disport themselves in the manner of the natives'*. Long hair was out – this was the sixties after all, even if it was the 1360s. Presumably about this time a parliamentary edict forced all town names to henceforth be spelled so awkwardly in English that to fit them into a song would be impossible. Or so it seemed. But once again the local populace triumphed. Today there are songs which somehow manage to crowbar Ulster names, such as Magheralin, Slieve na mBan, Ballyjamesduff and Carrickfergus, seamlessly into the lyrics, no mean feat. Like real estate, the three most important things about an Ulster song are location, location and location, and whether it's Carrowmurwaghnemucklagh in County Down or Moneymore in County Antrim, it's more than likely to have a song written about it.

Ireland is today recognised as having one of the richest traditional musical heritages in the world, and the northern part of the island has played a crucial part in preserving, fostering and evolving that tradition. Throughout every county you will find traditional Irish sessions, festivals (called fleadhs), concerts and ballad sessions. Almost every town will have ceili dances or set dances (there is a subtle difference) where visitors and novices are always welcome. Several centres will teach you to play a few tunes on the tin whistle or keep the beat on a bodhran (a type of side drum) or even introduce you to the forbiddingly specialist

TRADITIONAL MUSIC IN THE SIX COUNTIES

Traditional music in the Six Counties tends to be centred on what is loosely called Irish traditional music – largely the music of the nationalist, Catholic population, although substantial numbers of Protestants are players as well. The Protestant – or loyalist – community also has its own specific brand of music, usually called Ulster Scots or Scots Irish music. Played almost exclusively by those descended from the Scottish planters, the music reflects the historic musical links with Scotland, but also the influences absorbed from indigenous Irish music. This gives the tradition its own very individual character.

Traditional Irish music tends to be focused on the pub session – although contrary to popular belief, this is not a particularly ancient tradition. It probably started – wait for it – in London, in the late 1940s and 1950s. Of course Irish music goes back much further than this – it's just that before the 20th century it was almost entirely a solo tradition, played exclusively for dancers. The ould session simply didn't take place before the 20th century. Scots Irish music is very old – but has largely centred round a band tradition, although more informal sessions now take place.

Throughout the year, championships for pipe bands take place. Local Antrim outfit the Field Marshall Montgomery Band are regular holders of national and international titles, and regularly give concerts where the other great feature of Ulster Scots music, the huge, deafening Lambeg drum (named after an Antrim town), can be heard. Around the rhythm of this drum, unique to Ulster, a large body of fife music has been written – particularly in County Antrim.

Look in the local press or in local shops for posters advertising upcoming events.

activity of learning the uillean pipes, the indigenous form of bagpipes.

Comhaltas, which promotes Irish traditional music throughout the island, will furnish you with details of classes where you can learn traditional music: www.comhaltas. ie. The **Tí Chulainn Cultural Activity Centre** (An Mullach Bán BT35 9TT; ☎ 028 3088 8828; www.tichulainn.com) runs classes and workshops in all aspects of traditional music and dance. The **Francie McPeake School of Music** runs courses and classes throughout the year (☎ 028 9099 8964; www.francismcpeake.com).

Of course, this being Northern Ireland, music, like most other things, has a religious dimension. Many, but by no means all, practitioners and aficionadas of Irish traditional music are Catholic. The Protestant community tends more to Scottish music (or Ulster Scots music – see box), which is centred round pipe bands, accordion bands, flute bands – and the fearsome Lambeg drum. A lot of the sectarian ferocity has gone out of the annual Orange marches every summer, and some pipe bands have even teamed up with Irish players to produce a truly local sound. Either way, on your journey through the region you will be astounded at the integral part music plays in the every-day affairs of the people.

Poetry and literature

Music and dance are the two art forms with the highest profile in Northern Ireland – but there's also poetry and literature, especially the towering figure of Nobel prize winner **Seamus Heaney**, not to mention **Flann O'Brien**, **C S Lewis**, **Paul Muldoon**, **Derek Mahon**, **John Hewitt** and **Louis McNiece**. In this country of over-achievers in the literary field, several museums are dedicated to writing. But given that much of the inspiration for Irish scribes came in pint-form, you could say that Northern Ireland contains thousands of writers' museums in the form of its pubs.

FANTASTIC NORTHERN IRELAND PLACE-NAMES

By the start of the 17th century Uladh (or Ulster in English) was still the most Irish, Gaelic, Catholic and traditional province in Ireland. Despite the Plantation, Ulster retains more Gaelic names than anywhere else in Ireland, and indeed boasts the largest number of Celtic place-names in the world. Their translations from the original Irish have led to some curious English constructions:

- **Billy** – near Bushmills, County Antrim
- **Cullybackey** – County Antrim
- **Aghanloo** – near Limavady, County Derry
- **Carrowmurwaghnemucklagh** – near Maghera, Tollymore parish, County Down
- **Tamlagh O'Crilly** – halfway between Maghera and Kilrea, County Derry
- **Pot of Legawherry** – near Slieve Comedagh, Mourne Mountains, County Down
- **Grockbrack** – near Moneymeaney, County Derry
- **Moneymeaney** – County Derry
- **Errigal Keerogue** – near Ballygawley, Tyrone
- **Lisbellaw** – Fermanagh
- **Belcoo** – Fermanagh
- **Bonamargy** – County Antrim
- **Sessiadonaghy** – County Tyrone
- **Termon McGrath** – County Fermanagh
- **Augher, Clogher and Fivemiletown in County Tyrone** – (Eacharadh-Lobrainis, Clochar, Baile na Lorgan in Irish)

Oscar O'Flahertie Wills Wilde, educated at Portora School (p. 289), had sufficient intellectual authority to state at the US Customs, *'I have nothing to declare but my genius.'* The Mountains of Mourne weren't just the inspiration for Percy French; the rocks and loughs of County Down became transformed into Narnia by Belfast man **C S Lewis** (p. 83), while somehow the

10... great songs from Northern Ireland

1 **'Danny boy'** – a (mostly) traditional air, and officially the most widely listened-to Irish melody since it was played at Princess Diana's funeral (listed as the 'Londonderry air' in the order of service)

2 **'Red sails in the sunset' by Jimmy Kennedy** – written on the north coast of Ireland by the prolific songwriter from Omagh

3 **'Songs of love' (the Father Ted theme) by Neil Hannon** – put Father Jack and Father Dougal out of your mind and listen to one of the finest adagios to be written in the rock genre

4 **'The star spangled banner'** – said to have been derived from an Enniskillen marching song. It is also claimed that the great Irish harpist, Turlough O'Carolan, wrote the melody

5 **'Moondance' by Van Morrison** – Van the Man has been named by various international authorities as one of the seminal talents in rock and roll. Moondance is one of his finest numbers

6 **'The mountains of Mourne' by Percy French** – perhaps the top topographical song of all time, as well as giving a wonderful commentary on the strange, hard-to-grasp relationship between Ireland and England. An essential track to have on your MP3 before heading for County Down

7 **'There is a green hill far away' by Mrs Cecil Alexander** – The Green Hills are believed to have been in Tyrone, with the Sperrins acting as an allegory for Calvary

8 **'What a friend we have in Jesus' by Joseph Medlicott Scriven** – Banbridge-born Joe wrote this song after having suffered dreadful personal loss

9 **'The mountain thyme' ('Oh the summer-time is coming...')** – by Belfast man Francie McPeake. Many people erroneously believe this to be a Scottish song, but the great uillean piper Francie McPeake penned the ballad in Belfast

10 **'I wish I was in Carrickfergus'** – a traditional song (probably), and one of the most beautiful ballads in the Irish folk song canon. It has been recorded by a huge range of singers from Nana Mouskouri to Bryan Ferry

10... actors and actresses from Northern Ireland

1 **Stephen Rea (Belfast)** – a Presbyterian, Rea was married to former Provisional Irish Republican Army member and hunger striker Dolours Price from 1983 to 2003. His roles have included parts in *The Crying Game*, *Michael Collins* and *The Company of Wolves*

2 **Liam Neeson (Ballymena)** – a Catholic from the staunchly Protestant town of Ballymena, Neeson's roles have included Oskar Schindler, Rob Roy and Kinsey

3 **James Nesbitt (Belfast)** – from Broughshane in County Antrim, Nesbitt has appeared in *Cold Feet* and *Waking Ned*

4 **Kenneth Branagh** – born in the Tiger's Bay area of Belfast, Branagh is an Emmy Award-winning, Academy Award-nominated actor and film director

5 **Ciaran Hinds (Belfast)** – a talented actor, Hinds's roles have included parts in Jane Austen's *Persuasion*, Andrew Lloyd Webber's *Phantom of the Opera* and *Titanic Town*

6 **James Ellis (Belfast)** – played Bert Lynch in Z Cars, and has been a regular on the television screen ever since in a career spanning more than 45 years. His appearances include roles in *Doctor Who*, *Ballykissangel* and *One by One*.

7 **Roma Downey (Derry)** – best known as Monica, the main character of the television series *Touched by an Angel*

8 **Amanda Burton (Derry)** – best known as Sam Ryan in *Silent Witness*, Amanda has also appeared in *Brookside*, *Peak Practice*, and *The Commander*

9 **Stephen Boyd (Glengormley, County Antrim)** – the original choice to play James Bond 007 in *Dr No*, he played parts in productions ranging from *Ben Hur* to *Hawaii Five-O*

10 **Greer Garson** – born in London, had family roots Castlewellan, County Down – this is often given as her birthplace as she spent much of her childhood in County Down. Presented with the Academy Award for Best Actress in 1942 for her role in *Mrs Miniver*, the Guinness Book of Records credits her with the longest Oscar acceptance speech of all time, at five minutes and 30 seconds. After this, the Academy Awards instituted a time limit streets of Strabane inspired **Flann O'Brien** to his amazing flights of surreal humour.

But where does this prowess in the literary field come from? Various theories have been put forward. Maybe it's all to do with the vexed question of cultural identity, a product of the strange relationship between Ireland and England over the past 800 years. In the same way that the fusion of the Gaelic society and the Christian religion 2,000 years ago produced a specifically Irish identity and resulted in some wonderful art, the collision of Irish and English culture has had the same profound effect. **Seamus Heaney** recognised this when speaking about his own background in the North: *'I began as a poet when my roots were crossed with my reading. I think of the personal and Irish pieties as vowels, and the literary awareness nourished on English as consonants.'* But it could be something as simple as the lack of a 'yes' or 'no' in the Irish language – the argument being that if you can't say yes or no in your own language, when you come to speak another one you've already a head start when it comes to playing around with words. And before long you're winning Nobel Prizes like they're going out of fashion.

ULSTER HEROES

Although **St Patrick** wasn't an Irishman, he could be regarded as a classic Ulsterman. Born in Scotland (probably), he made Armagh his home and helped change the face of the world. What could be more Northern Irish? John Boyd Dunlop, born in Ayrshire, did exactly the same thing. He moved to Belfast, where he invented the world's first pneumatic tyre. Just like Christianity, the tyre spread throughout the world, with several different versions eventually available. There's a plaque in Dunlop's honour at 38–42 May Street, the site of his workshop.

Home-grown heroes begin with the legendary **Cú Chulainn**, a figure in the early Ulster sagas. Born Setanta (whence the satellite channel name) Cú Chulainn, or the

Hound of Ulster, is the central figure in the *Táin Bó Cuailgne*, or the *Cattle Raid of Cooley*. The story centres round the great brown bull of Connacht and the great white bull of Ulster, and Queen Maeve's efforts to secure the latter. Not content with forming the basis of the great Ulster sagas, these stories also made their way to Iceland: *'The Irish brought to Iceland their literature and their learning – of which the Scandinavians had nothing,'* Halldéor Laxness Iceland's Nobel prize winner says. *'The sagas are our cultural foundation. Without them we would just be another Danish island.'*

The Six Counties have produced many heroes over the millennia. **George Best**, generally regarded as one of the finest soccer players of all time, was arguably the first soccer superstar, while **Pat Jennings** earned the reputation as the finest goalkeeper of his generation.

Northern Ireland has its scientific heroes too. World-renowned physicist **Professor Jocelyn Bell**, a Belfast Quaker, detected during research an aberrant signal from space, a signal that was regularly pulsing. Temporarily dubbed 'Little Green Man 1' the source was eventually identified as a rapidly rotating neutron star, the first discovery ever of pulsar. Unforgivably Ms Bell was overlooked for the Nobel prize for physics in 1967. Instead her boss scooped the main prize, leading to the award being called, justifiably, the 'No Bell' that year. Undaunted, Jocelyn has stayed at the forefront of her discipline.

Northern Ireland's heroes have come from both sides of the religious divide, and from every class. The region's unique mix of culture, religion, politics and nationhood has brought many a problem and much sadness – but it has also produced a dynamic, volatile population for whom creativity seems to have been an inevitable by-product.

As Belfast poet and writer John Hewitt put it:

'Kelt Briton, Roman, Saxon, Dane and Scot, time and this island tied a crazy knot'.

10... Northern Ireland historical figures

1 St Patrick – the Apostle of Ireland, the first Cardinal Archbishop of Armagh, and the man who spread Christianity throughout the island from his base in Armagh. One of Ireland's three patron saints, he will, according to legend, decide your fate in the afterlife should you have any Irish blood running through your veins

2 Cú Chullainn – originally called Setanta, this legendary Ulster hero is the central figure in one of the great Irish sagas, the *Cattle Raid of Cooley*. He crops up throughout the whole of the region as The Hound of Ulster, protecting the ancient province from all comers

3 King Billy – also called William III, Prince of Orange, victor at the Battle of the Boyne

4 John Duns Scotus – theologian and philosopher, probably born in Downpatrick, although Scotland also claims him. But Duns is the old name for Down, and 'Scotus' in the Middle Ages was the Latin term for 'Irish or Gaelic'. John had a profound influence on Catholic thought, but a schism with influential figures in the church led to his name being corrupted to 'dunce', the origin of the word

5 Johannes Scotus Eriugena (c. 815–877) – philosopher, John the Irishman, probably born somewhere in Ulster

6 Edward Carson – Dublin lawyer who defended the Marquess of Queensberry in the libel proceedings brought by Oscar Wilde. He became leader of the Ulster Unionists in 1910 and was instrumental in the foundation of Northern Ireland

7 James Craig – Viscount Craigavon, Northern Ireland's first prime minister

8 Rev Ian Paisley – at the forefront of Northern Irish politics for 50 years, eventually becoming First Minister

9 John Hume – Nobel laureate (for peace) and widely seen as one of the pivotal figures in bringing peace to Northern Ireland

10 Bobby Sands – MP for Fermanagh and South Tyrone, Robert Gerard Sands was an IRA volunteer imprisoned for the possession of firearms. His death on hunger strike in 1981 attracted worldwide media coverage

1

Belfast and around

a. Central and North Belfast
b. Outer Belfast

Unmissable highlights

01 Visit Odyssey's W5 'interactive and discovery centre', where you can interact with all sorts of weird and wonderful exhibits, p. 86

02 Dine with the quality at Belfast's only Michelin star restaurant, Deane's Restaurant, p. 72

03 Wander through Milltown Cemetery, the main Republican graveyard in Belfast, p. 79

04 Browse through the literary collections of the Linen Hall Library, one of the most fascinating libraries in these islands, p. 63

05 Have a pint in the Crown Liquor Saloon undoubtedly one of the world's great watering holes, p. 73

06 Dander down to Harland and Wolff Shipyards to see where the Titanic was built. (H&W's unofficial motto: 'She was alright when she left Belfast'), p. 58

07 Take a trip to the Ulster Museum to muse on artefacts from Early Ireland. Also loads of stuff nicked from other countries, p. 62

08 Visit Belfast City Hall, commemorating events from the *Titanic* to the Great War, p. 59

09 Visit the great murals in the republican heartlands – and in a spirit of religious even-handedness, visit the loyalist murals in east Belfast, p. 75

10 Walk up the mile-long drive to Stormont, a place which wouldn't have looked out of place in Ceaucescu's Bucharest, p. 80

BELFAST AND AROUND

Few cities in Ireland or Britain can boast anything like as varied and beautiful surroundings as Belfast. The dramatic setting of the city on the shores of **Belfast Lough**, with the huge volcanic outcrop of **Cave Hill** as a backdrop, has few rivals in Europe.

Unfortunately, that's where Ulster's capital beauty more or less begins and ends. *'Belfast,'* wrote E M Forster in 1936, *'stands no nonsense.'* Correct. This hard, Victorian, industrial metropolis has no fripperies, few elegant boulevards, little in the way of jack-the-lad architecture. But it does have character. This strange, complex place has produced characters as diverse as C S Lewis (Narnia fame), footballer George Best, musicians Van Morrison and James Galway, and actor Kenneth Branagh.

Dublin man Jonathan Swift knew Belfast well. While living at Lilliput Cottage near the bottom of the Limestone Road in the shadow of Cave Hill, he imagined that the mountain resembled the shape of a sleeping giant safeguarding the city. A small step from that to Gulliver in the land of Lilliput. The shape of the giant's nose, known locally as *Napoleon's Nose*, is officially called McArt's Fort probably named after Art O'Neill, a 16th-century chieftain who controlled the area.

Cave Hill offers the best view of the city across Belfast Lough – the giant gantries of the shipyard, the birthplace of the *Titanic*, line the horizon, eventually leading the eye towards the green hills of north **Down**. During the latter half of the 20th century the natural beauty of Belfast's surroundings clashed jarringly with the ugliness of the barbed wire, the sand bags and the miles of corrugated iron which steadily accreted. Now things are slowly returning to normal, although Belfast is still home to several miles of **peace lines** – bulwarks higher and longer than the Berlin Wall ever was, and in place to keep the two warring communities apart in what are still called 'interface areas'.

Most areas of the city are, however, perfectly safe to visit – probably safer than most parts of Britain. Because Belfast has turned progressively to culture and craic. The relative peace of the past few years has resulted in a huge upsurge of restaurants, cafés, clubs and pubs. And here's the funny thing – because Belfast has been largely untouched by the now defunct Celtic Tiger economy to the south, and there has been no huge influx of tourists, in many ways Belfast is probably the most Irish of Ireland's four main cities: the others being Dublin, Cork and Galway. The ultimate irony – if you want to see an old Irish city, you have to go to the British one.

CENTRAL AND NORTH BELFAST

After an eventful recent past, the centre of Belfast has metamorphosed into a vibrant city with dynamic pubs and classy restaurants. Traditional must-sees include the handsome **Belfast City Hall**, commemorating events from the *Titanic* to the Great War, and the **Linen Hall Library**, by the City Hall, with its comprehensive lowdown on Irish history.

The **River Lagan** – on which much of Belfast's fortunes were founded – divides East Belfast from the rest of the city. The recent **Laganside** development is dominated by the futuristic **Waterfront Hall**, the centre-piece of concert venues, coffee shops, restaurants, hotels and art galleries. Sip a skinny latte decaff here and watch the grey fog creep up the **Lagan**. Pillars of mist will drift silently across the **Harland and Wolff Shipyard** to surround two huge yellow cranes, reputedly the largest in the world. This was where the *Titanic* slipped anchor and sailed out to the Irish Sea, never to return.

Drinking establishments in Belfast are not difficult to come by. Lurking between its time-darkened buildings you will find traditional old back street pubs, up-market brasserie bars, and frenetic music houses catering for all rhythmic tastes. The city's oldest pub, **Kelly's Kitchen** lies at the very centre of matters. With cellars dating from 1720 (possibly the oldest in all Ireland) this was a meeting place for the United Irishmen leading up to the 1798 Rebellion. You'll undoubtedly find someone at the bar to tell you all about it – and where they went wrong.

No visit to Belfast would be complete without a pilgrimage to the glorious **Crown Liquor Saloon**, Great Victoria Street. Without doubt one of the great bars of the world, this gem of Victorian splendour is still a vital part of Belfast's everyday life. It's what you might call a theme bar – the theme being drink and conversation. Meanwhile **The Golden Mile**, stretching up **Great Victoria Street** to just beyond **Donegall Square** (the name is the result of a centuries-old spelling mistake) boasts every conceivable type of eatery from balti to boxty (the traditional potato pancake of Ulster).

The restaurant critic Clement Freud reminisced about a trip to Belfast some years ago. He was much taken by a sign in a pub that said, 'Pint, pie and a kind word – a quid.' Clement duly ordered the special, was served an immaculate pint of stout and a serviceable enough-looking pie; but the chat didn't seem too forthcoming. 'Hey! What about the friendly advice?' he called to the barman. The barman came back, leaned over the bar, and conspiratorially whispered to him, 'If I were ye, I wouldnae bother eatin' the meat pie.' An unlikely scenario in culinary Belfast these days.

WHAT TO SEE AND DO

Walking tours

One of the best ways of seeing Belfast – being a compact city – is by walking tour. The Northern Walking Partnership (☎07797994600; www.northernwalking. com) and Ulster Rambles (☎ 078 2850 5662; www.ulsterrambles.com) provide guided tours both within and beyond the city limits.

Queen's University Belfast

Queen's University Belfast opened for business in 1849. The University forms the focal point of the Queen's Quarter area of the city, one of Belfast's four cultural districts. A visitor centre in the Lanyon Building houses a variety of exhibitions, and provides information on the university as well as selling gifts and souvenirs.

Queen's University

QUEEN'S UNIVERSITY BELFAST: University Road BT7; ☎ 028 9024 5133; www.qub. ac.uk. Guided tours of the university are available by arrangement.

The Botanic Gardens

The Botanic Gardens, another triumph for the old Victorians, opened in 1827, and is something of a miniature Kew Gardens – the difference being that there aren't a million other people trying to cram into the **Palm House** – most of the time you will likely have the place to yourself. This iron and glass Victorian structure was added to the garden in the mid-19th century. It was designed by Richard Turner – he was indeed the architect responsible for the Great Palm House at Kew Gardens. Today, Belfast's Palm House houses an extensive variety of tropical and exotic plants. The **Tropical Ravine** is home to a jungle of tropical plants and a squadron of tiny terrapins, while the surrounding 25 acres boast water lily ponds, rose walks, gigantic fern trees – and even bananas flourishing in the hothouses.

THE BOTANIC GARDENS: www.belfastcity. gov.uk/parksandopenspaces. Entry: free; 7.30am to sunset; Palm House open 10am–12pm, 1pm–4/5pm Mon to Fri, 2–5pm Sat/Sun/bank holidays.

The Botanic Gardens

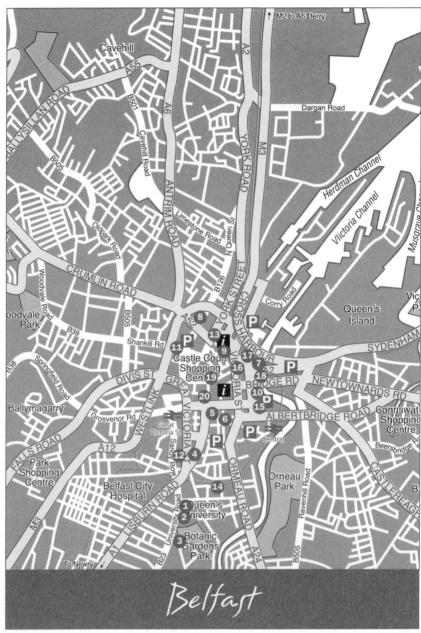

Belfast

Things to see and do
1. Ulster Museum
2. Queen's University
3. Botanic Gardens
4. Crown Liquor Saloon
5. Linen Hall Library
6. City Hall
7. Lagan Lookout
8. Clifton Street Cemetery
9. St Anne's Cathedral

Entertainment
10. Waterfront
11. Black Box Cathedral Quarter
12. Opera House

Shopping
13. Sheldon Arts, Donegall Sq East
14. Lawrence Street

Places to Stay
15. Hilton, Lanyon Place

13. The Merchant, Waring Street
14. Malmaison

Eat and Drink
13. Tedford's
14. Kelly's Cellars, Bank Street
15. Deane's Howard Street

Visitor Information
i Tourist Information Centre, St Anne's Court

The Cathedral Quarter

Belfast's new cultural heartland is the Cathedral Quarter, originally called Sailortown, surrounding the impressive **St Anne's Cathedral**. This attractive enclave – cobbled streets, inspiring architecture ranging from industrial to ecclesiastical – is home to cutting edge art festivals, such as the annual Cathedral Quarter Arts Festival, the Belfast Gay Pride Festival, the Big River Blues and Jazz Festival, the Children's Festival and the Belfast/Nashville Songwriters' Festival.

The Quarter extends out to the edge of the old merchant quarter of the city, traditionally the centre of Belfast's trade and warehousing district. This sprung up directly from the prosperous linen and shipbuilding industries, so the quarter still retains some of Belfast's oldest buildings and thoroughfares. The area fell into disrepair during the 20th century with the decline of traditional industries and the onset of the Troubles, but more recently it has re-emerged from both economic stagnation and civil turmoil. Essential sights include the **Cathedral** (see below) and the **Albert Clock** – which, until recent spoil-sporty renovation, had as impressive a list (because of subsidence) as the Tower of Pisa.

Two of Belfast's oldest thoroughfares, **Hill Street** and **Waring Street**, thread their way through the area. **St Anne's Cathedral** or Belfast Cathedral is a Church of Ireland (Protestant) cathedral. Here you will find the earthly remains of Edward Carson, architect of Ireland's partition, and the man who prosecuted Oscar Wilde in his sodomy trial in Dublin. You may prefer to admire the masonry, which can boast natural stone from each of Ireland's 32 counties. In 1924 it was decided to build the west front of the cathedral as a memorial to the Ulstermen and women who served and died in the First World War. (The militaristic nature of Ulster's Church of Ireland cathedrals may come as something of a surprise to visitors.)

In April 2007 a 40m stainless steel spire was installed on top of the cathedral. Named the Spire of Hope, the structure is illuminated at night and is

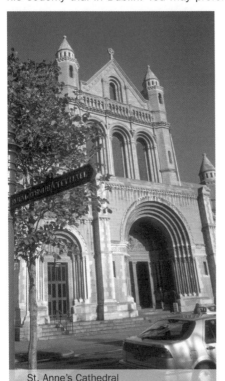
St. Anne's Cathedral

ST ANNE'S CATHEDRAL: Donegall Street, Belfast BT1 2FG; ☎ 028 9032 8332; www.belfastcathedral.org: Entry: free; open to visitors 10am–4pm on weekdays and before and after Sun services; daily Prayer Service Mon to Sat at 1pm; celebration of the Eucharist at 1pm on Wed, Feast and Saints' days; services of healing 8pm most Mon and 1 pm Fri; free parking for those attending Sun worship.

part of a wider redevelopment of the Cathedral Quarter. The base section of the spire protrudes through a glass platform in the Cathedral's roof directly above the choir stalls, allowing visitors to view it from the nave.

The *Titanic* tour

Belfast was the birthplace of the most famous ship since Noah's Ark. Many places in the city have connections with the ill-fated behemoth – memorabilia and memorials are dotted throughout the city, while the **Ulster Folk and Transport Museum** in **Cultra** (North Down, p. 247), and the **Linen Hall Library** both have artefacts and literature relating to the *Titanic*.

The **Lagan Boat Company** offers riverside tours beginning at the quay beside the **Big Fish**, a sculpture on the Laganside that celebrates the return of the salmon to the Lagan. This huge ceramic-skinned fish, installed at the waterside at **Donegall Quay** near the **Lagan Lookout** and just opposite the handsome **Custom House**, is by the artist John Kindness. The skin is decorated with texts and images relating to the city.

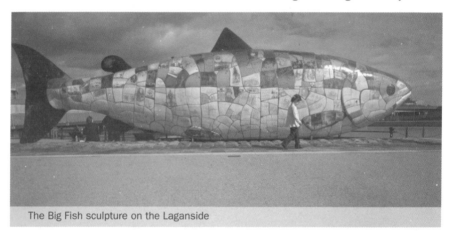

The Big Fish sculpture on the Laganside

The river tour chugs up the Lagan past the **Harland & Wolff** shipyard with its huge cranes, the biggest in the world – Samson and Goliath, or sometimes to the locals Big Ian and Wee Ian (a reference to Ian Paisley and his son). Tour guides will state – with a straight face – that any criticism about the *Titanic* seaworthiness will be met with the riposte, *'Well, she was alright when she left Belfast.'* They will also tell you about the County Down newspaper that covered the loss, including a man who lived locally in Donaghadee. The headline duly appeared: 'Local man lost at sea'.

LAGAN BOAT COMPANY: 48 St John's Close, 2 Laganbank Road, Belfast BT1 3LX; ☎ 028 9033 0844/07718 910 423; www.laganboatcompany.com: Entry: adults £10, concessions £8, family ticket £28 (2 adults + 2 kids), extra children £6 each.

The **Thompson *Titanic* Trail** is situated in the **Thompson Dry Dock** where the great Whitestar liners were built. The trail also includes the Pump-House audio-visual experience. The site is based in the Northern Ireland Science Park.

Black cab tours

Jump into a black cab for a day out in one of Europe's most historically turbulent cities – you can ask the driver to concentrate on *Titanic* spots, or choose from any number of themed tours: political tours, Narnia tours, mural tours, Van Morrison tours.

Coney Island pays tribute to Van's wanderings in County Down:

> *Coming down from Downpatrick*
> *Stopping off at St Johns Point*
> *Out all day birdwatching*
> *And the craic was good*
> *Stopped off at Strangford Lough*
> *Early in the morning*
> *Drove through Shrigley taking pictures*
> *And on to Killyleagh*
> *Stopped off for Sunday papers at the*
> *Lecale district, just before Coney Island*

Belfast City Hall

The poet James Maurice Craig expressed it thus:

> *Red brick in the suburbs, white horse on the wall,*
> *Eyetalian marble in the City Hall,*
> *O Stranger from England, why stand so aghast?*
> *May the Lord in His mercy be kind to Belfast.*

The impressive City Hall utterly dominates the centre of Belfast – as indeed it was meant to. A dominating statue of Queen Victoria in front of the building gazes regally down towards Belfast's main thoroughfare, **Royal Avenue**, while inside the Italian marble glistens. Whether the Lord has been kind to the city is another matter – certainly the 21st century has been more benign than the 20th – but there can be few better places to contemplate this theory than here at the fulcrum of the city's affairs.

Belfast City Hall is an ornate edifice made of Portland stone and topped with an enormous copper dome now covered

THOMPSON TITANIC TRAIL: *Titanic's* Dock & Pump-House, Northern Ireland Science Park, Queen's Road, Queen's Island, Belfast BT3 9DT; www.*Titanictrail*.com.

BLACK CAB TOURS: 07829 738239; www.belfastcitytours.com. Taxi tours include: Belfast Black Taxi Tours ☎ 077 6293 6704; Black Taxi Tours ☎ 028 9064 2264 or ☎ 077 9977 7888; Black Cab Tours NI ☎ 028 9087 5978 or Original Black Taxi Tours ☎ 028 9058 6996. Entry: £8–£12 per person or around £30 for the cab and depending on length of tour.

BELFAST CITY HALL: Donegall Square, Belfast BT1 5GS; ☎ 028 9027 0456; www.belfastcity.gov.uk. Entry: times of tours vary – call for details or visit the website.

Belfast City Hall

CELEBRITY CONNECTIONS

George Ivan Morrison OBE, came up with the masterly stroke of dispensing with the 'I' in his name early in his career. Today he is universally known as **Van Morrison** or Van the Man. He was born on 31 August 1945, in Hyndford Street, Ballymacarret in East Belfast, the only child of George Morrison, who worked at Harland & Wolff's shipyard, and Violet Stott Morrison, a singer and tap dancer in her youth. Van Morrison's family origins are the Ulster Scots population that settled in Belfast, and in his songs he often mentions Caledonia – his backing bands have been variously called the Caledonia Soul Orchestra and the Caledonia Soul Express.

Originally the front man with Belfast band Them ('Here Comes the Night' and 'Gloria'), Morrison is widely considered one of the most unusual and influential vocalists in the history of rock. Much of his material is influenced by American soul and rhythm and blues, such as 'Brown Eyed Girl' and 'Moondance'. The Celtic tradition, jazz, and stream-of-consciousness narrative – the latter borrowed perhaps from James Joyce – are also influences. Many of the places of Van Morrison's childhood, such as Cyprus Avenue, Fitzroy Avenue, Hyndford Street, Sandy Row and Orangefield (the boys' school he attended) are mentioned in his songs.

entirely in verdigris. The interior is lined with Greek as well as Italian marble. An exquisite banqueting hall and a large mural symbolizing Belfast's industrial history are centrepieces of conducted tours, which are free and an excellent way to learn some of the city's history. The *Titanic* **Memorial** stands just outside the main building.

Clifton Street Cemetery

Opened in 1797 as the 'New Burying Ground', the Clifton Street Cemetery holds the remains of rich merchants, paupers, unionist politicians, republican rebels, famous inventors, an American diplomat, an escaped American slave, and the man who coined the phrase 'the Emerald Isle'. The cemetery also contains unmarked mass graves where thousands of victims of cholera and fever were buried during the 1840s.

For Irish people, the most famous personage taking his eternal rest here is Henry Joy McCracken. Remembered in the popular eponymous ballad, McCracken was a United Irishman in the 1798 Rebellion, and hanged for his trouble on the gallows in **High Street**, **Belfast**. Beware, however; two graves bear the name of McCracken. One reads simply: 'The Burying Place of Henry Joy McCracken'; admirers of the rebel often mistakenly leave flowers there; however the United Irishman actually lies further up the cemetery. There's usually a copy of his song fluttering about on the tombstone:

> CLIFTON STREET CEMETERY: Belfast BT15 2BP; for conducted tours ☎ 028 9020 2100; www.glenravel.com.

An Ulster man I am proud to be, from the Antrim glens I come
And although I've laboured by the sea, I've followed flag and drum
I've heard the martial tramp of men, I've seen them fight and die
Ah lads it's well I remember when I followed Henry Joy

Body-snatching at Clifton Street Cemetery

Not long after the cemetery opened body-snatching became a major problem at Clifton Street. Doctors, still trying to understand how the human body worked, would pay up to £7 for a fresh corpse, and not be overly concerned about its origins. Body-snatchers would strike at dead of night, dig up a grave, and steal the corpse. It would then be packed in a barrel of brine and shipped to England or Scotland, labelled 'bacon'. As the problem worsened, bereaved families attempted to protect the bodies of their loved ones as best they could. Rich families built elaborate tombs, heavy tombs, tombs guarded by iron railings; poorer families simply stayed at the graveside until they were sure the body had begun to decompose.

A fellow United Irishman lying in repose, William Drennan, is generally recognised as the original author of the term 'Emerald Isle' for Ireland. It comes from his poem 'When Erin first rose', written in 1800:

> *Arm of Erin! Prove strong but be gentle and brave*
> *And uplifted to strike, still be ready to save*
> *Nor one feeling of vengeance presume to defile*
> *The curse of the men of the Emerald Isle.*

Surprisingly, Drennan denied that his poem was the first appearance of the phrase, but unfortunately threw no further light on the subject. Whoever was responsible, generations of songwriters, poets and not forgetting the Irish tourist board, have reason to be grateful to him or her.

Wet weather

ULSTER MUSEUM: Botanic Gardens BT9; ☎ 02890 383000 or 383001; www.ulster museum.org.uk. Entry: free; open 10am–5pm Mon to Fri, 1pm–5pm Sat, 2pm–5pm Sun, year round.

The Ulster Museum

The Ulster Museum in the **Botanic Gardens** is one of the best half dozen places in the world to get to grips with Irish history, from Early Erin onwards. It's not all Celts, however – an Egyptian mummy – **Princess Takabuti** – complete with teeth, skin and hair, plus a ghostly grin, is still one of the main attractions. She's also called 'Belfast's oldest bleached blonde' because of her chemically discoloured hair.

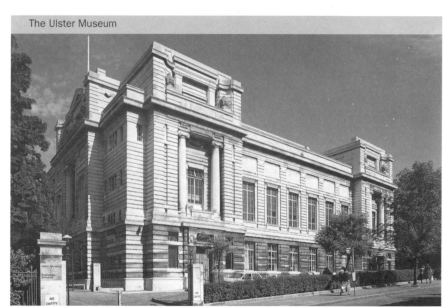
The Ulster Museum

The **Girona Treasure**, gathered from the Spanish Armada that foundered off the northerly seaboard of Ireland, is a graphic and glittering slice of history, while the art gallery houses European treasures both traditional and contemporary. You will also get the lowdown on linen, rope and glass manufacturing, industrial machines and Irish painting.

The Ormeau Baths Art Gallery

Belfast's premier contemporary art gallery, the space is located on the site of a Victorian bath house. The gallery programmes include a mix of solo and group shows; national and international in all art disciplines – exhibitions have ranged from Yoko Ono to Paul Klee, and of course Enniskillen-educated Oscar Wilde gets a look in too with his words: *'The object of art is not simple truth but complex beauty.'*

> **THE ORMEAU BATHS ART GALLERY:** Ormeau Baths Gallery, 18a Ormeau Avenue BT2 8HS; ☎ 028 9032 1402; www.ormeaubaths.co.uk. Entry: variable, depending on shows.

What to do with children...

Lagan Lookout Centre

Designed to protect Belfast from flooding, the **Lagan Weir** was the first completed component of the continuing river and docks redevelopment project. The raised, circular lookout centre explains the weir project and explores the river's vital role in the development of such diverse industries as linen, rope-making and shipbuilding. Carefully positioned windows around the centre point out Belfast landmarks.

> **LAGAN LOOKOUT CENTRE:** 1 Donegall Quay, Donegall Quay, Belfast BT1 3EA; ☎ 028 9031 5444; www.laganlookout.com. Entry: adults £1.50, children £0.75, family £4.00; open daily from 10am.

... and how to avoid children

The **Linen Hall Library**, a venerable old institution, was established in 1788 *'to improve the mind and excite a spirit of general inquiry'*. It is one of the most absorbing libraries in these islands. Apart from housing a valuable resource on the 1798 Rebellion (an early librarian, United Irishman Thomas Russell, one of the rebel leaders, was executed in 1803), the Irish and local studies collection includes a copy of everything written about Northern Ireland politics since 1966 – 250,000 items in all, the definitive archive of the

The Linen Hall Library

recent Troubles. There are also copies of the oldest English language newspaper – and one of the oldest in the world still published – the *Belfast Newsletter*, which rolled off the press in 1737.

Some of the more offbeat exhibits on show at the library include the IRA's A–Z handbook, chocolate bars commemorating loyalist violence at Drumcree, secret communications hidden in loo rolls and on cigarette papers between the republican hunger strikers in the Maze prison and the IRA leadership outside, and the Hang-David-Trimble posters, complete with a picture of the ousted unionist leader with a noose drawn around his neck. There's enough here to offend everyone, but the library is strictly non-partisan – everyone is offended equally. There are babies' propaganda bibs with loyalist slogans, a vicious children's alphabet ('A is for Armalite that sends them all running...'), a lolly shaped like a foot with the advice to 'kick the Pope', a letter of support from the Ayatollah Khomeini to mid-Ulster MP Bobby Sands (they eventually named a street in Teheran in honour of Bobby Sands), and plastic bullets as big as cucumbers.

Entertainment

Marching

Belfast is a vibrant centre for both Irish traditional music and Ulster Scots music. The marching season (May to October) is marked by parades from all the loyalist areas, particularly East Belfast, Sandy Row, the Shankill and Finaghy. The season culminates on 12 July, but minor parades are held throughout the season. On 12 July huge bonfires are lit in the most staunchly loyalist areas. Effigies of Republican heroes and Irish tricolours are burnt. The local press, particularly the *Belfast Newsletter*, carry details of parades.

A Parades Commission convenes regularly to decide which particular marches are too contentious to go ahead. The marching season in recent history was a synonym for civil disturbance. Over the past few years the violence has abated, and on a good day the Orange marches can be a fascinating spectacle, tinged with not a little irony. Thousands of loyalist folk get their bowler hats and sashes on, pick up their accordion, flute or bagpipes, and head to a hostile neighbourhood to proclaim their Britishness. The Parades Commission website (www.paradescommission.org) is a good place to see what marches are on, and how contentious they're likely to be.

Live music

Belfast is a major centre for folk and traditional music. During the Troubles people couldn't travel far for fear of violence – or just the sheer drudgery of going through security checks – so a huge upsurge in 'home grown' entertainment resulted. This was fastened onto the already long history of traditional music in Belfast – the McPeake

The best of... NORTHERN IRELAND'S HISTORY AND HERITAGE

THE HISTORY AND CULTURE OF NORTHERN IRELAND IS ETCHED IN THE VERY LANDSCAPE OF THE COUNTRY. PRACTICALLY NO FIELD OR OPEN LAND IS WITHOUT ITS RUINED CASTLE, HIGH CROSS OR NEOLITHIC REMAINS. THE IVY MAY BE GROWING OVER THESE FADING STONE STRUCTURES, THE SHEEP MAY BE GRAZING AROUND THEM – BUT THEY SPEAK OF A LENGTHY, RICH AND AT TIMES TROUBLED HERITAGE.

Dunluce Castle, County Antrim

Top: The Boa Man, Boa Island; Middle: Traditional fiddle making, Cushendall;
Bottom: Enniskillen Castle

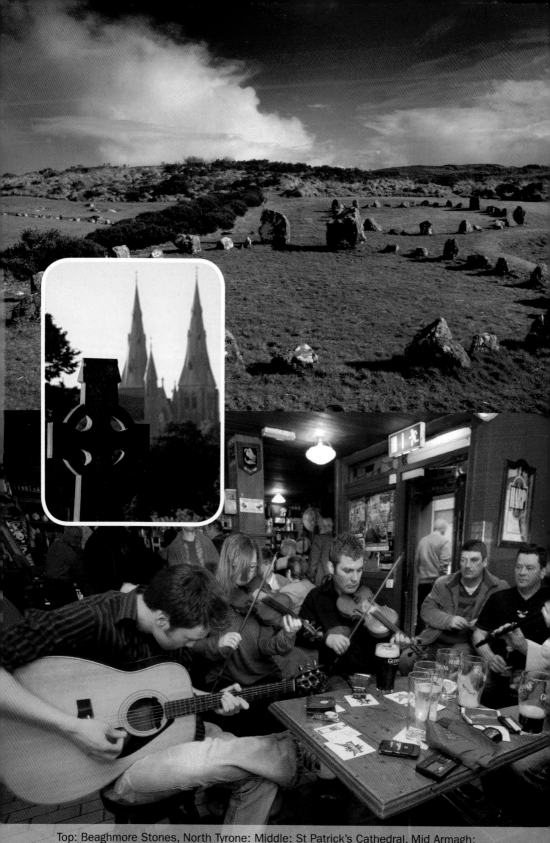

Top: Beaghmore Stones, North Tyrone: Middle: St Patrick's Cathedral, Mid Armagh;
Bottom: Madden's Bar, Belfast

Top: Slemish Mountain, South Antrim; Middle: 'Let the Dance Begin'
Millennium celebration sculpture, Strabane; Bottom: Narrow Water Castle

family, for instance, kept Irish music going when it had almost been forgotten in the rest of Ireland, while fiddler Sean Maguire from Belfast (who died recently) is seen as a seminal figure in consolidating the contemporary Irish fiddling style. The fourth generation of the McPeake family still perform. Particularly celebrated for preserving the uillean pipe tradition, you will likely hear them performing their grandfather's song 'Wild Mountain Thyme'.

Any number of pubs feature Irish music, ballad groups, sessions, and folk music of every sort throughout the city.

- **Pat's Bar** – 19–20 Princes Dock Street; ☎ 028 9074 4524; one of Belfast's most famous gathering places for traditional musicians.
- **Madden's Bar** – 74 Berry Street; ☎ 028 9024 4114 – similarly steeped in music. Live traditional music is featured most evenings during the week.
- **Rotterdam** – 52–54 Pilot Street; ☎ 028 9074 6021, www.rotterdambar.com; as above, live traditional music.
- **Errigle Inn** – 312 Ormeau Road; ☎ 028 9064 1410; has regular rock, folk and American music.

This is the third century that **Robinson's Bar** (Great Victoria Street BT2 7BA; ☎ 028 9024 7447; www.robinson'sbar.co.uk) has been servicing Belfast's thirsty people. A pub full of charm and character, the part known as **Fibber Magee's** presents traditional music and ballad bands seven nights a week. On the top floor, **Roxy's Night Club** tears away every Friday night, while the basement is home to the BT1 club. With three different bars, the **Botanic Inn** (23–27 Malone Road, Belfast BT9 6RU; ☎ 028 9050 9740 has sessions, live bands, DJs, dances – as well as big-screen sport and pub quizzes.

Concerts, theatres and cinemas

Belfast is well supplied with concert venues, theatres and cinemas. The premier theatre for musicals, opera, ballet, comedy and pantomime is the **Grand Opera House**

The Grand Opera House

(Great Victoria Street, Belfast BT2 7HR; ☎ 028 9024 1919; www.goh.co.uk). Twice bombed to bits and rebuilt, the Opera House is a hugely opulent exception to the functionality of most of Belfast's architecture. This jewel box of Victoriana and imperial taste boasts satin chairs, gold elephants on the ceiling, nymphs, cherubs and Indian Shivas, with a frieze of Sanskrit on the walls. Pure theatre from start to finish.

- The **Belfast Waterfront Hall** – 2 Lanyon Place, Belfast; ☎ 028 9033 4455; www.waterfront.co.uk; one of Northern Ireland's principal concert venues. It's also a good place for a nice cup of tea.
- **The Black Box** – 18–22 Hill Street, Cathedral Quarter BT1 2LA; ☎ 028 9024 440; www.blackboxbelfast.com; a showcase venue where local artists perform alongside a line-up of modern and abstract theatre, drama etc. Not the place for a sing song.
- **The Queen's Film Theatre** – 20 University Square, Belfast; ☎ 028 9097 1097; www.queensfilmtheatre.com; the only full-time provider of non-mainstream cinema. It has a friendly atmosphere, two screens, and is fully licensed.
- **Movie House Cinemas** – 14 Dublin Road, Belfast; ☎ 028 9024 5700; www.moviehouse.co.uk; located in the heart of Belfast's restaurant and club district, has 10 screens. Many art-house and independent films are screened as well as more mainstream movies.

Nightlife

Belfast these days has a feisty nightlife. Clubs include **Kremlin** (96 Donegall Street, Belfast; ☎ 028 9031 6060; www.kremlin-belfast.com), Ireland's biggest and most popular gay club. Open five nights a week, ranges from drag cabaret to live gigs. **La Lea** (43 Franklin Street, Belfast; ☎ 028 9023 0200) is where Belfast's young, up-for-it clubbers congregate. **The M-Club** (23–31 Bradbury Place; ☎ 028 9023 3131, www.mclub.co.uk) is in the heart of the Belfast's nightlife district. Recent winner of 'The Club of the Year Award', this lively, sophisticated club pulls in punters from all over Ireland. **The Box** nightclub (Odyssey Pavilion, 2 Queen's Quay; www.theboxnightcub.com) is a massive club running at the weekend. **The Roxy** (38–42 Great Victoria Street; ☎ 028 9024 7447) is where New York chic meets industrial Belfast with low metallic lights and the remorseless thrum of techno and dance-floor anthems.

Sport

The principal GAA stadium in Northern Ireland is Casement Park, home to senior Antrim Gaelic football and hurling teams. Named after one of the participants of the 1916 Easter Rising, Sir Roger Casement, the ground has a capacity of 32,600. For tickets to events, visit www.gaa.com.

The main international soccer ground is Windsor Park, also the home of club side Linfield. For fixtures, see www.irishfa.com. Northern Ireland's main ice hockey team, the Belfast Giants, can be seen in action at the Odyssey (www.belfastgiants.com). The Ulster rugby side, which have been European champions, perform at Ravenhill Park in Belfast. For tickets and fixtures list, see www.ulsterrugby.ie.

CELEBRITY CONNECTIONS

George Best, born in East Belfast, in the same area which produced Van Morrison, was a professional footballer with Manchester United and the Northern Ireland international side. The wayward Belfast genius is universally regarded as the one of the truly great players in the history of the game, one of its most talented ball artists. He retired at the age of 27, leaving the tantalising question of what could have been achieved had he played on for another five years or so.

Having said that, George was always proud of his record, pointing out that he played over 11 seasons for Manchester United, won two league championships, and one European Cup – when he almost single-handedly annihilated Benfica. But the former European Footballer of the Year's off-field activities, which centred round wine, women and song (mostly the former two), attracted as much publicity as his on field exploits. Even Best himself acknowledged that his adventures with the opposite sex may have contributed to his true potential having not been fulfilled. *'If I'd been born ugly,'* he is quoted as saying, *'Pele wouldn't even be spoken of in the same breath as me.'* He used to tell the story of chatting up a young lady at a night club, who proved to be impervious to his famous charm. Trying the age old chat-up line he asked: *'Where have you been all my life?' 'Well,'* she replied, *'for most of it I wasn't born...'*

He was one of the first celebrity footballers, but his extravagant lifestyle led to problems with alcoholism that curtailed his playing career and eventually led to his death in November 2005 at the age of 59. Belfast's city airport is named after him.

Belfast's two main golf clubs are **The Royal Belfast** (Station Road, Craigavad; ☎ 028 9042 8165; www.royalbelfast.com) and the **Malone Golf Club** (240 Upper Malone Road, Dunmurray; ☎ 028 9061 2758).

Festivals

Held annually in November, the **Belfast Festival** (www.belfastfestival.com) is primarily run by Queen's University Belfast. Founded in the 1960s the festival grew through the years expanding to a two-week long event. Every conceivable type of music has been presented over the years – ditto comedy, drama and film. The festival is held at several venues across the city, including the **Mandela Hall**, the **Naughton Gallery**, the **Queen's Film Theatre** and the **Whitla Hall** at Queen's, as well as the **Grand Opera House** and the **Waterfront Hall**.

Other Belfast festivals include:

- The **Cathedral Quarter Arts Festival** (www.cqaf.com), takes place in January and features rock, poetry, drama. Takes up almost the whole month.

- **St. Patrick's Day Carnival** (17 March) begins at Belfast City Centre (☎ 028 9024 660; www.belfastcity.gov.uk) and winds through Belfast. It features a parade, free music concert (featuring a mix of pop and traditional music), and floats.
- The *Titanic* **Made in Belfast Festival** (www.belfastcity.gov.uk/Titanic) takes place in April (coinciding with the original launch day of 10 April) and includes a week-long celebration and commemoration of the great ship, its tragic fate, the people who perished on it, and the Belfast people who built it. Featured are *Titanic* tours, special exhibitions, lectures and music.
- The **Belfast Maritime Festival** (☎ 028 9024 6609; www.belfastcity.gov.uk/maritimefestival/index.asp) annually features a flotilla of majestic sailing ships docking in Belfast in June. The festival also includes a 'continental market', music, sports, storytelling, face painting, circus performers and demonstrations.
- The **Belfast Film Festival** (www.belfastfilmfestival.org) is an annual festival taking place March-April. County-founded in the mid-1990s by former Provisional Irish Republican Army member Laurence McKeown and other fervent film-goers, the festival includes specialist films, 120 screenings, workshops, discussions, master classes and special events in a (usually) 10-day period.

🛒 Shopping

For Irish art, **Sheldon Art & Framing** (1a Donegall Square East, Belfast; ☎ 028 9032 4295) has a great store of limited edition art, canvas, open editions and original paintings and **Linen Hall Library & Coffee Shop** (17 Donegall Square North; ☎ 028 9032 1707; www.linenhall.com) sells a wide selection of paintings and prints from leading Ulster artists, plus unique mementoes. **Lawrence Street Workshops** (☎ 028 9023 4993) are located in an old stables courtyard in the Queen's Quarter. Established in 1989 by local artists and crafts people, the complex features a series of bustling workshops and an impressive showroom offering a diverse and fascinating range of two and three-dimensional crafts from paintings to furniture. All the works for sale are by local artists using traditional and contemporary skills. The workshops are also known for a unique range of recycled produce known as Upcycling, including beautiful glasses made from wine bottles and sculptures made from recycled plastic. Tours are by appointment only.

For that traditional standby for Ulster souvenir hunters, **Smyth's Irish Linens** (65 Royal Avenue; ☎ 028 9024 2232) and **The Irish Linen Stores** (14 Callender Street; ☎ 028 9032 2727) carry a full range of linen damask, doilies and other lacey things.

 # The best... PLACES TO STAY

BOUTIQUE

Ten Square

10 Donegall Square, South Belfast BT1 5JD
☎ **028 9024 1001**
www.tensquare.co.uk

Ten Square Hotel is an innovative boutique hotel famed for its character-packed rooms and inspired dining areas. Although as centrally located as you could get, the hotel inside is quiet and calming.

Price: From £90 for a double.

The Malmaison Belfast

34–38 Victoria Street, Belfast BT1 3GH
☎ **028 9022 0200**
www.malmaison.com

Offering a range of luxurious hotel rooms and elegant, opulent suites, Malmaison Belfast is a haven of gracious living. Built on a converted old seed warehouse, it combines history (offering original features such as iron pillars and beams) with the best of contemporary style. For a top boutique hotel in Belfast, it's unbeatable.

Price: From £79, breakfast not included.

HOTEL

The Europa

Great Victoria Street, Belfast BT2 7AP
☎ **028 9027 1066**
www.hastingshotels.com/europa

The PR for the four-star Europa Hotel calls it 'world famous'. And indeed it is – although the hotel's blurb doesn't actually tell you why. Understandable really, because it once had the reputation for being the most bombed hotel in the world. This was at the height of the provisional IRA bombing campaign, at a time when people said if you wanted your cocktail shaken, you just waited until the windows rattled and the floor shuddered as another car bomb went off outside. Another celebrated anecdote tells how a guest one evening phoned up reception saying, 'I'm afraid I'm having trouble with my shower.' 'Trouble?' said the receptionist. 'Jayz, you don't know the meaning of the word.' All changed now of course. Today the hotel is famed only for its sumptuous rooms, mellow bars – and local langoustines and scallops for dinner.

Price: From £200 for a double, from £135 for a single.

The Merchant

35–39 Waring Street, Belfast BT1 2DY
☎ **028 9023 4888**
www.themerchanthotel.com

In the heart of the Cathedral quarter, the Merchant is one of the city's few five-star hotels. Situated inside the Edwardian splendour of the Ulster Bank's former headquarters, the Merchant offers opulence and sophistication in equal measure. Don't forget to try the Merchant's porridge – whipped with double cream and infused with whiskey.

Price: B&B from £87.50–£225 per person sharing.

The Hilton

4 Lanyon Place, Belfast BT1 3LP
☎ **028 9027 7000**
www.hilton.co.uk/belfast

Another of Belfast's five-star hotels, the Hilton has everything you might expect from a Hilton, including luxurious bedrooms, elegant dining areas, and a romantic bar.

Price: From £129 for a double.

The best... PLACES TO STAY

The McCausland Hotel

34–38 Victoria Street, Belfast BT1 3GH
☎ 028 9022 0200

Two old Victorian warehouses converted into a luxury hotel on the banks of the Lagan have produced this haven of sophisticated accommodation and dining. The bistro offers contemporary Irish cuisine, the bar is exceptionally well supplied, and a post-prandial stroll just outside on Laganside offers a rejuvenated view of Belfast with its boutiques and bars.

Price: From £120 for a double.

B&B

The Old Rectory

148 Malone Road, Belfast BT9 5LH
☎ 028 9066 7882
www.anoldrectory.co.uk

The Old Rectory won the Aga Rayburn Best Breakfast Award in 2005. No wonder, the options include soda bread, locally smoked salmon, wild boar and apple sausages, free-range duck and guinea fowl eggs and black pudding. Four of the five bedrooms have an en suite and the other has a private bathroom. The drawing room is stuffed with books about Ireland, as well as cards, games and a piano.

Price: Doubles £75 from £39 to £49 for a single.

Ash Rowan Town House

12 Windsor Avenue, Belfast BT9 6EE
☎ 028 9066 1758

Run by Sam and Evelyn Hazlett, former restaurateurs, this Victorian guest house offers breakfasts such as omelettes, smoked salmon, kedgeree, mushrooms flambéed with sherry – or an Ulster fry-up with organic sausages and soda bread. Trouble is, you start to feel hungry again after about 24 hours.

Price: from £59 to £69 for a single; from £98 to £110 for a double.

The best... FOOD AND DRINK

▶ Staying in

St George's Market, the oldest covered market in Ireland, is a combination of farmers' produce (organic veg, organic burgers, tasty artisan cheeses) and food market with sweet stalls, fruit, traditional bread and the like. You can count on lots of free samples. Don't miss the local seafood – Belfast Lough prawns have never gotten the same publicity as their cousins the Dublin Bay prawns, but they're every bit as tasty – all they need is a good PR agent. Once you've had your fill of crustaceans, head for the wild mushroom risotto, or dainty handmade lemon and violet cakes.

You might even be able to pick up some pre-loved clothing from the secondhand stalls. This is one of the liveliest market scenes in Ireland.

Founded in 1954, **Direct Wine Shipments** (DWS), a family owned specialist wine importer and retailer, works with some of the most famous wine producers in the world, including Torres, Brown Brothers, Hugel and Vega Sicilia. Located in a large (and allegedly haunted) building in the atmospheric old docks area of Belfast, DWS regularly hosts wine courses and tastings as well as wine dinners with top chefs. Tours should be arranged in advance.

ST GEORGE'S MARKET: 12 East Bridge Street; www.belfastcity.gov.uk/georgesmarket. Entry: Fri 6am–2pm, Sat 9am–3pm.

DIRECT WINE SHIPMENTS: 5–7 Corporation Square, Belfast BT3 9LB; ☎ 028 9050 8000; www.directwine.co.uk.

Once upon a time eating out in Ulster meant chips with everything but even throughout this bleak period of gastronomy **Sawers** (Unit 7, Fountain Centre) kept the gourmet flag flying. As recently as the 1970s, this shop was one of the very few places you could buy anything as exotic as garlic or tomato puree. The shop has kept up the good work over the decades, selling local produce, seasonal goods – and of course garlic and tomato puree.

Drinking

The Irish theme pub can now be found everywhere in Europe. But in Belfast they have the cask-conditioned, batteries included, utterly genuine real thing. And in great numbers. Traditional old back street pubs – cosy, dark premises with a honeycomb of tiny rooms, ubercool clubs with techno music, bars serving food shot through with cholesterol, gastropubs for the Gaelic gourmet, lounges dedicated to Ulster's full sporting panoply, music pubs where the craic is guaranteed every night of the week, little snugs where the conversation crackles and wanders until the wee hours – Belfast has the lot. Here you'll find incorrigible informality, glowing hospitality – plus music and conversation that erupts spontaneously and pushes on through until dawn.

It is also home, arguably, to one of the best bars anywhere in these islands, the television and Muzak-free socialist gastro-pub/Irish traditional music boozer, the **John Hewitt,** in the Cathedral Quarter. The bar is probably unique in the world in that it's owned by a non-profit making non-governmental office – the Belfast Unemployed Resource Centre. The Resource Centre's managers had always relied on various grants to fund its work. In the mid-1990s they came up with the idea of generating some of their own funds by opening a pub on-site. John Hewitt, the late poet, socialist and Freeman of Belfast officially opened

THE JOHN HEWITT: 51 Donegall Street, Belfast BT1 2FH; ☎ 028 9023 3768; www.thejohnhewitt.com.

EATING OUT

RESTAURANT

Tedford's
5 Donegall Quay, Belfast BT1 3EF
☎ 028 9043 4000
www.tedfordsrestaurant.com

Tedford's Seafood Steakhouse, rich in maritime history, was built in 1843, overlooking the River Lagan. The first-floor dining room is done out like an ocean liner, and the cuisine – local fish, seafood and meat – is prepared imaginatively in a contemporary style. Dishes from around £9.

Metro Brasserie
13 Lower Crescent, Belfast BT17 1NR
☎ 028 9032 3349
www.crescenttownhouse.com

Wine bar, brasserie, restaurant and pub, there's a vegetarian menu alongside the extensive à la carte menu and extensive wine list. Aperitifs, postprandial liqueurs and Irish coffees can be quaffed in the Bar Twelve. Main courses from £8.

The Northern Whig
2–10 Bridge Street, Belfast BT1 1 LU
☎ 028 9050 9888
www.thenorthernwhig.com

This restaurant and popular city centre bar in the lively Cathedral Quarter was formerly headquarters of the *Northern Whig*. The newspaper, founded in 1823, was published until 1963. The restaurant's menu ranges from daily specials (roasts to pastas) as well as delicious tapas and paninis. Fish comes from County Down, beef from a farm in Armagh ('a particularly lovely wee farm' apparently), and vegetables from local farms around Belfast. Starters from around £5, mains for about double that.

Deane's
38–40 Howard Street, Belfast
☎ 028 9056 0000
www.michaeldeane.co.uk

Ornate Hollywood staircase, cultured chow and generally brassy surroundings. The food is equally showy – and good, earning Deane's Northern Ireland's only Michelin Star. Downstairs in the brasserie things are much simpler – and cheaper. The style of the food could be described as modern and contemporary. Main courses from £17.

Made in Belfast
Wellington Street BT1 6ET
☎ 028 9024 6712
www.madeinbelfastni.com

In the shadow of City Hall, this is part-boudoir, part art college space, part Manhattan club – you drink and dine while reclining on cushions or perched on chairs and crates. The menu is varied and interesting, but includes big-fisted favourites such as a steak burger in a Belfast bap with Welsh rarebit topping and Ballymaloe relish. On weekend nights you can sip cocktails to sounds from a local DJ. Main dishes from around £11.

CAFÉ

The Kitchen Bar
16–18 Victoria Square, Belfast BT1 4QA
☎ 028 9032 4901

This part American diner, part Spanish tapas bar, part Irish pub serves breakfasts that feature three kinds of homemade bread – wheaten, soda and potato farls as well as the finest bacon and sausages in Ireland; specialities include 'Paddy's pizza'– a slab of soda bread with a slice of boiled gammon, Coleraine cheddar and tomatoes topped with eggs. Also try the Irish stew with beef – served with towering escarpments of mashed potatoes. Breakfasts and Paddy's Pizza cost around £5.

the Resource Centre on May Day 1983, thus the name. In 2008 the John Hewitt won the CAMRA Pub of the Year Award.

Kelly's Cellars (Bank Street; ☎ 028 90 324835) in the very centre of Belfast, is ideal for that reviving pint of stout. With cellars dating from 1720 (possibly the oldest in all Ireland) Kelly's was a frequent meeting place for the United Irishmen in the run-up to the 1798 rebellion. Nearly 300 years after it was founded, Kelly's manages to place itself somewhere between everyman drinking pub, political meeting place, and historic museum. Folk music is regular fare at weekends. During the week it's the ideal meeting-up place – even if you aren't planning a rebellion.

The **Hatfield House** (130 Ormeau Road, Belfast BT27 2EB; ☎ 028 9043 8764; www.thehatfield.com) is very much a traditional Irish bar with original features, ornate ceilings and lavish craftsmanship carried out by the same lads who worked on the *Titanic*. The Hatfield is very big on sports and live entertainment is regularly part of proceedings. **McHugh's Bar and Restaurant** (29–31 Queens Square, Belfast BT1 3FG; ☎ 028 9050 9999) has the unique distinction of being the oldest building in Belfast, dating back to its establishment in 1711. It is multi-functional, with restaurant, lounge, music venue and club. But it's the bar which is the glory of the establishment – warm, welcoming and comfortably quiet.

No visit to Belfast would be complete without a pilgrimage to the glorious **Crown Liquor Saloon**, (46 Great Victoria Street, ☎ 028 9024 9476). This is without doubt one of the great bars of the world, a gem of Victorian splendour – wood panelling, brasswork, Italian tiles, real gas lamps. Some of the fixtures and fittings may appear extremely opulent. That's because shipyard workers helped decorate the bar with swag from the *Titanic* and other ocean liners. Today, the pub, which belongs to the National Trust, is still a vital part of Belfast's everyday life.

The Entries, a cluster of narrow alleyways or closes running off High Street and Ann Street, are all that remain of Belfast's oldest quarter. Once home to a thriving commercial and residential area, now only the pubs remain. **White's Tavern** (☎ 028 9024 3080) in Wine Cellar Entry is the city's oldest pub. The **Morning Star** (17–19 Pottinger's Entry, Belfast BT1 4DT; ☎ 028 9023 5986) is another of Belfast's ancient, historic pubs, first built as a coaching stop for the Belfast to Dublin post. Situated in the Entries, this was an essential stop for the mail coach – it should be similarly essential for anyone wanting to know what a traditional Belfast pub is like. The menu is probably the most adventurous and eclectic in the city – serving pan-fried crocodile, kangaroo and emu, as well as local dishes.

Another great rarity in the pub world is the **Winged Lion of St Mark** sitting proudly on the corner. The building is historically listed and can trace its history back to 1810, when it was mentioned in the *Belfast Newsletter* as being one of the terminals for the Belfast to Dublin Mail Coach. The downstairs bar has its original mahogany counter with its old terrazzo floor. **Bittles Bar** (70 Upper Church Lane, Victoria Square BT1 4QL, UK; ☎ 028 9031 1088; open 11am–11pm) is one of the smallest bars in Belfast with one of the largest selections of bottled beer. Today Bittles stocks a huge range of vittles: wheat beers, stouts, lagers, ales and ciders. For those who like a chaser with their pint, an extensive whiskey menu does the job. This is a key landmark in Belfast for dedicated drinkers, with cask-conditioned character as well as beer, and friendly service into the bargain.

OUTER BELFAST

Outer Belfast stretches in the east to North Down and the towns of **Holywood** and **Groomsport**, in the north towards Cave Hill and the **Antrim Plateau**. In the south and west the suburbs of the city give way to the rolling drumlins of **South Down**.

East Belfast begins at the great shipyards and dock areas lining the **River Lagan**. Being a powerhouse of the Industrial Revolution, Belfast was built for function rather than finery, and nowhere is it clearer than the endless Victorian terraced houses that eventually morph into modern residential areas. There's probably little of interest for the visitor in East Belfast until you reach Stormont, although if you're a Van Morrison fan you might want to pay a visit to **Cyprus Avenue** in **Ballymacarret**. Nearby is Van the Man's birthplace in **Hyndford Street**.

North Belfast's main point of interest is **Belfast Zoo** on the Antrim Road, and the area round **Cave Hill** – one of the oldest parts of the city. **West Belfast** is altogether more absorbing as this is the heartland of both staunchly republican Belfast and also the stoutly loyalist Shankill Road. History is writ large here: finally in the 20th century, 800 years of war, rebellion, colonial occupation, repression, plantation and simmering resentment distilled down into 30 years of violent struggle – centred largely round a handful of streets built in Victorian times.

For the past dozen years or so West Belfast – and indeed the rest of the Six Counties – has been at peace. Although tensions remain, even the most entrenched areas have begun to emerge from communal strife and turmoil.

WHAT TO SEE AND DO

Falls Road

The Falls Road, the main thoroughfare through West Belfast, stretches from **Divis Street** and **Castle Place** in Belfast city centre to **Andersonstown** in the suburbs. Its name is synonymous with the Catholic and republican communities in the city, and is one of the most famous streets in the North. It draws tourists the whole year round, but you are unlikely ever to feel swamped by them.

The predominantly Protestant neighbouring area of **Shankill Road** is

Mural depicting Frederick Douglass

Protestant mural

separated from the Falls by the 'peace line' which consists of huge ramparts – some as high as 25ft – made from concrete and wrought iron. These keep the warring factions apart.

Various taxi tours and walking tours visit the peace line, at the same time taking in the wall murals depicting republican heroes, international revolutionary figures, and legendary Irish icons. Any walk up Falls Road or into neighbouring side streets will reveal more murals, covering walls and gable ends. Portraits of Bobby Sands stand beside the 26+6=1 slogans (an allusion to the counties in both parts of Ireland), as well as revered historical figures such as James Connolly, *'The man who lived for socialism but died for Ireland'*, Jim Larkin (trades unionist leader) and Sir Roger Casement, the British civil servant who became an Irish rebel.

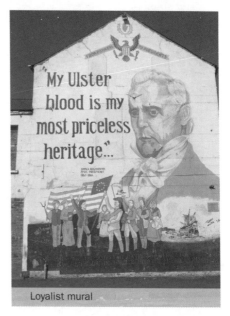
Loyalist mural

Today, very little heed is paid to tourists, and you'll have no problem taking photos of the murals. Be a little more wary, however, of taking photographs of the residents. Overall, however, you will find the locals friendly and helpful should you want directions – or a quick potted history of the area. Someone will probably point out **St Catherine's Primary School** on Falls Road, where Katie Melua went to school aged 8, after arriving in Belfast from the USSR.

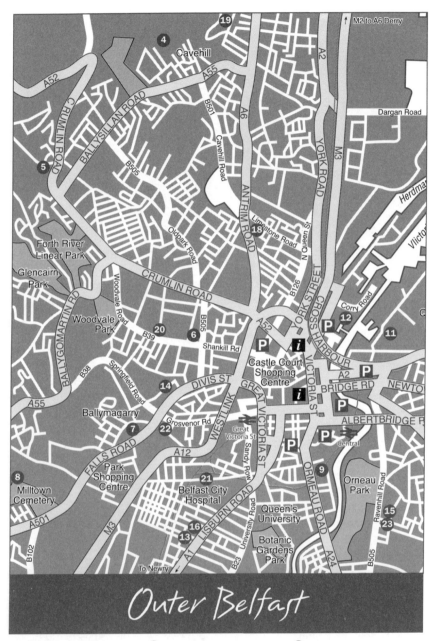

Outer Belfast

Things to see and do
1. Hyndford Street (Van Morrison's birthplace)
2. Aunt Sandra's Candy Factory
3. Harland & Wolff Shipyards
4. Cave Hill
5. Crumlin Road Gaol
6. Shankill Road Murals
7. Falls Road Murals
8. Milltown Cemetery

Entertainment
9. Errigle Inn
10. Dundonald Ice Bowl

11. Odyssey
12. Pat's Bar, Dock Street

Shopping
13. Lisburn Road
14. Conway Mill

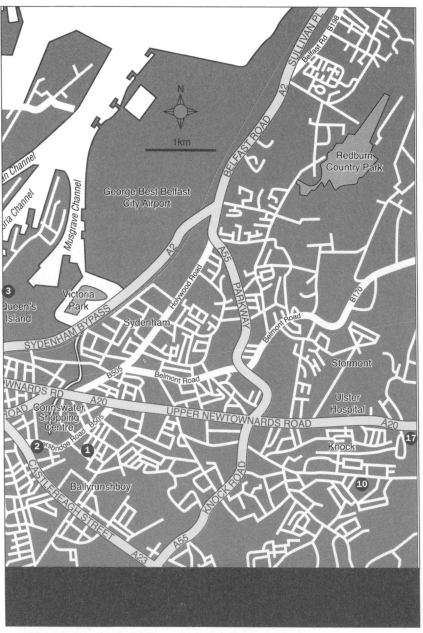

Places to Stay
- 15 Ravenhill House
- 16 City Resorts, Lisburn Road
- 17 Hastings Stormont Hotel

Eat and Drink
- 18 Owen McMahon's Butchers

- 19 The Cellar, Belfast Castle
- 20 The Berlin, Shankill Road

Visitor Information
- 21 Belfast City Hospital
- 22 Royal Victoria Hospital
- 23 Bike Dock

Other areas to view the full sweep of republican murals and nationalist art include **Beechmount Avenue** (just off Falls Road), the **Ballymurphy** district beyond the Upper Falls, and the **New Lodge Road** in North Belfast.

The **Sinn Féin shop** and office (53 Falls Road BT12 4PD) with its mural of hunger striker Bobby Sands MP, is often used by Sinn Féin politicians as a backdrop when giving television interviews. Another popular destination is the nearby **Solidarity Wall**, featuring murals mainly dedicated to revolutionaries inspired by or with connections to Irish republicanism (Palestinians, ETA and so on) and is located close to the newly refurbished Falls Road Leisure Centre and the Divis area.

TAXI TOURS INCLUDE: Belfast Black Taxi Tours ☎ 077 6293 6704; Black Taxi Tours ☎ 028 9064 2264 or 077 9977 7888; Black Cab Tours NI ☎ 028 9087 5978; Original Black Taxi Tours ☎ 028 9058 6996.

To see the famous murals, or indeed to visit any of Belfast's sights including the *Titanic* key spots, the peace line or

CELEBRITY CONNECTIONS

In the aftermath of the Georgian civil war, **Katie Melua**'s family moved to Belfast. It was here – first at St Catherine's Primary School on Falls Road, and later at the Dominican College, Fortwilliam in North Belfast, that Katie began writing songs. Because of her upbringing in politically unstable Georgia and troubled Belfast, Katie initially planned to become either a historian or a politician. However, her talent for music soon shone through at school.

When Katie subsequently told her teacher in England that she'd moved from Georgia to Belfast, he described the move as: 'From the frying pan into the fire', probably a natural enough assumption by someone who hadn't so far discovered the delights of Belfast. Katie for her part is on record as saying that she found the Belfast people extremely warm and welcoming, and that she made great friends there.

'I personally never saw anything or experienced anything that was part of the conflict,' she says. *'The only thing I saw were the soldiers patrolling the streets. That can be a bit strange, but for someone who's come from Georgia it didn't mean much. It's not as poor as some countries but not as rich as the UK. So to me, everything in Belfast was just so great and there was no trouble in my brother going to a Protestant school and myself a Catholic one.'*

The song 'Belfast' (Penguins and Cats) appears on the album *Call Off the Search*.

the Shankill Road, **black taxi tours** are to be highly recommended. Many of these taxi drivers plied their trade during the bleakest times of the Troubles, and have a fund of knowledge and anecdotes. The cost is usually between £8 and £12 per person, or around £30 per cab.

Milltown Cemetery

Milltown Cemetery was the scene of the Milltown Massacre on 16 March 1988, when loyalist paramilitary Michael Stone killed three mourners, one a Provisional IRA member. The funeral was that of Dan McCann, Seán Savage and Mairéad Farrell, IRA members killed by the Special

> MILLTOWN CEMETERY: 546 Falls Road BT12 6EQ; ☎ 028 9061 3972; The National Graves Association, Belfast, organise tours of the cemetery; call ☎ 07724 248 431 for details.

Air Service (SAS) in Gibraltar, all of whom are buried in the Republican Plot. The cemetery is synonymous with Irish nationalism. Most of the 10 Irish hunger strikers (1981) are also buried here, including Bobby Sands. IRA volunteers – and other splinter group paramilitaries – from every decade in the 20th century are buried here. It is the final resting place for those who were killed in action, died on hunger strike or were executed by either the British government or the Irish Free State.

Despite the iconic presence of the Republican Plot, Milltown Cemetery remains the graveyard of hundreds of ordinary Belfast men and women – including the parents of C S Lewis.

Shankill Road

The marching season – when Ulster's loyalists demonstrate their Britishness – runs roughly from June to October (it differs from area to area, and from year to year), but hits its peak during the 12 July fortnight. 12 July commemorates and indeed celebrates the victory of Protestant King Billy over Catholic King James at the Battle of the Boyne – just over the border in County Louth. There are few better places to watch this spectacle of Orangeism – which has been described as one of Europe's greatest expressions of folk pageantry – than on the Shankill Road, the epicentre of Protestant loyalism.

The road, which courses through predominantly working class areas, stretches westwards from central Belfast. Shankill's residents live in the many streets branching off the main road, largely lined by shops. The area is famous for its murals depicting Ulster loyalist sympathies. Here Princess Diana is still resplendent in black evening wear, not far from murdered loyalist heroes. King Billy of course is an old favourite, but some of the more inflammatory loyalist messages have been modified somewhat in these less turbulent times. The traditional cry of 'No surrender', however, has remained universally popular.

Many of the streets in the Shankill area, such as **Leopold Street**, **Cambrai Street** and **Brussels Street**, were named after places and people connected with Belgium or Flanders, where the flax for the linen industry was grown. Several loyalist paramilitary groups, such as the UDA and UVF, still have a presence on the Shankill, making it the focus of several power struggles. But, it should be stressed, the area is pretty much risk-free for the casual visitor – just maybe don't wear your Celtic top.

Northern Ireland's murals

Northern Irish murals have become a unique symbol of the entire area, although most are concentrated in Belfast and Derry. Almost 2,000 have been documented since the late 1960s, a monument to the region's religious and political divisions. Almost all of the murals promote either republican or loyalist political shibboleths, often glorifying paramilitary groups such as the IRA or the Ulster Freedom Fighters, while others commemorate victims of paramilitary or military attacks. Some are abusive – 'Don't be vague, kill a Taig,' some slightly more poetic – 'We will never forsake the blue skies of freedom for the grey clouds of an Irish republic.' Danny Morrison's 'With an Armalite under one arm and a ballot box in the other' is given plenty of coverage. This classic quote of terrorism, of winning your way in the world, is a recurrent message.

A few murals and slogans are not divisive – sporting figures George Best and Joey Dunlop (motor cyclist) are revered across the communities, and even C S Lewis's The Lion, the Witch and the Wardrobe makes an appearance. The most famous of the murals – and one of the earliest – is at Free Derry Corner, where the slogan 'You Are Now Entering Free Derry' was painted in 1969, shortly after the Battle of the Bogside. The more virulent slogans are now being covered up, with scenes representing peace and tolerance taking their place.

But it's still possible to see Princess Diana and other members of the Royal Family sharing wall space with loyalist paramilitaries on the Shankill, while on the Republican side murals commemorating events such as the Great Famine or internment without trial (which took place every decade in the 20th century) are still popular.

Fernhill House People's Museum

FERNHILL HOUSE PEOPLE'S MUSEUM: Glencairn Park, Belfast BT13 3PT; ☎ 028 28 9071 5599; www.fernhillhouse.co.uk. Entry: adults £2, children £1; open 10am–4pm Mon–Sat, 1–4pm Sun, group bookings available outside these hours.

The museum, in a recreated 1930s terraced 'kitchen house', depicts the social, economic and military history of the Greater Shankill area. The Home Rule crisis and the two World Wars – all articles of faith in the loyalist community – are recorded and presented imaginatively. More recent additions include the largest collection of Loyal Orders memorabilia in the world and the British Red Cross Exhibition

Parliament Buildings, Stormont

The extravagance of Stormont Parliament Buildings has bestowed on it the sometime description 'the biggest and grandest county council hall in the world'. Certainly, as

Parliament Buildings, Stormont

the legislative body of a community with just about enough people to fill a phone directory, it is impressively grand. A mile long drive – the Prince of Wales Avenue – runs through rolling parkland to arrive at a statue of Lord Edward Carson, Northern Ireland's first prime minister. Behind is the huge expanse of Stormont built in 1932 Greek classical style of Portland stone. This served as the seat of the Parliament of Northern Ireland until 1972, after which successive attempts at government also made their (temporary) home here.

Stormont is now where the Northern Ireland Assembly, created under the Belfast Agreement, plays its home matches. In the Executive Committee, or power-sharing cabinet, created under the agreement, nationalists and unionists share power in a form of 'consociational democracy'.

You can wander round the Great Hall or sit in on debates in the Assembly. But for a more comprehensive tour you must contact an Assembly member and ask to be sponsored. For a list of all MLAs and their contact details visit www.niassembly.gov. uk. MLAs are usually very happy to show visitors round and tell them a bit about the Peace Process, the legislative assembly, etc. You can choose from which perspective you want to hear about Northern Ireland and its legislative mechanics. You can walk from Lord Carson's statue to the other points of interest: **Lord Craigavon's Tomb**, the **Reconciliation Monument**, the **Glen Walk** and the children's playground.

PARLIAMENT BUILDINGS: Stormont, Upper Newtownards Road, Belfast BT4 3SF; public park open until 7.30pm daily.

Lagan Valley Regional Park

The Regional Park is a connected network of urban and countryside parks, heritage sites, nature reserves and riverside trails. Extending for 11 miles along both sides of the River Lagan between the south Belfast suburb of **Stranmillis** and the **Upper Locks** in County Antrim, its attractions include 19th-century **Malone House**, Upper Lisburn Malone Road (☎ 028 9068 1246; www.malonehouse.co.uk; free entry; Mon to Sat 10am–4.30pm;) which has a fine restaurant and art gallery.

Further south, past **Shaw's Bridge**, the **Giant's Ring** is still going strong after several thousands of years. A massive prehistoric earthwork, over 20m in diameter, a dolmen stands at its centre. This appears to be a major site of ritual importance – archaeological surveys here and among other sites nearby appear to testify to an early Irish tradition of severed (human) head cults, animal sacrifices and votive offerings.

LAGAN VALLEY REGIONAL PARK: 3 Lock Keeper's Lane, Milltown Road BT8 7XP; ☎ 028 9049 1922; www.laganvalley.co.uk. Entry: free; mostly open access.

The Regional Park's events programme runs from April to October and includes activities such as the Pond Dip – exploring life in freshwater ponds – guided rambles, discovery mornings and the butterfly discovery trail. All activities are free.

MALONE HOUSE: Barnett Demesne, Upper Malone Road BT9 5PB; ☎ 028 9068 1246; www.malonehouse.co.uk. Entry: free; Mon to Sat 9:00am–5:00pm, Sun 12:00pm–5:00pm.

Malone House

Malone House is an elegant, early 19th-century Georgian mansion set in the beautiful parkland and rolling meadows of Barnett Demesne in South Belfast. It's home to the Higgin Art Gallery which promotes a wide range of art.

Cave Hill

In a notably grave breach of social etiquette, the Earl of Essex in 1573 invited 300 members of the ruling O'Neill clan to a feast in Belfast Castle – and promptly had them murdered. This wasn't the first violent incident in the castle's history, so it was no surprise to anyone in the locality when it was destroyed in a subsequent act of aggression. Today's **Belfast Castle** (built c. 1870) has fared rather better than its predecessor. Designed by Sir Charles Lanyon in Scottish baronial style, it stands on the lower slopes of Cave Hill in the midst of a 750 acre estate. Today you can get

Napoleon's Nose at Cave Hill

married in this Victorian folly of a building (or even just have a cup of tea and a bun).

Cave Hill is the perfect spot for a picnic, with views across Belfast and beyond – even as far as the coast of Scotland on a clear day. And there's no knowing what heights the view might inspire you to. **Napoleon's Nose**, the distinctive human profile on the top of Cave Hill, inspired the local rector to write *Gulliver's Travels*. He was a regular visitor to the park as he lived nearby. Various hiking trails will take you to the best viewpoints, picnic areas, and not forgetting Neolithic hill forts – once again demonstrating that our ancestors loved a good view as much as we do.

> CAVE HILL VISITOR CENTRE: Belfast Castle, Cave Hill; ☎ 028 9077 6925; www.belfastcastle.co.uk. Entry: free; Mon to Sat 9am–10pm, Sun 9am–5.30pm.

Cave Hill Visitor Centre, within Belfast Castle, features a recreated 1920s bridal suite – plus an intriguing display of wedding pictures. A brief journey through the history of the area is on show – from Stone Age cave-dwellers, through to the 1800s when the most dominant crag was nick-named Napoleon's Nose. The story of the construction of Belfast Castle in 1870, which nearly bankrupted the aristocratic Donegall family – who once owned most of the city – is engagingly told.

C S Lewis Trail

Although C S Lewis gained much of his inspiration from further south in County Down, Belfast was his home, and many of the buildings associated with him make up the C S Lewis Trail (www.belfastcity.gov.uk – details of special tours are carried here).

CELEBRITY CONNECTIONS

Clive Staples Lewis, better known as **C S Lewis**, the creator of the Narnia novels, was born into an upper-middle class Protestant family in Belfast. Although Narnia is his best-known creation, Lewis turned his attention to many genres. In 'The Great Divorce' the author imagines what would happen if a group of damned souls were allowed to visit heaven on a sort of package holiday. It's often called Lewis's most perfect book, and worth a glance if you are undecided about the afterlife.

Lewis won a scholarship to Oxford in 1916 – but was immediately homesick for Northern Ireland. *'The strange English accents with which I was surrounded seemed like the voices of demons,'* he said. The writer saw front-line combat during the First World War before being wounded in Arras. His *Chronicles of Narnia* – including *The Lion the Witch and the Wardrobe* – were written from 1956 to 1960. He often cited the landscapes of the Mournes, Tollymore Forest and Slieve Gullion as having inspired his novels. He died on 22 November 1963 – the same day President Kennedy was assassinated.

The trail includes the family home **Little Lea** on Circular Road – you can't visit, and are specifically requested to 'please respect the privacy of the owners of private residences'. You can however visit **St Mark's Church**, (Dundela, Holywood Road, Belfast BT4 2DH) where young Clive Staples was baptised, his statue, **The Searcher**, outside Holywood Road Library, and **Campbell College** (by arrangement) where the writer went to school. He described Campbell as being founded *'for the express purpose of giving Ulster boys all the advantage of a public school education without the trouble of crossing the Irish Sea'.*

Several other sites on the trail are worth visiting, even without the connection of C S Lewis, such as the Linen Hall Library and Queen's University Belfast.

🌂 Wet weather

Crumlin Road Gaol

The execution chamber at Belfast's Crumlin Road Gaol bears what seems to be a very helpful message. 'Mind Your Head', proclaims the yellow sign. Despite not having been used for half a century, the execution chamber is still a chilling place to visit. This is where the Official Hangmen plied their grisly trade (see box below). The tools of their trade are locked inside a strong box: the heavy bag that acted as a counter-weight to the condemned man's body as he was strung up (no women were ever executed in the Crumlin), the hangman's noose, the white bag placed over the prisoner's head, and even pieces of chalk used to mark out his weight and position on the gallows. The equipment was last used by Harry Allen to execute Newry man Robert McGladdery in 1961. Next door is where the inmate spent his last day on earth, Cell 13. It was still used as an ordinary prison cell up until the 1990s.

The Lanyon-designed Crumlin Road Jail, a grade A listed building, is a symbol of Ireland's Troubles stretching back to the 19th century – it was built during the Great Famine. Prisoners incarcerated here include Irish suffragettes accused of trying to bomb a Church of Ireland cathedral just before World War I broke out. Other former inmates include Eamon de Valera, plus former First Minister, Rev Ian Paisley and President of Sinn Féin, Gerry Adams. The tour also features a descent into the eerie underworld – a trip to the entrance of a tunnel which took prisoners from their cells into the dock where they were tried and sentenced.

HMP Belfast, as it was officially known during its active period from 1846 to 1996 (and 'The Crum' by everyone else) was built on the same design as Pentonville Prison in London. During The Troubles several prison officers were killed by prisoners from both republican and loyalist sides.

CRUMLIN ROAD GAOL: The jail is open to the public on selected days, and all black taxi tours include it on their itinerary. Call North Belfast Community Action Unit (☎ 028 9072 6047).

Crumlin's hangmen

Albert Pierrepoint, arguably one of Britain's first commuters, carried out his trade in Britain, Northern Ireland and the Republic of Ireland. One day at an Irish execution he announced to the gathered group of prison guards and priests, *'I love hanging Irishmen – they always go quietly and without trouble. They're Christian men and they believe they're going to a better place.'*

Pierrepoint is often mistakenly called the last British hangman. It is certainly true he was the last official Chief Executioner for Britain, and, for a time, the unofficial hangman for the Republic of Ireland, taking over duties from his Uncle Thomas. However, executions continued in Britain until 1964, and until 1961 in the Six Counties. Robert McGladdery was the last person to be executed in the whole of Ireland, hanged in Crumlin Road Jail for the murder of Pearl Gamble in Newry. Harry Allen was the executioner, a part-time hangman and ice cream vendor until his employer summonsed him to his office one day and baldly told him, *'Hanging and ice cream, 'Arry m'boy. They don't mix.'* He was forced to choose between the two careers, and opted for the rope over the poke.

🚸 What to do with children...

Belfast Zoo
Overlooking Belfast Lough from the Antrim Road, Belfast Zoo is one of the most appealing in Britain or Ireland. The enclosures are spacious and attractively set on the sloping terrain, and viewing facilities are first class. The sea lion and penguin underwater viewing chamber will have you saying 'Aw!' more than you thought possible, ditto for the meerkats and red pandas.

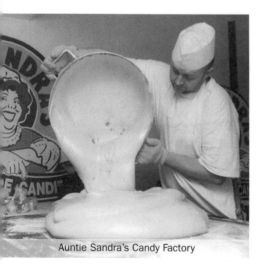

Auntie Sandra's Candy Factory

BELFAST ZOO: Antrim Road BT36 7PN; ☎ 028 9077 6277; www.belfastzoo.co.uk. Entry: adult £7.80, children £4.10, Oct to Mar £6.30/3.20; open daily 10am–7pm Apr to Sep, to 4pm Oct to Mar, last admission two hours before closing.

Auntie Sandra's Candy Factory
Auntie Sandra's is a unique Belfast sweet shop that looks the same as it did 50 years ago. All confectionary and chocolates (pan drops, humbugs, gobstoppers, fudge, yellow man, etc.)

AUNTIE SANDRA'S CANDY FACTORY:
60 Castlereagh Road, Belfast BT5 5FP;
☎ 028 9073 2868; www.auntsandras.
com. Entry: adults £4.50, children £3.50;
open Mon–Fri 9.30am/Sat 10am–4.30pm.

are made by hand to traditional recipes, some dating back more than a century. A viewing window into the small quaint factory allows visitors to enjoy tastes and smells of old-time sweetie-making at its best. The tour lasts approximately one hour.

The Odyssey

The Odyssey is a mega sports and entertainment centre situated on the former shipbuilding area of Queen's Island, now known as the *Titanic* Quarter. The complex includes:

- The Arena – Ireland's second biggest indoor stadium after the O2 Dublin, with a capacity of 14,000 for concerts and sporting events such as Belfast Giants ice hockey matches.

ODYSSEY ARENA: 2 Queen's Quay, Belfast
BT3 9QQ; ☎ 028 9076 6000 or 028
9046 7700. Entry: prices vary according to
activity.

- The Pavilion – bars, restaurants, nightclubs and a 12-screen multiplex.
- The Sheridan IMAX – the first three-dimensional IMAX in Northern Ireland
- Whowhatwherewhenwhy(W5) – children's interactive centre (see below)

WHOWHATWHEREWHENWHY (W5): Odyssey
Pavilion, 2 Queen's Quay; ☎ 028 9046
7700; www.w5online.co.uk. Entry: adults
£5.50, children £3.50; Mon–Sat 10am–
6pm, Sun noon–6pm.

Whowhatwherewhenwhy (W5)

Known as W5, this huge and vastly entertaining interactive scientific discovery centre is one of Belfast's most popular attractions. Some 150 different exhibits are crammed into five areas: WOW, START, GO, SEE and DO, where children can interact with all sorts of weird and wonderful exhibits. Activities range from creating your own animated cartoon to operating a lie detector; and if you fancy composing your own Irish song you can test your compositional skills on a laser harp.

If physics is more your thing, experience the force of lift and drag in a wind tunnel, before seeing how racing cars are made. You can even witness a fire tornado, and if your mind is still not boggled enough there's further wizardry in store.

The centre operates an extensive programme of events and activities, especially during the school holidays, featuring regularly changing exhibitions and live science demonstrations. An excellent photographic gallery also examines aspects of science and natural history.

The **Dundonald Ice Bowl & Pirates Adventure Golf** includes an Olympic-sized ice rink, 10-pin bowling, an indoor adventure playground and crèche facilities. Ice skating lessons are available, and young children can join the Polar Bear Club, an activity-based children's club held every Saturday. Birthday parties are a speciality with themed party rooms.

THE DUNDONALD INTERNATIONAL ICE BOWL: 111 Old Dundonald Road, Belfast; ☎ 028 9080 9100; www.theicebowl.com. Entry: skating £4.00 to £5.90 per person, family tickets available; Mon–Thurs 11am–5pm/ 7.30pm–10pm, Fri 11am–5pm/5.30pm–10pm, Sat 11.15am–1.15pm/1.30pm–4.45pm/ 6.30pm–10pm, Sun 11.15am–1.15pm/ 1.30pm–4.30pm/8pm–10pm.

Colin Glen Trust offers mini-beast studies, tree and wildflower identification, sensory walks, eco-trails and teddy bears' picnics throughout the year. All programmes are guided by Educational Rangers at this European award-winning forest park.

COLIN GLEN TRUST: 163 Stewartstown Road, Dunmurry, Belfast BT17 0HW; ☎ 028 9061 4115; www.colinglentrust. org. Entry: free; open daily 9am–6pm.

Streamvale Open Farm is a family-run, working dairy farm that offers children the chance to take part in animal feeding, pony and tractor rides, visits to the milking parlour, a mouse farm and a nature trail.

STREAMVALE OPEN FARM: 38 Ballyhanwood Road, Gilnahirk; ☎ 028/9048 3244; www.streamvale.co.uk. Entry: adults £3.95, children £3.50, family £13.50; Feb–May/ Sept–Oct, Wed/Sat/Sun 2–6pm; June, Mon–Sat noon–6pm Sun 2–6pm; July to Aug, Mon–Sat 10.30am–6pm, Sun 2–6pm.

... and how to avoid children

Clonard Church and Monastery

This beautiful French Gothic-style church and adjacent monastery, situated on the peace line between the Falls and the Shankill, is itself a haven of tranquillity – so calm and holy that even if you're not a believer you might find yourself stroking your chin and going, 'Hmmm...'

Completed in 1911, the church features a beautiful 6m wide stained-glass rose window, Portland stone and marble columns. Run by the Redemptorist Order, a Catholic community founded in Italy in 1732, the monks and priests played a crucial part in the peace process.

CLONARD CHURCH AND MONASTERY: 1 Clonard Gardens, Falls Road; ☎ 028 9044 5950; www.clonard.com. Opening hours Fri–Wed 6am–8pm, Thu 6am–10pm.

The best... PLACES TO STAY

HOTEL

Hastings Culloden Estate & Spa

Bangor Road, Holywood BT18 0EX
☎ **028 9042 1066**
www.hastingshotels.com

This top of the range, five-star hotel overlooking Belfast Lough is a haven of luxury and quiet comfort. The gardens are a tonic themselves, but should more relaxation be required, the spa and wellness centre are among the best in Ireland.

Price: B&B midweek, £90 per person sharing.

The Balmoral Hotel

Black's Road, Dunmurray
☎ **028 9030 1234**
www.balmoralhotelbelfast.co.uk

A friendly hotel on the outskirts of the city, the Balmoral is a comfortable three-star hotel, within striking distance of both the city centre and the County Down countryside.

Price: £100 for a double.

Hastings Stormont Hotel

Upper Newtownards Road, Belfast BT4 3LP
☎ **028 9065 1066**
www.hastingshotel.com

A fine hotel near the parliament buildings, this four-star establishment is comfortable and good value. Although it's well out of the city centre, it's well served by public transport, so it's a good place if you want to discover the countryside round Belfast.

Price: B&B midweek £60 per person sharing.

The Ramada Hotel

117 Milltown Road, Shaw's Bridge, Belfast BT8 7XP
☎ **028 9092 3500**
www.ramadabelfast.com

A well-appointed hotel, and a popular meeting up place in the south of the city, surrounded by the picturesque Lagan Valley Park. It also boasts Ireland's first Ayurveda Health and Beauty Centre.

Price: £69 for a double room.

B&B

Ravenhill House

690 Ravenhill Road, Belfast BT6 0BZ
☎ **028 9020 7444**
www.ravenhillhouse.com

Ravenhill House was built in 1886 and remains full of character. The breakfasts here are legendary complete with freshly squeezed organic fruit juices from orchards in County Armagh. Five bedrooms are available, all with en suites.

Price: £70 for a double, £45 for a single.

SELF-CATERING

City Resorts

361 Lisburn Road, Belfast BT9 7EP
☎ **028 9020 1088**
www.cityresorts.com

Five-star luxury apartments throughout the city (central and outer) with all mod cons.

Price: apartments from £57 per night all inclusive; from £325 per week all inclusive.

⚑ Entertainment

Féile an Phobail, also known as the **West Belfast Festival,** an Phobail, Teach na Féile, 473 Falls Road, Belfast BT12 6DD; ☎ 028 9031 3440) is an annual Belfast bash of Irish and international culture that takes place in and around Falls Road. Music, drama, dance and poetry are all part of one of Europe's largest community arts festivals.

Cultúrlann McAdam Ó Fiaich (216 Falls Road; ☎ 028 9096 4180; www.culturlann.ie) has a tourist information desk and a café restaurant plus regular music, drama and poetry recitals.

🛒 Shopping

Conway Mill (Conway Street – just off Falls Road; ☎ 028 9024 7276; www. conwaymill.org) a former 19th-century flax mill is now home to more than 20 small shops, art-spaces, ateliers and studios making and selling arts, crafts and furniture. **Fresh Garbage** (24 Rosemary Street; ☎ 028 9024 2350) is one of Belfast's most idiosyncratic shops, specialising in rock, Goth, punk, skater and ethnic clothing. Also in stock is a vast range of body jewellery, smoking accessories, slap, and unusual gifts. **Coral** (243 Lisburn Road; ☎ 028 9066 2323) is something of a Belfast institution selling just about the widest range of designer labels in Ireland.

The best... FOOD AND DRINK

▶ Staying in

Eatwell (413 Lisburn Road) is especially worthy of your attention as it's one of few places in the north where you can buy organic vegetables. Another popular option is **Walter Ewing's** victuallers (Shankill Road; ☎ 028 9038 1120), hugely respected by the restaurateurs who buy their supplies here. The smoked salmon here is seriously good, as are the haddocks. Try also **June's Cake Shop** (376 Lisburn Road, Belfast, Antrim), one of the great staples at the top of the Lisburn Road, packed to the rafters at lunchtime with office workers buying soups, sarnies and snacks. For meat visit **Owen McMahon's** (3–5 Atlantic Avenue; ☎ 028 9074 3525), a traditional butcher's serving terrific meat, sausages, pasties and pies.

EATING OUT

RESTAURANT

Shu
253 Lisburn Road, Belfast BT9 7EN
☎ **028 9038 1655**
www.shu-restaurant.com

A chic modern brasserie set in a handsome
Victorian terrace, serves up local produce
with European – particularly Mediterranean –
influences. Oysters, salmon, venison and trout
are all sourced locally, with the signature dish
being a glorious salt and chilli squid. Starters
cost from £8, main courses from £11.

Ryan's Bar & Restaurant
116–118 Lisburn Road, Belfast BT9 6AH
☎ **028 9050 9850**
www.ryansbarandgrill.com

Famed for its Irish-orientated menu, the
restaurant is bistro-type, with the emphasis
on good food, good craic. The restaurant's
signature dish is prime Aberdeen Angus steaks
and authentic boxty pancakes. Moderately
priced – mains cost from around £10.

The Cellar Restaurant & Belfast Castle
Antrim Road, Belfast
www.belfastcastle.co.uk

The Cellar Restaurant was recently described
as *'the best kept secret in Northern Ireland'*, and
it's true that as an eatery, Belfast Castle is not
often mentioned. But it's an atmospheric, first-
rate establishment, equally ideal for a morning
coffee or evening meal (open 9am–9pm).

Alden's
299 Upper Newtownards Road
☎ **028 9065 0079**

Alden's is one of the finest restaurants in East
Belfast – for that matter, one of the finest in
all Ireland. Expressive, friendly, tasty – you can
choose between the likes of lamb's kidney
and liver sage with champ (Ulster's version
of colcannon), or grilled scallops and ginger
sauce. Main dishes cost from around £12.

CAFÉ

Bennett's on Belmont
4, Belmont Road BT4 2AN
☎ **028 9065 6590**

An innovative, chic bistro-type place, serving
the likes of burger with celeriac remoulade(!)
or submarine roll made from roasted pork
loin and gherkins. The coffee served has
been said to be the best in Northern Ireland.
Snacks are available from £3 to £5.

Cargoes
Unit 4 Cranmore House, 613 Lisburn Road
☎ **028 9066 5451**

A several times award-winning restaurant-
café. Cuisine ranges from traditional to
adventurous. Established on the Lisburn Road
in 1993, it's reckoned to be one of the best
cafés in Belfast, ideal for breakfast, lunch or
a spot of decadent afternoon tea. Featuring
a tremendous delicatessen counter, with
meats and cheeses from around the world, all
produce is freshly prepared on-site. Lunch for
two, including coffee, costs around £20. A light
bite for two, including coffee, sets you back
around £12.

Takeaway

For a traditional chips wrapped in newspaper from a legendary chip shop, visit **The Willow** (54 Calvin street, Beersbeidge Road; ☎ 028 9062 4854).

DRINKING

Entry into the **Felons' Club** (537 Falls Road BT11 9AB; ☎ 028 9061 9875) used to be restricted to those with a prison record, or who'd had a spell of internment without trial. Changed days – now anyone is welcome, but you'd probably be better off not taking photographs, and you'll find yourself denied access to some bar areas unless you can prove you've been a guest of Her Majesty's. But the pub is friendly, somewhat male-orientated (sports bar, pool, race-talk, etc.), and they serve a good pint of stout. On the other side of the religious divide, the **Berlin Arms** (265 Shankill Road BT13 1FR; ☎ 028 9080 5552) has a real party atmosphere. The **King's Head** (829 Lisburn Road, Belfast B9 7GY; ☎ 028 9050 9958; www.kingsheadbelfast. com) is a comfortable, traditional drinking establishment just opposite the King's Hall events centre. The bar is warm and friendly, and the pub food, like the cuisine in the attached restaurant, is varied and good.

After a day's tramping on the Cave Hill pop into the cosy atmosphere of the **Cavehill Inn** (169–175 Cavehill Road BT15 5BP; ☎ 028 90370305). For a view back across the city, head up the Antrim Road to **Cassidy's Pub** (347 Antrim Road BT15 2HF; ☎ 028 9080 5552).

ⓘ Visitor Information

Tourist information centre: Belfast Visitor and Convention Bureau, 47 Donegall Place, Belfast BT1 5AD, ☎ 028 9023 9026, www.gotobelfast.com.

Hospitals: Belfast City Hospital ☎ 028 9032 9241; Royal Victoria ☎ 028 9024 0503; Ulster Hospital ☎ 028 9048 4511.

Doctors: Central Belfast – Kensington Medical Centre, 15a Donegall Road, Belfast BT12 5JJ, ☎ 028 9032 5679; Finaghy Health Centre, 13–25 Finaghy Road South, Belfast BT10 0BX, ☎ 028 9020 4440/1; Springfield Road Surgery, 70 Springfield Road, Belfast BT12 7AH, ☎ 028 9032 3571; a full list is available on www.neighbourhoodprofessionals.co.uk; doctors operate under the NHS.

Pharmacies: the two main pharmacies throughout Northern Ireland are Boots ☎ 028 9024 2332 and Gordon's ☎ 028 9032 0040. Belfast has hundreds of good independent pharmacies.

Police: In an emergency dial ☎ 999; otherwise contact the local PSNI station on ☎ 0845 600 80.

Parking: McCausland Car Park ☎ 028 90333777; National Car Parks ☎ 028 90244593.

Internet access: all 3, 4 and 5-star hotels have internet access. In addition public libraries all provide free access.

Bike rental: Bike Dock, 79–85 Ravenhill Road BT6 8DQ, ☎ 028 9073 0600, www.bikedock.com.

Local taxis: One of the main taxi ranks in Belfast city centre is at the City Hall. By law, all taxis in Belfast are required to display coloured licence plates; Please ensure that you always take a taxi that displays a coloured plate; black taxis display yellow plates and private taxis have a green licence plate displayed; Value Cabs ☎ 028 9080 9080; Gransha Taxis ☎ 028 9060 2092; Able Taxis ☎ 028 9024 1999; City Cab Taxis ☎ 028 9024 2000; Leaf Taxis ☎ 028 9031 4131.

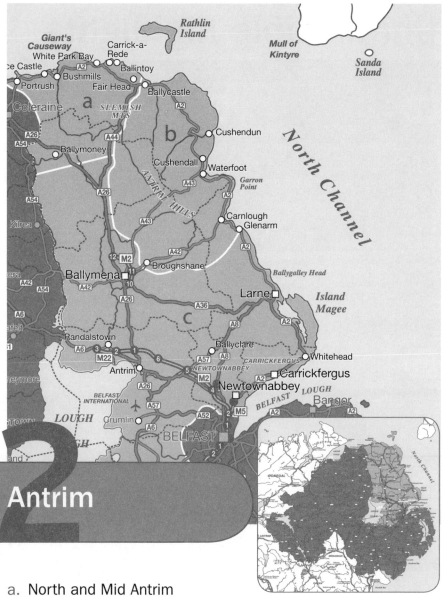

Antrim

a. North and Mid Antrim

b. Glens of Antrim and Rathlin Island

c. South Antrim

Unmissable highlights

01 Climb the rocks at Ballintoy Harbour, **the better to admire the magnificent white-limestone headland,** p. 99

02 Have a dram **at the world's oldest licensed distillery in Bushmills,** p. 101

03 Wander down Glenarriff, **the Queen of the Glens of Antrim,** p. 109

04 Watch the puffins and guillemots **off Ireland's most northerly inhabited point, Rathlin Island,** p. 113

05 Walk in the footsteps of St Patrick, **on Mount Slemish, where he tended sheep,** p. 126

06 Ponder the origins of the Giant's Causeway **– basalt eruption, or clash between the ancient titans who inhabited Ireland? You decide,** p. 96

07 Scare yourself witless **on the vertiginous Carrick-a-Rede Rope Bridge, which links Antrim to tiny Carrick Island,** p. 98

08 Wander in the shadow of ancient Dunluce Castle, **a formidable structure clinging to the Antrim Coast, originally built c1300,** p. 99

09 Drive along the Causeway Coastal Route, **recently chosen as one of the top 10 most spectacular drives in the world,** p. 97

10 Say a prayer **in the smallest church in Ireland, St Gobbans at the little village of Portbraddan,** p. 103

ANTRIM

Antrim is home to some of the most dramatic scenery in Ireland, including the Giant's Causeway (a UNESCO World Heritage Site), most of the 35 mile Causeway Coastal Route, and the magical, mystical Glens of Antrim.

History is never far away – St Patrick tended pigs on Slemish Mountain in the south of the county, and near the north coast stands another iconic Irish landmark – the oldest distillery in the world, Bushmills. Craic, culture and sport are in plentiful supply amidst this towering scenery. The Ould Lammas Fair is one of Ireland's oldest and most raucous festivals – a chaotic blend of horse-trading, Irish dancing and general debauchery is on offer. The middle of the county is home to the Cross Keys pub, one of the most respected venues for traditional music sessions on the entire island.

Rural backwaters (literally) are easy to find. The county borders Lough Neagh and the Lower Bann River – both providing ample opportunity for boating, angling and birdwatching. Nonetheless, the county stretches as far as two of Northern Ireland's five cities – Lisburn and Belfast. Which means that hotels, shopping and restaurants are in ready supply.

Antrim can claim two cities, but it is also dotted with dozens of postcard-grade villages such as Portbraddan, overlooking White Park Bay. This is home to what is reputedly the smallest church in Ireland, St Gobbans. Measuring only 12ft by 6ft, there's just about enough room to swing a cat, while saying your prayers. Glenarm comes complete with a castle you can call home for a weekend, while Cushendall is a thriving centre for traditional music with several festivals, fleadhs and sessions. In short, they're caning it the whole year.

Towards Ballintoy Harbour the limestone and basalt cliffs rise vertically out of the sea. From here you'll get terrific views across to Sheep Island. Britain, only 12 miles away, merely looks like a slightly bigger Sheep Island.

NORTH AND MID ANTRIM

North Antrim is dominated by two of Ireland's truly iconic sites – the Giant's Causeway and Bushmills Distillery. One has given rise to meandering legends, tales of giants, fantastic imagery, imaginary happenings and discussions about the Wee Folk. And funnily enough, the Giant's Causeway has done something similar. As well as cornering the market in spirits (in the widest sense of the word), North Antrim is a sportsman's paradise – golfing, fishing, horse-riding, surfing and motor sports all reach world class standards here.

North Antrim also boasts one of Ireland's main seaside resorts, **Portrush**, with clubs, pubs, discos – and of course shops that sell everything from surfing gear to fishing tackle; and not forgetting those seaside essentials, spades and pails. Even more than that, North Antrim is an area for exploring – brooding castles, glassy loughs, quietly flowing rivers, hidden beaches, magical glens and mysterious rock formations, and not just at the Giant's domain. In short, it's a first-class holiday destination – so long as you manage to avoid the banshee and her death-boding wail.

WHAT TO SEE AND DO

Giant's Causeway

The Giant's Causeway, for centuries a geological wonder known only to kelp gatherers and sheep herders, is one of the island of Ireland's three UNESCO World Heritage Sites, and the only one in Northern Ireland. It is an astonishing stony complex of octagonal basalt columns packed together. The tallest columns, collectively known as the Giant's Organ, are 12m high. Other formations are known as the Giant's Granny, the King and the Nobles, and the Chimney Pots.

Several theories attempt to explain the phenomenon. The most popular are: it was the work of the giant Finn MacCool; it was down to the Evil Ones, also called the Fomorians; it was the work of God; it is a geological phenomenon which happened 60 million years ago when molten lava erupted then cooled and shrank. Also, a book published in the 19th century claims that the formation was originally petrified bamboo trees, but this theory has not been as widely accepted as the previous explanations. It would be fair to say that the official information offered at the visitor centre categorically comes down on the side of the molten lava. This, despite creationists within both the Stormont Assembly (the jurisdiction's governing body) and the local council demanding the religious theory be displayed as well. Whatever the reason for this incredible basaltic extravaganza, the Giant's Causeway remains one of Ireland's most impressive, atmospheric and downright dramatic sights.

Giant's Causeway

A small bus will take you from the visitor centre to the main area of rocks where, once your mind has been deboggled, you can contemplate its origins at length.

GIANT'S CAUSEWAY: ☎ 028 2073 1855; www.giantscausewaycentre.com. Entry: free; Jul/Aug 10am–6pm , Sep to Jun 10am–5pm.

Local legends: Finn McCool and the Giant's Causeway

The main legend surrounding the formation of the Giant's Causeway – and there are several versions – centre around the giant Finn McCool (also spelt Fionn Mac Cumhaill). Finn built the Causeway the better to walk to Scotland in order to fight his Scottish nemesis, Bernandonner.

The story goes that Finn fell asleep before he could cross to Scotland; meanwhile Bernandonner came across to Ireland looking for Finn. His wife, Oonaugh, on seeing that the Scotsman was much larger than her husband, cleverly wrapped him up, and passed him off to Bernandonner as her baby. When he saw this enormous baby, the giant Scot, thinking that the father must indeed be a more gigantic giant than he was, headed back to Scotland with all speed, tearing up the Causeway as he went.

It's a plausible enough story if you see the Causeway of an evening, with columns of sea mist moving silently across the ethereal rock formations.

Causeway Coastal Route

The Causeway Coastal Route from **Belfast Lough** to **Lough Foyle** in County Derry is Mother Nature in one of her wilder moods. Natural wonders, great seascapes, elemental and empty land. A recent poll placed the Antrim Coast Road section of the Causeway Coastal Route in fifth place in a list of the world's most spectacular views. Some 80 miles of stunning coastline will transport you past rugged and windswept cliffs, spectacular scenery, fabulous unspoilt beaches and charming villages. It's a coastline sprinkled with historic castles, churches and forts. Many are now just ruins but each holds the memories of a heroic past, not to mention a melancholy history.

Every twist and turn in the road reveals new sights – over bridges and under arches, past bays and beaches and surreal rock formations. Inland lie the glens of Antrim, each glen with its own charm and mythology. **Larne** (see p. 127) is regarded

The Causeway Coastal Route between Carnlough and Cushendun

as the gateway to the Causeway Coast, but **Glenarm**, a few miles to the north, is the first 'Glens Village' you will come to. The road then travels through **Carnlough** and onwards to the very top of the island, overlooking Ireland's most northerly inhabited point, **Rathlin Island**.

Walking the Causeway Coast Way

The Causeway Coast Way is a way-marked route from **Portrush** to **Ballycastle** – some 52km (33miles) along the dramatic coastline from **Portstewart** to **Ballycastle**, one of the most invigorating walks in Europe. You will be following in the footsteps of fishermen, seaweed gatherers and coastal farmers. The route, is made up of paved paths, grassy tracks, good cliff paths, beaches and rocky sea shore, passes, seaside resorts and small fishing villages as well as the World Heritage Site and National Nature Reserve of the Giant's Causeway. You will also pass the ruins of **Dunluce**, **Dunseverick** and **Kenbane Castles** and the **Carrick-a-Rede Rope Bridge**.

CAUSEWAY COAST WAY: Map required: Ordnance Survey Discoverer Series (1:50,000), Sheets 4 & 5; visit www.walkni.com for details.

Carrick-a-Rede rope bridge

Carrick-a-Rede

For a diverting afternoon, you can scare yourself witless by crossing the vertiginous Carrick-a-Rede Rope Bridge, which links County Antrim to tiny **Carrick Island** some 24m away. Underneath, the angry waters of the Atlantic perform their party piece, pretending to be a giant jacuzzi. This is probably the scariest trans-Atlantic journey you'll ever make.

The bridge is just east of **Ballintoy Harbour**, well sign-posted off the main Causeway road. It's taken down in the winter, and reinstalled by the shepherds come March (the date is variable) with some pomp and ceremony. The locals like to joke that the bridge is the busiest trans-Atlantic route in the world – even if it only crosses 75ft of it.

> **CARRICK-A-REDE ROPE BRIDGE: ☎** 028 2076 9839. Entry: adults £3.30, children £1.80; open Jun to Aug 10am–7pm, Mar to May/Sept/Oct 10am to 6pm; the bridge is closed in difficult weather conditions.

Dunluce Castle

Dunluce Castle is a formidable structure clinging to limestone crags overlooking the Atlantic. Originally built around 1300, the castle has changed hands many times since then. The usual suspects are present and correct – Normans, Gaels, English, Scots, rebels, Planters, Ulster chieftains, etc. Many believe that Dunluce has one of the most dramatic settings of any castle in the world, an opinion that's hard enough to argue with. A fort probably stood here in Christian times, but it was the Normans who transformed it into the definitive castle we know today. Most of it is still just about standing, although sometimes you might imagine that just one more momentous Atlantic roller will dump the whole lot into the ocean.

Separated from the mainland by a 20ft chasm, Dunluce Castle was originally owned by the de Mandevilles, an early Norman family. The celebrated Ulster leader Sorley Boy O'Donnell then seized it and refurbished the place thanks to the Spanish Armada foundering on the Giant's Causeway nearby. And although nobody expected the Spanish Armada – to paraphrase Monty Python – the Spanish gold came in very handy, thank you very much.

> **DUNLUCE CASTLE:** A2 Coast Road, Portrush BT57 8SX; ☎ 028 7082 3333. Entry: adults £2, children £1; open 10am–6pm Apr to Sept, 10am–5pm Oct to Mar.

Portrush

At the most northerly point of the famous **Antrim Coast Road** lies Portrush. It looks out to the North Atlantic and there's not a tree between the town and the North Pole. Despite this, and notwithstanding the gales which occasionally blow in from Iceland, it's possible to have seaside holidays here the like of which you will

Dunluce Castle

not have seen since the 1950s. True, all the trappings of any other seaside resort in Ireland or Britain can be found – caravans, chip shops, hamburger vans, slot machines and discos – but somehow an unmistakable air of 1950s gentility pervades the place.

One of the town's most famous attractions, the **Royal Portrush Golf Club**, helps give Portrush a tinge of cosmopolitanism, a soupçon of sophistication. The course pulls in golfers from as far afield as Japan and America – Michael Douglas and his party, which included Dan Quayle, played a round here recently. Its popularity isn't hard to fathom. The 1st hole (the Tubber Patrick) is generally regarded as just about the best opening hole in all of links golf worldwide. A dramatic descent from a gloriously elevated tee leads into an amphitheatre of sand dunes. If you are lucky. If not, the Atlantic beckons.

This is the only course in Ireland where the Open (British) has been held, but it doesn't come cheap and they'll want to see your handicap certificate before they allow you to get your niblocks out.

Portrush is one of the main centres for **surfing** in Ireland. From April to November Trogg's Surf Shop on the Main Street (☎ 028 7082 5476; www.troggsurfshop.co.uk) will provide you with almost everything you need – surfboard, wetsuit, instructor, rosary beads. The thundering Atlantic Ocean, just outside the front door, will provide the rest.

> **ROYAL PORTRUSH GOLF COURSE:** Dunluce Road, Portrush BT56 8JQ; ☎ 028 7082 2311; www.royalportrushgolfclub.com. A round costs from £125 weekdays.

Joey Dunlop Memorial Garden

In Ireland, motorcyclist Joey Dunlop was a sporting figure equally revered in both communities, as much as George Best or Alex Higgins. In the international arena he had legendary status through his sporting prowess. In addition to winning five Formula One World Championships Joey made sporting history by setting a new world record of 26 wins in the Isle of Man TT Races. He is often described as the greatest sportsman Ireland has ever produced, in the most terrifying sport of them all. Into the bargain, he was a kindly, friendly, Antrim man of great modesty.

Joey died on Sunday, 2 July, 2000, racing in Estonia. Some 60,000 people from across the globe attended his funeral. You can pay your respects to one of the truly unifying figures in recent Northern Ireland history at the Joey Dunlop Memorial Garden in Seymour Street, Ballymoney.

Bushmills

The neat little village of Bushmills was served by the first electric tramway opened in 1883, and only closed in 1947. Whether this was to facilitate Portrussians on a pub crawl to the distillery, or merely an afternoon jaunt is hard to judge after this passage of time. The town is an ideal centre from which to explore the grandeur of the **Antrim Coast**. Nearby **White Park Bay**, a National Trust-run site with white chalk cliffs, grassy

Casks at the Bushmills Distillery

dunes, and foaming waves on clear water – is one of Europe's great sea vistas.

Bushmills Distillery

The origins of alcoholic beverages are lost in the mists of pre-history, but the evidence for an Irish dimension is compelling. The word 'whiskey' itself is derived from the Gaelic or Irish *uisge beatha* meaning literally 'water of life'. And if that's not proof enough (40% proof as it were) the oldest distillery in the world by a fairly long chalk is Bushmills. They've been manufacturing the electric soup here since 1608, and laughing all the way to the bottle bank ever since.

Whiskey facts

- The price of a bottle of whiskey remained fairly stable from about 1790 until 1914 when the modern phenomenon of inflation began. Back then a bottle would set you back about 3s 6d (16p). The barley from which whiskey is distilled is correctly called *Barliensis vulgaris*.

- Ireland once boasted hundreds of distilleries. However only three legal distilleries remain in Ireland today. They are Bushmills Distillery, Midleton Distillery in County Cork, and Cooley Distillery in County Louth. Ireland's whiskey trade suffered in the last century from the effects of the then Free State's independence which was followed by trade embargoes with Britain. Prohibition also wiped out the American market.

- It has been illegal to make poitin (or poteen) from 1760 when an Act of Parliament made the 'unlicensed private distillation of whiskey' an offence.

Bushmills was the first licensed distillery in the world, receiving its official papers in 1608. A tour of the premises hints at the magic formula behind this world famous brand. They say the most important ingredient is the water, and Bushmills H_2O still comes from **St Columb's Rill**, the tributary of the **Bush** on which the old stone buildings stand. During a guided tour of the premises you will pick up plenty of nuggets of information – including why Irish whiskey is smoother than Scotch. Scottish whisky (without an 'e') goes through the distillation process twice; Irish whiskey is a triple distilled tipple (try saying that after a double). This prolonged distillation gives Irish whiskey a smoother taste. You will also learn that the part of the distillate which evaporates away is known as the Angels' Share.

BUSHMILLS: ☎ 028 2073 3273; www.bushmills.com. Entry: adult £6, concessions £5, children (8–17) £3; tours every half hour; open Nov to Feb, Mon–Fri 9.30am–3.30pm, Sat/Sun 12.30pm–3.30pm, Mar to Oct Mon–Sat 9.15am–5pm, Sun 11am–5pm.

Stills at the Bushmills Distillery

The other factor in the distinctive Irish taste is that it is a combination of a single malt and a single grain – Scottish whiskies are blended. During your visit to Bushmills you will see another reason for the unmistakable Antrim taste – the long rows of Oloroso sherry casks where the drink is aged: some limited editions are aged there for a quarter of a century.

Irish whiskey vs. Scotch

The NATO phonetic alphabet was devised in 1956 in an attempt to internationalise the Allied Armed Forces alphabet. It eventually evolved as: Alpha, Bravo, Charlie, Delta, Echo, Foxtrot, Golf, Hotel, India, Juliet, Kilo, Lima, Mike, November, Oscar, Papa, Quebec, Romeo, Sierra, Tango, Uniform, Victor, Whiskey, X-ray, Yankee, Zulu.

Back then the British complained that 'whiskey' was spelt the Irish way (the Irish Republic has never been part of NATO), and tried to get the Scottish form 'whisky' inserted instead. But the use of 'whiskey' soon became almost universal, and the only Irish input into the alphabet remains intact. However, the Scots had the last laugh. Today the Bushmills and Midleton distilleries are owned by multi-nationals, and while there are scores of independent distilleries in Scotland, there is only one left in Ireland – the Cooley Distillery just south of the Armagh border on the Cooley Peninsula. Scottish whisky has also won in the vocabulary stakes: 'Irish' remains a mere adjective; 'Scotch' means whisky.

Traill monument

After leaving Bushmills Distillery, get your designated driver to turn left immediately on leaving the premises and drive along the B66 towards **Derrykeighan**. About 3 miles up the road look out for the Traill Monument, built around 1833. This set of stones will appear to swell and contract before your very eyes. It's due to an obscure law of physics – the one which deals with the human eye simplifying differing orientations, resulting in this strange optical illusion.

Wet weather

The Giant's Causeway & Bushmills Railway

This is a narrow-gauge line with three locomotives (two steam and one diesel) which follow the route of a 19th-century tourist tramway from Bushmills to just beside the visitor centre at the Giant's Causeway.

THE GIANT'S CAUSEWAY & BUSHMILLS RAILWAY: Bushmills BT57 8SZ; ☎ 028 2073 2844; www.freewebs.com/giantscausewayrailway.

Portbraddan

Portbraddan (also spelt Portbraden) boasts the smallest church in Ireland. Now, there are a few candidates for this title, but undoubtedly **St Gobhnans** (also spelt St Gobbans) is the most appealing, lying at the bottom of vertical cliffs, and overlooking White Park Bay – itself a stunning vista. The area round about is a rich habitat for naturalists. If the rain clears, you can venture out and see ferns and golden saxifrage growing by the streams which pour into the sea. Watch carefully and you will see seals in the bay and petrels on the cliffs.

St. Gobhnans, the smallest church in Ireland

What to do with children...

Barry's Amusement Park is an institution in the Six Counties. Ireland's biggest amusement park – as well as being one of the oldest – attracts children from all over the island to its classic carousel rides, ghost trains, dodgems and Ferris wheels.

BARRY'S AMUSEMENTS: 16 Eglinton Street, Portrush, County Antrim, Northern Ireland BT56 8DY; ☎ 028 7082 2340; www.barryamusements.co.uk. Entry: free entry but rides require 1–4 tokens at 50p each; open daily 10am–6pm June, 12.30pm–10.30pm July/Aug, open most Sat/Sun year round 12.30pm–9.30/10.30pm; see website for full calendar of opening days and times.

Waterworld (the Harbour; ☎ 028 7082 2001) has indoor swimming pools, water slides and spa baths. And **The Dunluce Centre** (10 Sandhill Drive, Portrush BT56 8BF; ☎ 028 7082 4444; www.dunlucecentre.co.uk) boasts what is billed as 'Ireland's only 4D special effects theatre'. There are also bouncy castles, treasure fortresses, face painting, organised games and Finn McCool's Playground.

Shean's Horse Farm (38 Coolkeeran Road, Armoy, Ballymoney BT53 8XL; ☎ 07759 320434) is a 400 acre spread at Armoy. The riding school caters for all ages and abilities – children are particularly encouraged, even if they've barely seen a horse before. Everything from jumping to trekking to looking after Dobbin is taught, and pony rides are provided for members of the family too young to trek.

Leslie Hill Open Farm (Macfin Road, Ballymoney BT53 6QL; ☎ 028 2766 6803; www. lesliehillopenfarm.co.uk) has nature walks, historic buildings with child-orientated exhibitions, playgrounds, pets' corner, horse and cart rounds – and a few things for the parents and grandparents to do too. But it's the children who are really catered for, with farm animals on their best behaviour, a deer park, nature trails and a café full of stuff children want.

... and how to avoid children

Nirvana Beauty and Day Spa (15 Isle Road BT51 4JH; ☎ 028 7032 8093; www.nirvanabeautyspa.com) offers a full range of very indulgent treatments for both men and women, including seaweed baths, chocolate facials, body massage, and aromatherapy, as well as more run-of-the-mill stuff such as jacuzzi and steam room.

Entertainment

Portrush is the entertainment capital of the North East. **Kelly's** (1 Bushmills Road; ☎ 028 7082 6633; www.kellysportrush.co.uk) is the number one venue. DJs from Britain regularly appear, and such is the rep, Ireland's young, up-for-it clubbers journey here from literally the four corners of the island. A Kelly's highlight is the Beach Party taking place at the end of June and featuring an extravaganza of clubbing (www. thebeachparty.co.uk). The **Fullerton Arms** (22 Main Street, Ballintoy BT54 6LX; ☎ 028 2076 9613; www.fullertonarms.co.uk) specialises in traditional evenings – both Irish and Ulster Scots sessions. Irish dancing during the summer months from local dancers is not to be missed.

The **Scenic Inn** (38 Fivey Road, Armoy BT53 8UT; ☎ 028 2075 1260), right in the middle of the North Antrim countryside, holds traditional sessions at the weekend; more often than not during the week spontaneous sessions break out. The Scenic Inn serves food from noon–9pm, so you need never miss a crotchet or a cran, a reel or a jig, through having to pop out for a bite. The **Springhill** (13 Causeway Street, Portrush BT 56 8AB; ☎ 028 7082 3361), Portrush's oldest bar, features music every night of the week: jazz, Irish traditional, club sounds, rock.

The best... FOOD AND DRINK

▶ Staying in

Like elsewhere in the Six Counties, Antrim is well supplied with small, locally sourced, independent butchers where you can buy pies made on the premises, ham cured on site, and sausages made from the finest livestock. Recommended butchers include:

The best... PLACES TO STAY

HOTEL

Glenmore House

94 White Park Road, Ballycastle BT54 6LR
☎ 028 2076 3584

This modern country house hotel is beautifully situated between Ballintoy and Ballycastle. Set in 95 acres of countryside, it's ideal for walkers and wildlife watchers. There are golf and trout fishing options too, and to save you walking too far in the evening, the Glenmore has its own restaurant and traditional Irish music sessions.

Price: from £25 to £40 per person per night.

Ramada Portrush

73 Main Street, Portrush BT56 8BN
☎ 028 7082 6100
www.comforthotelportrush.com

One of the best hotels in the area, the Ramada is reliably comfortable, has an excellent restaurant, and couldn't be more centrally located – have a wander down to the harbour after dinner, before returning for a nightcap in the cosy bar.

Price: From £65 to £178 per night.

INN

Bushmills Inn

9 Dunluce Road
☎ 028 2073 2339
www.bushmills-inn.com

In the centre of the famous whiskey-making village, this inn dates from the 17th century – so old world charm is guaranteed – as well as open turf fireplaces, gas lamps, and antique furnishings.

Price: B&B plus dinner from £59 per person sharing.

B&B

Whitepark House

Ballintoy BT54 6NH; ☎ 028 207 31482
www.whiteparkhouse.com

This B&B is actually an 18th-century country house, tastefully restored and richly decorated with only three rooms – so cosiness guaranteed. The landlord's definitive Ulster fry-ups are served in the morning at the bay window overlooking one of the finest views in the world. Tea and home-made shortbread is served in front of the open fire.

Price: £70 for a single; from £100 for a double.

SELF-CATERING

The Drum Gate Lodge

West Lodge Ballylough House, Bushmills, County Antrim BT57 8TP
☎ 00 353 1 670 4733
www.irishlandmarktrust.com

Until 1962, this lovely cottage was the gate lodge for the Ballylough Estate. Today it is a beautifully restored amenity with modern kitchen, cosy bedroom, and circular living room.

Price: from £350 to £440 per week.

UNUSUAL

Harmony Hill

Balnamore, Ballymoney BT53 7PS
☎ 028 2766 3459
www.harmonyhill.net

On the site of a old dry spinning mill, Harmony Hill has been fully converted into a charming country house. The restaurant is justifiably famous, bedrooms are comfortable and rustic.

Price: from £79 for a double.

EATING OUT

RESTAURANT

Smuggler's Inn Country House
306 Whitepark Road, Giant's Causeway BT57 8SL
☎ **028 2073 1577**

Surrounded by lovely gardens just across from the entrance to the Giant's Causeway, this restaurant has wide-windowed views of the coast. The cuisine is 'creative Irish', that is, local produce served with imaginative sauces. Baked salmon, grilled venison, and roast North Antrim duck with peach brandy are specialities. If you have no designated driver with you, the Smuggler's also has B&B. Cost £8–£15 for main courses.

Fullerton Arms
22 Main Street, Ballintoy BT54 6LX
☎ **028 2076 9613**
www.fullertonarms.co.uk

The Taggarts run their restaurant as if it were their front room. Craic, friendliness and a perfect pint of Guinness are all dispensed with ease, followed by oysters for starters and maybe some local beef for the main course. Expect to pay upwards of £30 per person for a three-course meal, plus wine.

GASTRO PUB

The Distillers Arms
140 Main Street, Bushmills BT57 8QE
☎ **028 2073 1044**
www.distillersarms.com

Housed in one of Bushmills oldest buildings, the Distillers offers modern Irish cuisine with imaginative flair – so much so that it's the recipient of several awards. The restaurant serves primarily seafood – local of course.

Lobster in the summer is an absolute seasonal treat. The roast rump of local lamb with Wysner's black pudding mash and red wine jus will set you back £15.95; lunch mains cost from £8.95; dinner mains from £13.95.

Sweeney's Wine Bar
6b Seaport Ave, Portballantrae BT57 8SB
☎ **028 2073 2405**

Despite its name, Sweeney's does the finest pub grub on the coast. Well-executed favourites include sea bass and chips, pastas, steak and kidney pie, and soups, but all done to a turn. If you are after comfort food – like bread and butter pudding or apple pie with fresh cream – this restaurant should be underlined in your diary with a curly red line and a few asterisks added for good measure. From £6 to £17 for main courses.

CAFÉ

Roark's Kitchen
Ballintoy Harbour, Ballintoy BT54 6NA
☎ **028 2076 3632**

Just beside the lovely harbour at Ballintoy, you can sip your tea and listen to the ocean crashing over the rocks just outside the window. Standard café fare – with a comprehensive choice of cakes and pastries. More substantial fare such as Irish stew (surprisingly rare in Ireland) or chicken and ham pie are also available. Afterwards lie full stretch on the harbour wall, your head towards the sea, and watch the jellyfish arriving in shoals; or at the very least the mackerel – innocent of their likely fate.

- **George Barr & Sons** – 43 Broughshane, Ballymena; ☎ 028 2565 2432
- **Bannside Meats** – 51 Main Street, Portglenone; ☎ 028 2582 2799
- **WJ Clawson** – W5 Bridewell Drive, Carrickfergus; ☎ 028 9335 1575

One of the best delis about is **Ben's Hot Food Deli** (Tower Centre, Wellington Street, Ballymena BT43 6AH; ☎ 028 2564 3399) – soups, sandwiches and voluptuous salads for under £5.

Drinking

Even if you aren't staying there the **Bushmills Inn** (9 Dunluce Road; ☎ 028 2073 2339) is an irresistible place to stop for a drink. A 17th-century pub, it's the perfect place to sit yourself in front of the fire, shlooter some Black Label Bushmills, and talk nonsense until the wee hours. The **Counties Bar** (73 Main Street, Portrush; ☎ 028 7082 6100) is part of the Comfort Hotel, but it is, as well, a terrific place for cocktails, wines from around the world, and of course whiskey from just up the road. The **Harbour Bar** (Harbour Road, Portrush BT56 8DF) is a lovely old-fashioned pub near the harbour, perfect for whiling the evening away with the locals.

Visitor Information

Tourist information centres: Antrim Tourist Information Centre, 16 High Street, Antrim BT41 4AN, ☎ 028 9442 8331; Portrush Tourist Information Centre, Sandhill Drive, Portrush, Antrim BT56 8BF, ☎ 028 7082 3333; Causeway Tourist Information Centre, 44 Causeway Road, Bushmills BT57 8SU; Country Antrim ☎ 028 2073 1855; General information from the local tourist board ☎ 02870 327720, www.causewaycoastandglens.com or www.discovernorthernireland.com.

Hospital: Antrim Area Hospital, Bush Road, Antrim, ☎ 28 9442 4000.

Doctor: Antrim Health Centre, Antrim Town, ☎ 028 9441 3910.

Pharmacies: Gordon's Chemist, 5 Main Street, Portrush, County Antrim BT56 8BL, ☎ 02870 822324.

Police: for emergencies dial ☎ 99 or ☎ 112; for non-emergencies call ☎ 028 7034 4122, Kilrea, Coleraine BT51 5LP County Derry.

Supermarkets: Portrush has a branch of Costcutters at 106, Main Street, Portrush BT56 8DA, ☎ 028 7082 5447.

Bike rental: nearest bicycle hire is G McAlister Cycles in Coleraine, 16 Glenleary Road, Coleraine, County Derry BT51 3QV, ☎ 028 7035 8443.

Local taxis: Andy Brown's (Portrush) ☎ 028 7082 2232; North West Taxis ☎ 028 7082 4446.

GLENS OF ANTRIM AND RATHLIN ISLAND

Madman's Window, which looks out over the Irish Sea to Scotland is part of the Causeway Coastal Road. No one quite knows why he went mad, or what his fate was – but the gaunt sentinel, in reality a curious rock formation, watches over the spectacular road which snakes from just beyond the seaport of **Larne** to **Portstewart** on the **Derry** border.

The Mull of Kintyre rises just a dozen miles away across the Irish Sea. Inland the nine **Glens of Antrim** snake their way up to the **Antrim Plateau**. The **Causeway Coastal Road**, recently adjudged one of the top 10 most scenic routes in the world, clings perilously to the limestone and basalt outcrops on the north-east coast of Ireland. The road winds through postcard-grade villages and glens with names that read like a poem: **Cushendun**, **Cushendall**, **Glenballyeamon**, **Glenarm**, **Waterfoot**. It passes under St MacNisi's School – high on **Garron Point** – the Jesuits' school which is the Harrow or Eton of Northern Ireland – and through **Glenarm** huddling beneath giant cliffs.

If you don't know the song, look it out before you come:

Soon I hope to return to my own Cushendall
'Tis the one place for me that can outshine them all
Sure I know every stone, I recall every tree
Where the green Glens of Antrim are calling to me.

Impossibly picturesque seaside villages like **Carnlough**, which might have appeared in Finian's Rainbow, consist of small pastel-washed houses; neat little shops (independently owned) vie for space with wee pubs made up from a honeycomb of tiny rooms. Journey along the magnificent engineering feat, known locally as the **Antrim Coast Road**, to **Red Bay**. Here during the penal times Mass was said in high caves in the hills, or in overturned fishing boats.

This route along Ireland's north-eastern seaboard – within living memory little more than a rough track bedded with basalt and chalk chips and pitted with potholes – is reckoned today to be one of the most spectacular roads in the world, in the same company as the San Bernardino Pass or the Monterey-Carmel coast road in California. The Antrim Coast Road can boast two advantages over the competition – first of all, lack of traffic. On weekdays, or during the autumn and winter (often the most spectacular time to visit) you'll all but have the road to yourself. Secondly, you won't find cod and chips in the same league as that sold by **McKillop's** in **Carnlough**. By the

Glenarriff

way, there's another implausibly beautiful harbour there, looking out over **Carnlough Bay** where you can sit and thoughtfully munch your chips.

WHAT TO SEE AND DO

Glens of Antrim

The Glens of Antrim (in Irish *Gleannta Aontroma*) or, simply, the Glens, are nine, or maybe 10 in number, running from the Antrim Plateau to the coast. The population hereabouts is descended primarily from native Irish and Hebridean Scots, rather than the lowland Scots of elsewhere in Ulster, which gives the place (music, language, outlook) a special character. The nine glens from northernmost to southernmost are: **Glentaisie**, **Glenshesk**, **Glendun**, **Glencorp**, **Glenaan**, **Glenballyeamon**, **Glenariff(e)**, **Glencloy** and **Glenarm**. **Glenravel** is often considered a tenth glen, although it fails on one crucial, unticked box – it doesn't open directly onto the sea.

Few places in Britain or Ireland hold more interest for geologists than the 100 miles of coastline which hug the North Channel and Atlantic. At **Fair Head**, the northeast extremity of Ireland, geology takes on a dizzying dimension with a 600ft plunge into the sea. Should you happen to fall off, you will pass sixteen different rock strata en route to the bottom. Often called Ireland's greatest rock group – and you thought it was U2 – black basalt, schist, red sandstone, white limestone, coal and yellow iron ore are all on show. But, and apologies to all geologists reading this, you're probably more likely to be interested in the beauty rather than the basalt. Because here is an intoxicating combination of colour, light, moving water and landscape.

Glenariff, the queen of the glens, has gushing waterfalls and a scenic path skirting the sheer sides of the plunging gorge. Three cascades, **Ess na Crub**, **Ess na Laragh** and **Tears of the Mountain** have viewpoints where you can sit and contemplate – and see if you can come up with something better than Thackeray's *Switzerland in miniature*. It's OK, but you feel he might have tried a little harder. The Nine Glens of Antrim each have their own individual character, and each is equally spectacular. Just like it says in the song, 'You'd imagine a picture of heaven it could be,/Where the Green Glens of Antrim are calling to me'.

Local legends: the myths of the Glens

Because of the ancient Gaelic influence in Antrim – a culture which had a more than passing interest in the supernatural – the Glens have more than their fair share of legends and folklore. The sheer effrontery of the landscape has probably helped as well – steep-sided valleys, surreal rock shapes and swirling mountain mists all contribute to a rich store of magic mythology. **Lurigethan Mountain**, which begins in Glenarriff, is one of the main settlements of the Wee People – or **Wee Folk**, but never leprechauns in these parts. BBC Northern Ireland has an early photograph of Glens boys dressed in petticoats to look like girls while travelling through this area – the fairies were famous for capturing boys.

The **Watershee** is also believed to inhabit the Glens. She usually appears as either a female fairy or a beautiful woman who lures weary travellers into bogs and loughs with her sweet singing, only to drown them and devour their unfortunate souls. Only the wearing of a cross or saying a prayer will protect human beings from her dark and evil ways. The **banshees** are slightly more benevolent, although a visit from them is equally unwelcome. They appear and begin wailing when a death is about to happen.

Many of the local place names reflect the folklore of the area such as Feystown (town of the fairies), Breen (the fairy palace) and Skeagh (the fairy thorn).

GLENARM CASTLE: Glenarm, County Antrim, Northern Ireland BT44 0BQ; ☎ 028 28841 203; www.glenarmcastle.com. Entry: adults £4.00, children £2.00; the castle can't be visited inside; Walled Garden is open May to Sept, daily 10am–6pm; free car parking.

Glenarm

Today the village of Glenarm looks as peaceable as any Sussex village, tucked snugly into its own green glen. Only a heavily fortified PSNI station – the old RUC barracks – reminds you that these bucolic surroundings have been witness to very dark deeds. Indeed, as you look across the harbour you will see some high castellated walls that predate the police barracks by several centuries – that's **Glenarm Castle**, where you can now lodge overnight in the Barbican Gate.

Glenarm is the oldest village in the Glens, the family seat of the MacDonnell family. The 14th earl of Antrim lives there now. To pay his home a visit, drive up the main thoroughfare of the town, Toberwine Street, and then head for the gothic, turreted building. Then it's across the drawbridge, through the Hammer Horror gates, and into a courtyard surrounded by battlements, look-out tower and flagpole.

The ancient 17th century Glenarm Castle of Randall MacDonnell is today very welcoming despite an 'itinerary' written in 1822 which states: 'Strangers are not permitted to enter without leave – and there is nothing to be seen worth the asking.' Obviously the spirit of

Céad Míle Féilte, or 'a hundred thousand welcomes', hadn't yet got off the ground. The barbican of Glenarm Castle is a quirky, Gothic miniature fortress – although our special knowledge of Northern affairs might tell us that, fairytale though it may look, the true story is somewhat different. Because, from its original building in 1242 right through to the 20th century, the castle has regularly been used for its original purpose, that is to say, military.

Unfortunately the main body of Glenarm Castle was badly damaged in 1929 by a blaze started by the housekeeper, so it is claimed, who kept a fire going constantly by her bedside. Today the castle is restored, and the barbican has been thoroughly modernized into accommodation. The turret staircase has been totally renovated and leads to a flat roof from where there are striking views of the village, the harbour, and out to the sea.

The surrounding estate is an 800-acre nature reserve which spreads upwards through the glen. A court cairn and several other Neolithic graves indicate that people have been living in these parts for the last 6,000 years or so. You can take the same path as our Stone Age forebears would have walked up through the glen, through over-hanging oak trees towards the open moorland of the Antrim Plateau. Within the Demesne walls you can visit the Walled Garden – one of Ireland's oldest walled gardens dating from the 18th century. Originally created to supply the castle with its fruit and vegetables, the Walled Garden is now filled with some beautiful horticultural specimens.

Cushendall

Cushendall is regarded as 'the capital of the glens' – at least the people in Cushendall regard it as such – because it stands just below the junction of **Glenballyeamon**, **Glenaan** and **Glencorp**. The best known feature of the town is the **Curfew Tower**. Now, although this looks every inch a Norman fortification, it is in fact a four-storey red sandstone copy of a Chinese building which the local squire, the very rich Francis Turly of Drumnasloe, saw on his travels. Mr Turly built his Chinese takeaway to be 'a place for confinement for idlers and rioters', altering the course of the **River Dall** 'to make Curfew Tower look more romantic'.

Cushendall has a shingly beach, good angling on the River Dall, and excellent deep-sea fishing with Ballycastle Charters.

Layde Old Church, about a mile north of the village overlooking a little valley, is part 13th century. It's a short walk along a cliff path from the beach. The churchyard has a stone cross in memory of Dr James MacDonnell – a descendant of the MacDonnell chieftains – and who was one of the organisers of the last great Festival of Harpists held in Belfast in 1792. For any lover of Irish music a pilgrimage to this site is an essential journey, because were it not for people like James MacDonnell who helped write down much

BALLYCASTLE CHARTERS: Contact Christopher P McCaughan, Claymore House, 6 Quay Road, Ballycastle BT54 6BH; ☎ 028 2076 2074; email cpmccaughan@aol.com. Entry: adults £15, children £10, day trips 10.30am – after 5pm £22.00 per person, minimum group size 6 maximum 12; evening trips Mon/Wed/Fri 7pm–10pm; no need to book, just arrive at the pier; transport/ accommodation can be arranged.

of the precious repertoire of the harpists – which stretched into antiquity – Irish music would have been sadly lost.

In Stone Street an old shop occupies a building that was formerly an inn. Our old friend Thackeray dined here, 'on a good dinner of fresh whiting, boiled bacon and small beer' – all for eightpence.

Cushendun

Cushendun is a very pretty seaside village famous for its Cornish-style cottages. The town was largely built between 1912 and 1925 to plans by Clough William Ellis – who also designed Portmeirion in North Wales. Nestling in the trees at the top of the village overlooking the old bridge is the parish church, sometimes called **John Masefield's Church**. The poet laureate spent holidays in the village and married a member of the Huguenot Crommelin family. Just outside the village is a small ivy-covered ruin called **Castle Carra**. In the 16th century, it was the scene of the climax of a quarrel between the two main Gaelic clans in Ulster, the O'Neills and the MacDonnells.

Shane O'Neill, also known as Shane (or Sean) the Proud, claimed sovereignty over Ulster. However Queen Elizabeth I was having none of it. She sided with the O'Donnells. So the O'Donnells invited Shane to Castle Carra, threw a banquet for him – and in a grave breach of post-prandial etiquette – killed him. They then sent his head to the Queen's Deputy in Dublin. A mile north, up the **Torr Head** road, **Shane O'Neill's Cross** on a cairn commemorates the event. To this day hereabouts the poem *Shane the Proud, the Prince of Tyrone*, has acute resonance:

> *I scorn your lady's honour,*
> *I scorn your titles vain.*
> *A prince am I of high,*
> *And of my own domain.*
> *I am Sean the Proud the Prince of Tyrone.*

Ballycastle

And for my next trick, ladies and gentlemen, I shall make this lake disappear.

Loughareema, near Ballycastle, on the inland road to Cushendun, is possessed of a highly unusual topography – a chalk 'plug hole' bunged up with peat. Which means you can bring a picnic and watch the entire lake vanish before your very eyes. This lonely and mysterious lake will appear, then slowly disappear as if someone has pulled out the plug. In dry weather the lough tends to go on extended leave; the best time to see it perform its trick is after very heavy rain. Cross the Glendun viaduct and after a steady climb to the moors, the road crosses a causeway over one end of Loughareema. The lough, in a remote part, was the scene of an accident in 1898 when a colonel, a coachman and two horses drowned on the causeway that crosses it. Their doomed carriage is said to haunt the lake to this day, thus neatly adding a supernatural phenomenon to the natural one.

But Ballycastle has plenty to offer besides a ghostly neighbourhood. It's a traditional seaside resort with many added extras – salmon and sea trout fishing,

The best of... NORTHERN IRELAND'S WATERSCAPES

WHETHER IT'S THE CRASHING ATLANTIC ON THE EXPOSED NORTHERLY COAST OF DERRY, OR THE QUIET MEANDERING BACKWATERS OF COUNTY FERMANAGH, NORTHERN IRELAND HAS SOME OF THE FINEST WATERSCAPES IN EUROPE. GREAT SEA LOUGHS ENTERTAIN GIGANTIC FLOCKS OF GEESE AS THEY MIGRATE THE WORLD; SPARKLING TROUT STREAMS PROVIDE SOME OF THE BEST FISHING AVAILABLE ANYWHERE.

Boating in Fermanagh's lakes

Top: Tollymore Forest Park, County Down; Middle: The Lower Bann River , County Antrim; Bottom: Keady Watermill , County Armagh

Top: Murlough Bay, County Down; Bottom: Sunset near Ballintoy Harbour, Antrim

Top: Lower Lough Erne, Fermanagh; Middle: Carrick-a-Rede rope bridge, County Antrim;
Bottom: River Lagan, Belfast

golfing, breathtaking views, a photogenic harbour, and the Marconi Memorial. The latter takes the form of a picnic site with stone tables and pillars shaped to symbolise radio waves and other tecky stuff. It's a long story, but in 1898 Gugliemo Marconi, carried out transmissions between **Rathlin Island**

Ballycastle Marina

and the mainland (of Northern Ireland) to prove to Lloyds of London that wireless telegraphy was practicable.

Ballycastle Charters offers full or half day fishing expeditions, as well as evening trips. Rod lessons are given, and transport to and from the quay can be arranged, as well as nearby accommodation (see p. 111). Ballycastle is crucially beyond Ulster's Bible Belt, a dozen miles from Scotland, and one of the finest places in these islands to enjoy a pint while contemplating the sea. And if the weather turns nasty, there's a wealth of pubs here: just remember the old north Antrim saying, '40mph winds outside, 40 per cent inside'. The hot toddies may also help you dispose of your reservations and join in a few verses of **The Ould Lammas Fair**.

Rathlin Island

Rathlin is Ireland's most northerly inhabited island. The island's attractions include bird watching, perhaps some hiking round the island, or scuba diving among the shipwrecks of the Spanish Armada, lying broken on the seabed. Don't miss out **Bull Point** at the western end of the island where the sight of thousands of guillemots covering the tops of the grey stacks of rock is just the thing for even the most jaded view junkie.

Legends and islands are inseparable, and Rathlin has its fair share including the famous arachnid anecdote. Robert the Bruce had his encounter with a spider in a cave on Rathlin. So taken was he with the spider's sterling efforts on the web that he (Robert) redoubled his efforts against the English.

Rathlin Island is a 50-minute boat trip across the sound from **Ballycastle** with **Rathlin Island Ferry Company** and only a dozen or so miles from the Mull of Kintyre in Scotland. It

Rathlin Island, Ireland's most northerly inhabited point

boasts lighthouses and high white cliffs round most of the coast. There's also a pub, restaurant, two shops and a range of fairly limited accommodation.

RATHLIN ISLAND FERRY COMPANY:
Ballycastle Ferry Terminal,18 Bayview Road, Ballycastle; Booking Line ☎ 00 44 28 20 769299; www.rathlinballycastleferry.com. Entry: adult £10 return, children over 5 £5 return, under-5 free; no cars.

Guillemots on Rathlin Island

BICYCLE HIRE: Soerneog View Hostel, Ouig, Rathlin Island, County Antrim BT54 6RT; ☎ 028 2076 3954. Entry: age 10+, child seats (for children up to 22kg) are available; helmets provided; book in advance.

RATHLIN ISLAND SEABIRD CENTRE: RSPB West Light Viewpoint; ☎ 028 2076 0062. Entry: free; Apr to mid Sep 11pm–3pm.

It won't be a luxury city break. This is an island whose weather is as stormy as its history, its surroundings as mournful as the wind that soughs through every nook and indeed cranny of the island. Rathlin boatmen are pleased to point out **Sloughna-More**, 'the swallow of the sea', a whirlpool at the southern tip of Rathlin where St Colmcille is said to have narrowly escaped drowning on a voyage from Ireland to Iona in the sixth century. A great way to see the island is by **bicycle** or you can take a **minibus tour** with McGinn's (☎ 028 2076 3451).

The cliffs of Rathlin are home to tens of thousands of seabirds whose incessant murmuring is a soundtrack to all outdoor activities on the island. The best place to see this abundant ornithology is at the **Rathlin Island Seabird Centre** at the west end of the island. Sheer volcanic rock-stacks are crowded with razorbills, guillemots, Manx shearwaters, fulmars, kittiwakes and puffins. Buzzards nest on Rathlin, and waders frequent the small reed-fringed lakes.

The caves in the Rathlin cliffs have magnificent interiors, some iridescent with reflected light, some with walls and pillars of white limestone. Most of them can only be reached by boat. The most famous is the afore-mentioned **Bruce's Cave**, beneath the **East Lighthouse**.

Rathlin's history is a tale of battles, massacres and troubles, brought about by its strategic position in the North Channel between Ireland and Scotland. 'The Hill of Screaming', got its name following a gruesome incident when a large force of Campbells landed on Rathlin in 1642 and slaughtered the MacDonnells. For a rundown on the island's history, head for the **Rathlin Boathouse Visitor Centre** (Church Bay, Rathlin Island BT54 6RT; ☎ 028 2076 2024; www.moyle-council.org) which has a fine exhibition on the social, economic and environmental history of Rathlin Island and its people. You will also meet the locals, find out what's happening on the island and sort out a day's **fishing**.

Fishing is one of the islanders' livelihoods, particularly lobsters, and local fishermen will be happy to take you along. All summer, mackerel are plentiful, with shoals of herring in the evenings. Out from the shore there's great **angling** for cod, haddock, skate and other big fish. There is also fantastic **scuba diving**. Contact Tommy Cecil (☎ 028 57 63915) for more information.

LOCAL KNOWLEDGE

Linda Heggarty, a vice principal at a local Quaker grammar school, was born and brought up in Ballycastle and knows everything there is to know about the area. Her interests range from walking along the beaches of North Antrim to enjoying local poetry. Here are her local recommendations:

Favourite pub – the House of McDonnell – a Ballycastle institution, as is its publican Tom O'Neill. This is a real must to visit if you are in the area.

Favourite shop – Wysner's in Ballycastle for their meat pies – there's nothing like them anywhere!

Favourite activity – I have many favourite activities in and around Ballycastle, like walking along the golf links in Ballycastle; or driving to Portbraddan or Ballintoy in Winter. In summer I love to watch the tennis at the Ballycastle Club.

Favourite Haunt – the Bushmills Inn with its local salmon, its not so local Pinot Grigio, and its always-burning turf fire.

Best tip for lunch – Morton's fish and chips, they really are to die for. Or better still, take a day trip to Rathlin, have a sandwich, and look at the art in local galleries.

Best view – when you're driving in from Belfast, that first view of Fair Head is pure magic! I love the clarity of Scotland on a bright winter's day. Or coming through Glenshesk and seeing it roll towards the sea.

Favourite drive – the coastal road from Ballyvoy to Cushendun and sweeping back into Ballycastle via Corrymeela and hugging the water all the way to Marconi's cottage.

Favourite treat – the local dulse! Or soft ice cream from Harry's van.

☂ Wet weather

If the rains come, then a worthy diversion is **Ballycastle Museum**. Housed in the town's 18th-century courthouse, it's a

BALLYCASTLE MUSEUM: 61A Castle Street; ☎ 028 2976 2942. Entry: free; Jul/Aug noon–6pm Mon–Sat.

Ballycastle Museum

fine collection of Irish arts and crafts, plus a short history of the area.

🏃 What to do with children

WATERTOP OPEN FARM: 118 Cushendall Road, Ballycastle; ☎ 0208 2076 2576; www.watertopfarm.co.uk. Entry: camping from £8–12.

Watertop Open Farm, about 10km east of Ballycastle is the ideal place to take children whether they know about farms or not. They'll be absolutely entranced, no matter what time of year, with lambing, sheep shearing, tending the ducks, grooming the horses. This is a working farm, but camping and caravan sites are available.

    Ardclinis Outdoor Adventure (☎ 028 2177 1340; www.ardclinis.com) in Cushendall provides a wide variety of outdoor activities, all with qualified instructors. Archery, rope course, canoeing, climbing and abseiling, bridge building and orienteering are all included, and older children can take part in powerboat handling.

Ropes course at Ardclinis Outdoor Adventure

🎭 Entertainment

Traditional music

The **Glens of Antrim** area is famous for traditional music. An organisation, Causeway Music (www.causewaymusic.co.uk) is devoted to promoting traditional sessions in the North Antrim area. Visit the website to find out what's going on.

    Pubs which regularly hold sessions include **McBride's** in Cushendun (2 Main Street BT44 0PH; ☎ 028 2176 1511), **Johnny Joe's** in Cushendall and the **Carrick-**

a-Rede in Ballintoy. The **Glencloy Inn** (Bridge Street, Carnlough; ☎ 028 2888 5226) was formerly known as Pat Hammill's, and as a famous music pub it is named in the song 'Sweet Carnlough Bay'. It features a variety of music at the weekend. The **Central Bar** (12 Ann Street, Ballycastle BT54 6AD; ☎ 028 2076 3877), right in the middle of town, has been famous for traditional music, ballads and sessions for over five decades. Mid-week session nights change with the season, but at the weekend there are always some lively happenings.

Festivals

The most famous festival in the area – indeed one of the most famous festivals in all of Ireland is the **Ould Lammas Fair** held at the end of August. The festival boasts an eponymous theme song which acts as a one-medium advertising campaign:

> *At the Ould Lammas Fair, boys,*
> *Were you ever there,*
> *Were you ever at the fair at Ballycastle, O*
> *Did you treat your Mary Ann*
> *To some dulse and yellow man*
> *At the Ould Lammas Fair in Ballycastle O*

Dulse is seaweed. Yellow man is basically like Crunchie without the chocolate. The song is known throughout Ireland, and the fair, originally a livestock market, has mutated over the years to include much more than trading in horseflesh.

The Ould Lammas Fair

The best... **PLACES TO STAY**

HOTEL

Londonderry Arms

20 Harbour Road, Carnlough BT44 0EU
☎ 028 2888 5255
www.glensofantrim.com

A historic old hotel, you can even stay in the room Winston Churchill slept in – en route, no doubt, to survey 'the dreary steeples of Fermanagh and Tyrone'. Downstairs it's open log fires, cosy snugs and a well stocked bar. Just outside the front door is the almost impossibly picturesque Carnlough Harbour.

Price: from £65 for a single; from £95 for a double; from £135 for a suite.

Cullentra House

16 Cloghs Road, Cushendall BT44 0SP
☎ 028 2177 1762

Want a terrific view of Scotland? Forget about going to the Highlands. Book yourself into the Cullentra and you will have great views of the Mull of Kintyre, Islay and Bute. Voted Northern Ireland Guesthouse of the Year, Cullentra House is about a mile outside Cushendall, and has only three en suite rooms.

Price: £30 for a single, £23 per person sharing a double.

The Glens Hotel

Coast Road, Cushendall BT44 0RU
☎ 028 2177 1223
www.theglenshotel.com

The Glens Hotel is a small family-run hotel with homemade cooking (local breads a speciality), and the emphasis on fish, seafood and local beef for dinner. A friendly place in the heart of the glens and a stone's throw from the sea.

Price: from £75 for a double.

FARMSTAY

Torr Brae

Torr Road, Torr Head, Ballycastle BT54 6RQ
☎ 028 2076 9625
www.torrbrae.co.uk

On the very unlikely chance that you are homesick, this is the place to stay. Because it's the closest accommodation in Ireland to Britain – only 12 miles away. Set on a farm, the surroundings are bucolic, the views spectacular, and the welcome warm and friendly.

Price: from £30 for a double.

B&B

Lurig View

38 Glen Road, Glenariffe BT 44 0RF
☎ 028 217 71618
www.lurigview.co.uk

A family-run business situated in Glenariffe. A handy place if you want to be near the coast, the pub and the restaurants.

Price: £30 for a single; £55 for a double.

SELF-CATERING

The Barbican

Glenarm Castle, Glenarm – bookings through The Irish Landmark Trust
☎ 00 353 1 670 4733

The Barbican of Glenarm Castle is now a self-catering weekend hideaway, shielded from the restless Irish Sea by crenellated walls and tall pines. A spiral staircase leads up to a modern, well-equipped kitchen/living room. On the floor below are the sleeping quarters with, needless to say, a fourposter bed. You'd be hard put to find a more romantic setting in all these islands.

Price: from £700 for a full week.

The best... FOOD AND DRINK

▶ Staying in

For seafood you could scarcely do better than the **Dalriada VG Store** (Dalriada Avenue, Cushendall; ☎ 028 2177 1496) in Cushendall. Owner Harry McAlister is following in the footsteps of his forefathers and continuing the 500-year-old family tradition of selling magnificent produce from his wee shop. Whether it's salmon, lobster or crab, you will find none tastier or fresher. Further down the coast the **Northern Salmon Company** in Glenarm (☎ 028 2884 1691) specialises in both smoked and fresh salmon.

Glens of Antrim Potatoes is a family-owned firm specialising in local growers – with a special line in organic potatoes (118 Middlepark Road, Cushendall; ☎ 028 2177 1396; www.goapotatoes.co.uk).

Wysner's, Ann Street in Ballycastle (☎ 028 2076 2372) is famous throughout the area for its lean meat (exceptionally good cattle-grazing on the Antrim Plateau guarantees it), its sausages and meat pies. Particularly to be recommended: Irish black puddings – light, tasty, and entirely delicious.

◀ Drinking

One of the finest pubs in the area, **McDonnell's** in Ballycastle, was founded in 1766. For generations the business was known simply as 'The Store' – groceries and household goods could be bought here as well. Now it's the full panoply of pints and drams. Next door is the **Antrim Arms**, with a comprehensive selection of whiskies and an atmosphere that seems geared towards conviviality and conversation. **Strand's Bar**, Ballycastle, is a fine wine bar if you've had enough Guinness for the day. And you probably have.

EATING OUT

RESTAURANT

Harry's Licensed Restaurant
10–12 Mill Street, Cushendall
☎ **028 2177 2022**

A friendly, no-nonsense sort of place serving lunch and dinners with, unusually for Northern Ireland, a vegetarian menu that has some enticing dishes on it. A tenner will see you rightly for lunch, as they say in these parts, not much more for à la carte in the evening.

The Marine Hotel
1–3 North Street, Ballycastle BT54 6BN
☎ **028 2076 2222**
www.marinehotel.net

The restaurant of the main hotel on the seafront in Ballycastle is something of an institution with locals, and popular with visitors. If you're in Ballycastle on business, this is where you stay. The restaurant, then, caters to a wide clientele and works wonders within that brief. The very freshest of seafood is on offer, as well as quirky variations on standard fare such as steaks, chicken etc. Starters cost from around £6, main courses from £12.

Wysner's
16 Ann Street, Ballycastle
☎ **028 2076 2372**

Good old-fashioned fare – sausage and champ (mashed potatoes with spring onions and cream) in the café downstairs; upstairs in the restaurant it's salmon, scallops, mussels etc. A reasonably priced establishment right in the middle of Ballycastle, it's popular with locals and visitors alike. Prices from around £6.

CAFÉ

Bruce's Kitchen
The Harbour, Rathlin Island
☎ **028 2076 3974**

If you've been out in the elements on Rathlin you will want hearty, big-fisted food rather than an amuse-bouche. Bruce will furnish you with fish (very fresh!), chips, steaks etc. The restaurant is licensed, and it's just the place to refuel after being battered by a brisk north-easterly. Open from Easter to October.

The Pantry
41A Castle Street, Ballycastle
☎ **0208 2976 9993**

An upmarket café, which means that as well as soda bread, potato farls and wheaten scones, paninis and pitta are also available. Housed in an old printer's shop, the café has a friendly atmosphere and is a particularly good spot for a late breakfast or lunch.

TAKEAWAY

McKillop's Chip Shop in Carnlough has won awards for its chips – served with everything from cod to pasties; by the way 'pasties' in Northern Ireland are sausage meat and vegetables deep fried in batter. (Perhaps because of the strong Scottish influence here, everything here seems to be deep fried in batter.)

ⓘ Visitor Information

Tourist Information Centre:
www.causewaycoastandglens.com.

Hospitals: Altnagelvin Hospital, Derry, ☎ 028 7134 5171; Antrim ☎ 028 9442 4000.

Doctors: Doctors operate under the NHS; a full list is available on www.neighbourhoodprofessionals.co.uk.

Police: in an emergency ☎ 999 or ☎ 112; for less urgent calls, Ballymena PSNI station ☎ 028 2565 3355 is the main station in the area.

Parking: Parking throughout the Glens – including Ballycastle – is easy and usually free.

Local taxis: Regency Cabs ☎ 028 9446 6666.

SOUTH ANTRIM

South Antrim, stretching from the northerly suburbs of **Belfast** to the shores of **Lough Neagh**, suffers somewhat from having such spectacular neighbours. Many people only know it because they land at the seaport of Larne, or arrive at one of Belfast's airports, and head for the Antrim coast. Yet South Antrim has many charms, including the historical site of St Patrick's apprenticeship in the pig industry – it's said he tended livestock on the slopes of **Mount Slemish** just north of **Carnalbanagh**. The south of Antrim borders **Lough Neagh** – the biggest lake in the these islands and one of the great angling centres of Europe – as well as following the **Lower Bann River** as it flows to the Atlantic.

The area is certainly not as immediately appealing as the surrounding countryside, but it has a tranquil feel about it these days, the people are friendly and welcoming, and it's a good place to discover and ruminate on the industrial heritage of Northern Ireland.

WHAT TO SEE AND DO

Lough Neagh

Lough Neagh, with an area of 400sq km, is the largest lake in Ireland or Britain. At its greatest length it is 32km long, and at its maximum width, 32km. Five of the Six Counties border the lough – only Fermanagh doesn't. Although the Lough is used for a variety of recreational and commercial activities, it is exposed and tends to get extremely rough very quickly in windy conditions. Due to the marshy foreshore, few roads follow the shoreline, and because there are few peaks in the surrounding countryside it can be difficult to get a complete view of the lake's immense size. The best viewpoints in County Antrim are around **Sandy Bay** (nearest town **Glenavy**).

A number of islands are scattered mostly close to the shore – **Coney Island**, **Croaghan Flat**, **Derrywarragh Island**, **Padian**, **Ram's Island**, **Phil Roe's Flat** and **The Shallow Flat**. None are inhabited, although **Oxford Island** (the largest) has an interpretive and discovery centre (see p. 142).

Here you'll find out not only which birds and fish you will come across on, in or round the lough, you will also hear about the great horse-god Eochu, Lord of the Underworld, who lives below the waters. It's unlikely you will spot him – there have been no recorded sightings of him for a few years now. But the legendary Finn MacCool does make an appearance here. Northern Ireland's resident giant is reckoned to be responsible for the similarity in shape of Lough Neagh and the Isle of Man. In a fight with a rival giant, Finn scooped out a handful of earth (thus making Lough Neagh) and threw it into the Irish Sea – the Isle of Man was the result.

Oxford Island, at Lough Neagh, is a haven for bird-watching

Helping the legends and myths along is an odd phenomenon, which unlike the giants and the horse-gods, you may very well see – and hear. 'Waterguns' – as the locals call them – are booming noises heard along the surface of the lough, and are associated with whirlwinds which occur during sultry weather. It's a very odd sound when you do hear it – and if you can't spot any wind disturbances on the surface of the lough, well then it probably was a horse god.

The **fishing** here is superb. Lough Neagh is Europe's greatest source of eels – the fish are exported to restaurants throughout the continent. It's an odd thing that visitors sometimes have difficulty in finding this huge expanse of water, because of the surrounding modest topography. Yet millions of tiny eels, the size of a fingernail, born in the Saragosso Sea, swim across the Atlantic, turn right up the Lower Bann River, and apparently have no difficulty in locating the lough. They do this unerringly every year. Other species which can be fished for in Lough Neagh include pollan (a freshwater herring), and salmon-trout, which commonly reach 14lb in weight.

Bird watching is another great Lough Neagh activity. The bird and plant life around Lough Neagh is exceptionally rich. The great crested grebe nests everywhere along the banks, while the south shore is the focus for vast numbers of winter diving ducks, including rare ferruginous and ring-necked ducks, red-crested pochard, and smew. Watchful herons can be spotted fishing everywhere along the banks, and all three native swans are on show – mute swans gliding effortlessly across the lough, whooper and Bewick's swans grazing just beyond the foreshore.

There can be few better ways to explore Lough Neagh than by pleasure cruiser. The **Maid of Antrim**, the **Trostan** and the **Island Warrior** all ply the lough's waters giving the chance to experience the unspoilt scenery, secluded bays and countless forms of wildlife along the **Lower Bann River**. Various trips also take in the towns of **Portglenone**, **Portneal** and **Coleraine** before returning.

THE MAID OF ANTRIM: 136 Ballynease Road, Portglenone BT44 8NU; ☎ 028 2582 2159; www.loughneaghcruises. com. Entry: cruises depart Apr to Oct with refreshments and bar service available on board.

The Maid of Antrim is the biggest purpose-built pleasure cruiser on the lough, licensed to carry 100 passengers, departing from **Ballyronan Marina** on the western shore of Lough Neagh

ECOS ENVIRONMENTAL CENTRE:
Broughshane Road, Ballymena; ☎ 028
2566 4400; www.ecoscentre.com. Entry:
free; open July/Aug 9am–5pm Mon–Fri,
10.30am–5pm Sat, 12–5pm Sun, Sept to
Jun 9am–5pm Mon–Fri.

Ballymena

South Antrim is the area once known as the buckle on Northern Ireland's bible belt, and the heartland of the Ulster Scots. **Ballymena**, was the centre of operations for Rev Ian Paisley – this was his constituency, and was the scene of much sectarian strife. On the eastern side of the town is a visitor centre that focuses on sustainable technology and alternative energy sources. The **Ecos Environmental Centre** offers a range of exhibits that will appeal to children, plus a duck pond and play area.

Carrickfergus

Northern Ireland's oldest town, Carrickfergus has been bombarded, burned, bombed and many times during its 900-year history, but little except the massive Anglo-Norman castle and the Elizabethan parish church remain to suggest this long history. The rest of the town is fairly unprepossessing, but the castle is certainly of major interest (see below). Nearby is **Kilroot**, famous because it holds the remains of the church where **Jonathan Swift** earned his first living (1694–6) as a vicar. It seems that Swift got his idea for Gulliver in Lilliput from the shape of Cave Hill above Belfast which looks like a resting giant. The vicar-cum-writer would have regularly passed this en route from Kilroot to his home in Dublin.

CARRICKFERGUS CASTLE: ☎ 028 9335
1273. Entry: adult £3, child £1.50; open
Jun to Aug 10am–6pm Mon–Sat, 12–6pm
Sun, Apr/May/Sept 10am–6pm Mon–Sat,
2–6pm Sun, Oct to Mar 10am–4pm
Mon–Sat, 2–4pm Sun.

Carrickfergus Castle sits on the harbour front, controlling the seashore. Once the centre of Anglo-Norman power in Ulster, Carrickfergus is a remarkably complete and well-preserved early medieval castle that has survived intact despite 750 years of continuous military occupation – it was seized in 1689 for

Carrickfergus Castle

CELEBRITY CONNECTIONS

Liam Neeson, born in Ballymena in 1952, is famous for his roles as Oskar Schindler in Steven Spielberg's *Schindler's List*, as Qui-Gon Jinn in George Lucas's *Star Wars Episode I: The Phantom Menace* and as the voice of Aslan in *The Chronicles of Narnia* film series. He has also starred in several other blockbusters including *Rob Roy* and *Michael Collins*. The only boy among four siblings, he was named Liam, the Irish equivalent to William, after the local priest. While at Queen's University Belfast, Neeson's talents shone through. At football. He was spotted by Bohemian FC (one of the premier teams in the Republic) and featured briefly in top-flight soccer when he came on as a substitute in a game against Shamrock Rovers. Neeson was not offered a contract at the club and the match remains his only performance in professional football.

Neeson subsequently flowered as an actor at the Lyric Players' Theatre in Belfast. After two years there, he moved to Dublin and joined the Abbey Theatre in 1977. In 1980, film-maker John Boorman offered him the part in *Excalibur*. Neeson then moved to London, where he continued working on stage, small budget movies and television series. He lived with the actress Helen Mirren at this time, whom he met working on Excalibur. Dame Helen is reported to have been much taken with Ballymena.

In 1998, Neeson turned down an offer by Ballymena Town Council to honour him. He said that the controversy which erupted over plans to offer him Freedom of the Borough had made it 'inappropriate' for him to accept. Ballymena, whose MP is Rev Ian Paisley, is overwhelmingly Protestant. Neeson was quoted as saying in an American magazine the previous year that he felt 'second class' as a Catholic growing up in Ballymena, something that caused great annoyance to some of the councillors – hence the row. He did, however, accept an OBE in the 2000 New Year's Honours list.

King William of Orange who stepped ashore here in 1690. A plaque on the pier marks the spot, a revered site by one section of the community. At the time Carrickfergus was the only part of the North where English was spoken. The castle, built as a strong and mighty fortress – not just to ward off the rebellious insurgents but also to make the point that those who built it were now the power in the land – is today open to the public as a museum.

St Nicholas's parish church – where the poet Louis McNiece's father was vicar – is contemporaneous with the castle. Just off the market place, some 12th-century features remain, including pillars in the nave. A statue to Sir Arthur Chichester,

Slemish Mountain, still a place of pilgrimage on St Patrick's Day

landlord of Belfast (quite a title, really) stands in the north transept. A small effigy of his brother, Sir John Chichester, who had his head chopped off at **Glynn** near **Larne** in a McDonnell ambush in 1597, is part of the same monument.

Glynn was the location for Northern Ireland's first talking picture *The Luck of the Irish*, something that Sir John Chichester would surely have had something to say about, had he survived his beheading.

Mount Slemish

Slemish stands in the centre of County Antrim, and it was on its slopes that the captive Patrick herded sheep and pigs for Milchu, a local chieftain. In his Confessio, Patrick describes his early days in the Rev Ian Paisley's constituency: 'Now after I came to Ireland daily I herded flocks and often during the day I prayed. Love of God and his fear increased more and more, and my faith grew and my spirit was stirred up so that in a single day I said as many as a hundred prayers, and at night likewise, though I abode in the woods and then in the mountain.'

Slemish, standing some 1437ft high, is near the town of **Broughshane** and visible for miles around, being the only peak in the rather flat landscape. A well-marked path leads to the top. The North of Ireland writer Sam Hanna Bell once wrote of Ulster: 'Where every hill has is hero and every bog has its bones.' And Mount Slemish has the biggest hero of all.

Antrim

The county town of Antrim sits on the River Sixmilewater, and is worth a stop for the **Antrim Castle Gardens**, an attractive 17th-century ornamental garden, now minus its castle, and for the **Antrim Lough Shore Park**, west of the town centre, which offers wonderful views of Lough Neagh, and walking trails around the Lough.

Just outside Antrim town in **Steeple Park**, a mile from the centre, stands one of the most perfect 10th-century round towers. These tall circular towers, which taper towards the top in characteristic fashion, are a unique feature of the Irish countryside. They include a doorway about 12ft from the ground, served by a wooden ladder which could be hastily pulled up behind those fleeing the Viking raiders. Round towers were built between the 9th and 12th centuries.

Islandmagee

Islandmagee is not actually an island but a 7-mile-long peninsula. Nonetheless it has its own very specific atmosphere, a distinctive separate feel about it. The witches

Cottage on Islandmagee

tried at Carrickfergus assizes in 1710 – the last witch trial in Ireland – were from Islandmagee. And when you go there, well, you are not surprised.

On the east side of Islandmagee, basalt cliffs called the **Gobbins** were the site in 1641 of a particularly gruesome incident. Soldiers from the garrison in Carrickfergus rounded up local inhabitants and threw them into the sea.

Just opposite Larne is Ballylumford Power Station. A strike here in 1974 by loyalist workers brought about the fall of power-sharing (in the political sense, that is) set up by the Sunningdale Conference. Thus Northern Ireland was sentenced to 20 more years of mayhem and murder. The Good Friday Agreement, which has finally brought peace to the North, has been called 'Sunningdale for slow learners'.

Larne

At the head of Belfast Lough, Larne is Northern Ireland's main car ferry port, with services to Stranraer and Cairnryan – about an hour away by fast ferry. The drive-on drive-off ships brought into service after the Second World War were the first such vessels in the world. Apart from that footnote in maritime history, Larne doesn't have an awful lot to detain you, although it's worth remembering that the wife of the stationmaster here at the beginning of the 19th century was **Amanda McKittrick Ros**. This austere County Down woman, born in 1860, is quite simply the world's worst novelist. Her books gloriously consist of plots of utter nonsense propelled forwards by the most preposterous dialogue. One of Ms McKittrick Ros's great gifts was to manufacture words – she would speak of 'prequintate' events, 'montogular dress', 'incendious' people or 'manifestful' views. Curiously enough she lived in a village called **Clintagooland** – a name seemingly straight from one of her books, but in fact the genuine article.

Doagh

On a hilltop 3km north-west of the village of Doagh, is a standing stone about 5ft high, in the middle of which is a hole approximately 4 inches in diameter. The monolith is possibly as much as 500 years old, and local folklore since time immemorial states that the **Holestone** will bestow everlasting love on those who clench hands through it. It's a particularly popular part of the 'St Valentine Tour' – St Valentine's bones lie in a Carmelite church in Dublin.

Whitehead

Whitehead is a small seaside resort on the 'corner' of **Belfast Lough**. It's pleasant enough, and having had a dander on the beach and bought an ice cream, head south on the coast road towards **Belfast**, to White Head itself. From the 60m cliff edge you get a good view of Belfast's topography and in stormy weather (you may not have to wait long) the **'Bla' Hole'** provides canon-size booms caused by waves from the Irish Sea dashing into a cave.

☂ Wet weather

Irish Linen Centre and Lisburn Museum is an award-winning museum in the city's 17th-century Market House. Ulster linen is famous throughout the world, and Lisburn was at one time the centre of this important industry of the area. At the museum you'll get an idea of the impact of the entire enterprise, and the consequences of its near demise after the invention of synthetic fibres. There's also a varied exhibition on topics of local history and the arts in Antrim, and an opportunity to buy craft, including, of course, linen products.

Weaving workshop at the Irish Linen Centre

IRISH LINEN CENTRE AND LISBURN MUSEUM: Market Square, Lisburn BT28 1AG; ☎ 028 9266 3377; www.lisburncity.gov.uk. Entry: free; open Mon–Sat 9.30am–5pm.

Ballance House (118A Lisburn Road, Glenavy BT29 4NY; ☎ 028 9264 8492; www.ballance.utvinternet.com) is the birthplace of John Ballance, who went on to become prime minister of New Zealand in the 19th century. The exhibitions within the house also explore the ties between Ireland and New Zealand, the impact Irish people had on New Zealand, Maori culture and of course John Ballance's role in the development of New Zealand.

County Antrim can boast (just about) another president – this time an American one. The parents of the seventh US President, Andrew Jackson, left Carrickfergus in the 18th century. The family home in **Bonnybefore** was destroyed in 1860, but has since been rebuilt. The replica cottage now houses the **Andrew Jackson Centre** which explores the links between the Ulster Scots and the USA.

Ballance House, birthplace of John Ballance

ANDREW JACKSON CENTRE: ☎ 028 9336 6455. Entry: free; Apr to Oct 10am–4pm/ 6pm depending on season.

What to do with children...

Carnfunnock Family Fun Zone is probably one of Northern Ireland's most comprehensive children's leisure parks (age range 2–12) with miniature railway, 18-hole mini golf, remote control boats, laser clay pigeon shooting, bouncy castle, and bungee harness etc. There's enough here to keep the whole family occupied for hours.

> **CARNFUNNOCK FAMILY FUN ZONE:** Carnfunnock Country Park, Larne; ☎ 028 2858 3269; www.carnfunnock.com. Entry: prices vary according to activity; open from St Patrick's Day to Mid Nov weekends only, daily during school holidays 11am–5.30pm.

✗ ... and how to avoid children

You can buy Hilden Ales throughout Northern Ireland, but even better you can visit the **Brewery and Tap Room. Hilden** is a little village near **Lisburn**, and in the visitor centre see how the ales are made. It is interesting to hear how the Devil's Buttermilk is made – that's how the MP for the area, Ian Paisley once described all alcoholic drink – but the real interest is in

> **HILDEN BREWERY VISITOR CENTRE AND TAP ROOM RESTAURANT:** Hilden House, Hilden, Lisburn BT27 4TY; ☎ 028 9266 3863. Entry: admission £4.50, concessions £3.50; tour times 11.30am and 6.30pm all year Tue–Sat and bank holidays.

sampling the stuff. That you can do to your heart's content at the Hilden Brewery Visitor Centre. Even better, there's an award winning pub and restaurant as well.

📺 Entertainment

Toomebridge (or the Bridge of Toome) is mentioned in one of the most famous rebel songs in the Irish folk ballad repertoire: 'For young Roddy McCorley goes to die/On the Bridge of Toome today.' Thankfully Toomebridge is more musically famous these days because of the **Crosskeys Pub** (40 Grange Road, Toomebridge, 40 Grange Road; ☎ 028 7965 0694; www.crosskeys-inn.com). Founded in 1742, for the last half century it has been a fulcrum of Irish traditional music, particularly fiddle music. Sessions take place on weekend nights.

    East Antrim Traditional Music School (Monkstown Community School, Larne, www.eatms.co.uk) runs sessions and workshops throughout the year. You can pop along as spectator, learner or performer – all are welcome.

The best... PLACES TO STAY

HOTEL

The Dunadry Hotel & Country Club

2 Islandreagh Drive, Dunadry BT41 2HA
☎ **028 9443 4343**
www.dunadry.com

The four-star Dunadry is one of Northern Ireland's finest hotels, set in 10 acres of beautiful grounds. Friendly service, relaxed atmosphere – and two first-class restaurants the Mill Race Bistro and the Linen Mill Restaurant.

Price: from £82 for a double.

Galgorm Resort & Spa

136 Fenaghy Road, Galgorm, Galgorm Resort & Spa BT42 1EA
☎ **028 2588 0080**
www.galgorm.com

A hotel complex full of old traditional features interspersed with the most modern of spa and wellness facilities. The 19th-century manor house is set on the banks of the River Maine, and the atmosphere is a mixture of the sumptuous and the rustic – huge timber beams, log fires, monumental staircase, and of course lots of fluffy towels.

Price: from £85 for a double.

Dobbin's Inn Hotel

6–8 High Street, Carrickfergus
☎ **028 9335 1905**
www.dobbinsinnhotel.co.uk

An atmospheric, informal old hostelry which has been on the go for four centuries and comes complete with priest's hole (for hiding in) and an original 16th-century fireplace.

Price: from £45 for a double.

Ballygally Castle

Coast Road, Ballygally, Larne BT40 2QZ
☎ **028 2858 1066**
www.hastingshotel.com

A lovely, historic hotel – so much so that this is reckoned to be one of the most haunted castles in Ireland. The ghost that visits is said to be Lady Shaw who passes her time knocking at doors of the different hotel rooms. Built in 1625, many of the original features are still on show – the original beam ceilings and antique pine furniture. Maybe Lady Isobel Shaw, the former lady of the castle, wants to keep her eye on things.

Price: from £70 for a double.

FARMSTAY

Hillview Farm

35 Stoneyford Road, Lisburn BT28 3RG
☎ **028 9264 8270**

This large country house abuts a working farm – so produce is guaranteed fresh. Fully modernized, the house is cosy and friendly, with a play area for children and residents' lounge.

Price: from £45 for a double.

B&B

Marlagh Lodge

Moorfields Road, Ballymena BT42 3BU
☎ **028 9443 3659**

Truly memorable home cooking, and a cosy welcoming ambience are the hallmarks of this B&B guesthouse.

Price: £45 per person per night.

The best... **PLACES TO STAY**

SELF-CATERING

Brookhall Cottages

86 Ballinderry Road, Lisburn BT28 2QT
☎ **028 9262 1712**
www.brookhall.com

In the private grounds of Brookhall Historical Farm, these cottages – part of which used to comprise the gate lodge – retain their original period character. Both cottages hold up to six people. The grounds are beautifully relaxing – you can stroll through the gardens, walk round the farm, or go fishing for trout in the lake.

Price: low season £150 for three nights, £250 for a week; high season £185 and £300.

Ballealy Cottage

Randalstown, Lough Neagh
Contact: The Irish Landmark Trust
☎ **00 353 1 670 4733**
www.irishlandmark.com

Ballealy Cottage is a 19th-century estate cottage on the Shane's Castle Estate. Built for the local estate keeper around 1835, its sturdy blackstone appearance hasn't changed much on the outside since then. Inside, however, it has been perfectly restored, but with all added conveniences – central heating, cooking range, fridge, en suite bedrooms, washing machine etc. The cottage is surrounded by a working farm.

Price: from £364 to £546 for a week.

The best... **FOOD AND DRINK**

▶ Staying in

Tom Gilbert's Ballylagan Organic Farm, **Ballyclare** (☎ 028 9332 2867; www. ballylagan.com) is one of the finest organic outlets in the Six Counties. A wide range of produce from the farm is available as well as imported fruits, dried food – all of certified organic standard.

Templepatrick Farmers' Market (☎ 028 9443 2513) happens from 9am to 1pm at **Coleman's Garden Centre**, **Templepatrick** every day. In **Lisburn** a small farmers' market takes place near the main square. Northern Ireland-produced cheeses are on offer, as well as home-baked bakery, organic produce, local jams and honey. The **Country Harvest Delicatessen** (The **Tramways Centre**, **Glengormley**, ☎ 028 9083 9338) is a huge deli selling everything from pastas to honey, vegetables, fruits, spices – and of course a good variety of Northern Ireland produce from cheeses to chutney.

EATING OUT

RESTAURANT

Oregano Restaurant
29 Ballyrobert Road, Ballyclare BT39 9RY
☎ 028 9084 0099
www.oreganorestaurant.com

An award-winning restaurant which has become a landmark for gastronauts in South Antrim. Signature dishes include a starter of roast wood pigeon and puy lentils, or main dishes of chargrilled rump of Finnebrogue (local County Down) venison. Main courses cost from £9.

Raffles Restaurant
822 Antrim Road, Templepatrick, Ballyclare BT39 0AH
☎ 028 9443 2984
www.templetonhotel.com

An elegant restaurant in the three-star Templeton Hotel, Raffles has established itself as one of the finest tables of modern cuisine in the North. An award-winning eating place, it has a wide range of vegetarian options as well as the pick of freshwater fish from nearby Lough Neagh.

GASTRO PUB

Joymount Arms
17, Joymount Street, Carrickfergus BT38 7DP
☎ 028 9336 2213

Wonderful pies, seafood platters, ploughman's lunches (with local cheeses) and homemade desserts make this an ideal place to start your exploration of one of Ireland's most historic towns. From £6 upwards.

The Grouse Inn
2–12 Springwell Street, Ballymena BT43 6AT
☎ 028 2564 5234

A comfortable, friendly restaurant on the outskirts of Ballymena, popular with the locals. Standard fare – steaks, salmon, and a few vegetarian options, but all done with a touch of flair. Mains cost from £8.

CAFÉ

Solomon Grundy's Café & Restaurant
Tower Centre, Wellington Street, Ballymena BT43 6AF
☎ 028 2565 9602
www.solomongrundys.com

This popular establishment has been serving the people of Ballymena for the best part of a quarter of a century. Regarded as a family friendly restaurant, it serves hearty food in comfortable surroundings. A designated play area is provided for very young children, and there is a children's menu as well. Mains from £7.

🍺 Drinking

The **Hilden Brewing Company** has been brewing ale in County Antrim since 1981. Currently it produces three beers – Hilden Ale, a dark pale ale, Molly Malone, a red beer, and Great Northern Porter, which has won plaudits all over the beer drinking community (sizeable) in Northern Ireland. It is possible to visit the brewery (see p. 129). **Hague's** in Chapel Street, Lisburn (☎ 028 9266 3588) is a comfortable pub in the city centre, an excellent oasis from the busy shopping centre nearby. Lisburn is one of Northern Ireland's four cities, but is generally regarded as a stolid, no-nonsense sort of place. But Hague's is ideal for a great pint of Guinness, a chat and a read of the newspaper.

The village of **Rasharkin** in the Antrim countryside is a sleepy little place, but **Mullaghan's** (53 Main Street BT44 5PY; ☎ 028 2957 1163) is a wonderful country pub to pick up local knowledge on a range of topics from fishing to Gaelic games. **McNally's** (62 Hillhead Road, Toomebridge BT41 3SP; ☎ 028 7965 9872) is another lovely little village pub, an ideal place for a pint and maybe a sandwich. But they don't come more traditional than **McGeown's** (22 Main Street, Glenavy BT29 4LW; ☎ 028 9442 2467) – cosy bar, turf fire, stone walls, black, black Guinness and plenty of craic.

ℹ️ Visitor Information

Tourist information centre: Antrim Tourist Information Centre, 16 High Street, Antrim BT41 4AN, ☎ 028 9442 8331; General information from the local tourist board ☎ 02870 327720, www.discovernorthernireland.com.

Hospitals: Antrim Area Hospital, Bush Road, Antrim, ☎ 28 9442 4000.

Doctors: Antrim Health Centre, Antrim Town, ☎ 028 9441 3910; The Gables Medical Centre, 45 Waveney Road, Ballymena BT43 5BA, ☎ 028 2565 3237; Scotch Quarter Practice, Carrickfergus Health Centre, Taylor's Avenue, Carrickfergus BT38 7HT, ☎ 028 9331 5835.

Police: ☎ 028 7034 4122, Kilrea, Coleraine, County Derry BT51 5LP.

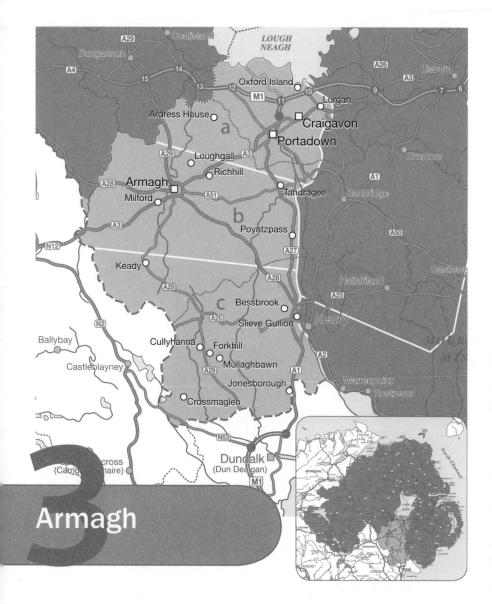

3

Armagh

a. North Armagh

b. Mid Armagh and Armagh City

c. South Armagh

Unmissable highlights

01 Climb Slieve Gullion, which dominates this land of poetry and legend, p. 165

02 Visit the Kilnasaggart inscribed stone, the oldest Christian field monument in Ireland, p. 168

03 Join in a traditional music session at the Welcome Inn, Forkhill, reputedly the longest running traditional sessions in these islands, p. 174

04 You've a choice of visiting two St Patrick's cathedrals in Armagh, the ecclesiastical centre of all Ireland, p. 153

05 Meet the stars at Armagh Planetarium and Observatory. Monks in Armagh were responsible for some of the earliest weather records in the world, p. 151

06 Get to the core of the matter with a walk through Armagh's orchard country, p. 138

07 Fish for rainbow trout in Tullynawood Lake, Keady, p. 172

08 Visit the Clontygora Court Tomb built around 4500BC. A nearby Republican memorial from the recent Troubles helps puts history in context, p. 169

09 Visit Tayto, Tandragee – the home of the flavoured potato crisp, p. 158

10 Listen to story-telling in the pubs round Crossmaglen, Cullyhanna and Mullaghbane, p. 169

ARMAGH

The early Celts made Armagh one of their strongholds. When
St Patrick arrived he took to the place like a duck to water – of
which there was a plentiful supply – and without further ado
established his ministry here.

The city of Armagh remains the ecclesiastical centre of the island with echoes
of the patron saint of Ireland, as well as Brian Boru, Queen Macha and the
Book of Armagh. The unique, ethereal atmosphere of Armagh has an appeal
for anyone, partly because this is still a living, working community. Unlike many
European cathedral cities, Armagh isn't just a preserved shell with little more
than souvenir shops and tea rooms to offer.

County Armagh is a traditional music centre – sessions abound, and often
include the primordial art of storytelling, an artform undertaken by what is
known as a *seanchaí*. The ancient sport of road bowling (it rhymes with fowling)
can also be glimpsed. Gaelic sports are very popular in the county – Armagh
has one of the strongest Gaelic football sides in the whole of Ireland, and the
area has a hallowed place in the annals of soccer. This is where the penalty
kick was invented in the 19th century.

The north of Armagh is apple country, a welcoming area, a place to drift and
wander between orchards and loughs with no plans, no hurry. Lough Neagh is
home to the wonderful Discovery Centre on Oxford Island. Here you can delve
into the natural history of the Lakeland – its birdlife, fish stocks (massive and
diverse) and varied vegetation. Some of the earliest weather records in the
world were kept by Armagh monks, and Armagh Observatory, in the star-gazing
business for a thousand or more years, is still at the cutting edge of inter-
stellar research.

South Armagh for long decades in the 20th century was a no-go area. Not only
did security forces and representatives of the State give the region a wide
berth, basically if you didn't have family there, you didn't visit. All changed
now, it's a destination for lovers of folklore, traditional music, ceili dance – and
geology. Slieve Gullion is a textbook example of a very specific volcanic rock
formation. Something, indeed, for everyone.

NORTH ARMAGH

Thomas Carlyle famously said in 1849 in his Irish Journey: 'Armagh is as like Madagascar as England.' And 160 years later the north of the county lives up to that observation in many respects – it was here that the Orange Order (one of the oldest surviving political organisations in Europe) was founded, and until the Peace Process of the mid 1990s, the area was blighted with violence and chaos. Today defiant Union Jacks continue to flutter alongside Ulster flags on Protestant housing estates and in Protestant villages the kerb-stones will be painted red, white and blue to proclaim their Britishness. Since the Good Friday Agreement – which more or less ended the Troubles – all has been relatively calm in North Armagh. Bitterness still remains in some quarters but – to be blunt about it – this is a private squabble, and the tourist can happily avoid any involvement.

Nowhere could seem more peaceful, more bucolic, than the middle of the county, wherein lies Armagh's apple country. Few scenes in Ireland are more pastoral – the delicate white and pink of the apple blossom, the green patchwork of the fields, the orchards stretching across the gentle drumlin country in soporifically beautiful procession. Apple cultivation has a long history in these fertile lands – they've been growing here for the past 3,000 years. Our old friend legend has it that St Patrick himself planted an apple tree at **Ceangoba**, an ancient hill north of **Armagh City**. And William of Orange momentarily became William of Apple when he quenched his thirst with the famous local cider. Even though King Billy had the forthcoming Battle of the Boyne on his mind, he had time to comment favourably on the juice of the apple. Today the main apple crop is the Bramley – probably County Armagh's most famous gift to the world, aside from the penalty kick in soccer.

WHAT TO SEE AND DO

Apple tour

A tour round the 'Orchards of Armagh', including stop-offs for traditional tea/coffee, apple tart and fresh cream, is a good way to get the lie of the land. A local guide will present the whole lowdown on apple history and horticultural in Armagh. The **Apple Blossom Tour** takes in the pretty villages of **Loughgall** and **Richhill**, each with a very odd combination – a dramatic past (both ancient and recent) overlaid with a studied gentility.

APPLE BLOSSOM TOURS: Barbara Ferguson; ☎ 028 3755 1119 or 07740 511 442; info@armaghguidedtours.com. Entry: tour costs £15 (including tea/coffee, apple tart and fresh cream) during apple blossom season beginning May; other tours of the orchards are undertaken throughout the year.

Lurgan

One of the many orchards in Armagh

Lurgan is the largest town in the area, although often overlooked by visitors. But to get to grips with some of the subtler aspects of Ulster life, stick it on your itinerary. Its Georgian architecture, compelling heritage, and easygoing ambience make it a worthwhile stopping off point. The history of Lurgan has given the town a unique character, beefed up by the esoteric fact that its most famous personality, by a very long chalk, is a dog.

Lurgan, originally a Plantation town (referring to the 17th-century plantation of Ulster by the English and the Scots), was founded by John Brownlow, a miller from Nottingham – later to become Lord Lurgan. Today the **Lord Lurgan Memorial Park** (www. lurganpark.com) is an essential pilgrimage if you are a greyhound-racing aficionado. The centrepiece is **Brownlow House**, a magnificent 19th-century Elizabethan-style manor house. But dog-lovers will barely notice the honey-coloured mansion with its tall chimney pots as you hurry to the front of the house to pay your respects to Master McGrath. Overlooking the lawns lies the Master's grave and monument. Three times winner of the Waterloo Cup, Master McGrath is widely regarded as the greatest greyhound of all time, and without doubt the county's most famous personality. His progeny includes Mick the Miller, whose stuffed remains stand in the Natural History Museum in London.

The reverence in which Master McGrath is held in Lurgan could scarcely be overstated – a stained glass window in his honour stands behind the pulpit in the **Shankill Parish Church**, **Main Street**, **Lurgan** (Church of Ireland); the town council placed his likeness at the top of its coat of arms, and there's even a famous ballad in the dog's honour, written after yet another successful outing for the Master in England. Just two of the verses give a flavour of the song:

Lord Lurgan stepped forward and says he, 'Gentlemen.
If there's any among youse has money to spend
For your damn English nobles I don't care a straw
Here's five thousand to one on Master McGrath.'
Then McGrath looked up and he wagged his ould tail
Informing his Lordship he never would fail
'Don't fear, noble Brownlow, don't fear them agrá
I'll soon tarnish their laurels,' said Master McGrath...

The Hampton Park-like Brownlow House was designed by the Scottish architect Playfair (responsible for many of Edinburgh's fine buildings) and is one of the grandest

Lurgan Park

houses in Armagh. As well as its canine connections, Brownlow House looms large in the history (and terminology) of the region in one other significant aspect. This is the headquarters of the Imperial Black Chapter of the British Commonwealth – an organisation similar to, but separate from, the Orange Order. In the wealth of names for Protestants and Catholics in Ireland, the Black Chapter has led to the widespread practice of calling Protestants 'blacks', something that can regularly catch visitors out. Northern Ireland is regularly referred to as 'the Wee Black North' in the Republic.

Many bombastic parades – with flute bands, accordion bands and pipe bands – take place in and around this area during the marching season, roughly speaking from June to September. It's a colourful pageant – and has been called one of the great community folk festivals in Europe. When the people in these bands sing 'God Save the Queen', they make it clear they're going to save her whether she likes it or not.

The cast-iron **Colebrookdale Fountain** in Lurgan Park was originally erected in 1888 in Lurgan town centre to celebrate Queen Victoria's Jubilee. It was moved to the park in the mid 1920s to make way for the war memorial. While other similar cast iron fountains survive around the world – from Christchurch, New Zealand to Weston-super-Mare, Somerset – no other fountain is known to survive with its original lampposts. The roses planted adjacent to the fountain were bred in the North mostly in the 20s and 30s at a time when Dickson's of Newtownards and McCready's of Portadown were prominent breeders. They remain to this day two of the most important families in the history of rose-growing.

Near Brownlow Park, just off Edward Street, **Shankill Parish Church Old Graveyard** provides, as it were, the last word on epitaphs. A few feet from a tall black marble memorial a flat 18th-century slab with no name bears just the one Latin word 'Tacet' ('she is silent') – reputed to be the husband's only comment on his wife. The **Quaker Meeting House**, **Main Street**, **Lurgan** (the first Quaker headquarters in the Six Counties) has a plaque outside commemorating James Logan, scientist, son of a local Quaker headmaster, and one of the founders of Pennsylvania.

Portadown

Portadown, on the **River Bann**, derives its name from the Irish 'Port na Dun', Port of the Fortress, with a history stretching back some 4,000 years. Its modern foundations, however, began in the 17th century when manufacturers and traders arrived in town. That trading ethos continues, with Portadown today a thriving shopping centre with a variety of daily markets and fairs.

Coney Island, the only island which is still inhabited on Lough Neagh

The triangle formed by Portadown and the south shore of **Lough Neagh** is an area of laneways still with many traditional stone cottages. South of the little village of **Maghery**, archaeologists have found evidence of an ancient road made of oak trunks. Locally called **St Patrick's Road**, it is traditionally used for pilgrims headed for **Coney Island**. Reputedly St Patrick frequented Coney Island for peregrination, prayer and meditation.

Maghery Country Park and Coney Island

Situated on the shores of **Lough Neagh**, the park covers an area of 30 acres comprising 3 miles of woodland walks and picnic areas, plus islands including **Coney Island** and **Oxford Island**. The whole area is a haven for birdwatching, fishing, walking and boating. **Coney Island**, the only remaining inhabited island on Lough Neagh, is a wooded islet lying less than a mile offshore from the park at the mouth of the **Blackwater River**. This is where the Blackwater enters Lough Neagh, an area or 'stand' renowned for trout, salmon and dollaghan. Fortunately in the world of the trout, salmon and dollaghan, the area is not renowned for humans, so the fishing is very good indeed. The island is administered by the National Trust, and can be visited by arrangement (☎ 028 3832 2200).

Coney Island is considered to be one of the most westerly outposts of Norman occupation after their arrival in Ulster. However, it was never within **the Pale**, the area of administration radiating out from Dublin, and only stretching as far as the neighbouring county of Louth (now in the Republic). The restless natives of Ulster were always considered 'beyond the Pale', usually given as the origin of the phrase. The ruins of a Norman keep on Coney Island, with evidence of an attached church, overlook the small **Maghery Canal**. History continued unabated over the centuries with numerous seditious incidents. In November 1830, Ribbonmen (Catholic militia men) attacked an Orange band nearby, puncturing their drum. The Orangemen retaliated by burning the Catholic village of Maghery to the ground. This was no blueprint for good community relations, and skirmishes continued sporadically right up to the modern day Troubles.

Lough Neagh Discovery Centre

LOUGH NEAGH DISCOVERY CENTRE: Oxford Island National Nature Reserve BT66 6NJ; ☎ 028 3832 2205; www.oxfordisland. com. Entry: free; open in daylight hours; boat trips to Coney Island available by arrangement.

Oxford Island has 4 miles of footpaths, five birdwatching hides, woodland, ponds, flower-strewn meadows, picnic and play areas. **Lough Neagh Discovery Centre** (with bird hides and binoculars) tells you all about the natural history of the island and lough. A loughside café gives panoramic views over Lough Neagh, and you are free to picnic anywhere, from the shoreline to shady woodland. Picnic tables are dotted throughout the island, and barbeque facilities will get your sausages done in jig-time.

At various times throughout the year exhibitions are featured, free of charge. Everything is covered – from fish to Finn McCool (local giant who formed Lough Neagh by scooping up a clod of earth from Ulster and throwing it into the Irish Sea). The Isle of Man was thus formed.

Local legends: Coney Island

Local folklore has it that the famous Coney Island in New York is named after the Armagh island – an honour, it would have to be pointed out, also claimed by County Down's Coney Island (and a few other Coneys besides).

Sadly, the American Coney Island is most likely to be an English misconstruction of the Dutch name, Konijn Eiland. Mind you, don't mention that in the bars of Lurgan – they'll have you believing that Konijn was a regular in the Corner Inn in Tandragee before stocking up on potato crisps and setting off for America.

Loughgall Country Park

Loughgall Country Park is set in a 188-hectare estate of open farmland and orchards that includes an 18-hole golf course and 37-acre coarse fishery. There's a bridle path, walks, children's play area,

LOUGHGALL COUNTRY PARK: 11–14 Main Street, Loughgall BT61 8HZ; ☎ 028 3889 2900; www.loughgallcountrypark.com. Entry: free; open dawn till dusk.

children's adventure trail, outdoor exercise/trim trail, tennis courts and football pitch.

It's an ideal place for anglers – all lawful methods of fishing are allowed, but fish must be returned to the water. A daily permit is available from the on-site shop for £3, a yearly permit costs £25.

Canoeing

Northern Ireland has some particularly well-organised canoe facilities, including five marked trails. The **River Blackwater trail**, which starts at Maghery where the Blackwater joins Lough Neagh, passes through the countryside of Tyrone and Armagh. Visit www.canoeni.com for canoe hire centres, guided trips and places to stay. Craigavon Watersports Centre (☎ 028 3834 2669; full address below) has a wide selection of canoes, kayaks and umiaks for hire.

Craigavon Golf & Ski Centre

Craigavon Golf & Ski Centre is set in impressive wooded surroundings near the shores of **Lough Neagh**. Facilities include three golf courses, a floodlit driving range and putting green. A premier outdoor artificial ski slope provides a 300ft main slope, nursery slope and snow tubing facilities.

CRAIGAVON GOLF & SKI CENTRE: Turmoyra Lane, Lurgan BT66 6NG; ☎ 028 3832 6606. Entry: prices vary according to activity, age, time etc; opening times: golf dawn–dusk all year; ski 9am–9pm all year, Sat/Sun 9–5pm.

Loughgall

Loughgall, where the Orange Order was founded, is in the middle of Armagh's orchard area. To be exact, it's surrounded by 5,000 acres of fruit trees whose blossom lights up the countryside from late April through to early summer. In season, signposts are erected to guide visitors on apple blossom tours. For more information on the Orange Order, there's a museum at the Ancestral Home of Dan Winter, where a fight took place in 1795 between the Peep O'Day Boys (Protestants) and the Catholic Defenders. From this melée – known as the Battle of the Diamond – the Orange Order arose. Until this decisive event, Protestants had been represented by various groupings. But unity was established thereafter, with formal discussion taking place at nearby **Sloan House**.

You can find out all about it at the **Ancestral Home of Dan Winter** (1 The Diamond, Loughgall BT61 8PH; ☎ 028 3885 2171 or 028 3885 1344; www.danwinterscottage. co.uk), former home of one of the founders of the Order. The listed vernacular farmhouse was re-thatched and restored in 2000 with a large proportion of the original fabric conserved. The cottage has been maintained by the Winter family down the years. On display are relics from the Battle of the Diamond, plus old farming and dairy artefacts. The original timber used in the cottage has been dated to reveal that this is probably one of the last houses to use Irish oak as a building material.

The Troubles bit hard in this part of North Armagh. **Lurgan** and the associated towns of **Portadown** and **Craigavon** made up part of what was known as the 'murder triangle'. Loughgall was part of it. Like many of its neighbours in Armagh's rural north, it is strongly Protestant. In 1987, the village was the scene of a British army ambush in which eight IRA men died. Today it's hard to believe the trouble that this genteel, tranquil town has seen.

Poyntzpass

Poyntzpass was the birthplace of the famous 17th-century rapparee (guerrilla soldier-outlaw), Redmond O'Hanlon. An important figure in the Irish Rebellion of 1641 he was the son of Loughlin O'Hanlon, rightful heir to the castle at **Tandragee** – now the Tayto Crisps factory. The name of Poyntzpass comes from one Lieutenant Poyntz who fought an engagement here in 1598 against an Irish force. Charles Poyntz eventually became the High Sheriff of County Armagh and was knighted in 1636. Queen Elizabeth and Princess Diana are both family.

Despite Lieutenant Poyntz's military endeavours and his royal lineage, Poyntzpass distinguishes itself martially because of being the home town of the first ever winner of the Victoria Cross, David Lucas. He lived at **Druminargle House** which stands one mile outside the village. As a 20-year-old midshipman in the Royal Navy with the Baltic Fleet, Lucas became the first recipient of the medal on 26 June 1857, presented personally by Queen Victoria. She heard of Lucas's bravery – he'd thrown a live shell with its fuse hissing into the sea where it exploded – and decided to mark the pluck of the Irish personally. This historic event is commemorated on a memorial tablet erected at **Poyntzpass Royal British Legion Hall**. Lucas finished his career in the Royal Navy reaching the rank of Admiral.

Poyntzpass is situated in an area of tiny loughs, drumlins and rural charm. Its Village Trail takes in the three pubs and five churches (Catholic, Church of Ireland, Presbyterian, Baptist and Independent) that serve a population of some 400 souls. (Which is some going even by Northern Ireland standards.) The trail – which is sign-posted – also includes an intriguing Victorian signal box and early 19th-century school. Perhaps not quite so intriguing, but worthy of mention nonetheless – Poyntzpass is the only town in the whole of Ireland with a Z in its name.

Wet weather

Ardress house

Ardress House near Portadown is a 17th-century manor house with ornate plasterwork by Michael Stapleton, a good collection of paintings, a sizeable working farmyard and fine wooded grounds. Nestling in the apple orchards, this is a terrific place to

Ardress House

visit whatever the weather. Built in the 17th century as a farmhouse, Ardress was re-modelled in Georgian times. On display is the 1799 table originally made for the speaker of the Irish Parliament (in Dublin), and on which King George V signed the Constitution of Northern Ireland on 22 June, 1921.

To relax from the momentousness of this pivotal event in Irish history, step outside into the horticultural haven of the gardens and demesne, with scenic woodland and riverside walks attached. A small museum has an important collection of farm machinery and tools.

ARDRESS HOUSE: 64 Ardress Road, Anaghmore, Portadown BT62 1SQ; ☎ 028 8778 4753; www.nationaltrust. org.uk main/w-ardresshouse. Entry: £4.40, children £2.20; opening times: House 15 Mar to 28 Sep 2–6pm Sat/Sun and bank and public holidays only; Apr/May/Sept 2–6pm Sat/Sun; Easter week same times; June to Aug daily except Tues, same times.

What to do with children...

Craigavon Watersports Centre offers expert tuition in water-skiing, windsurfing, canoeing, sailing and banana boating. Numerous exciting but safe canoe trails track through Lough Neagh and the Blackwater. Canoes, kayaks and umiaks are all available for your voyages of discovery.

CRAIGAVON WATER CENTRE: 1 Lake Road, Craigavon BT64 1AS; ☎ 028 28 38342669; www.craigavon.gov.uk. Entry: times and cost vary depending on activity.

Tannaghmore Animal Farm, Silverwood, Craigavon provides children with close encounters of an agricultural kind: farmyard animals, including cattle, sheep, goats, pigs and poultry, traditionally found on farms in Ulster 100 years ago, wander about in unconcerned fashion. Many of the breeds on show are now rare or close to extinction, including: Irish Moiled cattle, one of the very rarest breeds of

TANNAGHMORE ANIMAL FARM: Silverwood, Craigavon; ☎ 028 3834 3244 or 07801292803; www.craigavon.gov.uk/ Tourism/tanaghmore.asp. Entry: free; open daily 10am–one hour before dusk.

cattle in the world; Dexter cattle, one of the smallest breeds of cattle in the world; and Saddleback pigs, known throughout Ireland as 'Belties'. Fowl include geese, hens, turkeys, ducks, pheasants, guinea fowl and peafowl.

The **Barn Museum** has displays of farming activities in County Armagh from bygone days. The farm is right beside the Craigavon Lakes, (great for walking) and a playground is situated in the gardens adjacent to the farm. Older children (and adults) will enjoy karting in a variety of machines on different terrains at **Superdrive Motorsport Centre** (7 Derryneskan Road, Portadown BT62 1UH).

... and how to avoid children

A good way to avoid children – indeed a good way to avoid anyone – is to head out to **Brackagh Bog**, situated in the fenlands between Portadown and Lough Neagh. This is emphatically not for children, as the area is composed of bogland, water meadow and deep pools – and is particularly susceptible to soft, insistent drizzle. Get your waterproofs on, because this habitat is of particular interest to naturalists. The 900 acres of bogland (known locally as the Birches) contain many rare plants such as bog asphodels and field orchids, as well as the ubiquitous bog cotton dancing in the breeze.

Entertainment

I am of Ireland,
And of the holy land of Ireland
Good Sir, pray I thee
For of saint charité
Come and dance with me
In Ireland.

Those anonymous words were written in the 14th century, more than likely in the Armagh area – a locality long famous for its dancing. Several of the local townlands in North Armagh gave birth to some of famous ceili bands of the 1940s and 1950s: The McCusker Brothers, Johnny Pickering and Malachy Sweeney bands all plied their trade here. Today set dancing and ceili dancing (there is a subtle difference) are still going strong. Traditional sessions and set-dances take place at the **Corner House** (Embankment), Derrymacash, ☎ 028 3834 1817. For other details visit www. setdancingnews.com. **Jameson's** (1–3 Thomas Street, Portadown; ☎ 028 3839 2692) presents entertainment nightly, disco (1960s, 1970s music), dance music and blues music every Friday night.

Lurgan Park is home to annual summer events such as the Lurgan Agricultural Show, and the Lurgan Park Rally, noted as the largest annual motor sport event in Northern Ireland and a stage in the Circuit of Ireland Rally.

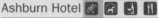

 The best... **PLACES TO STAY**

HOTEL

Ashburn Hotel

81 William Street, Lurgan BT66 6JB
☎ **028 3832 5711**
www.theashburnhotel.com

A long established hotel run by well-known hoteliers the McConaghys who own a handful of hotels in the area. Comfortable, and just about the friendliest hotel you could hope to come across.

Price: from £50 for a double.

Newforge House

58 Newforge Road, Magheralin, Craigavon BT67 0QL; ☎ **028 9261 1255**
www.newforgehouse.com

Once belonging to the owners of the local linen mill, the 200-year-old Georgian Newforge House has been beautifully restored by the ancestors of the Mathers family. The result of the Mathers' work is this elegant, comfortable country house.

Price: from £110 to £150 for a double.

B&B

The Bleu Apple

12 Cannagola Road, Portadown, Craigavon BT62 1RG
☎ **028 3885 2188**

The Bleu Apple is set in the midst of two acres of gardens, orchard and patio areas. At the luxury end of the B&B range, this establishment was pampering people long before the word was hijacked by wellness centres and spas.

Price: from £48/£76 for single/double.

SELF-CATERING

Dobsons Corner-Ballydougan Pottery Courtyard Cottages

171 Plantation Road, Ballydougan, Craigavon BT63 5NN
☎ **028 3834 2201**
www.balldouganpottery.co.uk

These beautifully restored 4-star cottages in the old pottery guarantee comfort and tranquillity. The main cottage sleeps 5. Bramley Apple Cottage, Gaskin's Grove cottage and Wheat Loft Apartment are all 4-star accommodation in the same complex.

Price: from £355 to £435 for a week.

Clenaghans

48 Soldierstown Road, Aghalee BT67 0ES
☎ **028 9265 2952 or 07912 033190**
www.clenaghans.com

Four-star self-catering, with everything from king-size beds to central heating. This is old Ireland as she used to be, with old stone buildings located in the middle of nowhere, snug little pub and ancient farm buildings.

Price: B&B £90 for two people for one night; £345 for two people for seven nights.

Callan Cottage

Callan Cottage, 128 Ballygassoon Road, Loughgall, Armagh BT61 8JU
www.callancottage.com/

Nestled between an old apple orchard and the banks of the Callan River, this is a wonderful country retreat with all mod cons, and a few un-mod cons such as an atmospheric turf fire.

Price: from £180 for three nights (minimum stay).

The best... FOOD AND DRINK

▶ Staying in

With 100 years of growing fruit under their belt, this family-run business certainly knows its onions when it comes to apples. **Barnhill** apple juice is a blend of traditional varieties grown, harvested and pressed on the family farm (Barnhill Farm, 23 Drumanphy Road, Portadown BT62 1QX). This naturally cloudy juice is made exclusively from whole fruit, with no added preservatives, sweeteners, colourings or water. New flavours have been created by blending apple with the juice of other whole fruit such as raspberry, blackcurrant and blackberry. You can stock up here at the farm – and yes, a cordial greeting can be expected.

Moyallon Foods, a family business, supports individual, small and medium scale producers in the locality who use free-range and organic farming techniques in rearing livestock. Moyallon makes an array of meaty goodies. The dry, cured bacon is done in the old fashioned Irish style, and if you want a burger, you won't get better than the beefy Aberdeen Angus variety made here. Moyallon also sources a number of other delicious products, including rare breed free-range pork, lamb, venison, game, artisan cheeses and smoked Irish salmon.

MOYALLON FOODS: 76 Crowhill Road, Craigavon BT66 7AT; ☎ 028 38349100; www.moyallonfoods.com

Ell's Fine Wine (42 Dobbin Road, Portadown; ☎ 028 3833 2306) boasts some 700 wines available at their outlet. Their area of expertise is Australia and Portugal, but they also offer some very good value wines from France. Stock up well here – this is one of the best wine merchants in the Six Counties. (Wine consuming in Northern Ireland is probably about 10 years behind Britain, and places such as Ell's, while increasing in number, are still fairly few and far between.)

For meat products head for **John R Dowey** (20 High Street, Lurgan; ☎ 028 3832 2547). This butcher's shop and delicatessen sells excellent homemade pies, sausages, salads and organic fresh eggs. **Errol Lenaghan** (15 Church Street, Poyntzpass; ☎ 028 3831 8885) is one of the top butcher shops in the area, concentrating on beef from the rolling pasturelands of North Down and lamb from the Mournes and Cooley Mountains. Black pudding, white pudding and sausages are all specialities.

Portadown has a fair every Friday and Saturday at the market held in the **Millennium Court** complex on **William Street**. Everything from local produce (breads, cheeses, vegetables) as well as a limited amount of crafts – homemade candles, jewellery etc. **Tandragee Garden Centre** (55 Market Street, Tandragee; ☎ 028 3884 0677) sells a wide selection of locally produced vegetables and fruit – including, of course, apples. Every variety of local Armagh apple is available, as well as local pears and plums.

EATING OUT

RESTAURANT

Avanti
**Seagoe Hotel, 22 Upper Church Lane,
Craigavon BT63 5JE**
☎ **028 3833 3076**
www.seagoe.com

Fresh local food – all the meat comes from a
local butcher's – has helped Avanti to several
awards. Traditional meat and fish dishes are
the speciality in this fine restaurant. Main
dishes cost around £15.

Clenaghans
48 Soldierstown Road, Aghalee BT67 0ES
☎ **028 9265 2952 or 07912 033190**
www.clenaghans.com

Clenaghan's Restaurant is every bit as
atmospheric as the attached accommodation.
The cuisine is locally sourced but given
impeccably adventurous treatment – main
courses such as duck lasagne or fresh
halibut with linguini pasta. There's a great
choice for vegetarians including butternut
squash risotto, mushroom and caraway
cutlets, deliciously prepared Mediterranean
vegetable stews. Main courses begin at
around £15. The wine list is comprehensive,
from £14 per bottle.

The Famous Grouse Country Inn
Ballyhagan Road, Loughgall BT61 8PX
☎ **028 3889 1778**
www.thefamousgrouseloughgall.co.uk

A country restaurant with a traditional theme,
situated in the heart of the orchard country,
the Famous Grouse is justifiably named
famous. The atmosphere is relaxed and
friendly and the combination of quality local
produce and well-prepared food make this
one of the best-known restaurants in the
area. The use of fresh fish 'with a hint of the
Med' is a feature. Starters from around £7 to
£9, main courses from £11 upwards.

Chilli Pepper
**Tandragee Golf Club, Markethill Road,
Tandragee BT62 2ER.**
☎ **028 3884 1763**

This restaurant takes a hearty and very
earthy approach to classic Irish cooking – the
result is a winning menu of well executed
favourites. Main courses begin around £12.

Pot Belly Restaurant
**58A Banbridge Road, Tullylish, Gilford
BT63 6DL**
☎ **028 3883 1404**
www.potbellyrestaurant.co.uk

Overlooking the banks of the River Bann and
housed in a converted Linen Mill dating from
the 1800s this restaurant has lots of history,
charm – and good cooking. The 'pot belly'
in the name has nothing to do with calorie
calamities – it refers to two wonderful old pot
belly stoves in the dining room. An eclectic
menu includes medallions of pork fillet,
sautéed and served with a parsnip and apple
puree. Cost around £15 per head.

CAFÉ

Yellow Door Deli
74 Woodhouse Street, Portadown BT62 1JL
☎ **028 3835 3528**
www.yellowdoordeli.co.uk

This deli-café and artisan bakery – something
of an institution in the area – serves soups,
sandwiches, Irish stew and speciality breads.
Or you could pick up a gourmet hot-smoked
salmon salad, some Irish soda bread, a
bottle of white wine and head to Oxford Island
nature reserve on Lough Neagh for a picnic.
Meals from £6.50 to £9.50.

🍸 Drinking

The traditional, atmospheric **Charlie McKeever's** (28–29 Woodhouse Street, Portadown; ☎ 028 3833 2054) has been a landmark pub in the Portadown area since 1944. **Portmor House**, 44 Main Street, Blackwatertown, is an inviting mix of locals, fisherfolk and boating people. The conversation and craic is usually around 90. ('The craic was ninety' is a ubiquitous measure of any evening's entertainment throughout Ireland. However, 90 is the only value it can have. No point in mentioning to your landlady that 'the craic was 90, with gusts up to 140.' Even if there were.

Sally McNally's (91 Markethill Road, Portadown BT62 3SH; ☎ 028 3884 0230) run by John and Lisa McNally, has gradually expanded from a two-roomed pub into a meandering complex restaurant with loads of nooks and crannies, and equal amounts of charm and character. Whether it's a leisurely pint, a dinner for two or a quiet Irish coffee on the sofa – you will find somewhere to relax at Sally's.

ℹ️ Visitor Information

Tourist information centre: Armagh Tourist Information Centre, Old Bank Building, 40 English Street, Armagh BT60 7BA, ☎ 028 3752 1800, www.armagh.gov.uk.

Hospital: Craigavon Area Hospital, Lurgan Road, Portadown, ☎ 028 3833 4444.

Doctors: Dr J Leetch, Portadown Health Centre, Tavanagh Avenue, Portadown, Craigavon BT62 3BU, ☎ 028 3835 0269; Dr A Turtle, 6 Greenview, Richhill, Armagh BT61 9PD, ☎ 028 3887 1701; a full list is available on www.neighbourhoodprofessionals.co.uk; doctors operate under the NHS.

Pharmacies: the two main pharmacies throughout Northern Ireland are Boots ☎ 028 9024 2332 and Gordon's ☎ 028 9032 0040; in addition most towns (even small ones) still have independent pharmacies.

Police: In an emergency ☎ 999; otherwise contact the local PSNI station on ☎ 0845 600 80.

Parking: Outside the centre of Portadown and Lurgan, parking is free and widely available.

Bike rental: Richhill Cycles ☎ 028 3887 1066.

Local taxis: Pet's Cabs ☎ 028 3833 8866 or 3839 2020; RJ Cabs ☎ 028 3834 8599.

MID ARMAGH AND ARMAGH CITY

It was once the very centre of Europe with its great teaching monastery and missionary abbey – now you can't even get a direct flight there. Armagh City, the ecclesiastical centre for both the Church of Ireland and the Catholic Church in Ireland is today a tranquil, untroubled city, dreaming perhaps of its glory days in the 5th century when St Patrick established his mission here.

Several centuries before Gutenberg had invented movable type, revolutionising the world, Irish monks were beavering away in their attempts to save Western civilisation. Rome lay sacked, London was a muddy backwater; meanwhile Goths, Visigoths, Vandals and assorted barbarians continued to lay waste to much of Europe's literary and ecclesiastical treasures. Fortunately the great monasteries of Ireland helped preserve some of this academia. One book surviving from this era is on show at Trinity College, Dublin. The great *Book of Armagh* was written by Ferdomnach, a scribe at the School of Armagh, 1,200 years ago. The manuscript, containing some of the oldest surviving specimens of Old Irish, is believed to have originally belonged to St Patrick. It contains a transcription of his life, the New Testament and various historic annals.

The name Armagh comes from Ard Macha, or 'Macha's Height', after a legendary pagan queen. According to tradition she built a fortress on top of this southern Ulster hill some time in the middle of the first millennium BC. Today, the pagans – royal or otherwise – have decamped and Armagh city is the centre of Christian Ireland, with two cathedrals each called St Patrick's.

WHAT TO SEE AND DO

Armagh City
Armagh Observatory boasts one of the oldest star-gazers in the world, the Troughton Equatorial Telescope, built in 1795. Armagh Observatory has been watching this space for a thousand or more years – the monks were keen observers of the heavens, and indeed Irish monks were responsible for some of the very first climate records we have, later compiled in the Annals of Ulster (mostly cloudy with a few sunny spells, clearing from the west

ARMAGH OBSERVATORY: College Hill, Armagh BT61 9DG; ☎ 028 3752 2928; http://star.arm.ac.uk. Entry: free; grounds open 9.30am–4.30pm; guided tours to the main Observatory building can be arranged by appointment only.

later). Perhaps because of the existence of these records, Archbishop Richard Robinson, the rich and influential Church of Ireland Primate from 1765 to 1794, decided to include an observatory in the plans for his primatial city. The historical main building is an architectural gem surrounded by beautiful gardens. Two sundials 'still keep accurate time' and visitors have free access to the dome that houses the main telescope.

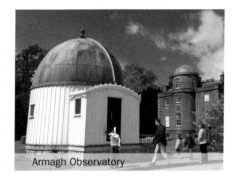
Armagh Observatory

As befits any self-respecting city as ancient and spiritual as Armagh, the place has a generous helping of ghosts, gore and the grotesque. **Ghost tours** are held throughout the year, wending their way through the centuries-old streets and stopping by various historical sites to hear tales and stories of the darker and grislier side of Armagh's past.

> GHOST TOURS: The Living History Department, Palace Demesne, Armagh BT60 4EI; ☎ 028 37 529629.

En route you'll be able to peer at some of Ireland's finest Georgian-Regency architecture – the **Archbishop's Palace**, the **Royal School**, **College Hill**, the **Observatory**, plus some very fine private dwellings, particularly in the **Mall**. The latter was a venue for horse-racing, cock-fighting and bull-baiting until the 18th century. But Archbishop Robinson decided it wasn't fitting at all

From popes to penalties

Today Armagh may be a quiet backwater – but it could have all been so different. The city is often called the 'Irish Rome' – and the title almost literally came true. In 1948, the Irish ambassador to the Vatican reported that Pope Pius XII was 'in a mood of deepest pessimism' about the very real possibility of a Communist government coming to power in Italy. So worried was the Holy Father that he contemplated moving the Holy See – lock, stock and apparel – to Ireland. He is reported to have said, 'Ireland is the only country I could go to – only there would I have the atmosphere and the sense of security to rule the Church as Christ wants me.' In the event, the Communist challenge was defeated. The Vatican remained the Eternal City instead of Armagh, and the Pope continued to take his holidays in Castel Gandolfo and not Ballycastle.

Something that probably didn't come into the Pope's considerations is the village of **Milford**, about 2 miles south-west of the city. This is where the modern penalty kick in soccer was invented. The idea was first put forward in 1890 by goalkeeper William McCrum who played for local side Milford Everton. McCrum had become disillusioned with the 'win at any cost' ethos sweeping through the game, and on 2 June 1891 the penalty kick was born. To date, no fitting memorial to this seminal world event has been erected, although a bronze statue is planned.

to have such a rough element enjoying themselves in the heart of this ecclesiastic, academic city. So he transformed it into an elegant Georgian park, most of which survives today. The rough elements' current whereabouts are not known.

In the **Palace Stables Heritage Centre and Palace Demesne**, a restored Georgian stable block set on the Palace Demesne, you will experience Georgian history brought to life by a host of fascinating characters just arrived from the 18th century. The Heritage Centre is behind the Primate's Palace, the home of the Archbishop of the Church of Ireland until the 1970s. You can see how the stables operated in the 1800s, or take a choice of signed walks through the Demesne. The **Franciscan Friary** in the palace grounds, founded by Archbishop O'Scannail in 1263, was destroyed in 1561 by Shane (the Proud) O'Neill. Some of the ruins remain, as do some important graves, including that of Gormlaith O'Donnell, wife of one of the head honchos of the area in the 14th century.

> **PALACE STABLES HERITAGE CENTRE:**
> The Palace Demesne, Armagh BT60 4EL;
> ☎ 028 3752 1801; www.visitarmagh.com.
> Entry: adults £4.75, children £3; open
> 10am–5pm Mon to Sat, Apr to Sept; and
> 12pm–5pm Sun, Jun to Aug.

Armagh's two cathedrals

Armagh is today probably the only city in the world with two cathedrals with the same name; James Ussher and St Malachy (see box below) were archbishops when there was only one, and their names appear on the roll call of clerics in the older **St Patrick's Cathedral** (Church of Ireland). Then along came the Reformation – the Protestants kept the established church; the Catholics had to go and build their own one.

Armagh has a claim to being the oldest recorded settlement in Ireland, the name commemorating Queen Macha who had a fort there, probably about 600BC. The prestige and antiquity of the town in all likelihood inspired St Patrick to choose it as the site of his principal church about AD445. His first church, Druim Saileach (Sallow Ridge), is thought to have been built on a site now occupied by the **Bank of Ireland** on **Scotch Street**, around which a substantial monastic community grew.

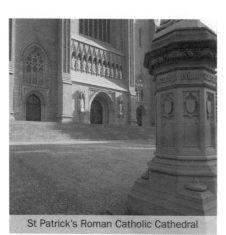
St Patrick's Roman Catholic Cathedral

St Patrick's Church of Ireland Cathedral has been destroyed and rebuilt 17 times. It was substantially restored between 1834 and 1840 by Archbishop Lord John George Beresford and the architect Lewis Nockalls Cottingham. A slab on the north transept wall commemorates Brian Boru, High King of Ireland killed at the Battle of Clontarf (1014). This was the fight which finally rid Ireland of the Norsemen, so Brian Boru is a revered figure in Ireland to this day.

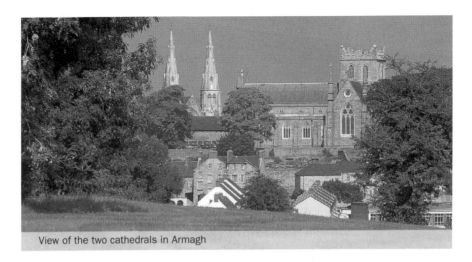
View of the two cathedrals in Armagh

The **Cathedral Library** contains an astonishing range of swag. A long manuscript dating back to about 1360 is written in colloquial Italian. The writer, Brother Stephanus, testified that he took it down faithfully as a direct dictation from St Catherine of Siena while she was in the throes of a mystical ecstasy. A copy of *Gulliver's Travels* – corrected in Swift's own hand – takes pride of place beside the *Claims of the Innocents*, basically pleas of mercy to Oliver Cromwell. The library also has an Ogham stone (an ancient type of Irish writing stone, possibly dating back to pre-Christian times) and a collection of ancient bells and silver maces. There's enough here to keep the spiritually inclined or historically curious occupied for weeks.

SAINT PATRICK'S CATHEDRAL (CHURCH OF IRELAND): Cathedral Close BT61 7EE; ☎ 028 3752 3142; www.stpatricks-cathedral.org. Entry: free; open Apr to Sep 9.30am–5pm, Oct to Mar 9am–4pm.

The **Catholic Cathedral of St Patrick** stands on a hilltop within walking distance of the Church of Ireland cathedral. Construction began in 1840, but it took 70 years to complete the lofty building with its two imposing spires.

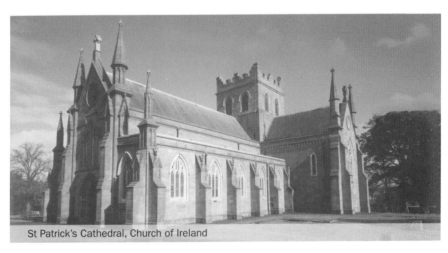
St Patrick's Cathedral, Church of Ireland

Armaghgeddon

The cathedral is a curious example of a building that changes architect and style half way up. The bottom half was designed in 1838 in the English Perpendicular Gothic style by Thomas Duff of **Newry**; the top half, designed in 1853, is in the French Decorated Gothic style, by J J McCarthy of **Dublin**.

Inside, a prevailing air of dignity fills the cathedral. Intricate coloured mosaic covers every square foot of walls and ceilings – and some 20 Irish saints and 50 angels are represented in marble. The red hats of Armagh's five deceased cardinals hang from the ceiling, and outside in the tranquil, leafy graveyard are buried Ireland's Catholic Archbishops of Armagh.

> **ST PATRICK'S CATHEDRAL (CATHOLIC):** Armagh BT61 9DL; ☎ 028 3752 3638; www.armagharchdiocese.org. Entry: free; audio-visual display in the museum, but telephone booking is essential.

Armagh Planetarium

Armagh Planetarium comprises a **Hall of Astronomy**, an **Eartharium**, and an **Astropark**. In the Hall of Astronomy the Digital Theatre boasts the world's most advanced digital projection system, Digistar 3. A customised sound system designed by BOSE, a state-of-the-art LED lighting system and purpose-built reclining seats make this a hugely enjoyable three-dimensional stellar treat. You can travel to the International Space Station, outwards to Mars in the three-dimensional stereo room and see stereoscopic animations of Solar System exploration. The Astropark is a scale model of the Universe where visitors can walk through the Solar System and into the Milky Way and beyond.

> **ARMAGH PLANETARIUM:** College Hill BT61 9DB; ☎ 028 3752 3689; www.armaghplanet.com. Entry: adults £6, children £5; open 1pm–5pm, Tues to Fri, 11.30am–5pm Sat/Sun.

Patrick Moore, astronomer and broadcaster was appointed director of the newly constructed Planetarium in 1965.

ST PATRICK'S TRIAN: 40 English Street, Armagh BT61 7BA; ☎ 028 3752 1801; www.saintpatrickstrian.com. Entry: adult £4.75, child £3; Jul/Aug 10am–5pm Mon–Sat, except noon–5pm Sun; Sept to Jun 2–5pm Sun.

St Patrick's Trian

The Trian derives its name from the ancient division of **Armagh City** into three distinct districts, or 'Trians'. They were known as **Trian Mor** (to the south and west), **Trian Masain** (to the east) and **Trian Sassenach** or Saxon (to the north). The city today has an **English Street**, **Irish Street** and **Scotch Street** which roughly mark the boundaries of these Trians.

St Patrick's Trian Visitor Complex features three major exhibitions, basically giving a potted history of Ulster – Neolithics, Celts, pagans, Gaels, Patrick, Vikings, Normans, English, Scottish, European Union. No Romans, though as they never made it across the Irish Sea. An audio-visual presentation portrays 'Belief' throughout the world, with particular emphasis on Armagh as the Christian capital of Ireland, and its contribution to the re-spreading of the Gospel throughout Europe after the Dark Ages. The Book of Armagh is also on show, albeit only digitally. The interactive displays allow the visitor to find out about this ancient manuscript through touch-screen computers.

Armagh County Museum

One of the most distinctive buildings in the city, Armagh County Museum's collection reflects the lives of those people who have lived or worked in or are associated with the

ARMAGH COUNTY MUSEUM: the Mall East, Armagh BT61 9BE; ☎ 028 3752 3070; www.armaghcountymuseum.org.uk. Entry: free; open Mon–Fri 10am–5pm, Sat 10am–1pm and 2–5pm.

county. Everything from military costumes to wedding dresses are on show, and an impressive art collection includes works by many famous Irish artists.

Royal Irish Fusiliers Museum

ROYAL IRISH FUSILIERS MUSEUM: Sovereign's House, the Mall, Armagh BT61 9DL. Entry: free; open 10am–12.30pm and 1.30–4pm, Mon to Fri, year round.

This elegant Georgian residence houses the collections of the 'Eagle-Takers', the first regiment to capture one of Napoleon's imperial eagle standards, in 1811. Later known as the Royal Irish Fusiliers, the museum displays the story of this regiment raised from Armagh, Cavan and Monaghan militias from 1793 to 1968. An absolute must if you are interested in military history, and still a good bet even if you're not as the building itself is worth seeing.

Gosford Forest Park

Gosford Forest Park, formerly **Gosford Demesne**, comprises some 240 hectares of diverse woodland and open parkland set in gentle rolling drumlin countryside. Several way-marked trails, horse-riding paths and orienteering routes wend their way through the grounds. The very imposing castle is not open to the public, but is still a fine sight. Construction began in 1819 and finished in the 1850s. The seat of the Earl of Gosford, it is a sumptuous and stately structure in the Norman style, built of granite from the nearby **Mullaglass** quarries.

At various times the castle was used as winter quarters for a travelling circus, also as a store for the Public Record Office. Eventually, in 1958, it was acquired by the Northern Ireland Forestry Commission. The British Army was stationed in the castle in the 1970s under heavy fortification during the recent Troubles – there can be few castles around originally built as a residence that have to revert to the military function for which most castles are built.

> **GOSFORD FOREST PARK:** Markethill BT60 1UG; ☎ 028 3755 1277/ 028 3755 2169; www.gosford.co.uk. Entry: free except car parking; open daily 10am–sunset.

Richhill

Midway between Armagh city and Portadown, Richhill is a regular winner of the title 'Ulster's best-kept village'. **Richhill Castle**, one of Ulster's most famous haunted castles, has been investigated by the Northern Ireland Paranormal Society many times. One of the first unfortified castles built in Ireland, it is a fascinating 17th-century Dutch-gabled manor house, and, as with most Big Houses, the former owners were industrialists. The impressive wrought iron gates were transferred to Hillsborough (the then British Governor's residence) in 1935. The castle is only open to the public on special occasions such as lectures, festivals or paranormal investigations. For details visit www.nipra.co.uk.

Blackwatertown

Associated with one of the most decisive Elizabethan battles, an engagement between the Earl of Sussex and Hugh O'Neill, Blackwatertown sits on the top of a drumlin, surrounded by apple orchards. As you enter the lovely little village, you'll see the church of **St Jarlath's** on the right, with its serene 17th-century graveyard. St Jarlath's is known locally as Clonfeachle – *feachle* is the Irish for tooth. Legend has it that St Patrick came through Blackwatertown one day, lost a tooth, looked for it, but never found it. So tell the children to keep their eyes peeled.

The best way to see this area is by bicycle – the roads are traffic-free in a way that will make you think that Northern Ireland is closed for the day. It isn't – there just aren't many people living round here. The roads are good, undulating and hedge-lined. Other sporting pursuits include fishing in the **Blackwater** – noted both for coarse fishing and salmon. Blackwatertown is also one of the main centres for **road bowling**. For details ask the locals – Seamus Hegarty's, the local newspaper shop, will have all the details.

Navan Fort, the traditional Royal seat of the Kings and Queens of Ulster

☂ Wet weather

The Navan Centre, Fort and King's Stables

The Navan Centre interprets one of Ireland's most important ancient monuments, **Navan Fort**. This was the traditional royal seat of the Kings and Queens of Ulster, and the province's ancient capital. The tour begins in the 'Vanished World' of lost myths; then it's into the 'Real World' of archaeology, before entering the 'Other World' to hear the legends of the Ulster Cycle – great tales of derring-do, giants, heroes and of course the odd fairy.

THE NAVAN CENTRE: Killylea Road, Armagh BT60 4LD; ☎ 028 3752 1801; www.visitarmagh.com. Entry: Apr to May/ Sept Sat 10.00–17.00, Sun 12.00–17.00; Jun to Aug Mon–Sat 10.00–17.00, Sun 12.00–17.00.

⋯ What to do with children...

Tandragee Castle

The flavoured crisp was invented in Ireland by Joe 'Spud' Murphy, who, some 50 years ago, came up with the idea of cheese 'n' onion at his Tayto factory in Dublin. Joe passed away in 2003 – he had retired to Marbella, and was buried at sea in the Mediterranean. As his body was lowered into the depths, cheese 'n' onion potato crisps were tastefully sprinkled on the waves. Today you can visit the Tayto Factory at Tandragee Castle, at one time the Duke of Manchester's home. You'll see how the whole process from potato to crisp is cunningly engineered.

TAYTO FACTORY: Tandragee Castle, Main Street, Tandragee BT62 2AB; ☎ 028 3884 0249; www.tayto.com. Entry: adults £5, senior citizens/students £4, children (5–16) £3; opening times and tours Mon–Thu 10.30am/1.30pm, Fri 10.30am; closed public holidays.

Take a tour of the Tayto factory and see the crisps being hand cooked

... and how to avoid children

Armagh Public Library (43 Abbey Street, Armagh BT61 7DY; ☎ 028 3752 3142; www.armaghrobinsonlibrary.org) is one of the oldest libraries in Ireland, established in 1771 by Archbishop Robinson. In addition to the archbishop's personal library of 17th- and 18th-century books, particularly in history and theology, archival material traces the Christian heritage of Ireland and Europe. Here you will find transcripts of the few writings that the Apostle of Ireland left behind:

I, Patrick, a sinner, the simplest of country men.... was taken away into Ireland in captivity with ever so many thousands of people.

You can read how St Patrick was taken into slavery in Ulster just as Roman civilisation was falling apart in Britain (the Romans never made it to Ireland). He escaped, but had a vision in which a man brought him a letter and as he read he seemed to hear the voice of the Irish: 'We beg you, holy boy, to come and walk among us once again.' And it completely broke my heart and I could read no more.

The Armagh Public Library has the rest of this incredible story – which had huge implications for European Christendom as the Roman dispensation collapsed. The library also holds ancient Irish artefacts – stone axes, flint arrowheads and bronze implements.

Entertainment

Armagh can today justifiably claim to be Ulster's cultural capital. Its festivals – the **William Kennedy Piping Festival**, the **John Hewitt Summer School**, the **Charles Wood Summer School** – have become internationally famous, while its **Halloween and Apple Festival** is one of Northern Ireland's primary Samhain (pronounced 'Sow-wain' and meaning Halloween) festivals in a country where Halloween is taken very seriously – and has been these last 5,000 years or so. An Apple Blossom festival at the beginning of May celebrates the importance of the apple in County Armagh (its nickname is the Orchard County).

The **Market Place Theatre & Arts Centre** (☎ 028 3752 1821; www.market placearmagh.com) presents a year-round programme of arts and entertainment, workshops, classes and visual art exhibitions. The **Armagh Pipers Club** (14 Victoria Street, Armagh BT61 9DT; www.armaghpipersclub.com), which has been promoting traditional music in the area since 1966, is one of the city's major cultural organisations. The Club is now a centre of excellence in the practice of teaching traditional music, catering for over 200 pupils of all ages who attend weekly music classes, as well as promoting concerts, sessions, and Europe's top international Piping Festival.

The best... PLACES TO STAY

HOTEL

Armagh City Hotel

2, Friary Road Armagh BT60 4FR
☎ **028 3751 8888**
www.armaghcityhotel.co.uk

A fondly regarded hotel in the area, music is featured at the weekends, and traditional sessions during the week contribute to a lively atmosphere. Set in an elevated position overlooking Ireland's oldest city, the hotel has won numerous awards over the years.

Price: B&B from £69 for a double.

Charlemont Arms Hotel

57–65 English Street BT60
☎ **028 3752 2028**
www.charlemontarmshotel.com

Armagh City's other hotel, this family-run establishment is in the very centre of the historic old part of the city. It's fairly historic itself – the Charlemont, named after a local ruling family, is now in its third century of accommodating.

Price: from £70 for a double.

INN

The Montagu Arms

9–19 Church Street, Tandragee BT62 2AF
☎ **028 3884 0219**
www.montagu-arms.com

The family-run establishment, situated in the shadow of Tandragee Castle, has won several awards. The six en suite bedrooms in this old inn-cum-hotel-cum-restaurant are all comfortable and well-appointed.

Price: from £29.38 per person for a double.

B&B

De Averell House

3, Seven Houses, 47 Upper English Street BT61 8DW; ☎ **028 3751 1213**
www.deaverellhouse.co.uk

Centrally located, within 10 minutes' walk of the cathedrals, this is a comfortable family-run establishment. Only six rooms are available, so a cosy intimate atmosphere is guaranteed. All rooms are en suite, and well equipped.

Price: £45 for a single; £75 for a double; from £100 to £120 for a family room.

SELF-CATERING

Tandragee Gate Lodge

36 Tandragee Road, Markethill BT61 9DS
☎ **028 3752 4256**

This former gamekeeper's lodge, situated at the edge of Gosford Forest Park, is a comfortable, friendly and well-appointed cottage in the heart of Armagh. Guests have free access to Gosford Forest Park, which offers its visitors a rich variety of facilities for walking, cycling and horse-riding.

Price: from £200 to £300 for a week, with one unit sleeping between three and five.

School House

Armagh Road, Tandragee BT62 2AB
☎ **028 3884 0249**

A five-star converted cottage with luxurious fittings, elegant furnishings and state-of-the-art kitchen, etc. Only one unit which sleeps eight (four bedrooms), but on the other hand when they say 'fully-equipped' they mean it includes a full size snooker table.

Price: £500 for a week.

$\mathcal{The\ best...}$ **FOOD AND DRINK**

▶ Staying in

Forthill Farm (80 Ballymore Road, Tandragee BT62 2JY; ☎ 028 38 840 818; www. forthillfarm.co.uk) supplies the best of quality free range pork and beef from traditional breeds. The free range pigs and cows are produced naturally, reared without the use of antibiotics, hormones or growth promoters.

In Armagh a variety of organic greengrocers supply a wide range of vegetables and fruit, including:

- **Oliver Organic Greengrocers** – 51 Thomas Street, Armagh BT61 7QB; ☎ 028 3752 2461
- **Patrick McGee** – 2 Lower English Street, Armagh BT61 7LJ; ☎ 028 3752 6907
- **R. Thompson & Son** – 58A Hamiltonsbawn Road, Armagh BT60 1HW; ☎ 028 3752 2707
- **Hawthorne Ernest** – The Garden Stores, 52 Scotch Street, Armagh BT61 7DF; ☎ 028 3752 2776

For meat, **David Flanagan's** shop (1 Scotch Street, Armagh; ☎ 028 3752 2805) is a must. As well as their own cured gammons and beef from their own herds of Limousin and Blond Aquitaine cattle, the butcher's has an impressive deli side too.

Takeaway

Both the **Dolphin Takeaway** (100 Main Street, Markethill BT60 1PL; ☎ 028 3755 1540) and **Traditional Fish & Chips** (1 Moy Road, Armagh BT61 7LY) are regarded as the very best chippies in this area.

▶ Drinking

Groucho's Café Bar & Music Lounge (1, The Square Richhill BT61 9PP; ☎ 028 3887 1874) is one of the main drinking establishments in a town which in the past wasn't just famous for its linen trade, markets and fairs, but also for horse racing, hunting and fighting birds (feathered type). Linked to **Richhill Castle** by tunnel, these premises share much of the history and secret comings and goings-on in the Big House. Evolving for some 350 years, this may be one of the finest, most diverse

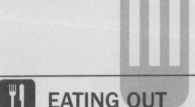

EATING OUT

RESTAURANT

The Old Barn
5 Mowham Road, Markethill BT60 1RQ
☎ 028 3755 2742

The Old Barn Restaurant is an old stone building dating back to 1871, originally built as a grass seed warehouse. It's a good place for light lunches or Sunday dinner, serving traditional and local food. Prices are moderate – a full Sunday dinner is around the £7 mark.

Courtrooms Restaurant & Coffee Lounge
7 Main Street Markethill BT60 1PL
☎ 028 3755 2553
www.courtroomsrestaurant.com

Located in the Old Courthouse just off the A28 main Armagh Newry road and within walking distance of Gosford Forest Park. And you might need the walk to work off the calories – homemade cakes and sweets are a specialty. The atmosphere here is friendly and relaxed, and you can probably eat yourself to a standstill for £10.

Manor Park Restaurant
2, College Hill The Mall, Armagh BT61 9DF
☎ 028 3751 5353

An attractive early 19th-century stone-fronted building beside the entrance to the Observatory is home to this famous French restaurant. The menu includes local seafood, beef and lamb, and also Blacklion duck. Set lunch from £5.95; set Sunday lunch £12.95; set dinner from £24.50. House wines from £10.

Stonebridge Restaurant
74 Legacorry Road, Richhill BT61 9LF
☎ 028 3887 0024
www.stonebridgerestaurant.co.uk

Situated in a listed former residential home, the Stonebridge concentrates on traditional Irish cuisine with the odd continental adventure and an à la carte menu. Starters cost from £3.25; mains from £9.50; desserts £3.95; set menu £18.95.

The Pilgrim's Table
40 Upper English Street, St Patrick's Trian, Armagh BT61 7BA
☎ 028 3752 1814

A terrific place for lunch or snacks if you are visiting the Trian. The menu changes regularly but includes items such as potato and leek soup, steaks, savoury tarts, salads and Irish bread. Arrive early for fresh scones hot from the oven.

The Palace Stables Restaurant
Palace Demesne, Armagh BT60 4EL
☎ 028 3752 9634

For lunch only, but this is a lovely restaurant with traditional menu – favourites include soup and wheaten bread, along with sandwiches, sausage and champ (potato, cream and spring onions). Lunch costs from about £6.

café bars in Ulster. There's also a wide range of entertainment from local artists, songwriters and live bands.

The **Corner Bar** (Kiln Road, Silverwood) is a quaint country pub, full of village life. There's a good friendly atmosphere and a great mixture of chatty locals in the bar. Food is served daily, and an excellent pint is poured *'like a candlelit procession down your throat',* as one barman had it. Spontaneous music sessions regularly take place. **Lynes's Bar** (The Square, Richhill BT61 9PP; ☎ 02838 871874) is great for a quiet drink during the day, and it's buzzing at night; **Damper Murphy's** (48 Lower Irish Street, Armagh BT61 7EP; ☎ 028 3752 8199) is a lovely old city pub. **McKenna's Bar** (21 Lower English Street, Armagh BT61 7LJ; ☎ 028 3752 2645) is the place to get deeply involved in a discussion on GAA sports with the locals.

Basil Shiels Bar & Lounge (80 Dundrum Road, Tassagh BT60 2QE; ☎ 028 3753 8259) is a unique experience even by Armagh's exemplary drinking standards. Renowned for selling only bottled beers and spirits (no draught), this adherence to the old ways is a reflection of the character of the hostelry. Some of the local regulars have been staggering home from here for more than half a century. During the summer months a traditional session takes place on Wednesdays.

ⓘ Visitor Information

Tourist Information Centre: 40 English Street, Armagh BT61 7BA, ☎ 028 3752 1800, www.visitarmagh.com.

Hospitals: Craigavon Hospital 68 Lurgan Road, Portadown BT63 5QQ, ☎ 028 3833 4444; Towerhill Hospital, Tower Hill, Armagh BT61 9DP, ☎ 028 3752 2381.

Doctors: Drs Dorman, Chambers, McCollum & Fearon, Willowbank, Crossmore Road, Keady, Armagh, County Armagh BT60 3RL, ☎ 028 3753 1248; Abbey Court Surgery, Dobbin Lane, Armagh, County Armagh BT61 7QP; ☎ 028 3752 1450.

Pharmacies: JW Gray, 15–17, Upper English Street, Armagh, County Armagh BT61 7BH, ☎ 028 3752 2092; Boots the Chemist, 15 Scotch Street, Armagh, County Armagh BT61 7PU, ☎ 028 3752 3199.

Police: Lurgan Police Station, 62 Church Place, Lurgan, County Armagh BT66 6HD, ☎ 0845 600 8000.

Supermarkets: Sainsbury's, The Mall West, Armagh, County Armagh BT61 9AJ; HA Emerson & Son, 55 Scotch Street, Armagh, County Armagh BT61 7DF.

Local taxis: Diamond Taxis, 12a Lower English Street, Armagh, County Armagh BT61 7LJ, ☎ 028 3752 5204; Armagh & Crispy Taxis, 127 Railway Street, Armagh, County Armagh BT61 7HT, ☎ 028 3752 7171.

SOUTH ARMAGH

In South Armagh's verdant countryside lies a tranquil valley traditionally known as the Gateway to Ulster – **Bealach Isteach Chúige Uladh**. This defile has long been associated with an ancient frontier dating as far back as the earliest record of man's habitation in Ireland. Here, in this lovely, lonely valley Cú Chullainn and the Red Branch Knights (of ancient Ulster saga fame) did their derring-do, Brian Boru and O'Neill-the-Great marched en route to do battle for Ireland, and St Patrick passed on his thoughtful way to set up his mission. He subsequently called Armagh 'my sweet hill'.

From Neolithic times through the turbulence of the Middle Ages and on to the recent Troubles, South Armagh has rarely been out of the news. Because of its fearsome reputation over the past 40 years few people ever visited – only if you had family there. This has had an unforeseen benefit. South Armagh is today unspoilt and largely undiscovered – a magical destination for visitors looking for tranquillity, and who want to see Old Ireland as she used to be. South Armagh has a particularly strong folk tradition including story-telling, Irish dancing, poetry and music. Traditional sports are also strong – Armagh boasts a top class county Gaelic football team, winning a brace of All-Ireland titles, while the quiet laneways are the ad hoc stadiums for the sport known as road bowling. You'll also see curious gable-ends that look as if they're half-built; these are the venues for another native sport, court handball.

International visitors have long made the journey to South Armagh – even during the long years of the Troubles – for one specific reason: to see a textbook example of a ring-dyke system. **Slieve Gullion** is required viewing for geologists from around Europe and beyond. Strictly speaking it should be called 'The Paleocene Slieve Gullion Igneous Complex – comprising a layered central intrusion surrounded by a slightly older ring dyke.' Suffice to say, that several million years ago a volcanic extrusion left a circular ring of mountain so mystical looking that it inspired the ancient scribes of Ireland (some 2,000 years ago) to write the epic saga *Táin Bó Cuailgne* or *Cattle Raid of Cooley*. Slightly more recently, it helped inspire Belfast writer C S Lewis to conjure up lions, witches and wardrobes in the far off land of Narnia.

This corner of the smallest of the Six Counties offers superlative hill-walking, unsurpassed fishing, striking landscapes and one of the strongest cultures in the whole of the island. From ceili dancing to ballad singing the people of South Armagh are proud of their heritage, and are only too glad to greet visitors with a truly Irish welcome.

Walking on Slieve Gullion

WHAT TO SEE AND DO

Ring of Gullion

The Ring of Gullion, designated as an Area of Outstanding Natural Beauty, forms a distinctive circle of hills around the majestic central peak of **Slieve Gullion**. It represents one of the best volcanic dyke systems in the world. When Ireland's share of molten lava was cooling down a few million years ago a little bit plopped up – just like boiling custard – but didn't plop down again. South Armagh was left with a central mountain surrounded by a ring of smaller mountains. From the top of Slieve Gullion you can see this formation in glorious wide-screen clarity. This beautiful, tragic landscape guards many a hidden mass rock – where the Catholic faithful came to pray after their religion was banned. St Oliver Plunkett sought refuge here – Archbishop of Armagh and founder of the Jesuits' Order in Drogheda, he was hanged, drawn and quartered in 1681 by the English, who accused him of being part of Titus Oates' Popish Plot.

To conquer the summit you'll only need average fitness. It's 1,800ft (573m) up, less than two hours' steady climb – all hill walking with none of the vertigo-inducing mountaineering that you might experience in the nearby Mournes. The well worn turf path is easy underfoot. At the summit ridge leading on to the top is a small lake, Calliagh Berra's Lough. Ultramarine blue in the sun if you choose the right day, as black as the surrounding peat hags if you choose wrong. It need hardly be mentioned that several legends attach to this lake. Ireland's oldest epic tale – the *Cattle Raid of Cooley* or the *Táin Bó Cuailgne* – passes right by en route to the rest of Ulster. The

The Brocken Spectre

If you're especially lucky you might see an additional highlight from the summit of Slieve Gullion: the **Brocken Spectre** (after a mountain in the Harz range in Germany). A huge image of yourself will appear, etched in rainbow colours in the clouds. As you move, it moves too. The phenomenon occurs when the sun is low and clouds or mist lie in the valley below you – a common enough meteorological set-up in these parts. Shadows cast from the peak are magnified and diffracted producing startling effects. Spectacular, not to mention a little spooky, when it does occur.

2,000-year-old tale is reputed to have travelled as far as Iceland, the inspiration for their great sagas. A short walk past the lake, another gentle climb, and you're at the peak – marked by a stone cairn built during the Victorian era, atop a court chamber constructed by Neolithic Armagh locals. Both great cairn builders, the Victorians and the Neolithics, separated by some 4,000 years.

The huge burial cairn on Slieve Gullion is known as the South Carn, and it bears a trig point and view indicator at 1,894ft (573m) – the perfect vantage point to survey the surrounding peaks of **Sturgan Mountain, Slievenacappe, Mullaghbane Mountain, Ballymacdermott Mountain** and **Slievebolea** – to name just a few. From the summit you can also see **Cam Lough** – one of the best examples of a glacial ribbon lake which has been designated as an area of Special Scientific Interest. It's also of great interest if you're into fishing – trout, pike, bream, rudd and perch are all available. The Ring of Gullion is also one of the largest European Dry Heath habitats in Northern Ireland. On the northern horizon lies a long silver ribbon of water which is **Lough Neagh**, to the south **Castletown River** and **Dundalk Bay.**

To descend from Slieve Gullion use the southerly slopes, which takes you down through Slieve Gullion Forest Park – pretty much a coniferous monoculture of Sitka spruce and European larch. Or you can stick to the heathland, and enjoy the more indigenous delights of gorse, heather and sphagnum moss – with always the chance of seeing a buzzard hunting for its dinner. During the Middle Ages great volumes of sphagnum moss were sent to Dublin – to be used as toilet paper.

The way leads past the ancient **Killevy Churches** and the nearby **Holy Well of St Moninna** who founded a nunnery hereabouts in the 5th century. Probably worth taking a slight detour from the main path to visit the site; the well is at the end of a quintessentially Irish laneway, overgrown with fuchsia and blackthorn and lined with moss-covered granite rocks. The grassy byway eventually leads up onto a knoll in the shadow of Slieve Gullion. The holy well itself is surrounded by a large cross and crucifix, a hawthorn tree, and a Douglas fir. In time-honoured – and pagan – fashion, the hawthorn has become a votive tree, festooned with ribbons, hankies and other scraps of material pilgrims have left in hopeful exchange for intercession.

Local legends: Finn MacCool

The warrior **Fionn Mac Cumhaill** (Finn MacCool) – another Hibernian hero – had dealings on Slieve Gullion. He was lured into the pool on the summit, emerging as a wizened, white-haired old man. His friends dug into the cairn on the top of the mountain to find the 'Calliagh Berras', the witch who caused the enchantment. After much persuasion she restored Fionn to his youthfulness, but his former head of red hair remained white.

Fionn Mac Cumhaill also occurs in the mythologies of Scotland and the Isle of Man. The stories of Fionn and his followers, the Fianna, form the Fenian Cycle or *Fiannaidheacht,* of the ancient Ulster sagas.

LOCAL KNOWLEDGE

Tom Quinn, a Bessbrook man, is a mine of information on every aspect of South Armagh life. He can – almost literally – reel off the name of just about every South Armagh dance tune, because Tom is that revered figure in rural Ireland: a dance master. South Armagh has one of the strongest traditional dance cultures in Ireland and over the past few years Tom has been helping to archive much of this heritage.

Favourite pub – O'Hanlon's in Mullaghbawn. It's been 400 years in the one family – some 15 generations. They have regular sessions and Phelim Brady, the Bard of Armagh drank here, as well as Redmond O'Hanlon the famous outlaw were all patrons of the establishment.

Favourite restaurant – Uluru Restaurant. It's an Australian restaurant, probably the only one in the Six Counties, serving delicious food.

Secret tip for lunch – McNamee's Bakery. They make the best home-made soups in the country. The wheaten bread is so special that it goes to America.

Favourite shop – Alexander's in Markethill: furniture, crystal, gifts, art, coffee shop. A terrific place.

Best view – from Ballintemple Viewpoint overlooking Camlough Lake and Camlough Mountain.

Quirkiest attraction – the fault line where Camlough Lake is – it hasn't been active for over 60 million years, mind.

Favourite haunt – Annaverna House, Ravensdale – just a couple of miles from Newry, just over the border in County Louth; it promotes Irish dancing, classical concerts, sessions, poetry workshops.

167

The Kilnasaggart Stone, the oldest inscribed stone in Ireland

Kilnasaggart Inscribed Stone

Just a mile outside Jonesborough stands what is probably the oldest Christian field monument in Ireland, and one of the oldest in the whole of Europe outside Rome. Marking the site of an early cemetery, the oldest inscribed stone in Ireland is set in a peaceful glen believed to be part of one of ancient Ireland's five great main roads. The **Slighe Midhluachra** ran from Royal Tara in the centre of the island through the Moyry Pass to Dunseverick in north Antrim.

The whole area west of Slieve Gullion is known as Gleann-na-Samhaisce, the **Glen of the Heifer**. The bovine in question always filled your bucket with milk, no questions asked. But one day somebody tried to take more than their fair share. The angry cow stamped her foot on the ground, staged a major strop, and left the valley forever. The shape of a hoof can still be seen on a stone beside the pillar stone. See for yourself. The inscription on the 2m tall standing stone reads: 'In loc so taninmarni Ternoc mac Ceran Bic er Cul Peter Apstel', which has been translated as: 'This place, bequeathed by Ternoc, son of Ceran the Little, under the patronage of Peter the Apostle.'

Ternoc's death is recorded in local annals as happening around 714–716, so a construction date of around AD700 seems probable. According to legend a crock of gold is buried below the pillar. Overturned by treasure seekers in the 1830s, it was reset shortly afterwards. The gold, fortunately, wasn't found. But it's still there, alright.

Moyry Castle

Overlooking Kilnasaggart and the Gap of Ulster is the well-preserved hulk of Moyry Castle. After fighting his way through the Moyry Pass in 1600, Lord Mountjoy wanted to secure the area, so built this no-nonsense fortification. Put up in something of a hurry, few signs of comfort are in evidence, not even a set of stone steps to service the three storeys – access was by ladder and ropes. It was built to last – and it has. Standing on a rocky outcrop on the eastern slopes of **Slievenabolea**, this squat, defiant castle sports a number of musket embrasures – windows for poking your gun out – and a 'machiolation', or murder hole from which uninvited guests (of which there were many) would be treated to boiling pitch or similarly unwelcoming drinks.

You're unlikely to be crowded out by other tourists visiting this grade A, 25-carat slice of history. Surrounded by bucolic meadows and hawthorn hedges, it's hard to imagine that just over 400 years ago the deafening roar of cannon and musket rent the air.

Moyry Castle

Come to think of it – you only have to go back just a couple of decades. Because as you turn to head back for the bus, you'll immediately see **Kilnasaggart Railway Bridge**. This carries the main Dublin to Belfast railway line, and glories in the reputation of being Europe's most bombed bridge. Never mind two world wars, or the Balkans, over the past 40 years this bridge was laid siege to so often that the Dublin-Belfast train became one of the few in the world to have a permanent helicopter escort.

Annaghmare Court Tomb, between Cullyhanna and Crossmaglen.

Neolithic court tombs are named after the distinctive semi-circle forecourt which stands at one end of a long stone cairn originally enclosing the burial chambers. Annaghmare Court Tomb, known locally as the Black Castle, is one of the best-preserved examples of the type. The horseshoe-shaped forecourt stands at the southern end of the tomb and is particularly notable for the excellent stone craftsmanship – intricate dry-stone walling fills the crevices between the larger boulders. The tomb has been used for burials at various times in the Neolithic Age; according to local gossip unconsecrated burials have taken place here in the more recent past. During excavations in 1963 a small standing stone – no more than a foot high – was discovered in the forecourt. The purpose of this unusual feature remains unknown.

Ballykeel Dolmen

An interest in prehistoric tombs will serve you well in Armagh. Near **Mullaghbawn** at the western foot of Slieve Gullion, Ballykeel Dolmen is an outstanding example of a portal tomb. The dolmen, built some 3,000 years ago, is made up of two portal stones with a sill between and a lower backstone supporting a huge capstone.

Crossmaglen

Two Crossmaglen men, the joke goes, once made it into the *Guinness Book of Records*. One was an only child and the other had a television licence. The humour in this joke – in the unlikely event that it has eluded you – rests on two perceptions: that Crossmaglen is predominantly Catholic and families are traditionally large; and that the normal rule of law as regards minor annoyances such as television licences, road tax, etc. is routinely ignored. Like all good jokes, there is a kernel of truth here. In the 2001 census 99% of the people living in Crossmaglen were Catholic, 0.8% Protestant. Presumably the remaining 0.2% is made up of atheists.

A picture will no doubt have emerged in your mind of a rebellious yet religious people with scant regard for the law. And at one time that would have been an accurate enough picture. But today Crossmaglen, the largest village in South Armagh, looks as quiet and idyllic as any Dordogne hamlet. The surrounding landscape is so verdantly picturesque that it's hard to believe that just a few years ago this was the scene of a bitter struggle between nationalists and British forces. The British Army base in Crossmaglen (XMG to the security forces), buried under tons of sand bags and barbed wire, made Castle Dracula look user friendly. Watchtowers such as Drumuckavall Hilltop Spy Post (otherwise known as Romeo Juliet II) could safely claim to offer the most expensive breakfasts in the world. Everything had to be helicoptered in daily by heavily guarded Lynx gunships, meaning that a plate of porridge cost in the region of £500. Crossmaglen finally bid God speed to the British troops just a couple of years ago.

Locals, with whom they were locked in mortal combat for 40 years, held up signs saying, 'Slan abhaile – safe home' as the helicopters clattered off and heeled towards Belfast for the last time. The Police Service of Northern Ireland still maintains the base, but the overt militarism has largely gone. Even the local baker's shop, McNamee's, has got its hot plate back.

Crossmaglen (*Crois Mhic Lionnáin* in Irish, or Lennon's Cross) is probably named after an 18th century local called Eoghain Lennon, famous as the owner of a shebeen or illegal drinking house. The square's name commemorates Cardinal Tomás Ó Fiaich, a local man who became Primate of All Ireland (head of the Catholic Church in Ireland), and who died in 1990. He was known for his Republican views – loyalists labelled him 'the Carmelite with the Armalite'. Today Crossmaglen is famed for its traditional music, its open air fair held on the first and third Friday of each month featuring local produce, and a horse fair held annually in September.

Creggan Churchyard, near Crossmaglen (well sign-posted), is home to some of Ireland's best known Gaelic poets. The Poets' Trail begins at the churchyard where Art McCumhaigh, Patrick MacAliondain and Seamus Mor MacMurphy are buried. The 8-mile trail also passes by O'Neill Burial Vault and **Roche's Castle**. For details of the Poets' Trail and other walking routes contact **Newry Tourist Office** (Town Hall, Bank Parade BT35 6HR; ☎ 028 3026 8877).

Bessbrook

Bessbrook, a picture-postcard Quaker village, is South Armagh's only Conservation Area – designated as an area of architectural or historic interest. One of the earliest 'model' villages associated with the Industrial Revolution, it was built from Mourne granite by a wealthy Quaker linen manufacturer John Grubb Richardson to house his workers. He decided to run his village on the 'three Ps' ethos – no pubs, no pawnshops and consequently no need for police. To this day the village has neither pub nor pawnshop – almost unique in Ireland. But its inhabitants are subject to the law – the Police Service of Northern Ireland now has a station there. At one time, Bessbrook linen was among the finest in the world, with the mill providing most of the employment in the village. In the frequently segregated communities of Northern

Ireland, Bessbrook is an unusually mixed village, with representation of Anglican, Methodist, Presbyterian and Roman Catholic denominations.

Derrymore House, a National Trust property in Bessbrook, is a late 18th-century thatched house in gentrified vernacular style set in over 100 acres of land. The house was described by Sir Charles Coote as 'without exception, the most elegant summer lodge', and is a must if you're interested in 18th-century architecture. The surrounding parkland was laid out by John Sutherland, one of the most celebrated disciples of Capability Brown. The banner of Bessbrook Star of Hope Temperance Loyal Orange Lodge 927, depicts Derrymore House, where the Act of Union was signed in 1800. The Treaty Room is open to visitors.

> **DERRYMORE HOUSE:** Bessbrook BT35 7EF; ☎ 028 8778 4753; www.nationaltrust.org.uk. Entry: (standard admission prices in brackets) Treaty Room Tour: adults £3.70 (£3.36), children £1.80 (£1.63), family £9.20 (£8.36), groups (£3.20); Treaty Room only open 4 May, 25 May, 12/13 July, 13 Aug, 2–5.30pm except bank and public holidays; last admission 30 min before closing.

On the outskirts of Bessbrook is **John McNeill's Craigmore Viaduct**, known locally as the Eighteen Arches, built in 1851. The Great Northern Railway, which opened in 1852, followed the ancient Gap of the North. Constructed from local granite, the viaduct still carries the Dublin-Belfast train link and with 18 20m-high arches spanning about half a kilometre, it was for a long time the longest bridge in Ireland. The viaduct remains one of the most impressive railway structures in Ireland or Britain.

Keady

Keady (from the Irish *an Céide* meaning 'a flat topped hill') is a small town very close to the border with the Republic. A tributary of the River Callan, the Clea,

> **KEADY HERITAGE CENTRE:** The Old Mill, 2 Kinelowen Street, Keady, County Armagh BT60 3SU; ☎ 028 3753 9928; www.keadyinitiatives.com.

The Old Mill in Keady

flows from Tullynawood Lake through the centre of the town. The river once powered the town's now defunct millwheels.

The **Old Mill** in the centre of the town has been converted into a modern visitor centre, café and community enterprise resource. The building is complete with its own millwheel and acts as the entrance to a beautiful riverside walk.

Keady holds something of mystical position in the annals of Irish music, being the home town of the late Tommy Makem. Along with Liam Clancy he formed the band the Clancy Brothers and Tommy Makem, more or less kick-starting the worldwide interest in Irish music. The town is also famous for the towering ballad 'The Hills of Greenmore', which begins, 'One fine winter's morn my horn I did blow / To the green fields of Keady for hours we did go...'

The quiet laneways around Keady are ideal for cycling or walking. The **Beetlers' Trail** is a circular route passing the site of an annual Road Bowling event (as can be seen from the white lines painted on the road) and eventually on to Tassagh Viaduct – one of the finest Victorian railway bridges still in existence. It's said that each of its 18 arches cost the lives of three workmen.

Jonesborough

Jonesborough is famous for its weekly Sunday open-air market, which can attract thousands of people. Everything from farmers' produce to illegal poteen (home-distilled whiskey) is on sale here.

Wet weather

For a wet day diversion head for the Tí Chulainn Centre (An Mullach Bán BT35 9TT; ☎ 028 3088 8828; www.tichulainn.com), which specialises in cultural activities and events and actively encourages visitors to participate in the culture of the area. You might find yourself learning a smidgen of Irish, or a few notes on the tin-whistle. You can also learn to dance – beginners and children are welcome; you might take home a few steps from Riverdance. The centre has an interpretative exhibition with archaeological, geological and environmental details of the area.

Alternatively, the **Chairdinéil Ó Fiaich Centre** (Slatequarry Road, Cullyhanna BT35 0JH; ☎ 028 3086 8757; www.ofiaichcentre.co.uk) recounts the life of the late Cardinal Tomás Ó Fiaich. A great pillar of the community during desperately hard times, the Cardinal was known as much for his 'common touch' as his nationalist politics. He died while leading a pilgrimage to Lourdes.

What to do with children...

Greenvale Equestrian Centre (141 Longfield Road, Forkhill BT35 9SD; ☎ 028 3088 8314) is a particularly child-friendly place for equestrian sports – trekking in the nearby Ring of Gullion, or hacking through the forest.

The best... **PLACES TO STAY**

BOUTIQUE

Dundrum House

116 Dundrum Road, Tassagh, Keady BT60 2NG; ☎ 028 3753 1257
www.dundrumhouse.com

This early 18th century manor is set in 80 acres of land with Callan River running through it. A comfortable, sophisticated place, with cosy lounges and a mellow bar, it's situated about six miles from Armagh city, with golf, angling, walking, cycling, and horse-riding in the locality.

Price: £38 single, £55 double.

INN

Cross Square Hotel

O'Fiaich Square, Crossmaglen BT35 9AA
☎ 028 3086 0508
www.crosssquarehotel.com

A comfortable old hotel in the centre of Cross (as it's known locally) with traditional music of a Friday night. Breakfasts are legendarily good in this family-run establishment.

Price: from £80 for a double.

B&B

Adrigole House

4 Bun Sliebhe, Maphoner Road, Mullaghbawn BT35 9TP
☎ 028 3088 8689

Good value glorified B&B right in Mullaghbawn village, with dinner served in the evening. No need to ask if it's licensed – this is South Armagh; of course it is.

Price: £30 per person per night.

Black Gap Farm

26 Divernagh Road, Bessbrook BT35 7BW
☎ 028 3083 0358

You won't find too many hotels in this part of South Armagh – but there is a good choice of B&Bs and farmhouse accommodation such as Black Gap overlooking Slieve Gullion mountain. Dog kennels are available if you don't want to take your pet down to the pub.

Price: £25 per night per person sharing; £30 for a single.

Bru an t-Sosa

32 Ballinaleck Road, Camlough BT35 7HU
☎ 028 3083 0727
www.bruantsosa.com

Luxury four-star accommodation on the shores of Camlough Lake with turf fires (turf supplied, but you can dig your own...), central heating, etc., plus your own secluded access to the lake – you can fish for your own dinner too.

Price: from £325 for a week.

...and how to avoid children

For peace and quiet, take a wander round the archaeological wonders of the **Dorsey**. Situated in the drumlins of South Armagh near Silverbridge this man-made boundary is estimated to be over 2,000 years old. It is part of a defensive wall, known as the Dane's Cast, which seems to have encircled Ulster from **Scarva** on the Down-Armagh border to **Donegal Bay** in the west. At various points known as **Worm Ditch** and the **Black Pig's Dyke** the ancient boundary consists of two parallel lines of large trench-like earthworks running east to west, about 4,000m in length and 300m apart with sections flanking either end.

The name Dorsey comes from the Irish 'dorsa' meaning doors or gates and refers to the passes through the earthworks. It is thought they were constructed to protect the important ancient route leading from the Plain of Louth to Armagh by people who regarded Navan Fort (near modern day Armagh City) as their capital. Two sections of the southern trenches have survived particularly well, featuring 1,300 various types of archaeological features. It's not spectacular, but totally intriguing.

Entertainment

South Armagh at one time had more ceili bands per head of population than anywhere else in Ireland. Ceili dancing, set-dancing, competition dancing (that's the stuff that looks like Riverdance), sean nós dancing (that's the very old style). It's also home to a wealth of traditional music, singing and storytelling. Any number of pubs have sessions both 'promptu and impromptu' as described outside one

Session in South Armagh

pub. **Paddy Short's** in Crossmaglen is a good starting off point. The uncle of Clare Short MP, Paddy is no longer with us, but his legacy of a pub is one of the hubs of South Armagh traditional music. **Mullaghbawn's O'Hanlon's Bar** has sessions at the weekend and encourages visiting musicians.

The **Welcome Inn**, (35 Main Street, Forkhill; ☎ 028 3088 8273) was originally called O'Neill's Welcome Inn after the original owner, Art O'Neill. Sadly, Art died in

The Welcome Inn

2005, the 30th anniversary of the traditional sessions which he began. The sessions continued right through the Troubles, its reputation attracting some of Ireland's top musicians. The MC for the evening introduces the musicians, the sean nós singers ('old style' unaccompanied performers specialising in highly decorative singing, usually in Irish), and the visitors *'home from South Australia, so give them a big south Armagh welcome'.* And of course the storytellers – shenachies are still very big round here. Session night at the Welcome Inn is an extraordinary cultural and social occasion.

Comhaltas Ceoltóirí Éireann

Comhaltas Ceoltóirí éireann, a non-profit cultural movement with hundreds of local branches around the world, is dedicated to preserving, promoting and developing traditional Irish music (Culturann na h Éireann, 32 Belgrave Square, Monkstown, County Dublin; ☎ 00 353 1280 0295; www.comhaltas.ie; 9.30am–1.00pm; 2.00–5.30pm every day). The organisation holds 1,000 weekly classes; every county in Ulster has at least one branch (http://comhaltas.ie/locations). Comhaltas (pronounced roughly speaking 'kyoaltass') also runs pub sessions and concerts. Its headquarters in Dublin house a comprehensive library of sheet music; rare footage, records and instruments are on show. The **Irish Traditional Music Archive** in Dublin (73 Merrion Square, Dublin 2; ☎ 353 661 9699; www.itma.ie) now holds the largest collection of Irish traditional music in existence. Rare recordings of the seminal names in traditional music are available, as well as footage of early 20th-century appearances.

The best... FOOD AND DRINK

▶ Staying in

McNamee's Bakery (Cardinal O'Fiaich Square, Crossmaglen; ☎ 028 3086 8412) cooks some of the finest bread in whole region. As well as supplying Crossmaglen and hinterland with their daily bread, coach tours make a special detour to give their customers a treat of soup, soda bread and sausage rolls. Its deli sandwiches are legendary – a McNamee's sandwich is best described as 'filling, with a little bread'. The shop also supplies supermarkets and the export market with its bakery. Not to be missed.

    John McEntee's butcher shop (15 Cardinal O'Fiaich Square, Crossmaglen; ☎ 028 3086 1780) serves the people from all round South Armagh. Meat pies, sausages and black pudding are made from local produce.

EATING OUT

RESTAURANT

Murphy's Bar and Restaurant
2 Drumintee Road, Meigh BT35 8JT &#8232
☎ **028 3084 8789**

A family-run restaurant established around 1838, Murphy's still retains some of its original features. Food is served in the bar at lunchtime – expect chunky meals of filling but fairly standard fare. Upstairs in the evening it's Chinese and local. Expect to pay about £10 a head.

Garvey's Ale House and Restaurant
58 New Road, Silverbridge BT35 9LN
☎ **028 3088 8220**
www.garveysbar.com

Ale house and one of the best places you'll find to eat in South Armagh, with imaginative twists on traditional dishes.

Belleek Country House
6 Main Street, Belleek
☎ **028 3087 8999**

Belleek specialises in fresh, local produce. It's an unassuming, friendly family restaurant with fairly moderate prices. They say that for a truly authentic Irish dinner your mother should be gently nagging you throughout the meal. At Belleek proceedings are so homely that you could imagine it happening (although it doesn't).

The Old Mill Restaurant
Kinelowen Street, Keady BT60 3SU
☎ **028 3753 9959**

Home-cooked food is served at the Old Mill – from breakfast-time right through to tea-time – as they still call around 5pm here. Whatever the time, the Old Mill will feed you admirably, with main dishes costing from around £6.

Drinking

South Armagh's pubs are renowned for their music (see entertainment above), including the **Welcome Inn** in Forkhill (which hosts one of the longest running traditional music sessions in Ireland), as well as **Keenan's**, Crossmaglen, **O'Hanlon's Bar**, Mullaghbawn, and the **Real McCoy**, Mullaghbawn.

For a traditional pub specialising in sporting matters, pop into the **Corner House**, Market Street, Keady, and for a quiet pint and a lovely view the **Callan River Inn** in Keady is the ideal place. The **Derryvale Inn**, Keady is renowned for a perfect pint as well as a great top shelf of Irish whiskies.

ⓘ Visitor Information

Tourist information centre: Armagh Tourist Information Centre, 40 English Street, Armagh BT61 7BA, ☎ 028 3752 1800.

Hospital: Craigavon Area Hospital, 68 Lurgan Road, Craigavon, ☎ 028 3833 4444.

Doctors: Drs Dorman, Chambers, McCollum & Fearon, Willowbank, Crossmore Road, Keady, Armagh BT60 3RL, ☎ 028 3753 1248; Dr RA Burnett, 67 Mullahead Road, Tandragee, Craigavon BT62 2LA, ☎ 028 3884 0578.

Pharmacies: McKeevers Chemist, 20 Davis Street, Keady, Armagh, County Armagh BT60 3RS, ☎ 028 3753 1665; Cheevers Chemists, 60 Kinelowen Street, Keady BT60 3TL, ☎ 028 3753 1276.

Police: Armagh Police Station, 1–2 City View, Newry Road, Armagh, ☎ 028 3752 3311; Keady Police Station, 38 Davis Street, Keady, ☎ 028 3753 1207; Tandragee Police Station, 10 Armagh Road, Tandragee, ☎ 028 3884 0232.

Supermarkets: Cox's Foodmarket, Windmill Corner, 1 Killylea Road, Armagh, County Armagh BT60 4AN, ☎ 028 3752 8128; Spar, Killylea Road, Armagh BT60 4AN, ☎ 028 3752 4026; Spar, 67 Kinelowen Street, Keady BT60 3TL, ☎ 028 3753 8982.

Parking: National Car Parks, Unit 20 Canal Quay, Win Business Park, Newry BT35 6PH, ☎ 028 3025 0909.

Cash point: Abbey National PLC, 19 Upper English Street, Armagh, ☎ 0845 765 4321; Bank of Ireland, 14 Main Street, Keady, ☎ 028 3753 1210; Northern Bank, 21 Main Street, Keady, ☎ 028 3753 8001.

Internet: Gaming World, 5a Thomas Street, Portadown, Craigavon BT62 3NP, ☎ 028 3835 1084.

Bike rental: Mc Convey Cycles, 183 Ormeau Road, Belfast BT71SQ, ☎ 028 90 33 0322.

Taxis: Castle Taxis, 68 Knockview Drive, Tandragee, ☎ 028 3884 1999; Cheers Cabs, 3 Kinelowen Street, Keady, ☎ 028 3753 1216; Gollogly Taxis, 5 Kinelowen Street, Keady, ☎ 028 3753 9080.

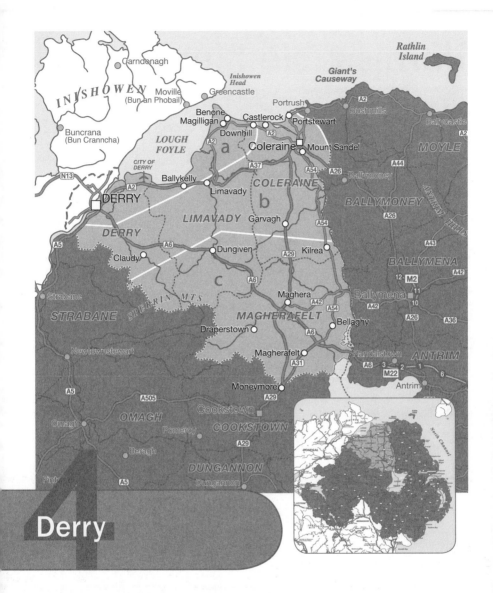

Derry

4

a. Derry City and coastal Derry

b. Mid and North Derry

c. South Derry

Unmissable highlights

01 Walk round the Walls of Derry, one of the few remaining walled cities left in Europe, p. 183

02 Picnic on Benone Strand, a 7-mile strip of sand on Derry's Atlantic coast, p. 188

03 Enjoy the view at Mount Sandel, near Coleraine. Ireland's very first settlers landed here before making their way inland some 9,000 years ago, p. 200

04 Mussenden Temple. The folly's blood-stained history guarantees a ghost fest, p. 190

05 Ponder at Bishop's Temple, Downhill. Local legend says that the only Irishman present in Jerusalem on the day Christ was crucified was born here, p. 190

06 See the sun set in Portrush, a view which inspired Jimmy Kennedy to pen 'Red Sails in the Sunset', p. 199

07 See the monument to Amelia Earhart, the first woman to fly the Atlantic, p. 191

08 Visit the statue of Dean George Berkeley in St Colomb's Cathedral. The philosopher believed that 'all reality is in the mind'. Makes you think, p. 187

09 In Limavady, visit the grave of Miss Jane Ross, who collected Danny boy, p. 202

10 Visit Free Derry Corner, which commemorates the bloody history of the city, p. 183

DERRY

Nothing could really prepare you for Derry, the world's most northerly Catholic city. Just a stone's throw from some of the finest beaches in Ireland, it is home to a school which has produced two Nobel prize winners, has of the few remaining walled cities in Europe, and boasts the biggest Halloween festival on the planet.

Derry City, for so long a byword for violence and chaos, has transformed itself this past decade or so into a vibrant metropolis, with edgy art galleries, innovative museums, contemporary restaurants and buzzy pubs. The city's night-life is mainly centred around the Waterloo Street areas where the craic seems to be at full throttle most nights of the week. The steep street is lined with pubs, Irish traditional and modern. But before heading for the cosiness of a city hostelry, you'll feel duty bound to take a stroll round the 17th-century city walls. Derry is the only completely walled city in these islands, and one of the finest in Europe. The muscular stone bastions have stood silent witness to terrible events, ranging from the Siege of Derry in the 17th century – which lasted 105 days – to Bloody Sunday in the 20th; the enquiry of which continues to this day.

The county of Derry has countryside which has inspired poet Seamus Heaney and playwright Brian Friel to write some of the greatest jewels in the English language, while the town of Limavady was the birthplace of the best known Irish melody of all, the 'Londonderry air', usually called 'Danny boy'. Music is certainly in the Derry air, literature too, but probably what strikes the visitor most is the friendliness of the people, and the fact that conviviality is the most pronounced feature of shops, pubs, restaurants and hotels.

DERRY CITY AND COASTAL DERRY

Although the Ordnance Survey maps all say 'Londonderry', in reality the overwhelming majority of people in the area (and beyond) call it Derry. This is not just shorthand, in the way people talk about LA or 'Frisco. To refer to the world's most northerly Catholic city as Derry is a political statement.

People have been living in this neck of the (literal) woods for over two millennia – the original name was *Doire Calgaigh*, 'the Oak Grove of Calgach'. In the 10th century it became Doire Colmcille in honour of a local 6th century saint. Colmcille, along with Patrick and Brigid, one of Ireland's three patron saints, was one of the heavy hitters in the early Christian church. Doire Colmcille was eventually shortened to Doire, Derrie or Derry. Soon, however, the city was to gain another name. Its troublesome prefix 'London', in honour of the Corporation of London's role in the 'plantation' of northwest Ulster, was adopted in the 17th century. However – and it's a very big however – people have long memories in these parts, and since the new name was imposed only recently (1613) it never really caught on. But whatever you call the county, it truly is a dramatic and uniquely attractive place, with history in plentiful supply. The Great Siege of 1689 had wide repercussions in Europe. It gave William of Orange crucial breathing space to regroup, paving the way for a decisive victory at the Boyne – the battle which secured William as King of England and damaged the prestige of Louis XIV in Europe.

From the ancient walls of the city, to the 7 mile golden sands of **Benone Strand**, to the only Irishman who was in Jerusalem on the day Christ was crucified (see p. 188), Derry City and coastal Derry live up to the words of the local anthem, 'The Town I Love So Well'.

And when times got rough, there was just about enough,
But we saw it through without complaining
For deep inside was a burning pride
For the town I love so well.

WHAT TO SEE AND DO

Derry City
Derry, perched at the top of the country facing the ocean, boasts a climate that could fairly be described as bracing. With a sky that usually means mischief, the wind whips off the Atlantic like a grudge. It has a constant presence here in Derry – indeed there's a rumour that one day the wind stopped blowing and everybody fell over.

Free Derry corner

Derry remains a predominantly Catholic/nationalist city (some 75% or more), and it's safe to say that in general, no Catholics call the city Londonderry, while a few Derry Protestants do. For visiting dignitaries – not wishing to diss one side or another – this duality causes problems. Bill Clinton, peace-processing in the city, managed to avoid calling Derry anything. Instead he continually referred to 'this beautiful city on the banks of the Foyle' – and he wasn't wrong there. Beautiful, but at times benighted. Meanwhile a local BBC DJ, Gerry Anderson, has coined the masterly name 'Stroke City' as in 'Derry-stroke-Londonderry', so as not to offend anyone.

History, both heroic and terrible, lurks round every corner of the city. Its hills and valleys have seen St Colmcille found his 6th-century church, gangs of labourers dragging rough-hewn stones across the **Bogside** to build the city's walls, King James' troops massing for the siege of 1689 in a crucial away tie. Later came the docks, shirt factories, linen mills and distilleries. Now all gone, but not before leaving their indelible mark on the bloodstained history of this dramatic city. The Troubles, needless to say, have also left their impression – **Free Derry Corner** in the Bogside has assumed Berlin Wall status, and despite the peace, Derry's PSNI station still looks as impregnable as a Norman fort.

No better way to see the city than walk the walk along the **Walls** – believed to be the last city walls built in Europe. The route begins at the **Guildhall** (home to the Saville Enquiry into Bloody Sunday) with its fine stained glasswork illustrating the city's history, past the **Harbour Museum**, then on to the **Apprentice Boys Memorial Hall**, and finally to **St Columb's Cathedral**. The only complete unbroken fortifications of any city in Britain or Ireland, the walls wend past the four original entrances to the city – **Shipquay, Ferryquay, Bishop** and **Butcher** gates. Stone watchtowers overlook the same areas that until recently British Army installations guarded. At Shipquay a plaque commemorates the ending of the Great Siege, in particular the death of

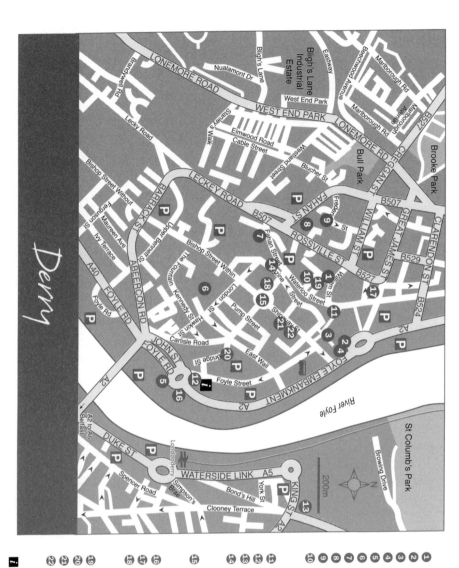

Derry

Things to see and do

1. Magazine Gate
2. Harbour Museum
3. Tower Museum
4. Guildhall
5. Shipquay
6. St Columb's Cathedral
7. Free Derry Corner
8. Museum of Free Derry
9. Bogside
10. Walls of Derry

Entertainment

11. Entertainment Nerve Centre
12. Waterloo Place
13. Waterside Theatre
14. Mason's Pub

Shopping

15. Austin's

Places to Stay

16. City Hotel
17. Merchant's House
18. Tower Hotel

Eat and Drink

19. Peadar O'Donnell's
20. Fitzroy's
21. River Inn Bar, Shipquay
22. Café Calm

Visitor Information

i Tourist Information Centre, Foyle Street

Michael Browning, master of the ship the *Mountjoy*, which eventually broke the blockade. Browning was a Derry man:

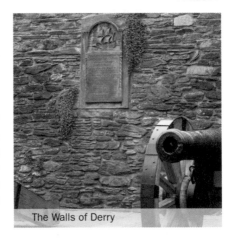
The Walls of Derry

> *Near this spot landed the body of Michael Browning, Master of the ship* Mountjoy. *Of Derry, killed in action at the breaking of the boom July 28th 1689 while leading the van of the relieving squadron against the forces of King James II & Louis XIV.*

> *He died the most enviable of all deaths in sight of the City which was his birthplace, which was his home and which he had just saved by bravery and self devotion from the most frightful form of destruction.*

Fresh flowers are regularly left at the plaque.

Tower Museum

Just inside **Magazine Gate**, Derry City, is the award-winning Tower Museum, housed in a 16th-century tower house (or fortified house, a first cousin, really, of a castle).

CELEBRITY CONNECTIONS

St Columb's College in Derry really is an extraordinarily over-achieving institution. One of the few schools in the world which can boast two Nobel prize winners – **John Hume** and **Seamus Heaney** – St Columb's is also alma mater to playwright **Brian Friel**, songwriter **Phil Coulter** (*Puppet on a String; Congratulations*), football manager **Martin O'Neill**, writer **Seamus Deane**, journalist **Eamon McCann** (the man who has been accused of starting the Troubles because he arranged the first Civil Rights march in 1968), Big Joe McLaughlin (better known as tenor **Josef Locke**) and assorted **Undertones**.

Another past pupil of St Columb's, musician **Charlie McGee**, was one of the most popular entertainers in Ireland during the 1940s and 1950s. Charlie traded under the name of 'Charlie McGee and his Gay Guitar' way back in those innocent days. His signature tune was 'The Homes Of Donegal', a hugely well-known song that saw him topping the bill at the Royal Albert Hall, and later sharing top billing with Slim Whitman at the Carnegie Hall in New York (where he was, reputedly, billed as Mr Homes from Donegal).

TOWER MUSEUM: Union Hall Place, Derry; ☎ 028 7137 2411. Entry: adults £4, children £2; open 10am–5pm Mon–Sat, 2–5pm Sun.

The views from the fifth floor are quite breathtaking, as indeed is the first-class Armada shipwreck exhibition. The Spanish fleet foundered on the north and west coast of Ireland after having been completely routed by the English navy. The disintegrating Armada is credited with bringing to Ireland's shores, among many other things, the potato, the swarthy looks of some Irish people, horses, hurling, Kerry people and whatever you're having yourself. They must surely have been big boats. On display are personal effects and marine paraphernalia from the Spanish ships. The Story of Derry Exhibition will give you a handle on Derry's 2,000-year history, from its evangelising Christianity to the Battle of the Bogside in 1969.

Museum of Free Derry

When British soldiers were deployed in Derry in 1969 they knew little about the place and were woefully unprepared. The troops, recently returned from British colonies, carried with them signs that read: 'Stop or you will be shot'. In Arabic. Their political masters knew precious little more. When Anthony Crossman heard about the Civil Rights riots in August 1969 he assumed it was St Patrick's Day 'because that's when the riots usually take place, isn't it?'

For more information and interpretation on the Troubles which erupted in Derry and quickly spread throughout the Six Counties, head for the Museum of Free Derry. You can journey through the Civil Rights struggle, the Battle of the Bogside, Bloody Sunday, the IRA, the curfews imposed by the British Army during the worst months of rioting. The curfew gave rise to the famous Derry joke, around 1973. It was 8.45pm, 15 minutes before curfew. A British soldier spots a youth on the streets, peers at him through the rifle sights, takes aim, and shoots the lad. His commanding officer is furious. 'Soldier! What on earth did you do that for? Curfew isn't for another 15 minutes.' 'It's OK, sir,' replies the squaddie. 'I know where the guy lives – and he was never going to make it home by 9.'

MUSEUM OF FREE DERRY: 55 Glenafada Accent Park, Derry BT48 9DR; ☎ 028 7136 0880; www.museumoffreederry.org. Entry: adults £3, concessions £2; open Mon–Fri 9.30am–4pm, Sat/Sun 1pm–4pm; open all year, but some slight seasonal variation in opening times.

The museum is housed in the recently renovated flats at the southern end of **Glenfada Park** just off **Rossville Street** – a place central to many of the events of Derry's wretched history.

St Columb's Cathedral

St Columb's Cathedral is Derry's oldest building, and the first post-Reformation church to be built in Ireland or Britain. It is one of the most visited tourist sites in the Six Counties. Named after the patron saint of the city, Donegal-born Colmcille, the Church of Ireland cathedral is built in what is known as 'Planters' Gothic'. This austere style is common throughout the Six Counties. In the porch the original foundation stone proclaims:

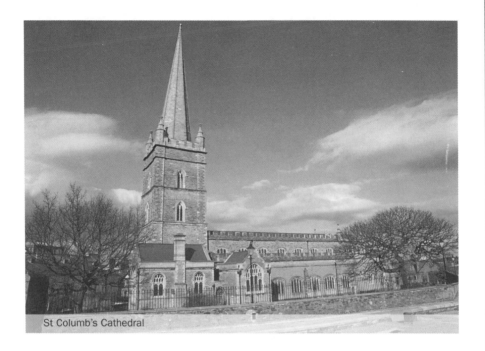

St Columb's Cathedral

If stones could speake
Then London's prayse
Should sounde who
Built this church and
Cittie from the ground.

Just beside the foundation is a hollow mortar shell fired during the Great Siege in the 17th century. The cathedral also contains, among many other fascinating artefacts, the locks of the gates slammed shut in the still controversial events of 1688. In England, the Anglican Church is associated with mild vicars, tea parties and scones with jam. Here in the Six Counties the very same church is all about turbulent priests, armed insurrection and military triumphalism.

When a new Bishop of Derry was appointed by James I back in the 17th century, his wife famously said: 'So to strange Derry: I pray to God it may make us all merry.' She is unlikely to have had her prayers answered in any positive sense – but history remains silent on her further adventures or lifestyle, so we'll probably never know. Speaking of Bishops of Derry's wives, one window in St Columb's celebrates the extraordinary song-writing talents of Mrs C F Alexander (1818–95), a Dublin woman who was domiciled in Tyrone before moving to Derry. Her hymns include 'There Is A Green Hill Far Away' and 'Once in Royal David's City'.

Ireland's most important philosopher, George Berkeley (after whom the Californian town is named) was Bishop of Derry. A groyne near the organ commemorates the man who said 'all reality is in the mind'.

Benone Strand

For summertime outings the beach at Benone Strand in Derry provides fantastic facilities, both natural and organised. Just beside the village of **Downhill**, Benone is a 7-mile strip of sand with a magnificent backdrop of mountain and cliff scenery on Derry's Atlantic coast. Washed by huge breakers it overlooks Donegal's Inishowen Peninsula just a few miles across the sparkling ocean.

Benone is a multiple recipient of the European Blue Flag and Seaside Award – the clean, firm, golden sands of Benone are without rocks, shingle or seaweed. And there's 7 miles of the stuff. And history abounds, you'll be unsurprised to hear, in this neck of the woods. To the westerly end of the **Strand** stands a **Martello Tower**, built to help see off Napoleon should he have expressed designs on Derry.

> BENONE TOURIST COMPLEX: Benone, Derry;
> ☎ 028 7776 0304; www.limavady.gov.uk.
> Entry: prices vary depending on activity and time of week and year.

The Benone visitor complex also has a supervised playground, outdoor paddling pool, and various play areas, two outside heated pools (seasonal), adventure play area, golf practice range, putting and bowling greens. A lifeguard service is on duty daily July and August, 11am–7pm.

Lough Foyle

Although Derry faces the Atlantic Ocean, **Lough Foyle** (a sea inlet) is relatively sheltered because of its narrow inlet. **Toucan One Cruises** (☎ 028 7136 2857; www. foylecruiseline.com) – on board a centrally heated, fully licensed cruiser – will take you up the Foyle for some stunning views of the city. You'll also hear stories of Derry's troubled times, including, of course, the most recent bothersome period. You'll hear how Edward Heath, prime minister at the time of Bloody Sunday, ordered Royal Navy aircraft warships to wait out at sea. To this day nobody is quite sure how he intended to deploy all that ordnance against civil rights marchers – after all, the city already belonged to Britain so gunship diplomacy was unlikely to work.

But it is interesting to mull over the very welcome changes in Irish–British relations over the years – and nowhere better to do it than a boat in Lough Foyle, between the two jurisdictions.

Downhill

Dún Bó, the fort of the cows, is an intriguing little village under the shadow of basaltic cliffs to the west of **Castlerock**. On the headland overlooking the village and on to **Magilligan Point** stands a castle that was built in 1780 by John Adams for the Bishop of Derry. Even by the standards of the North of Ireland, the Bishop was somewhat eccentric. So devoted was he to the improvement of relations between different religious groups that he organised horse races between clergy of all denominations on Magilligan Strand. A splendid idea, but one which, alas, had no lasting benefit for inter-religious relations. The bishop, who was also the Earl of Bristol, was a patron of the arts and a great continental traveller. However his religious beliefs and social

LOCAL KNOWLEDGE

Sinead McIntyre was born and brought up in Derry. After having graduated in English Literature at Glasgow University she followed various careers in London, before returning to Derry where she works as a guide and freelance PR. 'I love being back home,' she says. 'London was exciting, and full of opportunities, but Derry has a special atmosphere.'

Favourite pub: Metro, Bank Place for meeting young, lively pub-goers, and Badger's in Orchard Street for a quiet drink.

Favourite restaurant: Mange 2, Clarendon Street. This is a great restaurant and I wholeheartedly recommend it to anyone who's in the area.

Favourite haunt: Café Calm, for a coffee and a chat with friends.

Favourite activity: taking the dog Taoiseach for a walk through Ness Woods which has a lovely waterfall. Then coffee and cream cake at the coffee shop.

Best tip for lunch: get a tasty takeaway from the Mandirin Palace worth 20 quid and you get a free lunch voucher.

Best view: go to Gobnascale (top of the hill to locals) and you get a terrific view of Derry with its hills and two bridges.

Favourite walk: along the River Foyle between the two bridges.

Quirkiest attraction: the boat trip along the Foyle to Moville in Donegal.

Best kept secret: all the little rivers and loughs to fish in. There are hundreds within just a few miles of Derry.

Best treat: a trip to a beauty spa for a bit of pampering, then a nice meal and drinks at Beech Hill Hotel.

189

propriety were sometimes called into question, and he is thought to have been the target of Dom Gregory Dix's jibe that 'it is no accident that the symbol of the Bishop is a crook and that of an Archbishop is a double cross.'

Most of the **Bishop's Castle** today lies in ruins – giving it a poignant, evocative appearance. More seriously, it appears to be in imminent danger of slipping downhill and landing on top of the village of Downhill. The part known as **Mussenden Temple**, a building for which the word 'folly' could have been invented, commands a view across to the western isles of Scotland. The designer Michael Shanahan created it along the lines of the Temples of Vesta in Tivoli and Rome – and the exoticism doesn't stop there. A connection exists with a local legend. It's said that the only Irishman to be in

Mussenden temple at Downhill

Jerusalem on the day Christ was crucified, a wrestler, Conor MacCormac, was a local man.

With this sort of history it's unsurprising that Downhill is fecund ground for banshee followers, sprite spotters, Wee Folk fanciers and the like. Of course, ghost-hunting is an inexact science, so you likely won't see the awful Crom Cruach, headless aside his terrible black steed as he gallops past the temple intent on evil. Nor will you (probably) spot the slightly more visitor-friendly bog sprites which are particularly numerous in this area – but you never know.

If sprites, spirits and the otherworld are amongst your keen interests, you might as well spend a bit of time here. During its history the Bishop's Castle was apparently the scene of at least one terrible murder. A young lass, done wrong by the squire, was set upon by locals who showed her a quick route to the bottom of the cliffs. Her bereft sobbing can be heard to this day.

The Castle and Temple are about 8 miles north-west of Coleraine on the A2. Alternatively, take the **Derry-Portrush** train along the banks of **Lough Foyle** (be sure to sit on the left). The railway journey is the best way to see the 'polder', or reclaimed, appearance of the coastal strip between Derry and the mouth of the Roe – an unusual type of terrain to find in Ireland. The land was reclaimed in the 19th century for flax growing, and it remains a flat, fertile expanse of countryside. Get off at Castlerock or Downhill. The train journey is worth the effort, even if things from Ireland's otherworld prove elusive.

☂ Wet weather

Amelia Earhart Centre

Just outside **Muff** is a monument to Amelia Earhart, the first woman to fly the Atlantic. Pop into the nearby Earhart Centre for the complete gen on her epic journey across the ocean on 21 May 1932. And as for the name of the town and the Muff Festival – every joke imaginable has already been made.

> **AMELIA EARHART CENTRE:** Ballyarnet Country Park, Derry; ☎ 028 7135 4040. Entry: free, by telephone appointment.

Riverwatch

Riverwatch, located on the banks of the Foyle, is the governmental Loughs Agency's interpretative centre. (The 'Loughs' refer to the **Foyle** and **Carlingford Lough** to the south – the two sea areas administered jointly by the two governments). Displays and exhibitions tell the story of the loughs' wildlife – from salmon to shellfish.

> **RIVERWATCH:** Loughs Agency, 22 Victoria Road, Derry; ☎ 028 7134 2100; www.loughs-agency.org. Entry: free; open weekdays 10am–4pm (evenings and weekends on request).

🛝 What to do with children

Brunswick Superbowl in Pennyburn is a state-of-the-art 20-pin bowling centre. Also available is an Adventure Castle, a Super Freefall, all types of swings, and a maze. If you really want to make a day of it, facilities also include video games, pool tables – and free face painting at the weekend.

> **BRUNSWICK SUPERBOWL:** Pennyburn, Derry; ☎ 028 7137 1999. Entry: cost depends on activity; opens daily at 9am until late.

🎭 Entertainment

Festivals

Halloween is a Celtic invention, and nowhere is it taken more seriously (and light-heartedly) than in Derry. Come 31 October, the people here party like poltergeists. The **Banks of the Foyle Halloween Carnival** runs from the Saturday to Saturday which encompasses 31 October. Between 40,000 and 50,000 people turn up at the main event, the parade, most of whom will be in fancy dress – witches, ghouls, Gaels and banshees, as well as plenty of representations of Dracula – Ireland's other contribution

Halloween festivities in Derry

BANKS OF THE FOYLE HALLOWEEN
FESTIVAL: Tourist Information Centre,
44 Foyle Street; ☎ 028 7126 7284;
www.derryvisitor.com.

to the world of horror. The story of the extravagantly fanged count was written by Dublin man Bram Stoker.

There's a whole host of Halloween-related activities for children during the day, followed by a carnival parade with floats, costumes and band, and the festivities conclude with a massive fireworks display. (The first fireworks to be used on any large commercial scale were hand-held sparklers. These mimicked the early Christian custom – still found in parts of Ireland to this day – of striking flints against stone walls. This would light the way for the souls whose repose was about to be prayed for.)

Throughout Ireland bonfires are lit on Halloween, or Samhain as the early Celts called it. To pacify the restless spirits that would be out and about on Samhain, huge fires were built. These were composed of sacred plants – oak, mistletoe and holly were firm favourites. Also, it is widely believed, human sacrifices would be offered up to the spirits.

Every May bank holiday Derry City holds its Jazz and Big Band Festival (www.cityofderryjazzfestival.com). The festival takes places in venues throughout the city. A firm favourite on the bill is the Ulster Orchestra (and you can't get a much bigger band than that). Last year they gave the world premiere of Brian Byrne's composition 'Tales from the Walled City'.

Music and theatre

For traditional music, **Peadar O'Donnell's** and the **Gweedore Bar** (59 Waterloo Street, Derry BT48 6HD; ☎ 028 7137 2318; www.peadars-gweedorebar.com) – both part of the same concern and next door to each other – make up the fulcrum of traditional and contemporary music in Derry. Sessions are held every night of the week, as well as weekend afternoons at Peadar O'Donnell's. Rock bands are featured in the Gweedore Bar.

Sandino's Café Bar (1 Water Street, Derry; ☎ 028 7130 9297) features a mixture of live rock bands, DJs, traditional sessions and country hooleys, and **Mason's** (10 Magazine Street; ☎ 028 7136 0177) the home of Derry bands the Undertones and That Petrol Emotion, is still the focus of indie affairs in the city. The **Nerve Centre** (7–8 Magazine Street, Derry; ☎ 028 7126 0562; www.nervecentre.org.uk) has been described as 'one of the most dynamic and innovative multi-media centres anywhere'. The centre has been presenting the best of local talent, arts, performance and film for most of the past 20 years. It's a terrific place for an alternative night out – catch a cutting edge film and then chill out in the bar or café. The Nerve Centre also runs the annual Foyle Film Festival every November.

The **Waterside Theatre** (Ebrington Centre, Glendermott Road; ☎ 028 7131 4000; www.watersidetheatre.com), atmospherically housed in a converted factory and beautifully equipped, features drama, dance, comedy nights, children's theatre and live music, from classical to traditional.

🛒 Shopping

You can't leave Derry without visiting **Austin's**, the world's oldest independent department store. This has been the cornerstone of Derry City's Diamond area since 1830 – predating Harrod's of London by a full 15 years. Aside from admiring the original wooden staircase, polished balustrades and creaking escalator, this is a good place to load up with some decent local spoils – there's an impressive range of Irish crystal, linens and giftware.

AUSTIN'S DEPARTMENT STORE: The Diamond BT48 6HR; ☎ 028 7126 1817; www.austinsstore.com. Entry: open Mon–Wed 9.30am–5.30pm, Thu/Fri 9.30am–9pm, Sat 9.30am–6pm, Sun 1pm–5pm.

The best... **PLACES TO STAY**

HOTEL

Everglades

Prehen Road, Derry BT47 2NH
☎ **028 7132 1066**
www.hastingshotels.com/everglades

On the banks of the River Foyle, the four star Everglades comes complete with superb views across Derry City to the Donegal Hills. It has recently undergone an extensive refurbishment so expect every convenience – plasma telly, DVD, bathrooms you could get lost in.

Price: from £60/£90 for single/double.

Tower Hotel

Butcher Street, Derry BT48 6HL
☎ **028 713 71234**
www.towerhotelderry.com
email: reservations@thd.ie

The four-star Tower is the only hotel within Derry's walls, occupying a central location just off the Diamond. The stylish hostelry has been in business since 2003 and has already won an AA Rosette and RAC dining award for its bistro restaurant. It's a popular meeting place for Derry's literati and indeed glitterati.

Price: B&B from £70 to £110 for a double.

City Hotel

Queens Quay, Derry BT48 7AS
☎ **028 7136 5800; www.cityhotel.com**
email: reservations@cityhotelderry.com

A four-star hotel in the heart of the city with magnificent views over the River Foyle. The City Hotel offers full leisure facilities – including a health and fitness club with 15m swimming pool, jacuzzi, steam room, sauna, dance studio, gymnasium. Oh, and loads of fluffy towels (pronounced taarls).

Price: B&B from £99 for a double.

Beech Hill Country House Hotel

32 Ardmore Road, Derry BT47 3QP
☎ **028 7134 9279; www.beech-hill.com/**

An elegant rural manor house 2 miles outside the Walls of Derry. A tranquil atmosphere, luxurious accommodation and excellent four-star dining are all guaranteed.

Price: B&B from £120 for a double.

B&B

Merchant's House

16 Queen Street, Derry
☎ **028 7126 9691; www.thesaddlestore.com**

Generally regarded as one of the top B&Bs in Ireland, this historic Georgian building is about as far away from the old seaside B&Bs of yesteryear as you can get. Elegant antique furniture instead of George & Mildred cupboards, marble fireplaces in place of single-bar electric fires – and gargantuan breakfasts.

Price: from £35 per person.

SELF-CATERING

Derry Farm Cottages

74 Gortree Road, Drumahoe BT47 3LL
☎ **028 7130 1214**
www.derryfarmcottages.com

These luxury five-star cottages make an ideal base for both Derry City and the nearby Sperrin Mountains. All of the cottages feature stylish interiors and quality facilities (Managhmore cottage is equipped with Wi-Fi, VOIP and Sky.)

Price: from £450 to £575 for a week.

The best... FOOD AND DRINK

▶ Staying in

A Derry institution, the **Leprechaun** (23 Strand Road, Derry; ☎ 028 7136 3606) is just about the best deli-bakery-takeaway in the north-west. Whether it's soda farls or butter shortbread you're after, or just lasagne and chips, this is the place. Oh, and you'll also get a proper cup of tea here. Delicatessen products (from olives to colcannon) are displayed on huge wooden tables.

The **Sandwich Co.** (61 Strand Road, Derry; ☎ 028 7137 2500) serves its eponymous product on white bread, brown bread, soda bread, baguette, panini, ciabatta. The salads are tasty and imaginative, and the takeaway soup just the thing to warm you up on an invigorating Derry day. The **Boston Tea Party** (15 Craft Village, Derry) serves the best desserts in town. The Italian puds are delicious, as is the homemade apple pie. Takeaway soups, freshly baked cakes and a friendly service are assured.

♨ Drinking

The **Strand Road**, Derry City, is a major meeting place for the young people of the North-West of a weekend, and as such boasts some of the trendiest bars in town – the **Ice Wharf** (22–24 Strand Road, Derry; ☎ 028 7032 5820), the **Carraig Bar & Lava Lounge** (113–121 Strand Road), and the **Clarendon** (48 Strand Road), all feature the likes of plasma screens, music videos and late opening.

The **Townsman Bar** (33 Shipquay Street, Derry; ☎ 028 7126 0820) right in the centre of the city occupies the basement of a Georgian townhouse built back in 1741. It's old, comfortable and atmospheric, and boasts a fine top shelf of Irish whiskies.

The oldest pub in Derry City, the **River Inn Bar & Cellars** (36–38 Shipquay Street; ☎ 028 7137 1965) incorporates part of the City Walls in its structure. This ancient, nicotine-stained watering hole is just the place for some serious quaffing, and some not-so-serious conversation and craic.

McGilloways Seafood Wine Bar (145 Strand Road, Derry; ☎ 028 7126 2050) is as good as its word – a fine selection of booze, an expansive menu of bivalves and crustaceans. Friendly service is included in the price – cordiality and courteousness thrive in Derry; it's still possible to have an existential conversation with your barman here. Further up the coast **Bertha's Bar** (6 Sea Road, Castlerock BT51 4RE; ☎ 028 7084 8209) is a gem of a pub in a county studded with them. Order up a Guinness and listen to the Atlantic rollers crash on the beach outside.

EATING OUT

RESTAURANT

Best Western White Horse Hotel
68 Clooney Road, Derry BT47 3PA
☎ **028 7186 1438**
www.whitehorsehotel.biz

This award winning restaurant, featuring rustic Irish fare, has been a favourite with Derry's guzzlers and gourmets for decades. Comfortable surroundings and emphasis on the traditional – Guinness, oysters, bacon – will transport you back to a time when days had more hours. Prices are moderate – main courses cost around £10, and you will get an excellent bottle of wine for around £15.

Brown's Bar & Brasserie
1 Bond's Hill, Waterside, Derry BT14 6DW
☎ **028 7134 5180**
www.brownsrestaurant.com

Chef Ivan Brown has made this marinated-sea bass-with-chilli-chick-peas-and-tarragon restaurant a Derry essential-visit with his imaginative, ever-changing menu and comprehensive wine list. Cooking with flair, plus affability and ambience – everything you might desire, and expect, in a Derry eatery. Main courses cost from £12.

Fitzroy's Restaurant
2–4 Bridge Street, 3 Carlisle Road BT48 6JL
☎ **028 71266211**
www.fitzroysrestaurant.com

Everything from fish and chips to Moroccan kebabs – eclecticism isn't always a good thing in a menu, but here it works. Baked cod with leek risotto is particularly fine. It's cheap too – for under £8 you can eat like a king.

GASTRO PUB

The Linen Hall Bar
3–5 Market Street, Derry
☎ **028 7137 1665**

Facing the old Walls of Derry, this is one of the great restaurants in the Six Counties, with equally famous pub attached. Danny and Anne McIlvar pride themselves on their team of chefs who can produce everything from the most tempting amuse-bouches to straightforward, hefty steaks. Prices run from around £8 for main courses.

Mange 2
2 Clarendon Street BT48 7ES
☎ **028 7136 1222**
www.mange2derry.com

This family-owned restaurant in a Georgian-style dining room specialises in French fusion fare fashioned from local produce – sea bass from the Atlantic (conveniently located nearby), salmon from Lough Neagh, mussels from Strangford Lough. For afters, Mange 2 does crepes that will curl your toes. Expect to pay something over £18 for a couple of courses without wine.

CAFÉ

Café Calm
4 Shipquay Place, Derry BT48 6DH
☎ **028 7126 8228**

With a reputation as one of the most cosmopolitan coffee house in Derry, the place is full of locals, travellers and Donegal and Derry bohemians. But with a menu that should bring your snack in at under a fiver, there won't be many ladies-who-lunch about. From lattes to bagels, the friendly atmosphere makes this a very welcome pit stop amid the bustle of the city. Coffees from £1.50, sandwiches from £3.

ℹ Visitor Information

Tourist information centre: Tourist Information Centre, 44 Foyle Street, ☎ 028 7126 7284, www.derryvisitor.com.

Hospital: Altnagelvin Area Hospital, ☎ 028 7134 5171.

Doctors: Abbey Medical Practice, Abbey Street, Derry, County Derry BT48 9DN, ☎ 028 7136 4016; Quayside Medical Practice 82–84, Strand Road, Derry BT48 7NN, ☎ 028 7126 2790.

Pharmacies: Rathmore Pharmacy Unit 6/7, Rathmore Centre, Blighs Lane, Derry, County Derry BT48 0LZ, ☎ 028 7126 2195; Alliance Pharmacy, 47 Great James Street, Derry BT48 7DF, ☎ 028 7126 7399.

Police: 104–108 Spencer Road, Derry, ☎ 028 7136 7337.

Supermarkets: All the main Irish and British supermarkets can be accessed at the Foyleside Shopping Centre, Orchard Street, Derry, ☎ 028 7137 7575; Richmond Shopping Centre, Shipquay Street, Derry ☎ 028 7126 0525; Marks & Spencer, Dunne etc.; Tesco is at the Quayside Shopping Centre, Derry.

Parking: Foyleside Multi-Storey (1,620 spaces); Foyle Road (88 spaces); Quayside Multi-Storey (500 spaces).

Cash points: Nationwide Building Society, 11 Ferryquay Street, Derry BT48 6JN, ☎ 028 7185 0100; Bank Of Ireland, 12 Shipquay Street, Derry BT48 6DN, ☎ 028 7126 4992.

Internet access: Central Library, Foyle Street, Derry, ☎ 028 7127 2300.

Taxis: Derry Taxis ☎ 028 7126 0247; Delta Cabs ☎ 028 7127 9999.

MID AND NORTH DERRY

There was music there, in the Derry air
Spoke a language that we could all understand...

So wrote Derry man Phil Coulter, the very same Phil Coulter who co-wrote the Eurovision winner 'Puppet on a String' and Eurovision runner-up 'Congratulations', made famous by Cliff Richard. Indeed, music is a leitmotif of County Derry, whether it's 'Danny Boy', the most famous Irish song of all – written in **Limavady** – or 'Red Sails in the sunset' written by local resident Jimmy Kennedy. The area stretches from **Portstewart** – just by the probable site of Ireland's first inhabitants who landed some 9,000 years ago – along the banks of Northern Ireland's main river the Bann, eventually reaching the shores of the biggest lake in these islands, Lough Neagh.

This northerly part of the island also encapsulates one of the central paradoxes of the Six Counties – how two sets of people can be so murderously antagonistic to each other, yet so friendly to outsiders (no matter where they hail from). This generous assumption of goodwill towards strangers – very rare in the world of today – does not extend to your neighbour if he disagrees with you on matters such as Transubstantiation. It's a conundrum, right enough. In one church a quotation from Hebrews is emblazoned on the wall: 'Be not forgetful to entertain strangers: for thereby some have entertained angels unawares'. The Derry people have taken this message to heart, and are unfailingly friendly to strangers. Not sure about the neighbours, however.

WHAT TO SEE AND DO

Portstewart
The seaside resort of Portstewart is a welcome, nostalgic throwback to the genteel British seaside resorts of the 1950s. Not a lot has changed here over the years – indeed you might imagine that not much has changed since the novelist Charles Lever, who lived in the Main Street, entertained William Makepeace Thackeray here. The English writer was much impressed by the town, particularly its 'air of comfort and neatness' and its surroundings, although he did detect some traces of 'sanctimoniousness and sabbatarianism'.

Just outside the town, **Black Castle**, perched on a rocky outcrop overlooking the bay, gives views towards Inishowen Peninsula – and they're little short of mesmerising. Many poetic minds have admired this northerly vista. Songwriter Jimmy Kennedy from **Omagh**, was enchanted by this coastline. He was brought up in Portstewart, and one day in nearby **Portrush** he watched a boat putting out to sea heading for the **Inishowen Peninsula**. He wrote:

Portstewart Harbour

Red sails in the sunset way out on the sea,
Carry my loved one home safely to me.

In America when this song is performed, people assume it is set on some sun-swept beach in Hawaii; in Britain it's assumed to be about the Mediterranean. But no, 'Red Sails in the Sunset' is all about the **Derry** coastline. The boat in question was called *The Kitty of Coleraine*, named after another local song – which gives the story something of a pleasing symmetry. *The Kitty* is still said to be moored in **Portstewart Harbour**, although it now seems no one can remember which boat it is. However, anecdotal history indicates that the sails were in fact white, with the sunset turning them red. And indeed there is something almost iridescent about sunsets here. Walk through the streets of Portstewart just as the sun goes down and you'll be convinced somebody has turned on a giant floodlight to fill the streets with red light.

Despite its connections with music, it is the fantastic beach that's the main attraction – and has been for the thick end of 9,000 years. This was once home to Neolithic and Iron Age people (the first settlers to Ireland landed not far away at Mount Sandel). Flints, arrowheads and pottery shards have been excavated from beneath the sandhills – but so far no Neolithic buckets and spades.

The centre of Portstewart is resolutely Victorian, the main streets forming an Atlantic promenade winding round rocky bays. The impressive promenade has upper and lower walks, and at the westerly end St Mary's Dominican Convent, formerly O'Hara's Castle, gazes down on proceedings. The strand, looked after by the National Trust, leads to a winding cliff path linking Portstewart with its neighbour Portrush. The **Port Path**, a 3-mile coastal walk, is dotted with interpretive displays highlighting the natural history of the area. The path passes an ancient holy well, **Tubber Patrick**, where St Patrick reputedly stopped for refreshment. The architecture of Portstewart is Victorian, but it is somehow uniquely Irish, with castles, convents and holy wells part of the townscape.

The **Royal Portstewart Golf Club** (Strand Road, Portstewart; ☎ 028 7083 2015) is a venerable institution, founded in 1894. Its 36 devilishly tricky holes, even by Irish standards, are at the mercy of the elements. The Royal Portstewart consists of three courses – the Strand, the Riverside and the Old Course, all of which are truly world-class from a playing point of view, never mind the views. Still, even if your game is suffering from the vagaries of the weather the scenery is more than likely to offer compensations. And don't forget, for the ultimate compensation, **Bushmills Distillery** is just down the road.

CELEBRITY CONNECTIONS

Henry McCullough, guitarist, was born in Portstewart. He was Ireland's only representative at Woodstock, having been in Joe Cocker's band at the time.

Like Van Morrison and Rory Gallagher (another Ulsterman, from Ballyshannon in Donegal, 4 miles across the border), Henry started out in the music business by playing in a showband in the early 1960s – these were basically cabaret bands, excellent musicians who could turn their talents to anything from crooning to ceili, and concentrated on playing the hits of American and British artists.

Henry McCullough graduated from an Enniskillen band through the ranks of British rock, ending up in Paul McCartney's group Wings. His guitar solo on My Love is regarded by many as one of rock music's greatest solos, and his spoken words 'I don't know; I was really drunk at the time' can be heard on Pink Floyd's album *The Dark Side of the Moon*, at the end of the song 'Money'. Today the guitarist's music is bluesy, with country and Irish folk influences. McCullough has returned to live just outside Portstewart, and gigs regularly in Ireland and Scotland. His latest album is a collaboration with his old friend Eamon Carr, the former Horslips drummer and current rock critic with the *Evening Herald* in Dublin.

McCullough lives in a cottage in the countryside between Portrush and Ballymoney where he tends his chickens with his partner Josie.

Mount Sandel

On a high bluff overlooking the River Bann, the remains of a small collection of huts provide evidence of the first people who lived in what is now Ireland. The area is named after a fort, believed by some to be **Kill Santain** or **Kilsandel**, famous in Irish history as the residence of the marauding Norman king John de Courcy in the 12th century AD. But the small archaeological site east of the remains of the fort is of far greater importance to the prehistory of western Europe.

The Mesolithic site at Mount Sandel, excavated largely during the 1970s, bears evidence of human habitation here from around 7000BC, the earliest evidence of *Homo sapiens* in Ireland. Artefacts found at the site include flint axes, needles, and pick-like tools. But technology must have moved on apace. The immediate antecedents of these people built the great megalithic graves found in every one of Ireland's Counties, and most spectacularly at **Newgrange** in County Meath (a UNESCO World Heritage Site) and **Knowth**, also in County Meath. These were built by people who would have regarded the pyramids (about 4,000 years old) as new-fangled foreign contraptions.

Mountsandel Wood

Located on the Mountsandel Road Coleraine. Visitors approaching Coleraine, from Belfast, on the A26 should take first exit left off the roundabout at Wattstown Business Park onto Knocklynn Road. At the top of Knocklynn Road turn right and the entrance to Mountsandel Wood (with parking) is signposted off to the left.

Limavady

One essential port-of-call in Mid Derry is Limavady (*Léim an Mahadaidh*, or The Dog's Leap), a small town beautifully set in the **Glenroe Valley**. Surrounded by mountainous horizons, notably Binevenagh rising some 1260ft above Lough Foyle, the town is associated with the Thackeray poem 'Peg of Limavady'.

Fishing in the Roe Valley Country Park

Danny boy

'Danny boy' beautifully sums up the many ambiguities of Irish music. A collaboration between Miss Jane Ross, a piano teacher and a Protestant, and an itinerant fiddler whose name we can't be sure of, probably a Catholic, somehow resulted in one of the world's great folk melodies. This unlikely pair combined in 1851 in a project to preserve – or create, we can't be sure – one of the best known melodies in the world, the 'Londonderry air', more commonly known as 'Danny boy'.

Miss Ross reportedly jotted the air down from the fiddler, but whether she made up some of the tune is also not known. Her classical training would certainly account for some of the more un-traditional aspects of the melody line. No other collector of folk tunes encountered the melody as we now know it, and all known examples are descended from Miss Ross's version, which certainly seems to suggest that Limavady was the birthplace of at least some of the tune.

The lyrics are similarly puzzling – it should be sung by a woman, but it's invariably performed by a man. The fact that the most famous words – Danny boy – were written by an English lawyer who never set foot in Ireland only adds to the anomaly. Aside from Irish artists, 'Danny boy' has been recorded by Elvis, Bing Crosby, Jim Reeves, Sam Cooke, Connie Francis, Cher, Kiri Te Kanawa, Johnny Cash, Tom Jones, Roy Orbison and Willie Nelson to name only a very few.

> *Oh Danny boy the pipes, the pipes are calling,*
> *From glen to glen and down the mountain side;*
> *The summer's gone, and all the roses falling,*
> *'Tis you, 'tis you must go, and I must bide.*
> *But come ye back when summer's in the meadow,*
> *Or when the valley's hushed,*
> *and white with snow.*
> *'Tis I'll be there in sunshine or in shadow –*
> *Oh, Danny boy, oh Danny boy, I love you so.*
> *And when you come and all the flowers are dying,*
> *If I am dead, as dead I well may be,*
> *You'll come and find the place where I am lying,*
> *And kneel and say an Ave there for me;*
> *And I shall hear, though soft you tread above me,*
> *And all my grave will warmer, sweeter be.*
> *For you will kneel, and tell me that you love me,*
> *And I shall sleep in peace, until you come to me.*

However, it is the presence of Miss Jane Ross's house – she's buried in the Church of Ireland cemetery in the centre of the town – which makes this a de rigeur destination. Because Miss Ross, a piano teacher, along with a blind fiddler combined together in a project to preserve one of the best known melodies in the world – the 'Londonderry air', more commonly known as 'Danny boy'.

The **Roe Valley Country Park**, on the outskirts of Limavady, is a haven of riverside and woodland walks. The **River Roe** flows through the park – salmon and trout angling is a favourite pastime here. Picturesque **Largy Bridge** is the very location where the legendary 'leap of the dog' took place, thus bestowing on Limavady its name.

The **Dogleap Centre** is the main information centre in the country park, and contains the Countryside Museum and the Dogleap Centre itself, where the story of the valley is told. The Centre also contains a café and an audio-visual theatre. For the disabled visitor there is a specially designed trail emphasising the wildlife of the park. This includes an audio guide for blind and partially sighted visitors. There is also a disabled anglers' jetty by the river.

The Countryside Centre includes a museum with 19th century artefacts, with many historical monuments related to the 18th century linen industry. The park acts as a living history of Limavady – you can see where local genius J E Ritter began supplying the first direct current of electricity in Ulster. Remains of the once vibrant linen industry are also scattered about the estate.

> **ROE VALLEY COUNTRY PARK:** 41 Dogleap Road, Limavady BT49 9NN; ☎ 028 7772 2074; www.eshni.gov.uk Entry: open Oct to Apr, Mon–Sun 10am–5pm; May to Sep, Mon–Sun 10am–6pm.

Wet weather

The Green Lane Museum

The Green Lane Museum (☎ 028 7776 0304), situated within the Roe Valley Country Park, is an exhibition largely focused on the linen and agricultural industries of the locality. Rural heritage displays and craft demonstrations take place each Saturday during July and August.

The Green Lane Museum

The Garvagh Museum

The Duke of Wellington, aka Arthur Wellesley, is the only Irish-born prime minister Britain has ever had. But a few have had Irish roots – including Tony Blair, whose mother's family was from Donegal. Garvagh Museum (142a Main Street, Garvagh BT51 5AE; ☎ 028 2955 7924; www.garvaghmuseum.com) largely deals with another member of that select band – George Canning. The rural folk museum is situated in the **Bann Valley**, in the walled garden of Garvagh House, the former seat of the Canning family. George himself was the shortest-serving prime minister in British history, putting in a few months between April and August 1827.

The walled garden of the house has historic connections with Denis Hempson, the great blind harpist who lived in three centuries, being born in 1695 and dying in 1807. His legacy to Irish traditional music is incalculable. George Canning, a Dr Bacon and a Squire Gage (local gentry, apparently) purchased Hempson's first harp while he was resident in Garvagh. At the entrance to the museum a memorial to Hempson in the form of a granite pillar pays homage to the harpist. The museum has a collection that comprises almost 2,000 artefacts tracing the history of the Bann Valley from 3000BC through to the first half of the 20th century.

By the way, don't miss Garvagh's Pyramid. Erected by Lord Garvagh after having been on the Grand Tour of Egypt, this small pyramid is located on high ground in a bluebell wood, west of the car park at **Ballinameen Bridge**, at the south end of Garvagh. Intended as the burial vault for Lord Garvagh, it was never used. Now situated within **Garvagh Forest** on an elevated site, it is a strange edifice in a very peaceful setting. In the spring the hill is covered by bluebells.

What to do with children

The **Roe Valley Leisure Centre** (9 Greystone Road, Limavady BT49 0ND; ☎ 028 7776 4009; www.rvlc.co.uk) features a 25m indoor pool, children's splash pool, squash and badminton courts. The centre also features 'Hideaway Hall', an indoor adventure play area for children, featuring soft play equipment and ball playing areas.

Entertainment

In Portstewart, the liveliest of the traditional pubs, the **Anchor Bar & Skippers** (87–89 The Promenade; ☎ 028 7083 2003) draws a crowd ranging from students at nearby University of Ulster to bikers sussing out the area's motorcycle heritage. DJs man the decks until 1am. The **Roe Valley Folk Festival** takes place on Halloween weekend. Ceilis, concerts, storytelling, traditional sessions – as well as a chance for the children to learn an instrument or take up Irish dancing (☎ 028 777 40107; www.roevalleyfolkfestival. com). Portstewart holds a **Red Sails Festival** every July (www.redsails.co.uk). This is primarily a family event featuring everything form sandcastle-building competitions to folk music – and of course several renditions of Red Sails in the Sunset.

For motorcycling fans, the **North West 200** race (www.northwest200.org) is run on a road circuit taking in Portrush, Portstewart and Coleraine in May. Unlike Britain, on-road racing is allowed weekends in Northern Ireland. This classic race is attended by motorcycle enthusiasts from all over Europe and beyond. If you aren't one of them, you might just be better giving the area a miss that weekend, as every hotel, B&B and caravan site will be full of the biking hordes.

The **Danny Boy Festival** (www.limavady.gov.uk/visiting/danny-boy-festival) in Limavady takes place over the first May bank holiday. All types of music, not just 'Danny

The North West 200 race

boy' is on offer, as well as sport, entertainment and displays of rural crafts and tradition. For traditional sessions on various nights of the week (depending on time of year), the **Thatch Bar** (Catherine Street, Limavady; ☎ 028 7776 4876); **Flo's Bar** (Limavady; ☎ 028 7772 2746) and the **Alexander Arms Hotel** (☎ 028 7776 3443) Limavady are all rated as places where you can expect a good standard of music. More than likely you'll hear the towering ballad which is the national anthem of the area. No, not 'Danny boy' – but a poignantly beautiful love song, the 'Gem of the roe'.

🛏 *The best...* PLACES TO STAY

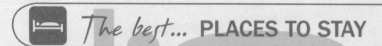

BOUTIQUE

Laurel Villa Townhouse

60 Church Street, Magherafelt, County Derry BT45 6AW; ☎ 028 7930 1459
www.laurel-villa.com

Seamus Heaney was born 3 miles from Laurel Villa and Blue Badge guide Eugene Kielt offers tours around the local area related to the Irish poet – these cost from £45 and include visiting places associated with the poet's life and works. Poetry readings from local Ulster writers are also held here and the five bedrooms are named after different Ulster poets. Breakfast is a full Irish.

Price: From £40/£70 for single/double.

HOTEL

Radisson Roe Park Hotel 🛗 🍴

Roe Park, Limavady BT49 9LB
☎ 028 7772 2222
www.radissonroepark.com

The North Coast's only four-star hotel until you get to Derry, is set on a historic 155-acre country estate. The complex includes an 18-hole parkland golf course, interactive golf academy, driving range and practice greens. The Fairways Leisure Club has an indoor heated swimming pool. This hotel is an ideal place for a golfing enthusiast.

Price: B&B from £60 for a double.

The best... **PLACES TO STAY**

Gort na Drum House

23 Gortnaghey Road, Dungiven BT47 4PY
☎ 028 7774 1289
www.gortnadrumhouse.com

Situated on the banks of the River Roe in the heart of the Sperrins, this is a truly rural retreat with first-class restaurant, so you don't need to stray too far from your base.

Price: from £75 for a double.

Raspberry Hill Health Farm

29 Bonds Glen Road, Killaloo, County Derry BT47 3ST; ☎ 028 7139 8000
www.raspberry-hill.co.uk

Facilities at Raspberry Hill include a hot tub, sauna, steam room and therapeutic spa bath. Sessions on weight loss, stress relief and fitness are run, and various massage treatments are available. A day at the spa costs £75. Guests can stay in one of seven bedrooms.

Price: from £115/£230 for single/double.

INN

Brown Trout Golf & Country Inn

209 Agivey Road, Aghadowey, Coleraine BT51 4AD; ☎ 028 7086 8209
www.browntroutinn.com

Owned and run by the O'Hara family for four generations, this old inn is now one of Northern Ireland's few golf hotels. Angling packages and pony trekking breaks can also be organised in the spellbinding surroundings.

Price: B&B from £40 per person.

B&B

Greenhill House

24 Greenhill Road, Aghadowey, Coleraine, County Derry BT514EU; ☎ 028 7086 8241
www.greenhill-house.co.uk

This Georgian house boasts views of the Sperrins. On arrival guests are greeted with a very civilised cup of tea and homemade cakes before being shown to one of the six bedrooms. Breakfast can be a traditional Ulster fry-up, smoked salmon or kippers.

Price: £40 for a single; £60 for a double.

Maddybenny Farm House

Loguestown Road, Portrush, Coleraine, County Antrim BT52 2PT; ☎ 028 7082 3394
www.maddybenny.com

This period farmhouse has four bedrooms, each with an en suite, and there is a BHS-approved riding school on site. There is a snooker room in the house, and breakfast includes an Ulster fry up.

Price: From £47 for a single; from £65 for a double.

SELF-CATERING

Drumcovitt Barn

704 Feeny Road, Limavady
☎ 028 7778 1224
www.drumcovitt.com

These quiet rural luxury cottages are an ideal place for unwinding. Four-star accommodation, complete with log fires, stunning views and a peaceful atmosphere. Guests can wander in the garden, explore the farm lanes and make use of the timber trail.

Price: from £360 in high season.

The best... FOOD AND DRINK

▶ Staying in

Culdrum Organic Farm (31 Ballytinagh Road, Aghadowey, Coleraine; ☎ 028 7086 8991; www.culdrum.co.uk) produces and rears everything organically – from parsnips to saddleback pork. Real chickens lay real eggs, and you can see your vegetables growing in the fields before you buy 'em. For the best sausages, head for **O'Kane Meats** (69 Main Street, Claudy; ☎ 028 7133 8944; www.okanemeats.com) who have won the prize for best sausage-making in Northern Ireland on several occasions. You can buy cooked meats here too – try a rack of local lamb. **Norman Hunter & Son** (53–55 Main Street, Limavady; ☎ 028 7776 2665) is quite simply one of the best butchers in these islands. Mind you the family have been in the business for some 165 years. All the meat is aged on the bone, and sourced locally. For organic fowl, head for **Keady Mountain Fowl** (Limavady; ☎ 028 7776 4157). Specialities include duck, geese, fresh eggs from the farm.

Hunter's Bakery (5–9 Market Street, Limavady; ☎ 028 7772 2411) is a member of the Artisan Bakers' Guild of Northern Ireland – so it specialises in the traditional bakery of the area, and that means wheaten bread, soda bread, potato farls. A bewildering array of cakes and pastries will have you dicing with obesity.

JE Toms & Sons (46 The Promenade, Portstewart; ☎ 028 7083 2869) is the place for fine pies, barbecue-prepared meats (roast 'em up on the beach!) and tasty sausages.

On the second Sunday of every month the **Causeway Speciality Market**, The Diamond, Coleraine, features the very best of local organic produce from County Derry, County Antrim and County Down – from farmhouse jam from Ballywalter to sheep milk cheese from the farmland round Claudy.

▶ Drinking

- **Brook's** – in Coleraine (21 Park Street), ☎ 028 7034 2550; lively town centre bar with friendly atmosphere and good bar snacks. Family-run by Dermot and Mary Guy, the pub is child-friendly.
- **Cooley's** – Seacoast Road, Limavady BT49 0LG; ☎ 028 7775 0265; has a wonderful old world atmosphere with large open fire and comfortable old furnishings.
- The **Glen Bar** – 639–643 Baranailt Road, Claudy BT47 4EA; ☎ 028 7133 7011; the bar has been in business for some 50 years so they know how to pull a pint of Guinness there.
- The **Arbutus** – tucked away in Kilrea, 13 Bridge Street; ☎ 028 2954 0140; a fine old pub as well as a terrific restaurant. Clientele includes anglers from the nearby Bann River – as well as locals waiting to dine upstairs in the award-winning restaurant.

EATING OUT

RESTAURANT

Macduff's Restaurant
Blackheath House, 112 Killeague Road, Blackhill, Coleraine
☎ **028 6586 8433**

Originally a Georgian rectory, the restaurant is situated in the cellar of the house. The chef/proprietor combines the best of country house cooking with today's lighter influences. Specialities include local game and the traditional Ulster dessert, Carrageen Moss.

The Cromore Halt
158 Station Road, Portstewart
☎ **028 7083 1919**
www.cromore.com

A centrally located, friendly restaurant selling good standard fare. Fish and cod are just the thing to warm you up after an invigorating walk along the strand. Inexpensive.

Rafters Restaurant
2–4 Kilrea Road, Swatragh BT46 5QF
☎ **028 7940 1206**

Rafters draws customers from all over the locality, not just for its famed pints of Guinness, but its Mediterranean cuisine with a Derry twist. King prawns fresh from the Atlantic are wrapped in filo pastry and served with delicate sauces; trout from nearby Lough Neagh is served with carefully crafted risottos. Main courses begin at £9.

GASTRO PUB

The Salmon Leap
Castleroe Road, Coleraine BT51 3RP
☎ **028 7034 2992**

The Salmon Leap on the River Bann is one of the oldest and most charming inns in the whole of the Six Counties. Home of the legendary Kitty of Coleraine (subject of equally legendary song), the Salmon Leap specialises in local produce, with of course the eponymous salmon taking the starring role. The extensive wine list has been assembled with knowledge and care. Fresh salmon and trimmings cost from £15.

The Lime Tree
60 Catherine Street, Limavady BT49 9DB
☎ **028 7776 4300**
www.limetreerest.com

Husband and wife team Stanley and Maria Matthews are well into their second decade of running this innovative restaurant. Stanley does the cooking, and takes delight in producing an imaginative, varied menu. The cuisine has a Mediterranean influence – although the produce is firmly local. Main courses cost from £14.95.

The Water Margin
The Boathouse, Hanover Place, Coleraine BT52 1EB; ☎ **028 7034 2222**

A bustling, buzzy eating place with everything to please the conservative Coleraine palate as well as plenty of zesty dishes for those who like something a bit more imaginative. Set supper, four courses £13.95; main courses from £10 to £15.

TAKEAWAY

McNulty's Fish and Chips
84 Main Street, Limavady
☎ **028 7776 2148**

Mr McNulty uses fish from the nearby stretch of water called the Atlantic and potatoes from, well, funnily enough, the Fens in England. Mr McNulty believes the Fen spud is more suited to the pure vegetable oil he uses for cooking.

ⓘ Visitor Information

Tourist information centre: 44 Foyle Street, ☎ 028 7126 7284, www.derryvisitor.com.

Hospital: Altnagelvin Area Hospital, ☎ 028 7134 5171.

Doctors: Portstewart Family Practice, 6 Lever Road, Portstewart, County Derry BT55 7EF, ☎ 028 7083 2149; Drs Carlin, O'Loan & Boston, Portstewart Medical Centre, 32 Mill Road, Portstewart BT55 7SW, ☎ 028 7083 2600.

Pharmacies: Paul McElhone, 22a The Promenade, Portstewart, County Derry BT55 7AD, ☎ 028 7083 2014; Alliance Pharmacy, 83 The Promenade, Portstewart BT55 7AG, ☎ 028 7083 2646.

Police: 104–108 Spencer Road, Derry, ☎ 028 7136 7337.

Cash points: Ulster Bank, 52 The Promenade, Portstewart BT55 7AE, ☎ 028 7083 2094; Northern Bank, 28 The Promenade, Portstewart BT55 7AE, ☎ 0845 6026553.

Taxis: Fab Cabs, 10 Carrickbeg Avenue, Portstewart BT55 7NX, ☎ 028 7083 5252; Portstewart Taxis, 54 Agherton Drive, Portstewart BT55 7JQ, ☎ 028 7083 3149.

SOUTH DERRY

South Derry is a gentle, rural land, boasting the landscape that inspired Seamus Heaney to write his poetry, and Mrs Cecil Alexander to write the song 'There is a green hill far away'. The landscape is the inspiration of that most beautiful of Irish songs, Slieve Gallion Braes, a poignant lament for times lost. Famine, forced emigration and poverty all took their toll:

As I was a-walking one morning in May
To view yon fair valleys and flowers gay
I was thinking on these flowers all going to decay
That grow around your bonnie, bonnie, Slieve Gallion Braes.

But it's not just song and verse that has emanated from this lovely land. More prosaically, the stockade style of US forts and the pet name for the Conservative Party come from Derry, and, to get back to music momentarily, it is home to some of the finest flute, accordion and pipe bands in the country.

The Sperrins Region, a gently contoured range of mountains straddling the border of Counties Tyrone and Derry, is an Area of Outstanding Natural Beauty, where the hedgerows are bright in spring and summer with the yellow gorse known locally as whin. But the area wears its importance lightly – the Sperrins' lack of major roads has left the area relatively untouched by tourism, indeed largely untouched by anyone. It provides myriad opportunities for walking, contemplating, hiking, chatting, cycling, pony-trekking and cycling. Nothing too challenging, mind. In fact the biggest challenge you'll have is keeping the smile off your face that you have such an area almost to yourself and your posse.

For those with a fascination for architectural heritage, the whole area breathes with the legacy of battles and struggles (from ancient to fairly recent), fortresses, castles and pre-Christian monuments. Like so much of Ulster, South Derry is proud, hard-working, mystical, poetic, contrary, battle-scarred – but its beauty is utterly mesmerising.

WHAT TO SEE AND DO

The Sperrins

There's no doubt that Killarney's Lakes and Fells are more famous, the Mountains of Mourne more lauded in song, and Macgillicuddy's Reeks in Kerry harder to spell – but the Sperrins in south County Derry have a charm all of their own. Easily enough climbed, **Mullaghclogher** (1896ft), and **Mullaghaneany** at 2070ft are both within the range of the averagely fit, with no great mountaineering expertise required. Your reward

Dungiven, the Sperrins

will be a panorama stretching from mid-Ulster to the hills of Donegal, from the shores of the Atlantic southwards to **Lough Neagh**. You won't be the first person to enjoy the view. Ireland's very first settlers landed somewhere near **Coleraine** (probably at **Mount Sandel, aka Mountsandel**) and made their way inland, following the mountain ridge of the Sperrins – some 9,000 years ago.

The area is archaeologically absorbing. One theory is that the first substantial human settlement in Ireland was in the townland of Crock, in the very south of the county. The area is verdantly beautiful, so it's no wonder they stayed. The loughs would have been full of fish, and the woodland full of alder, ash and hazel would have provided fuel, shelter and game. This is what is termed Neolithic affluence.

The Sperrins, or Sperrin Mountains, (from the Irish *Na Speiríní* meaning 'Spurs of Rock') are a range of hills making up one of the largest upland areas in Ireland. This expansive region has a population of only some 150,000, and is a designated Area of Outstanding Natural Beauty. Just to talk rocks for a moment, the Sperrins have a distinctive glaciated landscape which accounts for their rolling, undulating appearance. The **Glenshane Pass**, part of the A6 Belfast to Derry road, is in the mountains and has notoriously bad weather in winter.

Carntogher towers over the pass. Throughout the Sperrins many way-marked hiking trails and pathways pass through some of the most handsome – and emptiest – countryside in Ireland.

> **SPERRINS TOURISM:** The Sperrins Hillwalking Club, PO Box 45, Cookstown BT80 8YU; www.sperrinstourism.com; www.sperrins.co.uk; info@sperrins.co.uk.

Glenshane Forest

Glenshane Forest consists of just over 1,000 hectares of woodland lying to the west of Maghera, with several walking and cycling routes through the stands of spruce and pine. The forest area is made up of various conifer species but is mainly Sitka spruce due to the peaty upland soils. On the north edge is a large area of heather moorland. Here is the source of the **River Roe**, which flows down through the forest, through Limavady into Lough Foyle. Fishing in the River Roe is permitted within the forest limits. For licence details contact the Forest Service (www.forestserviceni.gov.uk/index/forests-in-northern-ireland). The river is important for salmon spawning during the winter months, as well as being home to a small population of otters – signs of their fish-feeding can be found all along the banks of the river; the trout fishing is also first class.

Glenshane Forest is a great spot for **birdwatching**. Buzzards can be seen in springtime displaying over the mature spruce trees in the valley, and in the springtime and early summer the sound of the cuckoo fills the woodland. Squabbling hooded crows fill the air with their chatter; while Ireland's smallest bird of prey, the merlin, patrols the woodland edges, reminding one of the Reverend William Inge's words: 'The whole of nature is a conjugation of the verb to eat, in the active and passive.' In the winter months, your only likely companions during heavy weather will be the regular, but shy, visitor to Ireland, the snow bunting. The moorland area is home to red grouse, wintering woodcock and snipe, with the call of the woodcock clearly audible to walkers on clear winter evenings.

GLENSHANE FOREST: Situated off the A6 Belfast to Londonderry road; around 8 miles from the Castledawson roundabout; parking at the lay-by beside the forest on the A6. Entry: free; open daily, 8.00am until sunset.

Bellaghy

Bellaghy has one of the best surviving examples of a Plantation Bawn, or fortified farmhouse. The massive circular tower and strong walls to protect the farm from disgruntled locals were built for the London Vintners' Company. After the Plantation the whole region west of Lough Neagh swarmed with 'kernes', or outlawed Irish swordsmen. Funnily enough it was about this time that the word 'Tory' entered the language. It derives from the Irish word *tóraidhe* meaning outlaw, or land thief. How it made the etymological step to becoming a name for the Conservative Party is unclear.

At the same time as the British were 'planting' Ulster and fighting off outlaws, America was similarly being colonised. Native Americans turned out to be as aggrieved as the Irish, and protection was soon needed. The US 'stockade style' owes a lot to the design of places such as Bellaghy Bawn.

Bellaghy Bawn, birthplace of the poet Seamus Heaney

Bellaghy Bawn was opened to the public in 1996 and features exhibitions on local natural history, the history of the Ulster Plantation and the poetry of local Nobel Laureate, Seamus Heaney. Although Celtic settlements would have been dotted round this area for millennia, Bellaghy was one of the first planned towns in Ireland. The village dates back to the 17th century, one of many areas settled and built under the authority of the Vintners Company of London. The company hoped to rename it 'Vintnerstown' but it didn't catch on and the English version of the original Irish name endured. In 1622, according to a manuscript of a Captain Thomas Ash, Bellaghy consisted of a church, a castle, a corn mill and 12 houses.

In the past there have been many disputes about Orange Order parades in the now mainly nationalist village. Recently all parades have been rerouted away from the main street. The parish is famous for its Gaelic football tradition, having won numerous titles.

BELLAGHY BAWN VISITOR CENTRE: Deer Park Road, Bellaghy, Magherafelt BT45 8LB; ☎ 028 7938 6812; www.ni-environment.gov.uk/bellaghy.htm.

Magherafelt

Magherafelt (from the Irish *Machaire Fiolta* meaning 'Plain of Fioghalta') is the biggest town in South Derry, with a population of just over 8,000. A plantation town built around a central diamond, its origins date back to 1425. Since then it's had a turbulent history, and during the recent Troubles, 11 people were killed in separate, desperate circumstances.

The town is described as 50/50 – half Protestant, half Catholic. The Protestant half of the town is responsible for some of the best known marching bands in the country, or possibly any other country. Dunamoney Loyalist Flute Band, formed in 1930, is rated as one of the very finest. Other bands include the Ballymoughan Purple Guards, Aughagaskin Flute Band and Magherafelt Pipe Band. The bands perform in public largely during the Marching Season, May to October, but with a crescendo in July; public performances are given at other times of the year – look in the local press for details, particularly the *Londonderry Sentinel* and the *Belfast Newsletter*.

Maghera

Maghera, with a population of just under 3,000, is about 75% Catholic. The Slaughtneil/Carntogher area around the town is unique for being the only rural community in Ireland outside the native Irish-speaking Gaeltacht where the majority of primary school children are educated through the Irish language.

The town of Maghera grew up around **St Lurach's Church**, founded in the year AD500, originally as a monastery. The town was a bishop's seat in the 12th and 13th centuries. However the church was allowed to fall into disrepair and is now a roofless ruin, but nonetheless very photogenic – especially with the Sperrins as a background. Within the ruins, as an insert to the west wall, is a sculpture of the crucifixion thought to date from the 10th century – making it one of the oldest in Ireland. St Lurach, unsurprisingly in the way of these things, is patron saint of the town.

Dungiven

Dungiven, located on the main road between Derry and Belfast, lies at the foot of Ben Bradagh, with the Sperrins rising to the south. Dungiven's castle, dating from 1839, was built by the Skinners Company of London. The ruined Augustinian priory of St Mary's, on a cliff above the River Roe, preserves the tomb of Cooey na Gall O'Cahan who died in 1385 – just about the finest medieval tomb in Ulster. It can be seen on the south wall of the chancel, and features an effigy clad in Irish armour, plus six mourning 'keeners' or weeping mourners.

The tune of 'Danny Boy' is thought to have originally belonged to the O'Cahan clan – legend has it that it was played at Cooey's wake. Nobody really knows for sure, but it would be fair to say that musicologists date the melody of 'Danny Boy' much later. Never mind them – as you stare at the grave, and as the wind howls off the Sperrins, you may find yourself humming the tune. Nearby, a thicket of thorn bushes hung with rags (votive offerings), conceals a bullaun stone, visited for wart cures.

Local legends: Ballaun stones

Ballaun stones are boulders usually about the height of post boxes, with one or more hemispherical depressions at the top. These are of uncertain significance. As they almost always occur near religious sites – in every county of Ireland – they evidently have some social significance. It is believed oaths, betrothals, and initiation ceremonies were carried on here. Healing also seems to have been part of their raison d'être. But the reason for their existence could simply have been to act as a useful communal site for a mortar and pestle. Or perhaps a mixture of all three – basically a one-stop shop for spiritual, medical and culinary requirements.

🌂 Wet weather

Draperstown is still a lively place on market days. A small linen museum at Upperlands, north east of Draperstown, contains original weaving and bleaching machinery.

UPPERLANDS LINEN MUSEUM: William Clark and Sons Factory Tour, Upperlands (3 miles north-east of Maghera); ☎ 028 7954 7200/028 7964 2214.

MONEYMORE MODEL VILLAGE: Manor House, High Street, Moneymore; ☎ 028 8674 8910. Entry: adults £3.00, senior citizens and children £1.00; Mar to Oct 12–6pm Mon–Sun.

Moneymore Model Village and Heritage Centre comes complete with figurines set in landscaped surroundings. The village depicts life in rural Ulster at the time of the Plantation.

Moneymore model village

CELEBRITY CONNECTIONS

Seamus Heaney, or 'Famous Seamus' to most people in Ireland, has pulled off the nigh impossible trick of being a famous poet without being dead. Holder of any number of fellowships, professorships and awards, he is the most recognisable poetic voice in the English-speaking world.

Seamus Heaney was born in 1939 into a family of nine children at the family farmhouse called Mossbawn, between Castledawson and Toomebridge in County Derry. In 1953, his family moved to Bellaghy, a few miles away, now the family home. His father, Patrick Heaney, owned and worked a small farm of 50 acres in the Sperrins. As a 12-year-old, Heaney won a scholarship to St Columb's College, after which he attended Queen's University, Belfast – an institution at which he also had two stints of lecturing.

Heaney's first poems were published in 1962. By that period in Northern Ireland stirrings of trouble to come were evident. Heaney was conscious of the pressure for him to become a spokesman for the Catholic community – instead he opted to move to Dublin, a decision he has addressed on several occasions. However, the poet has felt the need to emphasise that he is Irish and not British. For example, he objected to his inclusion in the 1982 Penguin Book of Contemporary British Poetry by writing: 'Be advised, my passport's green/No glass of ours was ever raised/To toast the Queen.' In 1995 Heaney was awarded the Nobel Prize for Literature.

What to do with children...

Maghera Leisure Centre Outdoor Play Park has three areas ranging from toddler up to teen age groups, and is supervised at all times. The park contains many features such as a zip line, swings, slides, tyre swing and climbing frames. The **Pirates Indoor Play Area** features a 'walk the plank' adventure, as well as many more piratical antics – although no hijacking oil tankers, not even pretend ones.

MAGHERAFELT DISTRICT COUNCIL: 50 Ballyronan Road, Magherafelt BT45 6EN; ☎ 028 7939 7979; www.magherafelt. gov.uk/leisure/maghera-leisure-centre. Entry: free; open 4.30pm–9pm Mon–Fri during term time; 10am–5.30pm Sat, 12.30pm–6pm Sun, 10am–9pm during school holidays.

... and how to avoid children

Volatile and dynamic, Ulster has for centuries been at the crux of the quarrel between Ireland and Britain, the intricacy of its history entangling its people and baffling the outside world. The **Plantation of Ulster Visitor Centre** (50 High Street, Draperstown, Derry; ☎ 028 7962 7800) is a sobering place to try to get to the bottom of the story – and trying to find out why deep religious and political divisions pertain in the north-easterly corner of Ireland to this day. The interpretive centre begins with a useful description of how and why the Plantation got underway in 1610. King James I observed that this colonisation would quieten Ulster, and free the province from the risk of further native rebellion and foreign invasion. He also observed that the plantation would, 'establish the true religion of Christ among men... almost lost in superstition.'

The Centre explains how the estates of the O'Neills and the O'Donnells (the earls of Tyrone and Tirconnell) and their chief supporters were confiscated. Their fiefdoms comprised an estimated half a million acres of land in the counties of Derry, Donegal, Tyrone, Fermanagh, Cavan and Armagh. English and Scottish Protestants were subsequently settled on the land thus confiscated. The Plantation of Ulster was the biggest and most successful of the plantations of Ireland.

Entertainment

Traditional music is particularly vibrant in the South Derry area. Recommended sessions include:

- **Mary's Bar** – Market Square, 10–12 Market Street, Magherafelt BT45 6ED; ☎ 028 7963 1997
- **Owen's** – Main Street, Limavady BT49 0EU; ☎ 028 7772 2328
- **Castle Inn** – Upper Main Street, Dungiven; ☎ 028 7774 1369
- **Carrig Rua** – Main Street, Dungiven BT47 4LD; ☎ 028 7774 1682

The best... PLACES TO STAY

HOTEL

Dungiven Castle

145 Main Street, Dungiven BT47 4LF
☎ 028 7774 2428
www.dungivencastle.com

Enclosed within 22 acres of immaculately landscaped gardens, this beautifully restored 15th-century castle has spectacular views over the Sperrin Mountains. A wealth of leisure activities are on hand nearby including golf, fishing, canoeing, cycling, hang-gliding, paragliding, and orienteering. Or you could just catch up on your reading in the magnificent Turret room, and while away the evenings over a glass of wine and dinner in the à la carte restaurant.

Price: a two-night B&B and one evening meal all inclusive for £120 per person.

B&B

Brooke Lodge

2 Laurel Brook, Aughrim Road, Magherafelt BT45 6NT
☎ 028 7963 4800
www.brooke-lodge.co.uk

The only guesthouse in Magherafelt awarded 3 stars by the Northern Ireland Tourist Board, so you're assured a comfortable stay in the heart of Derry. Brooke Lodge is a purpose-built luxurious guesthouse offering top quality accommodation with excellent facilities.

Price: from £25 to £35 per person sharing.

Clearwater House

11A Ballymulligan Road, Magherafelt, County Derry BT45 6ES
☎ 028 7930 0209

Clearwater B&B is a large, comfortable, four-star Victorian style guesthouse situated 1.5 miles from Magherafelt. Free transport is available to and from the town. There are three double en suite bedrooms including one family room with disabled facilities.

Price: from £30/£55 for single/double.

SELF-CATERING

The Grey Gables

103 Gelvin Road, Dungiven,
☎ 028 7774 1131

Two fully refurbished modern four-star self-catering apartments, with all mod cons – each apartment sleeps from four to six people. Excellent location.

Price: B&B from £25 per person sharing.

Jessie's Cabin

119 Legavallon Road, Dungiven BT47 4QN
☎ 07969 082781
www.scentedgeraniums.co.uk

The late Mr Scott built this detached chalet during the 1920s for when his cousin Jessie visited. Recently the chalet has had a complete makeover – it will comfortably accommodate up to four people.

Price: from £315 (£410 high season) for seven nights.

The best... FOOD AND DRINK

▶ Staying in

Derry, like everywhere else in Northern Ireland, loves its bread and pastry. The love of cakes and pastries in particular is a unifying force across the religious divide. **Ditty's Home Bakery** (Castledawson; ☎ 028 7946 8243; www.dittysbakery.com) has been making dough for 45 years, and is something of a landmark in the bustling village of **Castledawson**. Pastries, buns and cakes are all freshly baked, and their allure attracts visitors from far and near.

Moss Brook Farm (6 Durnascallon Lane, Magherafelt; ☎ 028 7963 3454) supplies organic and free-range sausages, bacon and gammon. You can buy them direct from the farm. For meat pies, it has to be **McKee's Butchers** (26 & 78 Main Street, Maghera; ☎ 028 7964 2559). Meat from the farm's own herds of Charolais and Limousin cattle is used for the pies. The beef here is hung for as long as a month, giving a superb flavour. Game and poultry are also available.

⬧ Drinking

The **Corner House** (6–8 Patrick Street, Draperstown BT457AL; ☎ 028 7962 8051) was originally a stopping off place for horses to be watered. It still services the thirsty (human) inhabitants of South Derry – a task it has undertaken since the 1860s. This is one of South Derry's main meeting places, so there's a lively atmosphere, particularly at weekends. **Jack's Bar in Walsh's Hotel** (Main Street, Maghera; ☎ 028 7954 9100) is steeped in folklore and history. Throughout the bar, drawings and writings highlight seminal events associated with the area. The stained glass, antique seating, open turf fire and friendly atmosphere are almost a working definition of snug.

The **Inn at Castledawson** (47 Main Street BT45 8AA) is perfect for a convivial drink with the locals, while the **Central Bar** (25 Main Street Bellaghy BT45 8HT; ☎ 028 7938 6363) is the place to catch up on the latest sports results – and have an astoundingly good pint. The **Cosy Corner Bar** (68 Gulladuff Road Knockloughrim, Magherafelt BT45 8NT; ☎ 028 79 644575) is as good as its word, as cosy as you could want. The **Flax Inn** (27 King Street, Magherafelt BT45 6AR; ☎ 028 796 31192) pays testament to the local linen industry, at one time an important employer in the area. The pub is one of the most popular in the area.

The **Hogan Stand Bar** (32 Moneyneany Road, Draperstown BT45 7DZ; ☎ 028 7962 8883) takes its name from one of the main stands in the Gaelic Athletic Association's main stadium, Croke Park. As such, the pub is the place to get a flavour of local sport. The **Shepherd's Rest** (220 Sixtowns Road BT45 7BH; ☎ 028 7962 8517 www.shepherdsrestpub.com) in the little village of Draperstown is a traditional, family run pub. A snug bar with open fires at the front, at the back a restaurant and lounge guarantees music on full overdrive at the weekend. Dancing suitable for all ages – no excuses for not dancing allowed!

 # EATING OUT

FINE DINING

Conservatory Restaurant
Ardtara Country House, 8 Gorteade Road, Upperlands, Maghera BT46 5SA
☎ **028 7964 4490**
www.ardtara.com

Situated on a 19th-century estate that once belonged to a linen magnate, this award-winning restaurant only seats up to 25 people – so it's cosy and intimate. Elegant cuisine fashioned from local produce is the order of the day. The two-course menu has a set price of £24, the three-course menu is £32.

RESTAURANT

Apparo Restaurant & Hotel
18 St. Patrick's Street, Draperstown BT45 7AL
☎ **028 796 28100**
www.apparorestaurant.com

The Apparo specialises in using only the freshest and finest local produce to produce contemporary cuisine – from farm to fork in less than a couple of miles. Beef stroganoff, lamb kebab and salmon baked with herbs and served with champ are all served in a warm and inviting atmosphere. Around the £12 mark for main dishes.

Gardiners Restaurant
7 Garden Street, Magherafelt BT45 5DD
☎ **028 7930 0333**
www.gardiners.net

Formerly a rugby club, Gardiners is now a smart, modern Irish cuisine restaurant with an impressive bar. The signature dish is smoked Lough Neagh eel on roasted onion soda bread – and is every bit as delicious as it sounds. Main courses start at £12.95.

GASTRO PUB

Mary's Bar
10 Market Street, Magherafelt BT45 6ED
☎ **028 7930 2616**

This lounge bar and restaurant is very popular locally. Dishes are created using local produce, and the menu ranges from traditional to adventurous. The carvery serves traditional roasts, downstairs is more bistro-like. Lunch costs from £4.95 to £6.95; dinner from £8.95 to £19.95.

ⓘ Visitor Information

Tourist information centre: Tourist Information Centre, 44 Foyle Street, ☎ 028 7126 7284, www.derryvisitor.com.

Hospital: Altnagelvin Area Hospital ☎ 028 7134 5171.

Doctors: Dr C J Collins, within Maghera Medical Centre, 25, Church Street, Maghera BT46 5EA, ☎ 028 7964 2579; Drs Glancy, Ingram, Walls & Diamond, within Bellaghy Medical Centre, 76 William Street, Bellaghy, Magherafelt BT45 8HZ, ☎ 028 7938 6228.

Pharmacies: Jos B Harkin, 108 Main Street, Maghera, County Derry BT46 5AF, ☎ 028 7964 2205; Alliance Pharmacy, 37 Main Street, Maghera BT46 5AA, ☎ 028 7964 2208; Boots The Chemist, 11–12 Meadow Lane Shopping Centre, Moneymore, Magherafelt BT45 6PR, ☎ 028 7963 4365.

Police: Police Service of Northern Ireland, 50 Coleraine Road, Maghera BT46 5BN.

Supermarkets: Toner Supermarkets, 16 Coleraine Road, Maghera BT46 5BN, ☎ 028 7964 2072; O'Kanes Centre Supermarket, 59–61 St Patricks Street, Draperstown, Magherafelt BT45 7AJ, ☎ 028 7962 8572; Iceland Foods, Meadow Lane Shopping Centre, Moneymore Road, Magherafelt BT45 6PR, ☎ 028 7930 1701.

Cash points: Alliance & Leicester plc, 9 Rainey Street, Magherafelt BT45 5DA, ☎ 028 7963 1931; Bank of Ireland, 21 St Patricks Street, Draperstown, Magherafelt BT45 7AJ, ☎ 028 7962 8237; Northern Bank, 58 Main Street, Maghera BT46 5AE, ☎ 028 9004 5960.

Taxis: Glenone Taxis, 2 Radharc An Chairn, Maghera BT46 5GZ; E G Taxis, 6 Moyola Gardens, Castledawson, Magherafelt BT45 8BB, ☎ 028 7946 9558; Westland Taxis, 2 Ashgrove Park, Magherafelt BT45 6DN, ☎ 028 7963 1640.

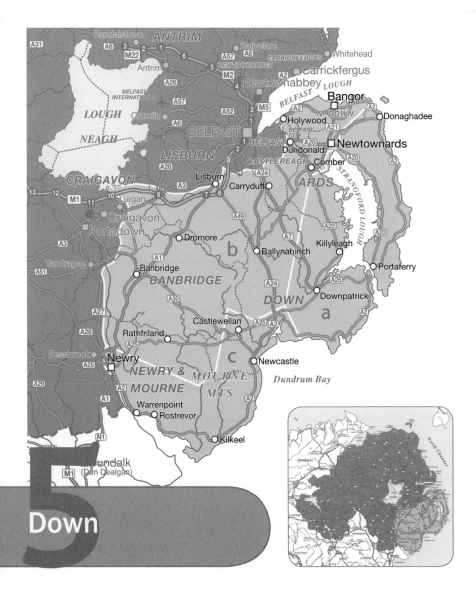

Down

a. East Down
b. Mid and North Down
c. South Down

Unmissable highlights

01 Climb Slieve Donard, Northern Ireland's highest peak with epic views of Ireland and Britain, p. 266

02 Admire the gothic follies and horticultural wonders of Tollymore Forest Park, p. 266

03 Wander through the millennia-old sand dune system at Murlough, p. 273

04 Say a prayer at St Patrick's Grave in Downpatrick. If you have any Irish blood in you, this is the man who will decide your fate on Judgment Day, p. 227

05 Have a mega-twitch at Strangford Lough – a quarter of the world's population of Brent geese winter here, p. 231

06 Shout 'Fore!' and take 14 on the Royal County Down Golf Course – one of the top 10 courses in the world, p. 274

07 Gaze up at Ireland's tallest tree – a western hemlock – in Castlewellan Forest Park, p. 268

08 Check in at the Slieve Donard Hotel – once one of the great railway hotels of Europe, now a haunt of the great, the good and the golfers, p. 277

09 Trace Heathcliff's origins at the Brontë Interpretive Centre. The hero of Wuthering Heights was based on Emily Brontë's uncle, who grew up near Rathfriland, p. 256

10 Visit the lovely village of Hillsborough, the seat of power in Northern Ireland, where the governor used to live in some style, p. 251

DOWN

The coast of Down is dotted with some of the most enchanting and idyllic seaside towns these islands have to offer. From Groomsport in the north of the county to Coney Island in the south, you will find resorts which manage to combine a 1950s British holiday atmosphere with a history which stretches back to the dawn of Christianity in Europe – and throw in a bit of Irish pub life too.

The county provides hill-walking and mountain climbing, sea angling and salmon fishing, and some of the finest links golf to be had anywhere – the Royal County Down was recently voted the number two course in the world. County Down also boasts the oldest state-owned forest park in Ireland – at Tollymore, just north of Newcastle, a haven of rare plants and Victorian follies, the inspiration for both C S Lewis and Edward Lear.

If gardens are your thing, you won't want to miss nearby Castlewellan which boasts the tallest tree in Ireland, a western hemlock, its branches stretching to the heavens. On the subject of heaven, we come to one of the main reasons that people from all over the world visit County Down – because here the architect of Christianity in Ireland, St Patrick, takes his eternal rest. In AD432 the Apostle came ashore where the Slaney River flows into Strangford Lough.

Eating out in County Down has improved out of all recognition in the last few years – Portaferry, Newcastle and Warrenpoint are destinations for gluttons and gourmets alike. Meanwhile Donaghadee is an essential visit for gastronauts – as well as trivia fans. It's the nearest Irish port to Britain – 21 miles across to Portpatrick in Scotland.

The Mournes are a big attraction for visitors from all over Europe. An extensive range, to tramp from one end to another would take days. Slieve Donard reaches some 2,700ft and is the highest peak in the North. The going can be relatively easy in the Mournes – as long as you choose the right route – so you get a chance to savour, not just the scenery, but some of the wonderful names Slievefadda, Slievemoughanmore, Pot of Pulgarve, Wee Slievemoughanmore and the Creaghts.

EAST DOWN

Most places traditionally associated with St Patrick – **Saul, Armagh, Downpatrick, Templepatrick, Lough Derg** and **Croagh Patrick** for example – are in the north of the island, and it was probably in Ulster that the Apostle did most of his missionary work, probably in the mid 5th century, when Christianity was just over 400 years old. St Patrick reputedly came ashore where the **Slaney River** flows into **Strangford Lough** in County Down. He began his mission to convert the Celtic Irish to Christianity nearby in the rolling hills of Saul. A simple church now stands on the site of the barn where he first preached (the word Saul has no biblical connotations – it's merely the English version of the Irish word 'sabhall' meaning barn). According to reasonably substantiated legend, the Apostle of Ireland takes his eternal rest nearby in the graveyard of **Down Cathedral**.

Even without its connection with St Patrick, this part of Down would be a stunning holiday destination because of the presence of one of Europe's great marine habitats, **Strangford Lough**. The northern end of this vast sea lough is quiet and sheltered – ideal for swimming and boating, while the southern end is wild and dramatic.

East Down is home to some of the Six Counties' finest restaurants, a world class opera festival, quiet fishing villages, glorious gardens and A-list birdwatching. The ideal place in fact for gardening gourmets who know their arias from their elbows. County Down's landscape and light has worked its strange sorcery on thinkers and artists alike. The man who founded the British Museum in London, Hans Sloan, was from **Killyleagh**, while Louis McNiece lies buried in the village of **Carrowdore**.

Belfast man Van Morrison has paid homage to the area in song:

Coming down from Downpatrick
Stopping off at St Johns Point
Out all day birdwatching
And the craic was good
Stopped off at Strangford Lough
Early in the morning
Drove through Shrigley taking pictures
And on to Killyleagh
Stopped off for Sunday papers at the
Lecale district, just before Coney Island.

He might just as well have been working for the East Down Tourist Board.

WHAT TO SEE AND DO

Downpatrick

Downpatrick, the county town with just over 10,000 inhabitants, lies in the heart of the rolling drumlin area of the **Lecale** district.

Although under British jurisdiction, Ulster is in fact more Irish than the rest of Ireland in several respects. It can lay claim to the heritage of St Patrick; further, Gaelic society lasted here much longer than in the rest of the island, accounting for the fact that Ulster has more Celtic place names than anywhere else.

Most provincial Irish towns – throughout the Republic – were founded by the Normans. This is not the case in Ulster, where traditionally towns and villages grew up round monasteries, abbeys and ancient markets. However, 15 Norman towns have been identified on or close to the coastlines of Antrim and Down. Downpatrick can be included in that number. It also has the distinction of being the lowest place on the island of Ireland, with the marshes surrounding the north east of the town recorded as being 1.3ft (0.4m) below sea level.

The modern name derives from the Irish *Dún Pádraig* meaning 'Patrick's fort', which once stood on the hill that dominates the town and on which Down Cathedral, the presumed burial place of St Patrick, stands today. An ancient assizes town, much of the town's Georgian architecture remains, particularly in **The Mall** and **English Street**. The thoroughfare runs up to the Cathedral past one of the oldest hotels in Ireland, **Denvir's**. The annual St Patrick's Day parade processes up this ancient route, past the lovely **Southwell School** built in 1733. Just a small word of warning: don't expect the place to be awash with Guinness and shamrocks. The Saint's Feast Day is something of a sober affair here, being primarily a religious concelebration.

Stained glass in Downpatrick Cathedral

The first semi-official celebrations of St Patrick's Day in Ireland only got going in 1903. The Times of London noted that public houses were closed and 'The day was accordingly distinguished by a very welcome, very general, and most unusual sobriety.' That's pretty much Downpatrick on 17 March.

Down Cathedral

The Cathedral Church of the Holy and Undivided Trinity, as Down Cathedral is pleased to call itself on formal occasions, belongs to the Church of Ireland. The Church of Ireland is the Irish sub-sect of the Anglican Church – in other words St Patrick is buried in a Protestant

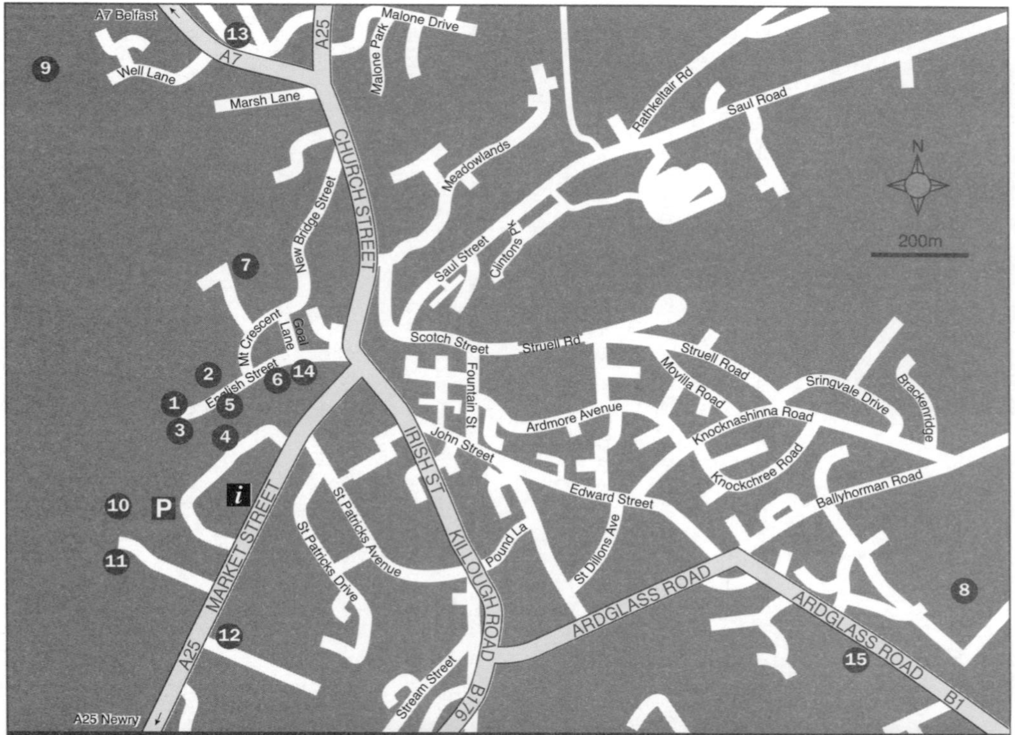

Downpatrick

Things to see and do

1. Holy Trinity Cathedral (Down Cathedral)
2. Down County Museum
3. St Patrick's Grave
4. St Patrick Visitor Centre
5. Southwell School
6. Georgian buildings, English Street
7. Down High School
8. Struell Wells
9. Quoile River
10. Down Railway Museum
11. Downpatrick Race Course

Entertainment

12. Patrick's Day Parade (English Street etc)

Shopping

13. Lowden Guitars

Places to Stay

14. Denvir's Hotel

Visitor Information

15. Downe Hospital
i. Tourist Information Centre, Market Street

St Patrick's Grave

churchyard, something which usually surprises first-time visitors to Ireland. The established order – the Protestant ascendancy – wanted to wield maximum power, which meant taking over the formerly Catholic abbeys, monasteries and cathedrals. Throughout Ireland – and not just in the North – the iconic churches are in the hands of this branch office of the Church of England: St Patrick's Cathedral in Dublin, the ancient **St Patrick's Cathedral** in **Armagh**, Christ Church in Dublin, **St Ann's Cathedral in Belfast**.

No surprise then, that Down Cathedral has had a history to which the word chequered barely does justice. Destroyed by earthquake, seized by the Normans, burnt by the Scots, destroyed again by the English, it then lay in ruins for the best part of 200 years. Lord Leonard Grey, the Lord Deputy of Ireland, stabled horses in the cathedral, basically destroying the place. He was hanged for his trouble just up the road. Nowadays it would be hard to imagine a more peaceful setting, the old stone cathedral surrounded by tall beech trees, with views across the **River Quoile** to the ancient **Cistercian Abbey of Inch**.

In the grounds of the cathedral a large granite slab marks the grave not only of the Apostle of Ireland, but also Ireland's other two official patron saints – St Brigid and St Colmcille. According to the ancient poem:

In burgo Duno tumulo
Tumulantur in uno
Brigida, Patricus, atque Columba pius
In Down three saints one grave do fill –
Brigid, Patrick and Colmcille.

Regrettably, it's unlikely the bones of any of these saintly personages occupy precisely this tomb, because, rather incongruously, the site was picked out and erected at the beginning of the 20th century by the Belfast Naturalists' Field Club. Granted they used local knowledge, putting the stone on the spot that was traditionally marked out. And ample evidence exists that St Patrick is buried somewhere in these grounds, according to some historians most likely under the main portal of the cathedral.

Christianity was only some 400 years old when **Cathedral Hill** in Down became a focus for the world's new religion. The year AD753 marks the earliest reference to an Abbot of Down, and it can be assumed he presided over the Celtic monastery whose ruins can be seen in the grounds of the current building. The abbey was plundered by the Vikings, and by 1016 a round tower had been built to stash the valuables. However both tower and church were destroyed when the place was struck by lightning and burnt to the ground.

When the Normans came to Ireland, John de Courcy, one of Henry II's men, set out for Down to conquer the North and lay claim to the tomb of St Patrick. In 1177 he ousted the local king Rory Macdunleavy, and founded his own Benedictine Monastery on Cathedral Hill. To this day the emblem of the nearby grammar school, **Down High**, uses de Courcy's emblem (a blue and yellow eagle) as its school badge.

The most striking feature inside the cathedral is the pulpitium topped by a magnificent organ, one of the finest in Ireland. At one time the cathedral would have held statues of St Patrick, St Brigid and St Colmcille as well as a statue of St Benedict. But since the Catholics were given their marching orders, only a statue of St Patrick remains. Some lesser individuals are honoured. Pride of place is given to the tombstone of Lord Edward Cromwell (uncle and godfather to Oliver), who died in 1607. His mission in this neck of the woods was to 'subdue the native Irish in Lecale'. Another curious adornment in this house of God is the phalanx of regimental colours of the 86th Royal County Down Regiment, later to become the Royal Irish Rifles. This military flourish is an odd characteristic of most Church of Ireland places of worship in Northern Ireland. As you progress further into the cathedral you will see a Bishop's Throne on the north wall; on the south side stands the Judge's Stall, so-called because the assizes used to be held in the cathedral.

At the foot of Cathedral Hill is the **Saint Patrick Visitor Centre**. A permanent interpretative exhibition centre features displays on the life and story of St Patrick. The main problem for any such enterprise is that facts about the patron saint are notoriously sketchy – even though he is central to the affairs of Ireland, North and South, in a way that few other patron saints are. Because of this influence – which pertains to this day – many august bodies have tried to tease out information on the Apostle of Ireland – a question which even came to the notice of the

THE SAINT PATRICK CENTRE: St Patrick's Square, Downpatrick BT30 6LZ; ☎ 028 4461 9000; www.saintpatrickcentre.com; Entry: adults £4.90, children £2.50; open 9.30am–5.30pm Mon to Sat, 10am–6pm Sun, Jun to Aug; 9.30am–5.30pm Mon to Sat, 1pm–5.30pm Sun Apr/May/Sept; 10am–5pm Mon to Sat Oct to Mar.

Dublin Institute for Advanced Studies in the 1940s. This body, set up by the then taoiseach Eamon de Valera, specialised in rambling cerebral discussion. It included some of Ireland's finest thinkers, plus several eminent Jewish and Eastern European philosophers fleeing the Nazis. The topic of Ireland's national saint was discussed in the most erudite terms. The philosophers finally came to a rather startling conclusion. As Tyrone man Flann O'Brien commented at the time, it was the Dublin Institute's singular achievement to prove that there was no God but two St Patricks.

Local legends: St Pat facts

According to legend, God will allow St Patrick to judge the Irish on the Last Day. Untroubled by this thought, Irish party-goers round the world celebrate Patrick's feast day with levels of craic and roll well in excess of sensible limits given the saint's significant role in granting admission to the hereafter.

Gargantuan volumes of Guinness and lager are consumed in honour of the man who spread Christianity throughout Ireland – although St Patrick himself would have been a complete stranger to merriment and revelry. Austere would probably be too chipper a word for the saint's religious outlook, so it's something of a mystery why he should have become one of the three most popular partying saints in the world – alongside St Valentine (also buried in Ireland) and St Nicholas.

Very little is known about St Patrick, the Apostle of Ireland and first Cardinal Archbishop of Armagh. The son of a minor Roman official, Patrick was probably born in Scotland. Aside from his missionary work, Patrick single-handedly launched the shamrock as Ireland's national logo – according to legend he used the three-leaved plant to convey the idea of the three-in-one Holy Trinity. This leads to a particularly succulent globule of trivia: the first motor race in these islands, the Gordon Bennett Tournament just over 100 years ago, centred on Athy in Kildare. The British participants, the Napier cars, were painted green in honour of the shamrock, and for the best part of a century British Racing Green remained the official colour of all UK Grand Prix cars.

At the other end of the speed scale, Patrick reputedly drove the snakes out of Ireland – hence his nick-name 'the snake charmer'. Regrettably, it's more than likely the snakes were absent from Ireland long before the arrival of St Patrick – like any offshore island, the species count is dramatically lower than on a continental mass. So as well as snakes being absent in Ireland, neither are there moles, toads, woodpeckers, weasels to name just a few.

Although many St Pat facts are disputed, it seems fairly certain he was responsible for spreading the Gospel in a country where, according to legend, no word for 'sobriety' existed. Indeed such was his success, Ireland became the only country to embrace Christianity without bloodshed or martyrdom. Well, almost without bloodshed: while baptising Aengus, King of Cashel, in 445, St Patrick unwittingly stuck the spike of his crozier through his new convert's foot. When later asked why he had not cried out, Aengus replied that he thought it was all part of the ceremony.

The St Patrick's Centre imaginatively examines the environment in which the saint lived – artwork and metalwork from the Early Christian period are an attractive feature. An excellent on-site shop sells Celtic-orientated artefacts, while the attractive café overlooking a herb garden is popular with locals as well as visitors.

St Patrick's Hill

About a mile north east of Downpatrick, at the mouth of the **Slaney River** (now called **Fiddler's Burn**), is the village of **Saul** where St Patrick began his mission to Ireland and where he probably died.

The St Patrick Centre

The barn at Saul was St Patrick's first church, but it had anything but a happy history. Burned by the Danes, it was rebuilt by St Malachy, sacked by Magnus O'Eochadha King of Ulster, and burnt to the ground again in 1316 by Edward Bruce. Nearby is a hill dominated by a huge granite statue in honour of the saint. From here a panoramic

The date of St Patrick's Day

The seventeenth of March was largely a day of religious observance until the 20th century, when the Bank Holiday (Ireland) Act 1903, passed by the British Parliament, was introduced by the Irish MP James O'Mara. However it seems unlikely that James had today's celebrations of pagan abandon in mind. Not long after he introduced the not-so-desperately popular law which required that pubs be closed on 17 March, a provision that held sway until the 1970s.

The first St Patrick's Day parade held in the then Irish Free State was Dublin's 1931 procession, reviewed by Minister of Defence Desmond Fitzgerald, but the religious aspect remained paramount. In 2008 the official Feast Day of St Patrick was 15 March, to avoid it clashing with Holy Monday, the day after Palm Sunday. The Apostle last had his timetable tampered with in 1940, when St Patrick's Day was observed on 3 April in order to avoid it coinciding with Passion Sunday. This chronological serendipity has always been regarded auspiciously. St Malachy of Armagh, a great prophesier, and Northern Ireland's version of Nostradamus, even formulated it into one of his predictions: peace, for long a fairly exotic concept in Ireland, would break out *'when the shamrock meets the palm'*.

In 2007 a power-sharing executive finally convened in Northern Ireland, and peace reigns now throughout the island. In 2008, Easter was as early as it's going to be this century, only one day later than the earliest it can be. St Patrick's Day missed out coinciding with Palm Sunday by just 24 hours. So the prediction of peace was only one year and one day out! Not bad, as medieval prophecies go.

Inch Abbey

view stretches from **Strangford Lough**, across most of South Down towards the **Mountains of Mourne**.

St Patrick's funeral procession was said to have begun from the church at Saul – two white oxen pulled his coffin to Downpatrick. Just beyond the village of **Raholp** is the ruin of a church associated with St Tassach, believed to have ministered the last rites to the dying St Patrick on 17 March, some 1,500 years ago or so.

Struell Wells

Just over a mile away from Downpatrick in Struell are the **Holy Wells of St Patrick**. These were, like so many Christian places of worship in Ireland, important to the pre-Christian Celts. The wily St Patrick co-opted this sacred spot – just as he had done on the **Hill of Tara** – and to this day Struell Wells remains a place of worship.

Inch Abbey

If you want to know where the most fertile land is anywhere in Ireland, look for the ruins of the biggest monastery, goes the old saying. This has now been updated somewhat: if you want to know where the best restaurants are, follow the local priest.

INCH ABBEY: ☎ 028 9181 1491; www.ni-environment.gov.uk/inch.htm. Entry: free; open 24h, year round.

The ruins of Inch Abbey certainly follow the older adage, being built on the fertile plains abutting the **River Quoile**. The extensive remains are of a Cistercian Abbey founded in 1180 by John de Courcy. Distant views towards de Courcy's cathedral town of Downpatrick complete the breathtaking scene.

Strangford and Strangford Lough

Strangford Lough – the largest sea lough in these islands – is a pit stop for some of the great feathered travellers of the world. An estimated quarter of the world's pale-bellied brent geese population arrive in Ireland every autumn from Greenland and the Arctic, and a large proportion of them fetch up in County Down.

Joined to the Irish Sea by the narrowest of channels, this 60sq mile inlet – with some 70 islands – also plays host to whooper swans from Iceland, widgeon and teal from eastern Europe, plus many more avian A-listers. Countless tidal rocky outcrops called *pladdies* dot the lough and mudflats, a haven for waders. In total it's estimated that this wetland supports some 25,000 wildfowl and 50,000 waders. Further information can be found at www.strangfordlough.org.

In 2007 Strangford Lough pioneered the world's first commercial tidal power station, installed in the narrows. The 1.2 megawatt underwater tidal electricity generator, part of Northern Ireland's Environment and Renewable Energy Fund scheme, takes advantage of the fast tidal flow. Although the generator is powerful enough to power up to a thousand homes, the turbine has minimal environmental impact. Almost entirely submerged, the rotors turn slowly enough so that they pose no danger to wildlife.

Local legends: the red hand of Ulster

Strangford Lough also earns a place in the annals of Northern Ireland's history in a particularly fraught area of tradition – its emblems. In a bid to win his rightful inheritance – away back in the mists of history – one Lamraid Lamh Dhearg took part in a race across Strangford Lough. As the contestants neared the winning post on the far shore, Lamraid decided to make an unorthodox move in a bid to guarantee victory. To make sure of being first he cut off his hand and threw it onto the shore. The Red Hand of Ulster subsequently became a potent symbol throughout the land.

STRANGFORD-PORTAFERRY FERRY:
Strangford Ferry Terminal, Strangford;
☎ 028 4488 1637; www.downdc.gov.uk.
The ferry takes about 12 minutes and from Strangford runs on the hour and half hour.

Strangford's name comes from the Old Norse word *Strangrfjörthr* meaning 'sea inlet with strong currents', and it's as good as its name. It's the westerly terminal for the **Strangford-Portaferry Ferry** across the lough, and the route across requires skilful negotiation of the currents.

Crab-wise the ferry skirts the entrance of the lough which is surrounded by drumlins – the egg shaped mounds that cover much of Down. 'Drumlin', by the way, comes from the Irish *droim* meaning ridge. The word was coined in 1833 to describe 'low ridges of superficial debris in the North of Ireland'. From the ferry you will get first-class views of the lough and surrounding landscape – this is a scenic sea cruise on the cheap.

The town of Strangford itself is made up of attractive 19th-century cottages and fine Georgian terraces, and is well supplied with fine restaurants and pubs. **Strangford**

Strangford

Castle, located near the harbour, is a 16th-century tower-house with murder-hole to deter unwanted guests. Just outside the town is **Audley's Castle**, a 15th-century castle on a rocky height overlooking the lough. Nearby **Audleystown Court Cairn**, just off the south shore of Strangford Lough, is a 3,000-year-old Neolithic court grave.

Killyleagh

Situated on Strangford Lough's southerly shore, Killyleagh's centrepiece is the magnificent **Killyleagh Castle**, which dominates the town. (The castle is closed to the public.) Originally a 12th-century fort used by John de Courcy, today it is the oldest inhabited castle in Ireland. The present building dates back to 1850, but incorporates two towers of an earlier castle in 1666. Remains of the original castle dating back to 1180 are also visible. The castle – designed by Charles Lanyon – was described by the writer Harold Nicholson over a century ago as 'pricking castellated ears above the smoke of its own village and towering like some chateau of the Loire above the tides of Strangford Lough'. Still sums up the place.

Killyleagh is the birthplace of **Sir Hans Sloane**, whose immense natural history collection was the nucleus of the British Museum, and after whom Sloane Square in London is named. He received his education in the castle's library. A statue of Sloane stands outside the castle.

Lecale Peninsula

The Lecale Peninsula is an ancient designation that covers an area of some 80sq miles between Downpatrick and **Dundrum**. Of significant historical and geographic importance, it is bounded by the **Quoile Marshes**, the **Blackstaff River**, the **Irish Sea** and Strangford Lough. Fishing is popular throughout the area – sea trout, bass, pollock and mullet are all widely available, as well as eel, perch, pike,

STRANGFORD GUIDING COMPANY:
Contact Stevie Kennedy, Pikestone Cottage, 40 Scaddy Road, Downpatrick BT309BP; ☎ 028 44828346; www.strangfordguidingco.com.

roach, rudd. Steve Kennedy runs the **Strangford Guiding Company**, specialising in saltwater fly-fishing. He is available for guiding, casting tuition, saltwater workshops, group expeditions.

Comber Angling & Country Pursuits (23 Bridge Street, Comber; ☎ 028 9187 0777) also has vast experience in fishing Strangford Lough and the Irish Sea. Coarse fishing can be enjoyed all year round in East Down. To get going, you will need a rod licence issued by the **Fisheries Conservancy Board** and a coarse fishing permit issued by the owner of the water. These can be bought from many of the tackle shops such as:

- **Field & Tackle** – 22 Dromore Street, Ballynahinch
- **Sports Centre** – 32 High Street, Ballynahinch
- **H W Kelly** – Market Street, Downpatrick

Castle Ward

Castle Ward, sometimes Castleward, is a National Trust property overlooking Strangford Lough. The most striking aspect of the house is its dual architecture. While the entrance side of the building is done in classical style, the opposite side is distinctly Gothic. Whether your artistic sensibilities are offended by the building or not, one thing is certain – Castle Ward makes for an absorbing day out. The house looks out on landscaped gardens, a fortified tower house, Victorian laundry, theatre, restaurant, shop, saw mill and a working corn mill. A Festival of Opera is held each year.

CASTLE WARD: Strangford BT30 7LS; ☎ 028 4488 1204; www.nationaltrust.org. uk/main/w-castleward. Entry: house and grounds: adults £6.50, children £3, grounds only £4.30/£2; grounds open 10am–8pm daily Apr to Sept, 10am–4pm daily Oct to Mar, house open 1pm–6pm Easter/Jul/Aug and Sat/Sun/holidays Apr to Jun.

The Strangford Lough Wildlife Centre is located in Castle Ward – the centre provides an entertaining and educational study and interpretation of the Lough's ecology.

Donaghadee

'Tooraloo, tooralay, and it's six miles from Bangor to Donaghadee', says the song, partly because for the best part of 300 years Donaghadee was the most important ports in Ireland. Donaghadee to Portpatrick some 21 miles away in Scotland was one of the shortest sea routes between Ireland and Britain. Well into the 20th century, you could still get a local fisherman to row you over to Scotland for £5. But the commercial days are largely over (the Larne-Stranraer route, followed by Belfast City Airport took over from the fishermen and local entrepreneurs) and today Donaghadee is a charming, quiet seaside town without much commercial traffic.

The **Lighthouse**, the work of Sir John Rennie and David Logan (of Eddystone fame) is worthy of a second glance not least because the Commissioners for Irish Lights gave Brendan Behan the job of painting it. Now, this is painting in the sense of painting the structure black and white, and not, for instance, doing a study in oils.

It would be fair to say Brendan was a reluctant worker. He eventually got his marching orders from the service at another County Down lighthouse (p. 274).

Grace Neill's Inn in the High Street undoubtedly came to Brendan Behan's notice. This is officially the oldest pub in Ireland, recognised by the *Guinness Book of Records*; what is not officially confirmed is the persistent claim that Peter the Great stayed here during his tour of Ireland, a visit undertaken to learn and take back the secrets of ship-building and linen making to Russia. However, the following definitely did visit Donaghadee: Keats, Daniel Defoe, Franz Liszt, and Wordsworth. Keats seems to have had the roughest time. Although he found the town itself charming, he was treated to 'ridicule, scorn, and violent abuse by the local people who objected to my mode of dress and thought I was some sort of strange foreigner.'

The Cleft Gallery (34 New Street, Donaghadee BT21 0AG; ☎ 028 9188 8502; ww.thecleftgallery.com) on the seafront exhibits the best of Irish art, with paintings available from £95 up to £12,000.

Copeland Islands

Most of Northern Ireland's islands are visible from the shore, affording them added allure – they're close, but just out of reach. The Copeland Islands are a perfect example. Some 4 miles off the coast from **Donaghadee**, these emerald green fragments are home to thousands of breeding seabirds and waders. This Area of Special Scientific Interest consisting of Lighthouse, Mew and Copeland Island, has an avian cast list featuring Manx shearwater, storm petrel, redstart. On an average day's walk round the islands you will see gannets dive-bombing, platoons of eider duck patrolling the rocks, and colonies of gulls wheeling endlessly over the Irish Sea.

Big Copeland supports the most diverse range of habitats of the three islands, but keen botanists will want to know that Lighthouse Island represents the southern limit for Scots lovage in Europe and the northern limit for sea purslane in Ireland. Grey seal and common seal can be found off the Copeland Islands in significant numbers. They utilise the off-shore islands and reefs as haul-outs and as pupping and mating sites.

Funnily enough Lighthouse Island doesn't have a lighthouse anymore, although Mew Island does. Over a century ago Lighthouse Island had a population of about 100 but now the only human residents are those who overnight at the reasonably cosy and comfy Bird Observatory. Visitors are welcomed, but advance booking is necessary. Access is by small boat from Donaghadee Harbour and most trips leave at 6pm on Fridays and return at 4pm on Sundays. Visitors may book a place on a weekend or for a week. There are also four or five day trips each summer, usually of a Saturday.

From June to September **MV The Brothers** (☎ 028 9188 3403; www.nelsonboats. co.uk) runs trips to the Copelands from Donaghadee. The company also runs sea-angling trips (mackerel a speciality, but you could get lucky with a sea trout) for £7, all bait and tackle provided.

COPELAND ISLAND BIRD OBSERVATORY: Secretary Neville McKee; ☎ 028 9443 3068; neville.mckee@btinternet.com.

Mount Stewart House

Mount Stewart House, standing on the western shores of Strangford Lough, has been a destination for punters (quite literally) for the best part of a century. A long, two storey classical 1820s building, the house is home to the George Stubbs painting **Hambletonian Rubbing Down**, one of the crowning achievements of equine art. When the National Gallery in London staged a major exhibition, 'Stubbs and the Horse' in 2005, this one great work was missing – considered far too valuable to travel. The painting, one of the greatest ever studies of victory, pain and triumph, was completed when Stubbs was 75.

The presence of Stubbs's iconic nag in County Down, however, is only one reason to visit this exquisite National Trust property. The house itself breathes a subtle beauty, while history and political relevance lurk in every room. The **dining room** has 22 Empire chairs used by the delegates at the Congress of Vienna in 1815. You will hardly need to be reminded that the Congress was a conference of ambassadors of the major powers of Europe that helped redefine the borders of the continent.

The dining room looks out towards one of the most stunning rooms at Mount Stewart – the private Chapel, with its stained glass windows, Italian paintings and decorations.

Despite the lavishness of the buildings and the presence of one of art history's iconic paintings, the reason most people visit this corner of County Down is to view the beguiling **gardens** – generally acknowledged as one of the great horticultural collections in western Europe. Seventy-eight acres comprising formal areas, terracing, pergolas, pavilions, woodland and a water garden encircle a large lake. This sheltered habitat has the serendipity to enjoy a sub-tropical local micro-climate. Mount Stewart experiences temperate island conditions, with the Gulf Stream feeding into Strangford Lough and guaranteeing frost-free winters. The atmosphere is humid, and in warm weather heavy dews ensure that tropical plants thrive. More than 100 eucalyptus trees, the most important genus at Mount Stewart, tower round manicured lawns, some topping out at 120ft. The garden probably has the most concentrated planting of *Eucalyptus globulus* in northern Europe – everywhere their resinous scent fills the air.

An eye-popping stand of blood red and orange rhododendrons leads to a whimsical collection of topiaries – an Irish harp, a shamrock, a sailboat, stags, the goddess Diana, and the Devil. Many tender greenhouse plants prosper outdoors in the mild climate – yuccas, unfeasibly large Paris daisies, jacaranda – while eight massive tree heathers line

Mount Stewart Gardens

the lawn. The demesne is divided up into many themes – a romantic Italian garden runs the full length of the south side of the house, while the Spanish garden comes complete with oleanders, bougainvillea, jasmine and a summer house decorated with blue tiles.

One of the most beautiful buildings in the grounds, the octagonal **Temple of the Winds**, is based on the building of the same name in Athens – although the Greek one doesn't have the dramatic views across Strangford Lough that the County Down Temple can boast. The only building in Ireland designed by James Stuart, the octagonal temple was inspired by the Grand Tour the 1st Marquess of Derry took in his youth.

Mount Stewart was originally the home of **Lord Castlereagh**, one of the dominant figures in late 18th-century and early 19th-century British and European history. Over the centuries some of the main players in Irish history have stayed here, including Michael Collins (sometimes called the father of modern guerrilla warfare) and Winston Churchill. The British Prime Minister's stay evidently seems not to have affected him sentimentally – during the Second World War he offered Eamon de Valera the Six Counties if the Taoiseach would foreswear neutrality and allow the Irish Free State – as it then was – to join the allies. Dev refused, knowing that after the war he had no means of containing one million disgruntled Protestants, many of whom would be armed and trained after their stint in the British Army.

Although the house has been around since the 18th century, the gardens were only designed in 1919 (just a teenager in gardening years). Created by Lady Derry, the enterprise required a small army of builders and gardeners. After a decade of clearing, planting, weeding, mowing, coppicing and hoeing, the gardens blended into the landscape as if they'd always been there. Mount Stewart is apparently the least visited National Trust property in the UK, an almost inexplicable fact because the gardens remain one of the most seductive places in these islands.

> **MOUNT STEWART HOUSE:** Mountstewart, Portaferry Road, Newtownards BT22 2AD; ☎ 028 4278 8387; www.nationaltrust.org. uk. Entry: house and gardens £6.50/£3, gardens only £5/£2; open 12–6pm daily Jul/Aug, 12–6pm Wed–Mon; Sept, Mar/Apr/May/Jun/Oct 12–6pm Sat/Sun/ holidays.

Wet weather

Down County Museum is located in the erstwhile 18th-century **County Gaol of Down**. In addition to walking through the restored prison complete with cells and incarceration equipment (to make your stay as uncomfortable as possible), 9,000 years of human history in County Down is on show in the exhibition 'Down Through Time'.

The gaol was opened in 1796 and until its closure in 1830, housed thousands of prisoners. The online prisoners' database allows you to check up if any of your ancestors were County Down ne'er-do-wells.

In addition to incarcerating many people for minor offences, hundreds of transportees bound for the convict colonies of New South Wales were held here before departure. The rebels captured after the battles of Saintfield and Ballynahinch during

DOWN COUNTY MUSEUM: The Mall, English Street, Downpatrick BT30 6AH; ☎ 028 4461 5218; www.downcountymuseum.com. Entry: free; open 10am–5pm Mon to Fri, 1pm–5pm Sat/Sun.

DOWN RAILWAY MUSEUM: Downpatrick & County Down Railway, Market Street, Downpatrick BT30 6LZ; ☎ 028 4461 5779; www.downrail.co.uk.

THE EXPLORIS AQUARIUM: The Rope Walk, Castle Street, Portaferry; ☎ 028 4272 8062; www.exploris.org.uk. Entry: adults £5.60, children £3.40, family £16; open 10am–6pm Mon to Fri, 11am–6pm Sat, 12pm–6pm Sun Apr to Aug; 10am–5pm Mon to Fri, 11am–5pm Sat, 1pm–5pm Sun, Sept to Mar.

the 1798 Rebellion were also jailed here in Downpatrick. The United Irishman, Thomas Russell, was executed here for his role in the abortive rebellion against the British in 1803.

Steam in the Heart of Down is a perfect wet day option. This Railway Museum, just a short walk from St Patrick's Visitor Centre, is Northern Ireland's only standard gauge heritage railway. From here a line runs towards **Inch Abbey** and on to **Ballydugan**. Day trips on the steam trains are advertised online. Particularly popular are the Halloween Ghost Train and the Christmas Day specials.

The **Exploris Aquarium**, Portaferry delves into the lives of the finny denizens of the deep, concentrating (although not solely) on local residents. Touch tanks allow visitors to feel and hold creatures as varied as rays and spiny starfish, while an open sea tank reveals a massive range of sea life. A marine discovery laboratory allows microscopic embryos to be observed. A whole section is devoted to jellyfish – which is entirely fitting as this section of the animal kingdom seems to be one of the few that is thriving because of climate change. They are, indeed, the very poster boys of global warming, with several new species being spotted round the north coast of Ireland in the last decade or so.

Seals are a regular feature of Strangford Lough – Exploris has a sanctuary for sick and orphaned seal pups, preparing them for a return to the lough.

Exploris Aquarium

What to do with children...

The **Quoile Countryside Centre,** just a couple of miles north of Downpatrick is an ideal place to take the kids for an introduction to the natural history of the area. As well as its exhibits on the wildlife of the **Quoile Pondage** – created when a barrage was built to prevent local flooding – various woodlands and wetlands trails explore the riverbanks. The centre also organises nature rambles and seal-watching trips on Strangford Lough.

> **QUOILE COUNTRYSIDE CENTRE:** 5 Quay Road, Downpatrick BT30 7JB; ☎ 028 4461 3280; www.ni-environment.gov. uk/quoile.shtml. Entry: free; reserve open 24h; visitor centre open 11am–5pm daily Apr to Aug; 1pm–5pm Sat/Sun Apr to Mar.

Delamont Country Park (Mullagh, Killyleagh; ☎ 028 4482 8333; www.delamontcountrypark.com) occupies 200 acres of woodland, countryside and beach on the shores of Strangford Lough. Open areas for picnics, outdoor adventure playground and Thomas-the-Tank-Engine style miniature trains are available. The park is also home to the largest heronry in Northern Ireland. Boat trips across the lough can be organised here – suitable for all age groups.

Clearsky Adventure Centre is based in the Castle Ward estate in a collection of converted old barn buildings within a 16th-century courtyard. The centre specialises in adventure activities and water sports: archery, laser clay pigeon shooting, abseiling, night-lining, sea kayaking and canoeing.

> **CLEARSKY ADVENTURE CENTRE, CASTLE WARD:** Demesne, Strangford, Downpatrick, County Down BT30 7LT; ☎ 028 437 23933; www.clearsky-adventure.com.

... and how to avoid children

Downpatrick Racecourse

Downpatrick Racecourse, within sight of Down Cathedral, is the oldest race course in Ireland, and one of the oldest in the world still in use. Racing began here in 1685, and the 1 mile, 2 furlong course has changed little over the years. It's all National Hunt and Flat racing with the most famous meeting the Powers Whiskey Ulster National Run held in February. Other meetings are held in March, May, August (Ladies' Day), September, November and December.

> **DOWNPATRICK RACECOURSE:** 24 Ballydugan Road, Downpatrick BT30 6SP; ☎ 028 4461 2054; www.downpatrickracecourse.co.uk.

Entertainment

A thousand years ago long ships carried Vikings to Ireland's northerly shores where they dominated the Strangford Lough area – and beyond – from the 9th to 11th century. Their leader was the only Viking king buried in Ireland, King Magnus, King of Norway (1073–1103). Nicknamed Magnus Barelegs, he formed an alliance in 1102 with King Murtagh O'Brien, King of Ireland. On 24 August 1103, having sailed his long boats in from Strangford Lough he landed near Downpatrick. As is the way of these things, the alliance unravelled and Magnus was subsequently killed. His remains lie in an unmarked mound just outside Downpatrick.

Today, the **Killyleagh Magnus Barelegs Viking Festival** at Killyleagh and Delamont Country Park, Downpatrick attracts hordes of Vikings from as far away as Scandinavia, Iceland and America. The festival takes place around the weekend of the autumn equinox, 21 September (www.killyleagh.org).

The **Dufferin Arms**, (35 High Street, Killyleagh; ☎ 028 4482 1182) is renowned for having one of the most eclectic Irish traditional sessions anywhere. The Saturday afternoon festivals are legendary – and feature musicians from both sides of the cultural divide, Ulster Scots and traditional Irish. Uillean pipes, double basses, harps, guitars, fiddles and pianos are all regularly spotted. To further add to this (somewhat) unusually cooperative situation, if you choose to sit al fresco, you may well experience a further musical treat. The musical wing of the local Orange lodge, the Inch Flute Band, regularly parade through the town (the marching season is roughly June – September). As you enjoy your Guinness on the veranda you may well be treated to a spirited rendering from the marching band of The Loyal Orange Heroes Of Comber. You can then retire to your snug to hear the traditional ensemble without missing a beat. The Good Friday Agreement in full living colour.

Shopping

Lowden Guitars (34 Down Business Park, Belfast Road, Downpatrick; ☎ 028 4461 9161; www.georgelowden.com) have been used by many satisfied customers throughout the world, including Eric Clapton, Van Morrison, Mark Knopfler and U2's The Edge. They're not cheap, but if you're interested and have a few grand to spare, you'll get a tour of the workshops before you buy.

The best... PLACES TO STAY

BOUTIQUE

The Mill At Ballydugan

Drumcullen Road Ballydugan BT30 8HZ
☎ **028 4461 3654**
www.ballyduganmill.com

Hidden away in the rolling drumlin countryside just outside Downpatrick, the site of this 18th-century flour mill is very atmospheric. Looking out onto ruined stone outbuildings, it resembles more a medieval castle than a former industrial complex. Bedrooms are appropriately furnished in traditional country style, with exposed beams and brass-and-iron beds.

Price: B&B £75 for a double.

INN

Denvir's Hotel

14–16 English Street, Downpatrick BT30 6AB
☎ **028 4461 2012**

In 1642 a retired soldier built this capacious coaching inn, and people have been enjoying the comfort and craic here ever since. Situated in Downpatrick's handsome Georgian thoroughfare English Street, the hotel is just yards down the hill from Down Cathedral and the grave of St Patrick.

Price: from £55 for a double.

The Cuan

Strangford BT30 7ND
☎ **028 4488 1222**
www.thecuan.com

Winner of the exceptional accommodation experience award at the Down District Council's Tourism Heroes awards 2007, the Cuan is just 50m from the sea and overlooking the Strangford village square.

Price: £47.50 for a single; £75 for a double.

SELF-CATERING

Killyleagh Castle Towers

Killyleagh BT30 9QA
☎ **028 4482 8261**

If you've never stayed in a castle before, this is your chance. The 17th-century towers are fully modernised inside – TV, fridge, washing machine, clothes dryer, hob, oven and a swimming pool and tennis court.

Price: from £200 for a week for a luxurious two-bedroom apartment, sleeping four people.

The best... FOOD AND DRINK

▶ Staying in

Finnebrogue Estate (Killyleagh Road, Downpatrick; ☎ 028 4461 7525; www.finnebrogue. com) is where to load up with what is generally reckoned to be the very best venison in these islands. Finnebrogue Oisín (*oisín* is Irish for young deer) is the meat of young deer between 9 and 21 months of age, from Finnebrogue's free roaming herd of red deer. Alternatively go for the organic sausages or bacon. While you're in the neighbourhood you should stock up with fruit, veg and cheese from **Churchtown Organics** (Ballycutler BT30 7AT; ☎ 028 4488 1128; www.churchtownfarmorganicproduce.com).

    Pheasants' Hill Farm (37 Killyleagh Road, Downpatrick BT30 9BL; ☎ 028 4461 7246; www.pheasantshill.com) supplies free-range, rare-breed meats. Dry cured hams and additive-free sausages are specialities. For the very best in bivalves, head for **Cuan Oysters** (Cuan Sea Fisheries, Sketrick Island, Killinchy; ☎ 028 9754 1461; www.cuanoysters.com). Cuan was one of the first commercial producers of Pacific oysters in Ireland or Britain, pioneering culture methods for very small hatchery-reared oyster seed. The company has been in the forefront of oyster making for 20 years.

▶ Drinking

Get your beer from the **Strangford Lough Brewing Company** (Braidleigh Lodge, 22 Shore Road, Killyleagh BT30 9UE; ☎ 028 4482 1461; www.slbc.ie). Its various brands are named after historical characters associated with this part of Ireland. Magnus Barelegs, a Viking King, has two beers named in his honour – Barelegs Brew and Legbiter, the latter the name of his sword. Naturally enough St Patrick gets many a mention.

    The **Dufferin Arms** (35 High Street, Killyleagh; ☎ 028 4482 1182) is made up of a honeycomb of snugs and bars, with terrific bar snacks available – all served with chips made from local Comber potatoes, generally agreed to be among the best in Ireland. The **Creel Bar in the Lobster Pot** (9–11 The Square, Strangford BT30 7ND; ☎ 028 4488 1288; www.lobsterpotstrangford.com) is another great boozer in this area, with live music on a Saturday night.

EATING OUT

FINE DINING

Pier 36
The Parade, Donaghadee BT21 0HE
☎ **028 9188 4466**
www.pier36.co.uk

Right on the quayside of one of the most picturesque harbours on the coast, Pier 36 is the perfect place to savour the best of seafood. Despite being a multi-award-winning restaurant, prices are not exorbitant: sautéed crab claws in garlic and chilli butter with homemade wheaten bread is £6.95, while main courses such as grilled fillets of sea bass on wild mushroom and hazelnut risotto begin around the £10 mark. The wine list is similarly reasonable, with a good Sancerre available from £19.95, or a Pinot for £12.50.

Balloo House
1 Comber Road Killinchy BT23 6PA
☎ **028 9754 1210**
www.balloohouse.com

A famous old 19th-century coaching inn, Balloo House enjoys a reputation as one of the finest country dining pubs in Northern Ireland. The place has genuine character and the old kitchen bar, with its flagstones and traditional range, makes a great setting. In January 2008, Balloo was announced as one of the *Bridgestone Guide*'s Top 100 Restaurants in Ireland. A smoked Lough Neagh eel, apple, beetroot in brioche sandwich costs £9.95, and the signature dish, seared Irish Sea scallops with local leeks, girolle mushrooms, crispy Jerusalem artichokes, and red wine vinaigrette will set you back £20.95.

RESTAURANT

Curran's Bar & Seafood Steakhouse
83 Strangford Road, Chapeltown, Ardglass BT30 7SB
☎ **028 4484 1332**
www.curransbar.ne

Originally the Curran family home, this establishment dates back to 1791. Curran's will endeavour to supply you with exactly the meal you want – whether it's a vegetarian extravaganza or lobster done the way your mother never used to cook it. Just give them a call 24 hours before you arrive. Or you could just settle for their famous seafood platter – a splendid collection of clams, smoked mackerel, mussels, crab-cakes, prawns, dressed crabs and langoustine, served with homemade wheaten bread. Slow-roasted lamb shank served with celeriac mash with winter berries costs £14.95.

GASTRO PUB

Grace Neill's
33 High Street, Donaghadee BT21 0AH
☎ **028 9188 4595**
www.graceneills.com

Grace Neill's, according to the *Guinness Book of World Records*, is the oldest pub in Ireland. Starters concentrate on local produce such as Portavogie prawns, Strangford Lough mussels and smoked salmon crepe gateaux. In fact, the only imported things in use here are the words 'crepe gateaux', specially brought in from France. Main courses cost between £10 and £20, starters around £5.

EATING OUT

The Lobster Pot

9–11 The Square, Strangford BT30 7ND
☎ 028 4488 1288
www.lobsterpotstrangford.com

To be expected, this restaurant's eponymous boast is that it has the largest lobster menu in Ireland – and it changes every week. You can have Lobster Tameriz, Lobster Thermidor, Lobster Trouville, Lobster Newburg, lobster salad etc. Oysters, skatewings and sea bass are the other specialities of the house. If you're not feeling particularly adventurous, traditional cod and chips will cost you £10.95, sirloin steak £16.95.

Paul Arthurs

66 Main Street, Kircubbin, County Down
BT22 2SP
☎ 028 4273 8192
www.paularthurs.com

Chef and owner Paul Arthurs has worked under Michelin-starred chefs Michael Deane and Robbie Millar. The food is exquisite and adventurous: try the pan-fried pigeon fillets with red wine, currant and champ for £16.95. 'Champ' is the local word for mashed potatoes, cream and spring onions. Another local delicacy, potato bread (usually called potato farls or fadge) is served with seared foie gras and streaky bacon (£11.50). A small but impressive wine list has bottles in the range of £10–£20.

CAFÉ

Edgars Restaurant

11–15 Main Street, Saintfield CT24 7AA
☎ 028 9751 1755

Colin and Emma Edgar's smart contemporary café-style restaurant specialises in fresh fish from nearby Ardglass, and beef from the local drumlin farms. Depending on the day of the week, you can order anything from fry to fresh cod, scampi, homemade burgers, rib-eye steak and chicken. For evening meals main dishes include slow-roasted Mourne lamb. Main courses cost from around £10, house wine from about £12.

DOWN

EAST DOWN

ⓘ Visitor Information

Tourist information centre: 53A Market Street, Downpatrick BT30 6LZ.
Hospital: Downe Hospital, Pound Lane, Downpatrick BT30 6JA, ☎ 028 4461 3311.

Doctors: Drs P Moore and U R Small, Health Centre, Pound Lane, Downpatrick BT30 6HY, ☎ 028 4461 3016; Donard Group Practice, 56 Main Street, Newcastle BT33 0AE, ☎ 0844 4773143; Stream Street Surgery, 40 Stream Street, Downpatrick BT30 6DE, ☎ 0844 8151050.

Pharmacies: Strangford Pharmacy, Unit 8, The Square, Strangford, Downpatrick BT30 7ND, ☎ 028 4488 1138; Gordons Chemists, 16 Railway Street, Newcastle BT33 0AL, ☎ 028 4372 2724.

Police: Police Service of Northern Ireland, 6 Saintfield Road, Crossgar, Downpatrick BT30 9HY, ☎ 028 4483 0210.

Supermarkets: Tesco, 21 Castlewellan Road, Newcastle BT33 0GW, ☎ 0845 6779487; ASDA Stores, Ballydugan Road, Downpatrick BT30 6DR, ☎ 028 4461 9606.

Parking: Adjacent to tourist information centre or Donard Park on The Strand.

Cash points: Ulster Bank, 115–117 Main Street, Newcastle BT33 0AE, ☎ 028 4372 3226; Ulster Bank, 23 High Street, Killyleagh, Downpatrick BT30 9QF, ☎ 028 4482 8207.

Taxis: Unicabs, 3 The Arches, Crossgar, Downpatrick BT30 9HD, ☎ 028 9751 0200; 1st Shimna taxis, 18 Railway Street, Newcastle BT33 0AL, ☎ 028 4372 3030/028 4372 6030.

MID AND NORTH DOWN

Mid Down is the heart of Ireland's drumlin country which stretches from the very south of Ulster in Monaghan (now in the Irish Republic) and almost up to Belfast Lough. Drumlins – small egg-shaped hills caused by the last Ice Age – stretch in serried ranks across the countryside, giving this area its nick-name County Up-and-Down. This part of Down also contains some of the region's prettiest villages and most gracious living – Hillsborough, Castle Ward, Hilltown and Waringstown are lovely places to wander about, while Bangor and Newtownards provide for more organised entertainment and diversion.

History there is aplenty too. Catherine O'Hare, the mother of the first European child born west of the Rockies – and delivered by Native American midwives – was born in **Rathfriland**, County Down, in 1835. Her enterprising spirit is par for the course in County Down. This area can be implicated in the birth of the USA, and the development of the tractor (see box below). And when Peter the Great travelled to this area in the 19th century to witness the linen industry at first hand, with a view to introducing it into Russia, he was immediately dubbed the Tsar of the County Down.

Mid Down is also the home of one of Ireland's favourite songs, 'The star of the County Down':

> In Banbridge town, in the County Down
> One mornin' last July
> Down a boreen green came a sweet colleen
> And she smiled as she passed me by...
> From Bantry Bay up the Derry quay
> And from Galway to Dublin town,
> No maid I've seen like my brown colleen
> She's the star of the County Down.

The lovely rolling drumlin landscape round south of Banbridge – from Loughbrickland to Rathfriland – is known as Brontë country. Here lived the numerous family – the father, uncles and aunts of the novelists Charlotte, Emily and Anne. The father of the three illustrious writers, Patrick, was born and brought up here. He was steeped in the folklore of Ulster, something he passed on to his daughters.

Mid and North Down is quite simply a soporifically beautiful rural area, stretching from the Irish Sea to the foothills of the Mountains of Mourne.

The Ulster Folk and Transport Museum

WHAT TO SEE AND DO

Ulster Folk Museum

The Ulster Folk and Transport Museum is situated on the road from Belfast to Bangor – probably just about the ugliest road in Ireland, passing through, as it does, supermarket generica, commercial warehousing and British Army barracks. But here in a roll of hills in **Cultra** just above **Belfast Lough** is an evocative slice of Old Ireland. Farmland is tilled and livestock reared using traditional methods of a bygone age. Crofters' cottages and small rural industries are a feature of the landscape, all meticulously re-created from authentic Ulster buildings.

The transport galleries hold a wonderful key for nostalgia fans. Trolley buses from Belfast, commuter trains from the old York Street Station – in the days before travellers were called commuters – compete for space with penny farthing bicycles, bone-jarring 1950s motor-cycles, trams, buses, fire-engines, aircraft and vintage cars. There's even a gull-winged DeLorean car, the ill-fated sports model made in the North by one of America's more flamboyant characters, John Zachary DeLorean. Of course no transport museum in Belfast could possibly be complete without some mention of the *Titanic*. The exhibition tells the whole story of the ship from her construction, loss, and subsequent legend, to the discovery of her rusted, empty hull on the Atlantic seabed in 1985. Celine Dion's 'My heart will go on' will burst forth from your lips.

On being told there was such a thing as the Ulster Folk Museum a former Tory minister once commented: 'What's that? Two damned Sten guns and a bag of potatoes?' But of course, he couldn't have been more wrong. This is a truly memorable day out, covering everything from the North's industrial and technological prowess to its valuable, ancient folk heritage.

Bangor

For more than 150 years, Bangor has been in the business of providing diversion for trippers and tourists. In 1858 Charles Dickens took time off from a lecture tour of Ireland to have a swim off **Ballyholme Beach** – part of 16 miles of beautiful coastline in north County Down.

ULSTER FOLK AND TRANSPORT MUSEUM: Cultra, Holywood BT18 0EU; ☎ 028 9042 8428; www.uftm.org.uk. Entry: adults £5.40, children (5–18) £3.40, under-5s free, family £15.20; open Jul to Sept Mon–Fri 10am–6pm, Sat 10am–6pm, Sun 11am–6pm; Mar to Jun Mon–Fri 10am–5pm, Sat 10am–6pm, Sun 11am–6pm; Oct to Feb Mon–Fri 10am–4pm, Sat 10am–5pm, Sun 11am–5pm.

County Down's pioneering spirit

Catherine O'Hare, the mother of the first European child born west of the Rockies – and delivered by Native American midwives – was born in **Rathfriland**, County Down, in 1835. Catherine and her husband Augustus Schubert were part of a group of 200 Overlanders heading west in search of gold. These intrepid explorers and settlers blazed the trail for the Canadian Pacific Railroad. Funnily enough, although Rathfriland has eight pubs, not one of them is named after her, nor does any memorial stand in her honour here in her home town. However in Kamloops, British Columbia, the main public park is named after this intrepid woman. Catherine's enterprising spirit is par for the course in County Down. This area can be implicated in the birth of the USA, the annual dating of Easter, and the development of the tractor.

Starting with the tractor, Harry Ferguson, from nearby **Dromore**, was the first man in Ireland to fly, way back in 1909. However, Harry made his name in agriculture rather than aviation. Mid-Down is famous for its drumlins. In a curious twist of progress, these fields helped usher in the technology which changed farming for ever – the tractor. A simple hitch system was required in restricted areas to make the tractor and its plough (or harrow etc) more manoeuvrable. Ferguson's invention was the forerunner of all subsequent tractor systems throughout the world, and in Europe heralded the slow decline of the working horse. The landscape would never be the same again – although there is some irony in the fact that Mid Down's landscape has changed less than most.

No irony, though, over the genesis of the USA – its birth happened here in County Down. It all came about, it is claimed, because of a catastrophic meeting that took place between Benjamin Franklin and Lord Hillsborough (then the acting Secretary of State for the Colonies) in the early 1770s in Hillsborough. They disliked each other intensely, and after no progress was made, Franklin returned home to convince the dissident colonists that there was no alternative but to initiate immediate revolution. The 'Declaration of Independence' in July 1776 followed shortly after Franklin's return.

Bangor **Marina** is one of the largest in Ireland. In 1944 a convoy of battleships, cruisers and destroyers assembled just off Bangor in preparation for the D-Day landings. Dwight D Eisenhower addressed the troops before they boarded the ships. In 2005, his granddaughter Mary-Jean Eisenhower came to the town to oversee the renaming of the marina's North Pier the Eisenhower Pier. A commemorative plaque takes pride of place on the central wall. Today, the area overlooking the marina and onwards along this part of the coastline is generally regarded as one of the most desirable areas in Northern Ireland to live in.

Bangor Boats does cruises round the harbour and surrounding coastline, departing most days (weather permitting) in the summer from the pontoon alongside the Pickie Pool and Eisenhower Pier.

The town has a long and varied history, having been the 'des res' not just of Belfast commuters, but also Bronze Age settlers. More recently, Victorian pleasure

Bangor Marina

seekers travelled on the new railway from Belfast to take the sea air. The town was the site of a monastery renowned throughout Europe for its learning and scholarship, later the victim of violent Viking raids in the 8th and 9th centuries, and then the new home of Scottish and English planters during the Plantation of Ulster in the 17th century.

BANGOR BOATS: ☎ 075 1000 6000/07779 600 607; www.bangorboat. com. Entry: various trips available – tours round the harbour, longer tours to the Copeland Islands (see p. 235), family fishing trips (mainly for mackerel), and bespoke tours along the coast.

The **Old Custom House**, completed in 1637 after James I granted Bangor the status of a port in 1620, is a visible reminder of the new order introduced by Scots settlers, and is one of the oldest buildings in Ireland to have been in continual use. The Annals of Ulster state that the monastery of Bangor was founded by Saint Comgall in approximately AD555 – the town of St Gallen in Switzerland is named after St Gallus who was from the Bangor Abbey.

Unfortunately, little is left of this great seat of learning – the early sundial outside **Bangor Castle** and part of a wall near **Bangor Abbey Parish Church (Church of Ireland)** are all that remain.

Groomsport

The name of Groomsport in the original Irish was *Port an Ghiolla Ghruama* – 'The Harbour of the Gloomy Individual'. Who he, or she was, isn't recorded – and predates the landing of Schomberg in 1689 with 10,000 troops. A monument commemorates the event. Groomsport was already going strong by then, a fishing and trading harbour. Today the village is a genteel, sheltered seashore village – situated 2km east of Bangor – with promenade, pretty harbour, cafés and children's play area.

COCKLE ROW COTTAGES: Just off Main Street, Groomsport; ☎ 028 9145 8882. Entry: free; open daily 11.30–5.30pm Jun to Aug; free entertainment 2–4pm Sat/Sun.

The **Cockle Row Cottages** – originally fishermen's cottages – help to preserve the old world atmosphere of the village, and are now open to the public. The cottages illustrate life for a fisherman and his family at the turn of the last century. They also house a seasonal tourist information centre and shop. A summer exhibition features work by several crafts workers making miniature ships, wood carvings, silver jewellery etc. Some local artists hold workshops where you can learn various crafts.

Summer shows are held for children, including Punch and Judy shows, magicians and storytellers.

Hilltown

Hilltown, a small village in the foothills of the **Mountains of Mourne**, has eight public houses in the main street. Which isn't bad going for a town of around 800 people, 97% of whom are Catholics. This preponderance of pubs is a legacy from smugglers who in the past would share out their contraband here. A footpath, called the **Brandy Pad**, leads from the village, through the Mournes and on to the Irish Sea.

Hilltown has a history of living outside the law – the outlawed Count Redmond O'Hanlon was killed in 1681 just outside the town. The village has a **livestock market** on alternate Saturdays, the Boley Sheep Fair and Festival in early July and a large sale of rams in September – just check how you're fixed for hand luggage before you buy one! Hilltown is very hilly right enough, but its name comes from Lord Hill, founder of Hilltown and Hillsborough. He later became Marquess of Downshire. The Hills founded the village in 1766 to provide workers for the developing linen industry.

Newtownards

Newtownards lies at the most northerly tip of **Strangford Lough**. In AD545, St Finian founded a monastery near present-day Newtownards. He named it Movilla (*Magh Bile*, 'the plain of the sacred tree,' in Irish) which suggests that the land had previously been a sacred pagan site.

The town of Newtownards is overlooked by the 100ft-high **Scrabo Tower** sitting atop a 530ft volcanic plug. Erected as a memorial to Charles Stewart, 3rd Marquess of Derry, it is open to the public, and houses a historical and local environment exhibition. When the Tower was built in 1858 the hilltop cairn – locally known as the house of Shane MacAnanty, King of the Ulster Fairies – was removed. In it were over 100 Viking coins – fairy treasure. The basalt-topped sandstone hill at Scrabo is one of the dominant features of North Down. The Tower now stands in Scrabo Country Park with its woodland walks and parkland through Killynether Wood.

SCRABO MEMORIAL TOWER: Scrabo Country Park, Newtownards; ☎ 028 9181 1491. Entry: free; 10.30am–6pm Sat–Thurs, Apr to Sept.

The **Somme Heritage Centre** is adjacent to the Clandeboye Estate. The Centre attempts to bring home the reality of the Great War and its effects on the community at home. It specifically commemorates the involvement of the 36th (Ulster) and 16th (Irish) Divisions in the Battle of the Somme, the 10th (Irish) Division in Gallipoli, Salonika and Palestine and provides displays and information on the entire Irish contribution to the First World War.

> **SOMME HERITAGE CENTRE:** Whitespots Country Park, 233 Bangor Road, Newtownards BT23 7PH; ☎ 028 4782 3202; www.irishsoldier.org. Entry: adults £3.75, children £2.75; open year round, 10am–4/5pm Mon to Thurs, open weekends Jul/Aug.

Newtownards Airport is home to the Ulster Flying Club — Northern Ireland's largest, non commercial training and flying organisations. The airport is used for an air display show every June.

Movilla Abbey, founded by Augustinian canons, is Newtownards' most ancient site. Nothing remains of the original monastery founded by St Finnian (sometimes Finian) in 540, but it is known to have been one of Ireland's most important monasteries. St Colmcille (aka Columba), and one of Ireland's three patron saints, studied here. The existing ruins – which you can wander round freely – only date back as far as the 15th century abbey. But history clings to you here like burrs. Built into the walls are a number of carved Anglo-Norman grave slabs. One bears an inscription in Irish – probably removed from the 10th century Abbot of Movilla, Dertrend. The church gables are almost intact with elaborately carved windows.

> **MOVILLA ABBEY:** 2km east of Newtownards on the Millisle road. Entry: no restrictions on visiting the site. Flying lessons can be booked here.

The graveyard holds the tomb of Colonel Paddy Blair Mayne, commando leader, believed to be the most decorated soldier in the British army in the Second World War and one of the founders of the SAS.

Hillsborough

Despite its connections with starting up the USA, Hillsborough is better known as the seat of unionist power in the North – this is where the representative of Queen Elizabeth II runs Britain's closest branch office. In days gone by it was a governor, now it's the Secretary of State for Northern Ireland. Hillsborough is everything a village should be with dainty shops, immaculately kept streets, a bookshop and a couple of excellent pubs. It is often called the antique-shop capital of Northern Ireland.

The historic centre of Hillsborough contains significant amounts of Georgian architecture – in fact, this is probably the most English-looking town in all of Ulster; some towns look unmistakably Scottish, others very Irish – but Hillsborough could be at home in Gloucestershire or Kent. Except maybe for the castles, forts and heavily protected PSNI stations. A prominent feature of the east and south approaches to Hillsborough is a 5-mile wall which encloses Hillsborough Fort, the **Park Dam**, an artificial lake, and the forest surrounding it.

Hillsborough Gardens

HILLSBOROUGH FORT: The Square, Hillsborough; ☎ 028 9268 3285. Entry: free; open Apr to Sept, Tues–Sat 10am–7pm, Sun 2–7pm; Oct to Mar, Tues–Sat 10am–4pm, Sun 2–4pm.

Built on the site of the old Magennis stronghold, the fort was founded in 1630 by Peter Hill and completed around 1650 by Colonel Arthur Hill. The fort consists of a square enclosed by an earthen rampart with outer stone facing. This stone facing rises above the rampart level to form a parapet wall. It was constituted a Royal Fort by Charles II. William of Orange spent several nights at the Fort on his way south to the Boyne in 1690.

Hillsborough Castle and Gardens

The 18th-century **Hillsborough Castle**, a two-storey Georgian mansion, has extensive gardens, and the demesne comes with a Victorian folly. You can see the gazebo

HILLSBOROUGH CASTLE: The Square, Hillsborough, County Down BT26 6AG; ☎ 028 9268 1309. Entry: guided tour: adults £5, children £3.50, grounds only £2.50; 11am–4.30pm May/Jun.

through the highly decorative wrought iron gates. It's also possible to take guided tours – see where the Good Friday Agreement was signed, and in the garden be thoroughly impressed by what is reputedly the largest rhododendron bush in Europe.

Local legends: King Billy

Many places lay claim to being the site of an extraordinary story – but as it is a matter of record that William of Orange, aka King Billy, stayed in Hillsborough on several occasions, perhaps the incident should best be related here. After the seismic Battle of the Boyne in 1690, a triumphant William of Orange is reputed to have subsequently met up with the disconsolate, defeated King James. King Billy comforted him with a few kind words. 'Ah sure, don't worry Jim,' he's reported to have said. 'It'll all be forgotten about in a couple of weeks.'

LOCAL KNOWLEDGE

Full-time musician, **Shaun Casement** was born in Killyleagh, deep in the heart of the County Down countryside, and spent his childhood there. At the age of 16 he began learning the guitar and started going to various local traditional music sessions.

Favourite pub – I recommend the Corner Inn in Crossgar – just a nice wee local.

Favourite restaurant – Balloo House in Killinchy. This is one of the places where I started my music career, playing in local sessions.

Best view – overlooking Strangford Lough towards Portaferry. The views here really are stunning.

Secret tip for lunch – Daft Eddy's. The lobsters are magic, and it's reasonably priced too.

Favourite activity – gardening and playing music. This is a great area for traditional music, and crosses the religious divide. And because so many people play in the locality, there's a huge variety of instruments from Scottish small pipes to harps. We even have a jazz double bass player who joins in on a Saturday afternoon.

Best walk – I like to ramble up to the top of St Patrick's Hill, just beyond Saul. There's a big statue of St Patrick at the top, and the views across to the Mountains of Mourne are beautiful.

Best kept secret – Inch Abbey, down by the Quoile River. It's so peaceful, and hardly anybody ever goes there – it's a great place to take you guitar and strum away.

Hillsborough Forest Park is the wildlife jewel of the area. A path takes you round the lake, which is crammed with swans and wildfowl. A prominent memorial to the **3rd Marquis of Downshire** (and closely resembling Nelson's column in Trafalgar Square, London) stands to the south of the village, visible throughout much of the surrounding area. However, the most breathtaking sight in Hillsborough is one that most people just glance at and pass by. The **Parish Church of St Malachy** lies in a glorious setting near the town centre. Dozens of stately old trees, mostly oaks, line a long, verdant lawn which stretches to the church steps. One of the finest examples of Gothic revival architecture anywhere, it was built by the 1st Marquis of Downshire between 1760 and 1774, in the hope that the church would become the cathedral of the diocese of Down.

In addition to its imposing setting, St Malachy's boasts two 18th-century organs, a peal of 10 bells and a number of works by notable craftsmen of the era and area. As with many Church of Ireland establishments, military flags are to the fore. Specifically the Colours of the County Down Battalion of Carson's Ulster Volunteers are prominently displayed.

Waringstown

Even in as politically turbulent an area as Northern Ireland there came a time in history when houses no longer needed to be fortified. In other words, an Irishman's home no longer needed to be his castle. The first mansion house in Ireland totally unfortified – without murder holes, stumble steps, turrets, moat etc – is believed to have been **Waring House**, built by the eponymous Mr William Waring in 1667. The house – a flaky, pink-painted mansion with tall Tudor-revival chimney – still presides over this typical small Ulster Plantation settlement.

The Waring family's fortune came from linen – as did most of the money in mid-Down. Flemish weavers were brought here, and several Dutch-style cottages, built specially for the workers, survive. Their white-washed walls and pretty gardens make this a lovely village to visit.

Slieve Croob

Slieve Croob is the largest of a small group of peaks in the middle of the county, to the north of the Mourne Mountains. Croob, the source of the **River Lagan**, which starts as a spring here, has been designated an Area of Outstanding Natural Beauty. As such, it is one of the finest walking and hiking areas in the country. Legend has it that 12 kings are buried at the summit of Slieve Croob. Every year the mountain is climbed by locals on the last Sunday in August, known as Cairn Sunday or blaeberry Sunday. Should you decide to join in this ancient rite, remember that it is de rigeur to bring a stone with you to help bury the kings. Several mountains in Ireland have similar peregrinations, although many have now taken on a Christian significance, such as the climb up Croagh Patrick in County Mayo on the last Sunday in July. But the Slieve Croob walk clings on to its pagan origins.

THE LEGANANNY DOLMEN: Situated off the B7, 7 miles south of Dromara, signposted from Dromara and Castlewellan.

The 5,000-year-old **Legananny Dolmen** (from *Liagán áine* or 'Pillar of Enya') megalithic monument or cromlech on the slopes of Slieve Croob, believed to be the portal grave of a chieftain, is the North of Ireland's best known and most photographed dolmen. The elegant tripod of stones is good starting off point for walking in Slieve Croob.

Banbridge

Banbridge is the industrial hub and market town of Mid Down, with one of the most curious centres in the entire region. **Banbridge 'Cut'** divides the wide main thoroughfare of Bridge Street and Newry Street. The underpass was cut out in 1834 to allow Royal Mail coaches to

The Crozier monument in Banbridge

pass through the centre. This has given the main street an odd double-decker effect. A statue to a Banbridge man, Captain Francis Crozier, stands in **Church Square**. The very Victorian-looking erection features four polar bears, which will probably remind you that Captain Crozier was the man who discovered the North West Passage in 1848.

Outdoor activities

Excellent areas for **fishing** in the Mid and North Down area include the southerly banks of Lough Neagh and the easterly shores of Strangford Lough. The River Lagan has its source in Slieve Croob, and

FINNEY'S FLIES: 8 Claremont Park, Moira BT670SF; ☎ 028 92 619313/07764 533823; www.finneysflies.com. Courses: All year round, every Mon/Wed/Fri.

also provides a variety of angling opportunities. For instruction in fly fishing – and for valuable local information on the best local sites – head for **Finney's Flies**.

The terrain of County Down is ideal for **horse riding.** In the soft countryside you can learn how to keep control of a skewbald Irish cob as she flies over a ditch, or have a more sedate ride on an Irish draught horse as she sweats and puffs up the side of a drumlin. This is

MILLBRIDGE RIDING CENTRE: 129 Glen Road, Comber, Newtownards BT23 5QT; ☎ 028 9187 2508. Has a wide variety of horses for a range of abilities.

prime equine territory, and horse riding is the ideal method for seeing the countryside at its most seductive and alluring.

Several **walks** criss-cross Mid and North Down (see also Slieve Croob), with one of the finest the North Down Coastal Path extending along the shoreline from Holywood to Bangor and on to Donaghadee. You can park the car or take a bus or train to join the coastal path at many places along its 16 miles. The route is extensively sign-posted and way-marked.

☔ Wet weather

Brontë Interpretive Centre

The area round **Rathfriland** is known as Brontë country. Ay oop! And you thought he wer't Yorkshire lad! But the fact is the hero of *Wuthering Heights* is based on Emily Brontë's memories of her uncle. Welsh Brontë, like Emily's father, grew up in the beautiful rolling countryside around Mid Down. Popular local legend has it that Uncle Welsh walked all the way to London on one occasion, armed with a big stick, to silence critics of his niece's novel. *Wuthering Heights* is generally regarded as one of the world's greatest novels, but not many people are aware of this County Down connection.

Patrick Brontë, Emily's father, was born on St Patrick's Day 1777 in **Emdale Cottage, Drumgooland**. His family was originally from Dundalk (now in the Republic) and originally called Prunty or *Ó Pronntaigh*. The son of a mixed (Catholic/Protestant) marriage, he was ridiculed as 'Papist Brontë'. But both the Presbyterian and Anglican clergymen of the locality realised his great literary talent and helped get him to St John's College, Cambridge. Subsequently he became vicar of Haworth, Yorkshire, where he regaled his illustrious offspring with tall tales and folklore from the land of his birth. All the Brontë sisters' novels owe something to their father's memories of his home in County Down. The Brontë countryside lies between **Banbridge** and **Rathfriland** (incidentally George W. Bush's great-great-grandmother came from Rathfriland).

The ruins of the cottage of Patrick's birthplace at **Emdale** are preserved and two other Brontë houses nearby are still occupied. The hilltop parish church and school at Drumballyroney where Patrick taught before going to England is now the

The Bronte Interpretative Centre

nucleus of the tiny **Brontë Interpretative Centre**. In **Glascar School** Patrick built his reputation as an innovative teacher in the 1790s. He was reportedly dismissed from his position after a rumoured romantic encounter with a student.

BRONTË HOMELAND INTERPRETATIVE CENTRE: Drumballyroney, Rathfriland; ☎ 028 4063 1152. Entry: adults £3, children £2; 12–4.30pm Fri–Sun, Apr to Sept.

The drive through this beautiful drumlin countryside is unsurpassable. The **Knockiveagh Brontë Homeland Picnic Site** (details from the Brontë Interpretive Centre) is an ideal place to contemplate the rolling hills and rough countryside where the young Brontë grew up. The picnic area occupies the ruins of a former shebeen, or illegal drinking premises.

A bit further on is **Alice McClory's Cottage**, the childhood home of Patrick's mother, Alice McClory. Alice and her lover Hugh used to court secretly and some say they eloped to their wedding in **Magherally Church**, near Banbridge. Here in the heart of rural Ireland Patrick Brontë heard the folklore of his native land. He was a fine writer himself, publishing several poems, but his literary importance lies in the storytelling gift he passed on to his three daughters – tales from his Irish childhood which fed and fired their imaginative genius.

What to do with children

Clementsmount Fun Farm (50 Ballydonaghy Road, Crumlin; ☎ 028 9442 2824; www.clementsmountfunfarm.co.uk) offers an extensive range of activities including cuddle bunnies, lambs, baby goats, chinchillas, pony rides, pedal go-karts, crazy golf, trim trail, indoor soft play, sand diggers and more.

Pickie Fun Park, Bangor is probably Northern Ireland's favourite children's venue with a host of traditional seaside pursuits. Facilities include swimming pool, paddle pools, giant (artificial) swan pedal boats on the (artificial) lagoon, bouncy castles, mini go karts, and the Pickie Puffer – a narrow gauge railway. A large adventure playground provides further fun.

PICKIE FUN PARK: Marine Gardens, The Promenade, Bangor BT20 3TA; ☎ 028 9127 0069. Most boats, rides and bouncy castle, all £1.50, play park free for under-14s.

The **Ark Open Farm**'s main aim is the preservation of rare and endangered species of domestic animals. Set in forty acres of unspoiled countryside it is home to approximately 200 animals of all kinds. Cattle, sheep, pigs, poultry, goats, donkeys, llamas, alpacas, ponies, rabbits, chicks, guinea pigs, pet lambs, kid goats and ponies to ride are all present and correct. The Ark Farm is the only one of its kind in Northern Ireland, specialising in animals no longer seen in the fields.

ARK OPEN FARM: 296 Bangor Road, Newtownards; www.thearkopenfarm.co.uk. Entry: adults £3.90, children £3.20; open Mon–Sat 10am–6pm, Sun 1–6pm, Oct to Mar close 5pm.

Entertainment

Parts of Mid Down, particularly the southerly end, are renowned for set dancing and ceillidh dancing. The following places all hold dances, for dancers of varying degrees of proficiency, and always welcome visitors.

- Sundays: **Ardglass Golf Club**, Castle Place, Ardglass BT30 7TP, 7–9pm
- Mondays: **Drumaness Parish Hall**, Edendariff Road, Drumaness, 8.30–10.30pm
- Tuesdays: **Russell GAA Clubhouse**, Old Course Road, Flying Horse Road, Downpatrick, 7.30–9.30pm
- Tuesdays: **Greenan's**, 1 Hilltown Road, The Square, Kilcoo BT34 5EZ, 8–10pm
- Thursdays: **St Joseph's Hall**, behind Ivanhoe Hotel, Saintfield Road, Carryduff, 8.30–10.30pm
- Fridays: **Irish National Foresters Hall**, Hilltown, 9.30pm–12.30am
- Fridays: **St Malachy's Hall**, Kilcoo, Newry, 9.30pm–1am

Prices vary, but generally range between £2 and £5.

At the end of August **Hillsborough** holds its **Oyster Festival** (www.oysterfestival.com). This weekend of bivalve revelry culminates in the World Oyster Eating Championship. Aside from bivalve, crustacean and mollusc treats, you can take part in a soapbox derby, tug of war or fancy dress, as well as enjoying bands, buskers and dancers. The **Planter's Bar** (4 Banbridge Road, Waringstown BT66 7QA; ☎ 028 3888 1510) in the beautiful historic town of Waringstown is a top entertainment venue in North Armagh. It features disco, live music and karaoke, as well as plasma TV screens.

For traditional music sessions **Lisbarnett House** (☎ 028 9754 1589) near Comber, on the Killyleagh-Comber Road, are held most Wednesday nights. Blue grass and country sessions are also held.

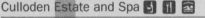

The best... PLACES TO STAY

HOTEL

Culloden Estate and Spa 🎵 🍴 🏖

Bangor Road, Holywood BT18 0EX
☎ 028 9042 1066
www.hastingshotel.com

The Culloden, just outside Belfast, is a former bishop's palace, now with a conservatory extension housing the Elysian Spa. Gym, swimming pool, jacuzzi and steam room are set in undulating parkland overlooking Belfast Lough. The spa offers more than just beauty treatments – reiki, reflexology and ear candling are all available, and the toe therapy is said to work wonders for insomnia and headaches. If you're staying overnight serious comfort is on offer – the beds are so big you might get lost in them; the bathrooms are covered from floor to ceiling in grey marble.

Price: from £200 for a double.

The best... **PLACES TO STAY**

Paul Arthurs

66 Main Street, Kircubbin BT22 2SP
☎ 028 4273 8192
www.paularthurs.com

Chef and owner Paul Arthurs has worked under Michelin-starred chefs Michael Deane and Robbie Millar, and as a result of the restaurant's location near Strangford Lough fish is prominent on the menu. The seven very comfortable bedrooms are each individually furnished. Staying and dining here is a wonderful experience.

Price: £50 for a single; £70 for a double.

La Mon Hotel & Country Club

41 Gransha Road, Comber BT23 5RF
☎ 028 9044 8631
www.lamon.co.uk

The La Mon Hotel is a family-owned four-star hotel famous for its award-winning cuisine and use of local produce. Breakfasts here are legendary, and the rooms are decorated in traditional style.

Price: from £60 for a single; £70 for a double.

FARMSTAY

Fortwilliam

210 Ballynahinch Road, Hillsborough
BT26 6BH; ☎ 028 9268 2255
www.fortwilliamcountryhouse.com

The house, dating back over 300 years, is furnished with antiques and period décor. Just over three miles from Hillsborough, all four bedrooms on this working farm overlook the gardens or farmland.

Price: £40 for a single; £60 for a double.

B & B

Clanmurry

Clanmurry Lower, Quilly Road, Dromore BT25 1NL
☎ 028 9269 3760; www.clanmurry.com

Built in 1820, this is a lovely family home owned since 1985 by John and Sara McCorkell. Clanmurry is comfortable and elegant, and the extensive gardens are ideal to relax in and breathe the sweet soft air of Down's drumlin countryside.

Price: £32.50 to £45 per person.

Edenvale House

130 Portaferry Road, Newtownards BT22 2AH
☎ 028 9181 4881
www.edenvalehouse.com

Edenvale House is surrounded by 7 acres of garden and farmland, and has a National Trust wildlife reserve opposite its gate. Its three bedrooms have views across Strangford Lough. The house is a three-minute walk from the village of Greyabbey. Breakfast includes homemade bread, and of course the full Ulster.

Price: from £45 per night per person sharing.

Beech Hill

23 Ballymoney Road, Craigantlet, Holywood
BT23 4TG; ☎ 028 9042 5892
www.beech-hill.net

This Georgian style house in the Holywood Hills is a 15-minute drive from Belfast city centre. The three bedrooms are decorated with antiques and have wireless internet access, flat-screen TVs and DVD players.

Price: £50 for a single; £85 for a double.

The best... FOOD AND DRINK

▶ Staying in

For seafood and shellfish, you'll find the very best at the **Drumgooland Smokehouse** (4 Gargarry Road, Ballyward BT31 9RN; ☎ 028 4065 0720; www.locallink.ie). A wide range of smoked foods, dressings and relishes is available. Drumgooland Smokehouse is noted for using tried-and-trusted traditional methods in its smoking process – the result is tasty produce of the highest quality.

Quails (13–15 Newry Street, Banbridge BT32 3EA; ☎ 028 4066 2604; www.quailsfinefoods.co.uk) have been purveyors of fine foods for over 110 years. In the heart of Banbridge, the family-owned business has spanned four generations, evolving from a small butcher's shop to a modern day food hall selling the highest-quality meat from its own farm and a range of foods from local and national high quality producers. **Primacy Food Village Farm Shop** (26a Primacy Road, Bangor BT19 7PQ; ☎ 028 9127 0083; www.primacymeatsfoodvillage.co.uk) is a traditional butchers, greengrocers, bakery with fresh local products paramount. The kitchen supplies freshly prepared ready-made meals, pies and quiches, all made with local produce.

Camphill (8 Shore Road, Holywood; ☎ 028 9042 3203) is a bakery that produces gluten-free bread, as well as the full sweep of traditional Irish breads. **Homegrown** (66b East Street, Newtownards; ☎ 028 9181 8318) is one of the best greengrocers around, with a huge range of local produce. **Knott's Cake & Coffee Shop** (45 High Street, Newtownards; ☎ 028 9181 9098) self-service café and bakery is hugely popular with locals who love the cakes, the sweet squares and the fresh cream buns. But there's savoury cooking too: beef olives; stuffed pork; pastry pies served with turnips and champ. Sandwiches are soft and chunky, packed with filling, and great old stagers such as coronation chicken sandwich get a decent showing. **McKee's Produce** (28 Holywood Road, Newtownards; ☎ 028 9181 3202; www.mckeesproduce.co.uk) sells cakes, meringues, home-made preserves, free-range eggs and chickens. And 99% of what they sell is sourced in Northern Ireland.

EATING OUT

RESTAURANT

Restaurant 1614
**The Old Inn, Main Street, Crawfordsburn
BT19 1JH
☎ 028 9185 3255
www.theoldinn.com**

One of the oldest inns in Ireland, this establishment has been going strong for the best part of 400 years. Food in the Old Inn is a mixture of hearty and adventurous. Being on Belfast Lough, seafood takes a starring role, although there are plenty of choices for fully-fledged carnivores and indeed herbivores. Try the special: gourmet menu tasting evenings £45 – five courses with wine to complement every course.

Daft Eddy's Bar & Restaurant
**Killinchy BT23 6QH
☎ 028 9754 1615**

Nestling off Sketrick Island in Strangford Lough, this famous bar and restaurant is within a couple of minutes' stroll from Strangford Lough. Renowned for its fresh food and friendly service, Daft Eddy's offers oysters and lobster along with daily fresh seafood and a host of other dishes all using local produce.

Slieve Croob Inn
**119 Clonvaraghan Road, Castlewellan
BT31 9LA
☎ 028 4377 1412
www.slievecroobinn.com**

This award-winning country inn is one of the finest in the county. Dishes range from traditional to the more exotic. However, one thing never varies – the stunning views of both Slieve Croob and the Mountains of Mourne, and probably just about the finest view you can get of Slieve Donard, the highest peak in the province. Prices are reasonable too, with fisherman's pie with salmon, prawns, cod and smoked haddock setting you back just £8.95.

The Halfway House
**80 Halfway Road, Banbridge BT32 4HB
☎ 028 9269 2351
www.halfwayhouse.co.uk**

This beautiful building, set in a beautiful rural backdrop, has been open for over 100 years and in the same family for four generations. The present owners Richard and Julianne Ferris have extended, improved and refurbished the Halfway House to its present glory. Main courses cost from £10.95.

GASTRO PUB

The Dirty Duck Ale House
**2–4 Kinnegar Road, Holywood BT18 9JN
☎ 028 9059 6666
www.thedirtyduckalehouse.co.uk**

The Dirty Duck is over 100 years old, with the original arrangements still in place – pub downstairs, restaurant upstairs. Views across Belfast Lough complement the cuisine – imaginatively cooked seafood, plus beef and pork from the fine grazing pastures of north Down. Main courses start at around £9.

CAFÉ

The Bay Tree Coffee Shop
**118 High Street, Holywood BT18 9HW
☎ 028 9042 1419
www.baytreeholywood.co.uk**

'Super Salads', chowder, bacon and mushroom croustade and pan-fried haddock fillets with parsley butter and mash are among the dishes which have made the Bay Tree one of the most popular eateries in the area. Probably most famous of all in this land where cakes and pastries have reached something of an artform are the homemade cinnamon scones, delicious and unforgettable.

♨ Drinking

The **Marquis of Downshire** (48 Lisburn Street, Hillsborough BT26 6AB; ☎ 028 9268 2095) is one of the most famous watering holes in the area. In summer the beer garden is thronged, in winter the big open fireplace is so inviting, the Guinness so good you will want to sit there all evening – and half the night if you get the chance. The **Old Inn**, Crawfordsburn (Main Street, Crawfordsburn BT19 1JH; ☎ 028 9185 3255; www.theoldinn.com) has provided liquid refreshment to locals and travellers for the thick end of 400 years. Those who have enjoyed hospitality here include Jonathan Swift, Dick Turpin, Peter the Great, Lord Tennyson, Charles Dickens, Anthony Trollope, and C S Lewis (the latter honeymooned here with his American wife.)

The **White Horse Inn**, Saintfield (49, Main St BT24 7AB) is part of the Whitewater Brewing Company (Northern Ireland's largest microbrewery) so needless to say real ale is part of the pub's charm – as well as its traditional surroundings and terrific cuisine. The **Hillside** (21 Main Street, Hillsborough BT26 6AE; ☎ 028 28 9268 2765) is renowned for its roaring coal fires in the winter and its atmospheric cobble-stoned beer garden in the summer. Being right in the centre of the lovely village of Hillsborough there's always a buzz in the pub. Three cask-conditioned ales are normally available and a selection of local Whitewater beers plus some from England.

ⓘ Visitor Information

Tourist information centre: 53A Market Street, Downpatrick BT30 6LZ.

Hospital: Downe Hospital, Pound Lane, Downpatrick BT30 6JA, ☎ 028 4461 3311.

Doctors: Rathfriland Surgery, 9 Castlewellan Road, Rathfriland, Newry BT34 5LY, ☎ 028 4063 0034; Drs McCloskey, Mockford and Ramsey, 1 Old Hospital Road, Banbridge BT32 3GN, ☎ 028 4062 3303.

Pharmacies: Gordons Chemists, 12 Linenhall Street, Banbridge BT32 3EG, ☎ 028 4066 2811; Boots The Chemist, 85–87 Newry Street, Banbridge BT32 3EA, ☎ 028 4066 2720; Gordons Chemists, 16 Main Street, Rathfriland, Newry BT34 5PS, ☎ 028 4063 0212.

Police: Banbridge Police Station, 14 Castlewellan Road, Banbridge BT32 4AX, ☎ 0845 600 8000; Police Service of Northern Ireland, 18 Downpatrick Street, Rathfriland, Newry BT34 5DG, ☎ 028 4063 0224.

Supermarkets: Barbican Fresh Foods, 34 John Street, Rathfriland, Newry BT34 5QH, ☎ 028 4063 1881; Tesco, 25a Castlewellan Road, Banbridge BT32 4AX, ☎ 028 4062 9301.

Parking: Downshire Road Car Park, Banbridge; NCP Unit 20 Win Business Pk, Canal Quay, Newry BT35 6PH, ☎ 028 30250909.

Cash points: Bank of Ireland, 17 Bridge Street, Banbridge BT32 3JL, ☎ 028 4062 2476; Abbey, 3 Margaret Square, Newry BT34 1JA, ☎ 0845 7654321.

Internet access: The Source Internet Café, Scarva Street, Banbridge, Down BT32 3DA, ☎ 028 4066 9250.

Bike rental: Cycle Hire, The Cycle Centre, 31a Church Square, Banbridge, ☎ 028 4066 2863.

Taxis: Ace taxis, 32 St. Marys Street, Newry BT34 2AA, ☎ 028 3027 8029; Bann Taxis, 94 Newry Street, Banbridge BT32 3HE, ☎ 028 4062 4794.

SOUTH DOWN

The Mountains of Mourne really do sweep down to the sea. The granite peaks stretch from the shores of Carlingford Lough northwards along the Irish Sea, for much of the way rising almost directly out of the sea. This gives them a spectacular appearance that belies their somewhat modest height. Altitudes with attitudes, like so much of Northern Ireland. These excellently stage-managed peaks do provide challenging climbs – the Everest Expedition of 1953 used the sheer cliff walls of the Pot of Pulgarve for preparatory work.

In the shadow of the Mournes two forest parks glory in the rep of their horticultural high jinx – Tollymore Forest Park and Castlewellan Demesne inspired not just Percy French but also Belfast writer C S Lewis (of *Chronicles of Narnia* fame) and the poet Edward Lear. Today you can walk along the same azalea-lined avenues, past the same time-weathered Victorian follies, and look out on the same astonishing panoramas which inspired these writers and poets.

Other high-profile visitors to South Down include the great and good of the golf world – their destination the Royal County Down. This course is generally agreed by the most objective of observers to be among the world's top 10 courses; among the less objective, it's believed to have been designed by God to get his handicap down. Recently it has been voted top course in the world outside the USA.

County Down has had to take the rough with the rough, so to speak. A politically volatile area for centuries, it is one of only two counties in the whole of Ireland still with a Protestant majority. However, South Down is predominantly Catholic. The United Irishmen who instigated the Rebellion of 1798 (only last weekend in Northern Ireland terms) were active here; more recently it was represented by Enoch Powell in the British parliament and before that by Eamon de Valera, the man who largely shaped independent Ireland. Despite this history of insurgency and political activity, South Down was relatively untouched by the recent Troubles. It retains a gentle, friendly face – but with enough spectacular sights to fill anybody's photograph album.

WHAT TO SEE AND DO

Mountains of Mourne
Famed in song and story, the Mountains of Mourne are among the most photogenic in these islands. Shaped by a million years of belligerent weather, the Mournes provide a haven for rock climbers, hill walkers, campers and geologists, as well as literary types. C S Lewis walked here, dreaming up tales about Narnia, while Percy French wrote:

I'll wait for my wild rose who's waiting for me
Where the Mountains of Mourne sweep down to the sea.

The Mourne mountains covered in snow

The stone from round here has long been prized in building construction – Mourne granite is being used to make the base of the 9/11 memorial in New York.

The **Mourne Wall** is a curious thing that stretches through the Mournes – a dry-stone granite wall which extends some 22 miles across 15 summits, enclosing the reservoirs of Silent Valley and Ben Crom. Standing 5ft along most of its length, it is impressive nonetheless, reaching as it does to the top of the highest mountain in the North, Slieve Donard. En route it scales the Castles of Commedagh – a mighty battlement of towers and turrets of solid granite – and then Slieve Coragh, Slievenaglogh, Slieve Meelmore and onwards into the mist. Not a pick of cement was used in the construction of the wall, begun in 1904. The men who built 'the black ditch of Mourne' lived through hard times in the early 20th century; thousands of local men earned a subsistence living heaving great boulders of granite across the mountainside. In the process they created a monumental structure quite unlike anything else in Ireland.

Doubtless, if this astonishing engineering feat adorned any other part of the island, tourists would be told it was built by the Wee Folk to keep the banshees out and appropriate souvenirs would be sold. But because it's in an area until fairly recently more connected with civil disorder in the public mind, it's unspoilt, undeveloped, and quite simply stunningly dramatic. Latest scientific research shows that the wall probably wasn't built by the Little People; so the question remains as to why it's there at all. The clue: the reservoirs. The Belfast Water Commissioners wanted the clear, plentiful water of the Mournes, so they built these giant reservoirs. As nationalists joked at the time, 'At last. A unionist plan that actually holds water.'

The dam things were duly completed in the days before sophisticated purification processes. So everything on four or two legs had to be stopped entering the catchment area. Up went the Mourne Wall, and it remains a triumph of craftsmanship. Most of it is as solid as the day it was built – despite the only mortar used in the entire length being in the three watchtowers on Slieve Meelmore, Slieve Commedagh and Slieve Donard. The strength of the wall lies in its cunning construction. Enormous 'footing stones' lie at the base, and two dry stone walls stand atop this, leaning against each other. Broad 'cam' stones along the top bind the two walls together – virtually impregnable to animals, human or otherwise. Only stones near to hand were used – so the path beside the wall provides easy going, being relatively free of stones to trip over. The wall is easily crossed today by wooden styles. This tremendous circuit of the main Mourne peaks was built by labourers who were poor and hungry. Paradoxically it was the work of these craftsmen which helped open up the Mountains of Mourne to hillwalkers, campers, orienteerers and rock climbers.

Today, a well-worn path follows the wall along its entire length. Other walls join up with the main wall – stiles are provided regularly to allow you to cross – and the entire network is a terrific orientation aid. And because the walls are now so weathered they blend in beautifully with the landscape.

Slieve Donard – the mammoth task of making Christians out of the people of Mourne fell to St Donard (died *c.* 506) who lived atop the eponymous mountain. To reach the site of his 'des res' you can follow the Mourne Wall from various points along its route. But the most direct way is to head for the coast. Your starting off point is the seaside resort of Newcastle, one foot above sea level. So, still some 2,785ft left to go. Follow the signs and head up along the Glen River. After some two hours your reward will be a view across Dundrum Bay which is singularly sweet: on a clear day you'll see most of Northern Ireland and the Irish midlands, the Isle of Man, and the Mull of Kintyre. If a local tells you that it's possible to see seven kingdoms from the top, it's a trick. That'll include the Kingdom of Mourne and the Kingdom of God. Play dumb, and you might get a pint of Guinness out of it.

The **Brandy Pad** (pad = path, hereabouts), an old smugglers' trail traversing the Mourne Wall, starts at the Bloody Bridge – the scene of an ancient battle, if you hadn't guessed – overlooking the Irish Sea. The remains of an ancient church and the old bridge which once carried the coast road can be seen from the pad as it wends its way upwards into the mountains. The route heads up through Poulaphouca – the Glen of the Fairies – on to the Hare's Gap and the slopes of Slievenaglogh. Walk along this path, and cross the Trassey River, and you will eventually come to Hilltown, a place which seems to have more than its fair share of pubs even by Irish standards – eight in the high street alone, which is going it a bit in a village of under 1,000 people. But this is where, according to legend, the smugglers, fresh off the Brandy Pad, repaired in order to celebrate a good night's work. Having safely stowed their liquor, tobacco, tea, silk and soap – often brought from the Isle of Man, sometimes Britain – the hardy smugglers would make their way to the pub. It's still a convivial watering hole, even if you haven't been smuggling.

Within striking distance of the Trassey Bridge are the Diamond Rocks. Look out here for Mourne Diamonds – beautiful pieces of smoky quartz and black mica crystals set deep in the granite. Any small crevice in the rock may yield this treasure. Impressive, glittering – but alas worthless in monetary value. Priceless, however, in the search for them.

Tollymore Forest Park

The Narnia films may have been made in New Zealand, but the inspiration for Belfast man C S Lewis was here in the southerly reaches of County Down – the Mournes, Slieve Gullion, and particularly Tollymore Forest Park. A 2-mile drive lined with Lebanese cedars and guarded by a Victorian barbican is the first clue that you're about to enter one of the great piles belonging to the Protestant Ascendancy – or the Raj in the Rain as they've been described. Tollymore Forest is festooned with monumental follies (literally) – gothic outrages, geometrical curios, grottos, obelisks and statues. The main entrance, with chunky round castellated turrets and quatrefoil loopholes, reflects the extravagant follies which lie inside. Enough to activate anyone's imagination.

The main car park, once the site of the Earls of Clanbrassill's Big House, is adjoined by the **Arboretum** with its hundreds of tree species – including a dwarf Norway spruce, the first specimen ever recorded and now more than 200 years old. Myriad horticultural superstars – obscure species of dawn redwoods, black junipers, maidenhair trees – jostle for space among rarities such as the Japanese white pine, the strawberry tree (native to Ireland but not Britain), and the vividly red katserra tree.

For a reasonably manageable tour of the demesne's curios, head for the **Azalea Walk**. After a few hundred metres you will come to a small, classical fountain. The water spouts from the mouth of a stone lion – according to local legend, Aslan. The path leads fairly steeply downhill now, underneath the **Horn Bridge**. With its tiny turrets, crenellations and shamrock-shaped embrasures, it looks for all the world like an overgrown toy castle. Through the bridge, and the hillside explodes in a profusion of rare plants and shrubs – another roll call of exotics such as blue pine, a wayfaring tree and locust bush. These rockeries are a result of some 200 years of planting, pruning, coppicing and weeding – and of course thieving. Away to the right is the oak grove which supplied wood for the main staircase of the *Titanic*.

The Hermitage in Tollymore Forest Park

At the bottom of the gardens turn left along the river, crossing at the **Old Bridge.** Head for the ornamental lake, overlooked by the Seven Sisters – gigantic silver firs which are the highest trees in the forest. Gawp at one of these cloud-piercing giants, and perhaps ponder a C S Lewis line: 'The garden and magic tree which lie to the west of Narnia, at the end of the blue lake.' From here take the road downhill to the **Ivy Bridge**. Built in 1780, each corner is decorated with an ornate stone sentry box. The route now hugs the fast-flowing Shimna River. Several more curios crop up – the tiny **Foley's Bridge** spanning a torrential waterfall; a stone chair engraved with Alexander Pope poetry; a glacial erratic (a huge split boulder) with biblical text inscribed.

The riverside path eventually leads to the oddest folly on the estate, the

Old Hermitage. Two chambers – each about 3m by 4m, and made from intricate stonework – straddle the path. Overlooking a deep pool on the Shimna, the faux hermitage is equipped with stone steps leading into a dark, coniferous forest. It looks like it's tumbled out of a fairytale – or a Chronicle. Heading further up the river you will come to the Meeting of the Waters – where the **Spinkwee River** joins the **Shimna**. Further along is **Parnell's Bridge** – named after Sir John Parnell, a relative of Charles Stewart Parnell, the first Irishman to really scare the British parliament. Just beyond Parnell's Bridge is the White Fort, a circular, stone-walled enclosure, probably a farmstead dating back to AD500–100, long before EU subsidies. The **King's Grave** is situated at the edge of the forest, just where the open mountainside begins. This round cairn dates back to between 1500BC and 1000BC.

> TOLLYMORE FOREST PARK: Two miles north-west of Newcastle – head for the village of Bryansford. It's about 4 miles from Castlewellan, and is well sign-posted from there; www.forestserviceni.gov.uk. Entry: free, but car parking costs £4; official opening hours are daybreak to dusk, although the gates are never closed.

Castlewellan

Castlewellan is a handsome enough market town with two squares, two old market houses, a brace of fine churches and half a dozen pubs. Although a fine base for exploring South Down, it has one added attraction marking it out as an indispensable destination – **Castlewellan Forest Park**. This 1,000-acre conifer and broadleaf wood boasts a lake (fishing and boating both recommended) nature trails, an orienteering route, and a castle built in the Scottish baronial style. But its most important asset is the world famous arboretum. Currently the home of Ireland's tallest tree – a western hemlock – its upper branches seem to pierce the clouds. Despite this, the claim is naturally enough disputed. What is irrefutable, however, is that here is the home of the ubiquitous cypress tree the Castlewellan Gold. The ancestor of this hedge and garden staple can be seen just beyond the ornamental pond.

> CASTLEWELLAN FOREST PARK: ☎ 028 4377 8664; www.forestserviceni.gov.uk. Entry: car park £4; open 10am–sunset.

Castlewellan Lake

Newry

Newry is sort of the largest city in South Down. 'Sort of', because it's one of the few towns or cities in the whole of Ireland split between two counties, in this instance Down and Armagh.

The name 'Newry' derives from the Irish *An tIúr* – The Yew, a reference to a tree St Patrick reputedly planted at the head of **Carlingford Lough**. The tree and Patrick's monastery are long gone, but Newry remains a place of cathedrals and steeples. Jonathan Swift, a regular commuter through the city, commented:

High church, low steeple,
Dirty streets, proud people.

To some extent the Dean, of *Gulliver's Travels* fame, was right. Although some of the still-cobbled streets are overlooked by handsome Georgian buildings, Newry has the feel of a hard-working market town. It became a city in 2000. This being Northern Ireland, two cities were awarded city status – one Taig (Newry) and one Prod (Lisburn), to use the vernacular.

The main Catholic place of worship in Newry on Hill Street, the **Cathedral of St Patrick and St Colman**, boasts striking architecture and vividly decorated stained glassed windows. This is the home church of Francis Campbell, Britain's ambassador to the Holy See, and the first Catholic to fill the post since the Reformation. Newry's **Town Hall** is built on a three-arched bridge astride the Clanrye River – the reason, reputedly, to settle inter-county rivalry; Down is upriver, Armagh is downriver. Newry saw its fair share of action during the Troubles – a continuation of its history. Since the bother began around 1169, Newry has been a military town – the headquarters of Edward the Bruce, a staging post for Shane O'Neill (the great Ulster Gaelic chieftain), the power base for Maurice McLoughlin King of Ireland, and a centre for the Anglo-Normans. Laterly it has been famous as a garrison town guarding the border at a pass in the **Slieve Gullion** mountains known as the **Gap of the North**. Situated close to the border, it's rumoured that during the Second World War the wily folk of Newry didn't observe the blackout curfew so that the Luftwaffe would be fooled into thinking the town was in the neutral Irish Free State.

The **Newry Canal** opened to traffic in 1741, linking the Tyrone coalfields (via Lough Neagh and the River Bann) to the Irish Sea. It was the first summit-level canal to be built in Britain or Ireland since Roman times. More crucially, it is reputed to have originated the word 'navvie', from navigator. Parts of the canal can be walked along, and it's a very popular fishing area.

Warrenpoint

For 800 years the lonely valley between **Fathom Hill** and the **Mountains of Mourne** has seen armed conflict. In 1979 it was the scene of the British Army's worst single loss in the North when 18 soldiers were killed here. To look at this place of almost Zen-like tranquillity now it's hard to fully take in the mayhem and violence wreaked here for

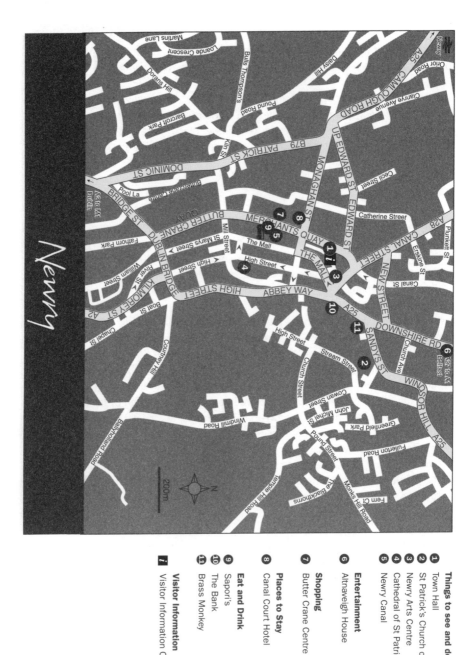

Newry

Things to see and do

① Town Hall
② St Patrick's Church of Ireland Cathedral
③ Newry Arts Centre
④ Cathedral of St Patrick and St Colman
⑤ Newry Canal

Entertainment

⑥ Altnaveigh House

Shopping

⑦ Butter Crane Centre

Places to Stay

⑧ Canal Court Hotel

Eat and Drink

⑨ Sapori's
⑩ The Bank
⑪ Brass Monkey

Visitor Information

ℹ Visitor Information Centre, Town Hall

Narrow Water Castle

centuries. Today, a plaque (usually vandalised) and several poppy wreaths mark the scene – adjacent to another plaque which gives information on **Narrow Water Castle**. Built in 1560 to protect the entrance to the Newry estuary, the fortified house faces the new Narrow Water Castle just across the water, a fortification originally built in the 13th century. Prior to that, the site had been a bridgehead for the Danes since AD790. It's possible to walk along the estuary via a footpath. The Irish Republic is just across the tidal river.

The elegant town of Warrenpoint bears little evidence of the trouble waged just outside its boundaries. So photogenic is this fashionable seaside resort – frequented by the Victorian middle classes in days gone by – it was used as a backdrop for Bundoran (in Donegal) in the film *The Butcher Boy*. Truly, this unchanged part of the island, still under British jurisdiction, looks more like Old Ireland than Ireland does. The town is centred around a harbour which came to prominence in the early 19th century as a port for Newry. Another plaque commemorates the thousands of emigrants who passed through the port en route to the New World. (South Down is big on plaques.)

During the summer months a **passenger ferry** operates between Warrenpoint to the village of Omeath in County Louth in the Irish Republic. The trip, amid truly spectacular scenery, takes about 15 minutes.

> **WARRENPOINT TO OMEATH FERRY:**
> ☎ 028 4175 3425/0781546 6498.
> Entry: adults return £4, children return £2;
> runs June to Sept, sailings run 11am–6pm;
> the ferry is well sign-posted in Warrenpoint
> and Omeath.

Rostrevor

Were towns obliged to apply for a licence before they could use the word 'nestle' in their official PR, Warrenpoint and Rostrevor would both immediately qualify. The nestling here is done between the **Mournes** and **Carlingford Lough**. Both towns look out towards the old Norman castles of **County Louth** in the Irish Republic, at one time the last outpost of the Pale. This was as far as Norman rule truly ran from the 13th century. Beyond the Pale resided the Gaelic warlords of Ulster, whose behaviour was, as you might imagine, beyond the pale. Today Rostrevor has a genteel air about it. A very mild micro-climate means that palm trees and mimosa – even the odd Chilean flame tree – grow here amidst the native oak and alder. The town is set round an elegant square where in summer months ceili dancing takes place.

In **Kilbroney Graveyard** on the Hilltown Road lies the remains of the grave of Giant Murphy, a local man reputed to have been over 8ft in height, who travelled the world displaying his enormous frame. Rostrevor is also the birthplace of Ben Dunne of the ubiquitous Dunne's Stores. Ben became famous for having given former prime minister of the Irish Republic Charles Haughey some 1.3 million pounds, giving rise to the quip: 'Ben there, Dunne that, Bought the Taoiseach.'

A walk through Rostrevor Forest will take you up Slievemartin and past the **Cloghmore Stone**. The 40 ton granite stone lies on the mountain ridge 1,000ft above Rostrevor. This huge stone – in actual fact a glacial erratic – is supposed to have been thrown at the hero of the Ulster Sagas, Fionn Mac Cumhaill – pronounced Finn MacCool. The more pragmatic members of the geology profession describe it as a spectacular deposit from the Ice Age. The stone is just off the main Slievemartin path, and is not easily missed.

Kilkeel

Kilkeel is the main fishing port in the area. The harbour is home to a large fleet of trawlers and some of the fattest seals you will see in Ireland. Kilkeel is what is known as a 'mixed' town – some streets are lined with Catholic businesses on one side, the other Protestant. In the Mourne Presbyterian church graveyard stands a headstone (1793) commemorating a revenue officer who 'fell by a ball discharged by an unknown murderer' – eloquent testimony to how seriously the smuggling trade was taken here.

The Neolithic **Kilfeaghan Dolmen** on the main Kilkeel to Newry road was built between 2000BC and 1000BC. The capstone is reckoned to be one of the biggest in Ireland with an estimated weight of between 35 and 40 tons. Four miles north of Kilkeel, the Silent Valley Reservoir's visitor centre (☎ 028 9074 1166) tells you all sorts of local water-related facts – such as the Silent Valley and Ben Crom reservoirs supplying most of Belfast and Down's water, some 30 million gallons of sweet, soft water. Northern Ireland's kettles never need descaling. And when someone asks you, as indeed they will, if you want 'a wee cup of tea in yer hand' (pronounced 'haun'), you can be sure it will be of the highest quality. A 3-mile circular Viewpoint Walk takes in spectacular scenes of the Mourne Mountains while the half mile Sally Lough stroll takes you up to the reservoir at Ben Crom – with, ahem, dam fine views.

Dundrum

Despite the dull modern bungalows guarding its approach – Dundrum is a postcard-grade harbour town at the edge of Dundrum Bay, overlooked by the sensationally sited de Courcy's Castle, built by the Normans in an effort to contain this part of County Down. Originally a Gaelic fortification, it was repossessed by the Magennis Clan, lost again to the English, and disputed in the 1798 rebellion.

CELEBRITY CONNECTIONS

Comedian and actor **Patrick Kielty** was born 1971 in Dundrum, County Down, and went to school in nearby Downpatrick before attending Queen's University Belfast. As well as stand-up and acting, Kielty has presented the likes of BBC's *Fame Academy*, and *Love Island* for ITV. Kielty was acutely affected by the Troubles. His father, businessman Jack Kielty, was murdered by the Ulster Freedom Fighters, a loyalist paramilitary group. Jack Kielty was to be the prime witness in British Central Television's defence of a libel action brought by a prominent UDA extortionist who was suing the television company over a broadcast of *The Cook Report*. Six men were eventually convicted of the murder.

Patrick Kielty formerly dated Amanda Byram, who has worked for the Irish TV channel TV3 and Channel 4 in the UK. He joked that due to the fact that she was from the Republic of Ireland their relationship received cross-border funding. In 2003, he was allegedly behind a stunt during which European Capital of Culture judges touring Belfast were greeted with the sight of a group of young Irish dancers, dressed in full regalia, jigging on every street corner they turned. Critics accused Patrick and his stunt of costing the city its chance of becoming European Capital of Culture.

Close by are the pristine beaches and sands which make up the 5,000-year-old sand dune system of Murlough. The National Trust has provided paths and notice boards detailing the natural history, geology and archaeology of the area – from Neolithic times to modern. Norman wisdom (not the comedian) brought the rabbit to Ireland's shores – it was farmed – or warrened – in Murlough's dunes for its flesh and coat. Thankfully it didn't replace the indigenous lagomorph, the Irish hare. This is a sub-species on its own (some argue that it should be a separate species). On formal occasions the Irish hare is pleased to call itself *Lepus timidus hibernicus* – and is larger and more gregarious (naturally) than the European, or Brown hare.

The varied habitats within the **Murlough Nature Reserve** (☎ 028 4375 1467; www.ntni.org.uk) are home to a wide range of animals and plants including badgers and stoats, delicate flowers such as the pyramidal orchid, carline thistle and rare and colourful butterflies. The sea buckthorn of the heathland attracts nesting willow warblers and whitethroats and in winter its orange berries are a valuable food source for wintering thrushes, such as fieldfare and redwing. Many species of wader, duck and geese visit the estuary, spring and autumn migration time being of particular interest. From the magnificent beach, sea watchers can observe more sea birds and in the summer and autumn both common and grey seals.

Newcastle

The high street in Newcastle is almost lapped by the waters of the Irish Sea; above the town the Mountains of Mourne provide a spellbinding backdrop. It's a view, you could imagine, which might support an entire postcard industry. Walk, cycle or trot on your horse far enough along the 6 mile strand and you reach Dundrum.

It was along this beach that Harry Ferguson – the County Down pioneer of the modern tractor – made the very first aeroplane flight in Ireland. In 1909 he took off from the sands in a monoplane built by himself. A large inscribed stone on **Newcastle Promenade** commemorates the event. Inexplicably, Ferguson decided there wasn't much future in flight. The environment was largely untroubled by air travel in 1909, a situation that was presumed likely to pertain – certainly as far as the Engineering and Scientific Association of Ireland was concerned. On 25 October 1909, that august body announced that flying through the air was 'not yet an accomplished fact', adding that it would never be of any practical use anyway. Whether this had any effect on Harry, unfortunately we don't know. But after his solo flight, three months after the Engineering and Scientific Association's pronouncement, he turned to the tractor and his famous 'three hitch system', necessary in the tight drumlin country of County Down.

The northerly extremity of Dundrum Bay is guarded by **St John's Point Lighthouse**. This is the site of the alleged encounter between the playwright Brendan Behan and his employer from Irish Lights. Brendan was employed to paint the lighthouse but after a liquid lunch he bedded down for a snooze. The foreman addressed the almost comatose Dublin man saying, 'Ah, sleep on Behan. For when you awake ye'll have no job.'

Activities

The **Royal County Down**, Links Road, Newcastle (☎ 028 4372 3314; www.royalcountydown.org) is one of the world's great golf courses, originally designed for £4 by Old Tom Morris. This is where Tiger Woods and Sergio Garcia *et al* practise before the British Open. Its notoriously vicious bunkers, pocking the greens like snipers' dugouts, are a test for the world's finest players. Founded in 1889 Royal

Royal County Down Golf Course

County Down is part of golf history. With the Irish Sea on one side and the huge edifice of Slieve Donard as a backdrop, you'll have your work cut out to concentrate on the six or seven blind tee shots. The 217 yard 4th hole is one of the most photographed in European golf. Gorse bushes and marram grass make it a beast, but the view from the back tee is some compensation.

Nearby, the **Mourne Golf Club** (☎ 028 4372 3218) provides cheaper links golf, but with pretty much the same high-grade views. **Warrenpoint Golf Club** (Lower Dromore Road; www.warrenpointgolf.com) is ranked as one of the top parkland courses in Northern Ireland. **Kilkeel Golf Club** (Mourne Park, Ballyardle, Kilkeel; ☎ 028 4176 2296; www. kilkeelgolfclub.org) has breathtaking views of the Mournes and the Irish Sea.

An Irishman's ideal day, they say, is to catch a fish which tells him the winner of the 3.10 running at the Curragh. Horses are part of the way of life in Ireland, and some of the best specimens in the world are bred here. The limestone leeched through the soil by the rain builds light, strong bones. Your children are unlikely to be impressed by that, but they'll surely get a thrill astride a bay mare as she treks along forest paths, mountain passes or wide, open stretches of virginal sand. Situated within 2,000 acres of woodland, open heath and beach rides, encompassing Castlewellan, Tollymore and the Mountains of Mourne, **Mount Pleasant Riding Centre** (Bannonstown Road, Castlewellan; ☎ 028 4377 8651; www.mountpleasantcentre.com) offers tuition and guidance for all ages, with trekking along traffic-free routes, galloping along the sands and hacking up mountain paths.

GAMEKEEPERS LODGE EQUESTRIAN CENTRE: Newry; ☎ 028 4176 4771; and TULLYMURRAY EQUESTRIAN RIDING AND EQUESTRIAN SERVICES NEAR CLOUGH; ☎ 028 4481 1880; Provide riding in the general area.

Wet weather

St Patrick's Church of Ireland, Stream Street, Newry, is an extremely significant building in these parts – it is almost certainly the very first Protestant church in Ireland, and one of the oldest churches in Ireland of any faith still in use. St Patrick's Church has been trying to get the Protestant people of Newry to give up their ould sins since 1575. The porch has a tablet dated 1578 bearing Sir Nicholas Bagnall's arms – the gentleman responsible for the church. The graveyard contains the grave of Sir Nicholas, who basically founded the modern town of Newry – inside a plaque attests to his efforts; meanwhile a United Irishman, one Cochron, hanged for his part in the 1798 Rising, lies nearby – not far away is the grave of Captain Alex Boyd, 'mortally wounded in a duel, 1807'.

Newry and Mourne Museum's eclectic collection and diverse literature features County Down's full sweep of

NEWRY AND MOURNE MUSEUM: Arts Centre, 1a Bank Parade, Newry BT35 6HP; ☎ 028 3026 6839. Entry: free; Mon–Fri 10.30am–1pm/2.00pm–4.30pm.

history – Neolithic dolmens, the town's Cistercian origins, Ulster's Gaelic order, the foundations of the merchant town, and its iconic canal. The folklore, folk traditions and working life of rural and mountain areas are explored through a varied programme of exhibits and exhibitions.

What to do with children...

Newcastle has plenty of seaside attractions – amusement arcades (with more than a touch of the 1950s about them), a promenade and a harbour largely devoted to pleasure craft. **Coco's Indoor Adventure Playground** (27A Central Promenade; ☎ 028 4372 6226; www.cocosplayground.com) is open May to September. **Castle Park**, just off the Main Street where the Shimna River flows into the sea, has miniature golf, a boating lake and tennis courts. The **arboretum** in **Castlewellan Forest Park** – 6,000 yews – encloses a full 2 miles of circuitous paths, one of the largest in Europe. You could attempt to be the first person to resist the temptation of calling it a-maze-ing.

...and how to avoid children

In Newcastle one sure-fire way of avoiding children is to head for **Soak Seaweed Baths** on the Promenade at Newcastle (☎ 028 4372 6002; www.soakseaweedbaths.co.uk) This traditional remedy for rheumatism, arthritis or just plain weariness consists of lying back in heated seawater amidst floating seaweed. Single sessions cost £20.

Entertainment

Altnaveigh House (51 Downshire Road, Newry BT34 1EE; ☎ 028 3026 5151; www.altnaveigh-house.org.uk) is a community and cultural development centre. Concerts include offerings from the Altnaveigh Pipe Band (Scottish type), and the Cross Border Orchestra. Rostrevor is best known for its folk music extravaganza, the **Fiddler's Green Festival** which takes place every July in Rostrevor. The **Maiden of the Mournes Festival** is held in August and the **Blues on the Bay Rock and Jazz Festival** every September, and the **Dundrum Busking Festival** takes place every August.

The best... PLACES TO STAY

BOUTIQUE

Slieve Donard Resort & Spa

Downs Road, Newcastle BT33 0AH
☎ **028 4372 1066**
www.hastingshotels.com

The serious grandeur of the Slieve Donard Resort and Spa stands in 6 acres of private grounds with epic views of the Mountains of Mourne and the Irish Sea. The main (Victorian) dining room may look as if it's the scene for an Agatha Christie mystery, but this is one of the foxiest hotels in these islands.

Price: from £190 for a double.

INN

Slieve Croob Inn

Seeconnell Centre, 119 Clanvaraghan Road, Castlewellan BT31 9LA
☎ **028 4377 1412**
www.slievecroobinn.com

Set in the small 'mountain' range of Slieve Croob – actually, just overgrown drumlins – the view here is, nonetheless, fantastic. If you want a rambling or cycling holiday in the soporifically bucolic pastureland of South Down, this is an ideal base. The main building is mountain lodge style; the 10 self-catering cottages accommodate couples and families.

Price: from £75 for a double.

Glassdrumman Lodge

Mill Road, Annalong BT34 4RH
☎ **028 437 68451**
www.glassdrummanlodge.com

In a dramatic hillside location just outside the coastal village of Annalong, and close to the great forest parks of Tollymore and Castlewellan, Glassdrumman, drips with aesthetic appeal. The backdrop of the athletic-looking Slieve Binnian with a patchwork of tightly walled fields running up the mountain slopes must appear in thousands of landscape paintings. Stand still long enough and you might find yourself painted into a masterpiece. Or at least on someone's mobile/camera.

Price: from £70 for a double.

SELF-CATERING

Tory Bush Cottages

Bryansford; ☎ 028 4372 4348
www.torybush.com

These clachan style cottages with white-washed walls and slate roofs are just outside the main gates to Tollymore Forest. Bicycle hire can be arranged.

Price: from £130 for a two-night stay.

UNUSUAL

Hanna's Close

Aughnahoory Road, Kilkeel BT34 4AH
☎ **028 9024 1100**
www.cottagesinireland.com

Hanna's Close is a meticulously restored clachan – the Ulster Scots word for a farming settlement, a closely knit collection of cottages, barns and outhouses. Built in 1640 the fully renovated cottages look out onto the open expanse of the Mournes – true bleak chic. The cottages sleep up to seven. All around is a working farm so your holiday companions will be sheep, hens and bullocks – two of whom definitely look as if they aren't bluffing.

Price: from £250 per cottage for a week.

The best... PLACES TO STAY

COACH HOUSE

Canal Court Hotel

Merchants Quay, Newry BT35 8HF
☎ **028 3025 1234**
www.canalcourthotel.com

Newry, in general, doesn't do cutting edge. But if you want a great place to stay or eat you could do worse than the Canal Court Hotel (four star) Merchant's Quay. Every town in Ireland has a hotel like this – once an old coaching house or the like, today it's a comfortable, lived-in hotel frequented by locals and travellers alike. They do a splendid Sunday buffet – only trouble is you might feel a bit peckish 24 hours later.

Price: from £130 for a double.

CAMPSITE

Meelmore Lodge

52 Trassey Road, Newcastle BT33 0QB
www.meelmorelodge.co.uk

Meelmore Lodge offers 5 acres of camping in the Mournes. With private access to the mountains, plus Hare's Gap and Spellack Slabs 3km from the camp, the site's location on the foothills of Slieve Meelmore make it ideal. If it's wet, light the turf fire, pour out a dram of Bushmills, and listen to the rain turning the land green.

Price: £5 per person per night.

The best... FOOD AND DRINK

▶ Staying in

Mourne Seafood Bar (10 Main Street, Dundrum, BT33 0LU; ☎ 28 4375 1377; www.mourneseafood.com) is a lively and informal seafood restaurant-cum-shop selling ultra fresh fish – so fresh that some of them still look surprised. Produce from local harbours of Kilkeel and Annalong, and mussels, oysters and cockles from their own shellfish beds on Carlingford Lough make this an essential pit-stop. The **Hilltown Chippy** (Main Street, Hilltown; ☎ 028 4063 8130) is generally agreed to be one of the best purveyors of chips in the western quadrant of the universe. Vegetarians beware – beef dripping is used for the fry-up, plus a quarter of a century's experience. This place would surely win the Nobel Prize for Chips were there such an award.

EATING OUT

FINE DINING

Buck's Head Inn
77 Main Street, Dundrum BT33 0LU
☎ **028 4375 1868**
www.thebucksheadinn.co.uk

For dinner, the Buck's Head in Dundrum serves sensational local food, and if it's fine, you can eat in their walled garden. Booking is advisable. The kitchen sources local produce including oysters from Dundrum Bay, County Down beef, and lamb from the Mournes. A set menu will set you back around £30 per person.

RESTAURANT

Sapori
16 The Mall, Newry BT34 1BG
☎ **028 3025 2086**

Pizzas were once billed in Northern Ireland as 'Italian Welsh rarebits'. Changed days now. The North's Italian population (quite substantial) has made the leap from fish and chip shops to authentic Italian restaurants. For first class pasta and pesto Sapori's takes some beating. Dinner costs from £20 to £25.

Duke Restaurant
Above the Duke Bar, 7 Duke Street, Warrenpoint BT34 3JY
☎ **028 4175 2084**

The Duke Restaurant deals in creative cuisine – and makes good use of its proximity to Kilkeel's fishing port. Contemporary and modern, the service, however, is friendly and down-to-earth. Average spend per person, including glass of wine is £20–£30.

CAFÉ

Seasalt
51 Central Promenade, Newcastle BT33 0HH
☎ **028 4372 5027**
www.seasaltnewcastle.co.uk

Bright and imaginative bistro, serving organic soups, steak-and-Guinness pie, with local produce a specialty. Coffee and views (of the Mournes, the strand, the Irish Sea) is also an option. Lunch menu from £2.25 to £6.50; tapas from £3.50; mains from £4.95.

BISTRO

Zest
22–24 Main Street, Newcastle BT33 0LY
☎ **028 4372 5757**

For a flavour of the area, Zest specialises in Ulster-Scots cuisine, a tradition of cookery that has been all but neglected in Northern Ireland. Try Cullen Skink, a Scots pottage of Finnan haddie, onions and potatoes. Zest operates as a standard daytime café, but you can bring your own wine. Prices are very reasonable, with soups around £4, main courses from £5.

🔲 Drinking

Whitewater Brewing Company (40 Tullyframe Road, Kilkeel BT34 4RZ; ☎ 028 4176 9449; www.whitewaterbrewing.co.uk) is the largest microbrewery in Northern Ireland, producing over a dozen different cask-conditioned ales and a lager. Its Clotworthy Dobbin Ale was judged one of the top 50 in the world in 2007 in the International Beer Challenge. Well-established bars where you can be guaranteed a session, or at the very least a bit of craic include the **Crown**, the **Madden**, the **Brass Monkey** and the **Bank** in Newry. Like most border areas, traditional music is fairly easily come by. The **Harbour** in Newcastle is recommended for spontaneous sessions, and the **Cloughmor Inn** in Rostrevor usually guarantees a lively weekend night.

On Thursday nights, a session takes place in the **Railway Bar** in Monaghan Street. Just outside the town, the **Cove Bar** on the Hilltown Road has its traditional music evening on Tuesdays.

① Visitor Information

Tourist information centre: 10–14 Central Promenade, Newcastle BT33 0AA, ☎ 028 4372 2222.

Hospitals: Downe Hospital, Pound Lane, Downpatrick BT30 6JA; ☎ 028 4461 3311; Daisy Hill Hospital, 5 Hospital Road, Newry, ☎ 028 3083 5000.

Doctors: Dr N F O'Connor, 56 Main Street, Newcastle BT33 0AE, ☎ 028 4372 3221; Warrenpoint Health Centre, Summer Hill BT34 3JD, ☎ 028 4177 3388.

Pharmacies: McKeever's, 11 Marcus Square, Hill Street, Newry BT34 1AE, ☎ 028 3026 2528; G Maginn, 9 Main Street, Newcastle BT33 0AD, ☎ 028 4372 2923.

Police: PSNI Station, 3 Belfast Road, Newry BT341EF, ☎ 028 4175 2222.

Supermarkets: Sainsbury's, The Quays, Newry BT35 8QS.

Parking: Newry is the only town in South Down where you may experience difficulties in getting a parking place – largely due to the number of shoppers, particularly at the weekend. The Quays has the biggest, followed by the Buttercrane Centre; during summer months Newcastle can occasionally become crowded – there is ample parking in Donard Park at the end of Main Street.

Cash points: On the main street in Newcastle, and outside the Ulster Bank in Castlewellan; in Market Square, Newry, several banks' branches have cash machines.

Internet access: Cyber Perk Internet Café, 11D Monaghan Street, Newry, ☎ 028 3025 2305.

Bike rental: Wiki Wiki Wheels, 10b Donard Street, Newcastle BT33 0AW, ☎ 028 4372 3973.

Taxis: Ace taxis, 32 St. Marys Street, Newry BT34 2AA, ☎ 02830 278029; Rock Taxis, 2b Rostrevor Road, Hilltown BT34 5UP, ☎ 028 4063 2000.

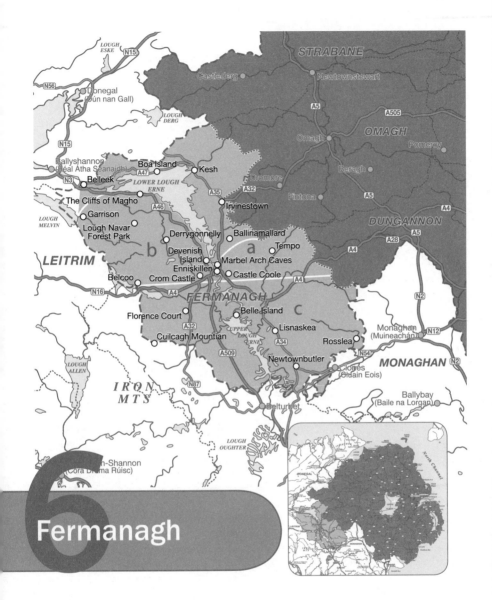

6 Fermanagh

a. Mid Fermanagh and Enniskillen
b. North Fermanagh
c. South Fermanagh

Unmissable highlights

01 Visit the original Irish yew in Florence Court, p. 312

02 Explore the Marble Arch Caves, a mesmerising underground waterworld, p. 315

03 Browse through some sheer pottery in Belleek. Fragile lattice-work china has been made here since the 18th century, p. 302

04 Go fishing in Fermanagh's Lakeland, an angler's paradise, p. 296

05 Have a holy enjoyable time on Devenish, the pious island in Lower Lough Erne, p. 297

06 Cadaragh Cemetery on Boa Island is home to the extraordinary stone statue of Boa Man, p. 297

07 Visit the military museum in Enniskillen Castle, the home of the Inniskilling Fusiliers and Dragoons, p. 287

08 Go hill-walking in the Cuilcagh Mountains, p. 312

09 Watch the herons at Crom Estate from the award-winning Loughside Visitor Centre, p. 314

10 Take a cookery course at Belle Isle Castle, a 17th-century Anglo-Irish pile in County Fermanagh, p. 316

FERMANAGH

Whether it's soaking up the spirituality in the lonely, lovely landscape, browsing through the history of Enniskillen, or just cruising for hours in solitude on the lough, Fermanagh is not to be missed.

But don't forget your wellies. The countryside is almost iridescently green; but invariably wet. The whole area is threaded by rivers, streams and loughs. Lough Erne and its catchment area takes up most of the county – a spectacular limestone tableland rises to the peak of Mount Belmore (366m or 1200ft).

Winston Churchill uttered what are probably the most famous words ever said about Fermanagh (and Tyrone). In 1922 he stood up and announced to the House of Commons: 'The whole map of Europe has changed, but as the deluge subsides and the waters fall short we see the dreary steeples of Fermanagh and Tyrone emerging once again.' It seemed an unnecessarily churlish thing to say, and it wasn't terribly accurate. Steeples there are aplenty, certainly, but the countryside of Fermanagh is so pastoral that the steeples give every view an almost Turner-esque beauty. Father John O'Donohue, poet, priest and author of Anam Cara, was a good deal more complimentary about the county: 'This is one of the most beautiful counties in the world. Its history is alive in the landscape. It has the spirit, humour and philosophy of its people.'

Historically part of the kingdom of the Maguires, Fermanagh was planted by English Anglicans rather than Scottish Presbyterians in the early 17th century, and this influence can still be detected in the towns and villages. The county suffered badly during the Great Famine of the mid-19th century, and it experienced significant sectarian violence during the recent Troubles. Between the ravages of history, the weather, the bitter aftertaste of the Troubles, people still kept coming here, arriving year in, year out. The reason was the fishing – adjudged to be among the very best in the world.

The **Marble Arch Caves** system is a mesmerising world of winding underground rivers, waterfalls and lofty subterranean chambers. If it's water you want, Fermanagh has gallons of the stuff. And if you're wondering what people do during the occasionally soft Fermanagh weather, why the answer is simple: read, fish, walk in the rain and go home happy.

MID FERMANAGH AND ENNISKILLEN

Nowhere in Ireland resonates with more unchanging tradition than Fermanagh. This was a view taken in the 15th-century poem 'Do mheall an sochar Síol gColla'. Translating from the Irish:

> I know a land whose hills should not be exchanged for any smooth plain
> .. whose fair thick woods sit about Fir Manach
> A forest of masts is on the Erne – it makes one start with joy to see them
> To see those green banks – one could gaze on them forever.

This peacefulness is why so many people have lately been discovering Fermanagh: soul-searching spiritualists, writers, romantic couples, poets – as well as sporting folk, anglers, sailors and energetic families. As W B Yeats put it: 'Come away, o' human child/To the waters and the wild,/with a faery hand in hand.' Old Willie knew a mystical place when he saw one.

WHAT TO SEE AND DO

Enniskillen

The only town of any size in Fermanagh, Enniskillen (with a population of 13,000), has basically stuck to its job these past 600 years or so – to keep an eye on the troublesome locals and forcibly dissuade them from the path of insurrection. The only stronghold in Fermanagh to escape destruction in the 17th century, today it's still a garrison town – many will remember the place in connection with the Remembrance Day bomb that killed 11 people in 1987. But despite its melancholy history, the city is today a friendly, relaxed place, one of the livelier rural towns, with a thriving nightlife.

Enniskillen (from the Irish *Inis Ceithleann* meaning 'Kathleen's Island') is located almost exactly in the centre of the county on the natural island which separates the Upper and Lower sections of **Lough Erne**. The steeples as mentioned by Winston Churchill are still here, dominating the town. Dreary on a wet autumn day, perhaps, but impressive none the less. **St MacCartan's**, also called **Enniskillen Cathedral**, is visible from just about everywhere in town. Inside, the old colours of the Enniskillen regiments are on show. (In general, visitors will be forcibly struck by the amount of room given to military memorabilia in all of the Church of Ireland's cathedrals in the Six Counties.)

Almost opposite St MacCartan's is **St Michael's Catholic Church**, built in the French Gothic style. The steeples continue with the **Methodist Church in Darling Street**, the **Presbyterian Church in East Bridge Street** and the **Convent Chapel** in Belmore Street. If you've only time to do one church, the latter has 15 nave windows in stained glass by Michael Healy, Lady Glenavy and Sarah Purser, three noted Irish artists.

Enniskillen's **Town Hall** only dates back to 1901, but it's of interest because of the presence of a plaque in the porch which commemorates Captain L E G Oates 'the very gallant gentleman' who sacrificed his life for his companions on Scott's Antarctica

CELEBRITY CONNECTIONS

Everyone knows something about **Oscar Wilde**, or at least a garbled version of one of his many quips. A conversational artist and wit, his one-liners have been pressed into service for more than a century. Oscar's connection with Ulster is twofold. Like fellow Dubliner Samuel Beckett he attended Portora Royal School in Enniskillen. Should you decide to pay homage to his old school you will be struck by the lustre of the poet's name inscribed on the honours board. Highlighted in gold, Oscar Wilde's inscription easily outshines his contemporaries'. However, this is not a deliberate highlighting of the writer and poet. Following Oscar's imprisonment in the 1890s for 'gross indecency with other men', his name was deleted. It was reinstated in the 1940s in slightly more enlightened times, accounting for its relative patina.

Which brings us to Oscar's other connection with the Six Counties. Another fellow Dubliner, Edward Carson, was the lawyer who defended the Marquess of Queensberry in the libel proceedings brought by Oscar Wilde. Carson destroyed Wilde's credibility in the witness box, and the writer was subsequently convicted of sodomy. Carson became leader of the Ulster Unionists in 1910, and was instrumental in the foundation of Northern Ireland. Wilde, like Beckett, fled to Paris, where he died in impoverished exile. True to form he disobeyed his doctor's orders – he was suffering from meningitis – and was quaffing champagne and opium until the end.

Nobel Laureate for Literature **Samuel Beckett** also attended Portora Royal School and later taught at Belfast's main Protestant public school, Campbell College. He wasn't really cut out for teaching, however – he described his pupils at Campbell as like clotted cream, rich and thick. Whether his time in Enniskillen and Belfast had much influence on him is not clear from his writing – he has been described 'as Betjeman fed intravenously on Benzedrine and force fed Guinness and Bushmills.' There are (possibly) oblique references to his time there.

Enniskillen

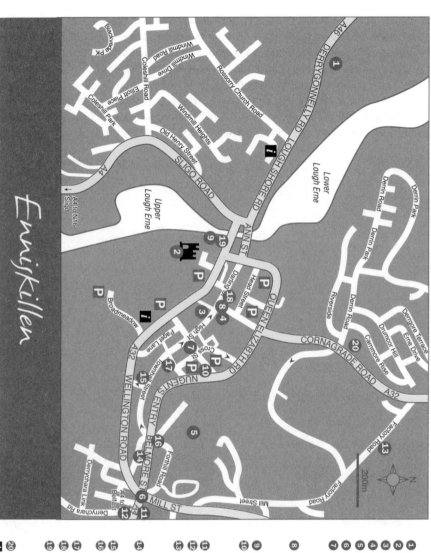

Things to see and do

1. Portora Royal School
2. Enniskillen Castle
3. St Michael's Catholic Church
4. St MacCartan's Cathedral
5. Cole's Monument Fort Hill Park
6. War Memorial
7. Town Hall

Entertainment

8. Blake's of the Hollow, Church Street

Shopping

9. Supermarkets, Erneside Shopping Centre
10. Butter Milk Centre

Places to Stay

11. Killhevlin Hotel
12. Belmore Court Hotel
13. Enniskillen Townhouses, Drumclay

Eat and Drink

14. The Horseshoe & Saddlers, Belmore Street
15. Flo's, Townhall Street
16. Patrick O'Doherty's Fine Meats, Belmore Street
17. The Linenhall
18. Café Merlot (in Blake's)
19. Le Bistro, Erneside Shopping Centre

Visitor Information

20. Erne Hospital, Cornagrade Road
i. Tourist Information Centre, Wellington Road

expedition in 1912 and an officer in the 6th Inniskilling Dragoons. Oates, aware his ill-health was compromising his companions' lives, told them, 'I am just going outside and may be some time' before walking out into a blizzard.

The **War Memorial** in Enniskillen in the centre of the town was the scene of the Remembrance Day Bombing (8 November 1987) when 11 people were killed and hundreds injured as a result of an IRA bomb. The Enniskillen bomb is acknowledged by some as a turning point in the Northern Ireland peace process.

Font Hill (or Fonthill)

This delightful Victorian town park at the east end of town comes complete with Victorian bandstand, clock tower and cupola. Nearby a statue to Sir Galbraith Lowry Cole, one of Wellington's generals in the Peninsular War, stands atop a Doric column. You can climb the spiral staircase (108 steps) to the top – where terrific views across Fermanagh's loughland await you.

> COLE'S MONUMENT: Font Hill Park. Entry: £1.50; open 1.30–3pm mid-Apr to Sep.

Enniskillen Castle

Enniskillen Castle was the former headquarters of two famous regiments, the Inniskilling Dragoons (or Dragoon Guards) and the Royal Inniskilling Fusiliers. 'Inniskilling' is not some bad pun with regards the main occupation of soldiers; it is merely an older misconstruction on the original Irish name *Inis Ceithleann*. The regiment's influence has (probably) been felt on the other side of the Atlantic – it has long been argued that the US national anthem, 'The star spangled banner', is derived from an Inniskilling marching tune.

Enniskillen Castle

ENNISKILLEN CASTLE MUSEUM: Castle Barracks, Enniskillen BT74 7BB; ☎ 028 6632 5000; www.enniskillencastle.co.uk. Entry: adults £2.95, children £1.95, students and senior citizens £2.50, family £7.95; open Mon 2–5pm, Tue–Fri 10am–5pm, Sat (May to Sep) 2–5pm, Sun (Jul/Aug) 2–5pm.

The museum is housed in the original castle – in the Keep of Hugh the Hospitable who died in 1438, presumably shortly after becoming Hugh the Hospitalised. His collection of stone idols and Ogham stones are still on view. Originally built by the Gaelic Maguires, the castle later became an English garrison fort and barracks. It now houses two museums – the **Fermanagh County Museum**, and the **Museum of the Royal Enniskillen Fusiliers**. On show are weapons, vehicles, uniforms, medals and silver from the regiment's long, tortuous history, along with stories of campaigns the soldiers have been involved in, from the jungles of Malaya – to, well, fighting with the Fermanagh locals. You will also hear the famous song sung by Enniskillen people the world over: 'Fare thee well, Enniskillen, fare thee well for a while…'.

Castle Coole

Even the most laid back tourist is likely to find themselves gasping at the riches of Castle Coole, just outside Enniskillen. One of Ireland's noblest neo-classical houses and the former family home of the Earls of Belmore, it is simply exquisite. If you only visit one stately home per year, this has to be very high on your shortlist. Inside, the opulence of the Regency interior with its rich decoration and furniture will have you musing that here is a place fit for a king – and indeed you wouldn't be far wrong.

The state bedroom was prepared for George IV, who in 1821 became the first monarch to pay a state visit to Ireland since Richard II of England way back in the 14th century. A visit below stairs (servant's tunnel, laundry, stable yard, butler's quarters) will give you some idea of how a Big House functioned. Presumably King George missed out on this part of the tour.

CASTLE COOLE: Enniskillen BT74 6JY; ☎ 028 6632 2690; www.nationaltrust. org.uk/hbcache/property169.htm. Entry: adults £5, children £2.50, family £13.50; opening times vary – visit the website for details.

Castle Coole

Wet weather

Portora Royal School

Portora Royal School for Boys, Enniskillen, is one of a number of 'free schools' founded by Royal Charter in 1608, by James I. Originally called Enniskillen Royal School its old boys include one Nobel Prize winner, Samuel Beckett, who learnt French here, the language he would later write in. Portora's other alumni include Oscar Wilde, Neil Hannon of the rock band Divine Comedy, who wrote the Father Ted theme music,

Portora Royal School for Boys

CELEBRITY CONNECTIONS

Neil Hannon, the front man and songwriter of the melodic rock band Divine Comedy, was born in Derry – the son of Church of Ireland vicar, Brian Hannon. The family moved to Enniskillen when Mr Hannon Sr was made Bishop of Clogher. The young Neil attended Portora Royal School, whose former pupils include Oscar Wilde and Samuel Beckett. Academic life was not really for him, and soon the world of rock beckoned. Fellow Fermanagh man and RTE broadcaster John Kelly described Hannon as 'someone whose music is entirely eccentric, irresistibly entertaining and quite perfectly crafted'.

The singer makes several warm references to his father in his work. The clergyman had been based in Derry at the time of Bloody Sunday and was in Enniskillen during that town's own War Memorial tragedy. The album *Fin de Siècle* draws on the experience of the Troubles. The track 'Sunrise' is a reference to the anomalies of life in Northern Ireland: 'I was born in Londonderry, I was born in Derry City too,' he sings, later adding, 'I grew up in Enniskillen, I grew up in Inis Ceithleann too...' As well as having success with his own band, Hannon has contributed material to enterprises as disparate as Ute Lemper and Doctor Who. He also composed the theme music for the comedy shows The IT Crowd, and Father Ted, the latter being a reworking of the instrumental break of The Divine Comedy's *Songs Of Love*. In the *Father Ted* episode 'A song for Europe', Hannon co-wrote and sang 'My Lovely Horse', a deliberately dire song, a pastiche of a Eurovision song.

PORTORA ROYAL SCHOOL: Portora Hill, Enniskillen BT74 7HA; ☎ 028 6632 7488; www.portoraroyal.co.uk. Entry: can be visited by arrangement; available for private functions.

and Evelyne Miller Henry Francis Lyte who wrote 'Abide with me'. There seems a wonderful symmetry that the two people responsible for 'Waiting for Godot' and 'Abide with me' should have gone to the same school.

Railway Museum & Headhunters' Barber Shop

Possibly one of the oddest hairdressers in the country, at the Railway Museum & Headhunters' Barber Shop, you can revisit the bygone days of steam – while you have

RAILWAY MUSEUM & HEADHUNTERS' BARBER SHOP: 5 Darling Street, Enniskillen BT74 7DP; ☎ 028 6632 7488; wwwheadhuntersmuseum.com. Entry: Tues to Sat 9am–5:30pm; closed bank holidays.

your hair cut. A diverting, if somewhat odd way to while a way an hour or so – particularly if you need your hair cut. And don't be fooled if they ask you if you're interested in the Track of the Week. It won't be a musical piece – more likely the up-line from Downhill to Castlerock or some such.

What to do with children...

The **Lakeland Forum** is the biggest leisure complex in the west of the Six Counties, with swimming pool, soft play areas, sports hall (badminton, squash) plus a variety

FERMANAGH LAKELAND FORUM: Kennedy Broadmeadow, Enniskillen BT74 7EF; ☎ 028 6632 4121; www.fermanagh.gov. uk. Entry: adults £2.50–£8 depending on facilities used, children from £1.50; open year round, 8am–6pm – hours vary according to facility used.

of water sports. The centre is situated on the shores of Lough Erne. Ample parking allows access to the facilities, jetties, picnic areas and canoe centre. The complex is open to everyone – holiday makers, locals, sportspeople and water activity enthusiasts.

The **Lough Erne Golf Resort** may not sound the likeliest destination for children but the centre's Escape to the Land of Lough and Legend programme and Luxury Kids Amenity Programme (for children aged 3–11 years) should keep everyone, including parents, well satisfied. Goodies include a Lough Erne Swan (to take home – a toy, not a real swan) a Cygnet robe and slippers, a Welcome pack, Lough Erne coloring book

The pool at the Lough Erne Golf Resort

and crayons (also to take home). Outdoor activities with information on the local area are included, board games and DVDs are available for hire, and there's swimming in the Infinity Pool from 10am to 4pm.

> LOUGH ERNE GOLF RESORT: Belleek Road, Enniskillen BT93 7ED; ☎ 028 6632 3230; www.loughernegolfresort.com; email: reservations@loughernegolfresort.com.

... and how to avoid children

Tempo, although a tremendous address for a drummer, was the home of Sir John Langham, the distinguished naturalist. But then this profoundly rural area would bring the naturalist out in anyone. Father John O'Donohue, poet, priest and author of *Anam Cara* (Celtic 'soul friend') described this as 'one of the most beautiful countries in the world. Its history is alive in the landscape. It has the spirit, humour and philosophy of its people.' But the lake-covered landscape is home to several Bronze Age standing stones. The most significant are known as the Grey Stones, about three-quarters of a mile west of Tempo in a place called Doon. The lower of the two stones is a red sandstone boulder with a 'bullaun' on either side. Bullauns were cavities in the stones, possibly used as mortars, but they may have had a spiritual significance – it is believed oaths and vows may have been taken here.

From here head about 2 miles further south-west to **Topped Mountain**. From the 910ft summit there's a terrific view of mid Ulster – don't linger long; after all there are only so many superlatives that you can use in a day.

Entertainment

Every 31 October, **Enniskillen Castle** holds a Samhain (Halloween) Extravaganza – you could scarcely find a more atmospheric place to hold a festival of spirits and sprites. The Castle also hosts a candlelit carol service in Irish at Christmas time. The innovative **Ardhowen Theatre** (Dublin Road, Enniskillen BT74 6HN; ☎ 028 6632 5440; www.ardhowentheatre.com) is situated on a panoramic lakeview setting, just a bend in the river away from the historic island of Enniskillen. The theatre offers a year-round programme of drama, music and dance including the annual Enniskillen Drama Festival. **Derrygonnelly**, a small village north west of Enniskillen, has a long history of traditional Irish music. Every year in early October a celebration of local and international talent is held in memory of the late musicians Eddie Duffy and Mick Hoy. Musicians come from all over Ireland and further afield to enjoy this festival that bases itself throughout Derrygonnelly's four pubs.

* **Doogie's Bar** – 66–70, Main Street, Derrygonnelly BT93 6HW, ☎ 028 6864 1615.
* **Knockmore Bar** – 47–48, Main Street, Derrygonnelly BT93 6HW, ☎ 028 6864 1531.

The best... **PLACES TO STAY**

HOTEL

Lough Erne Golf Resort

Belleek Road, Enniskillen BT93 7ED
☎ **028 6632 3230**
www.lougherngolfresort.com

The Lough Erne Resort is a one-stop shop, featuring everything from sports to spas. Fluffy towels, heavenly massages, uplifting aromas – as well as breathtaking views of the lough – can be indulged in after a few rounds on the Nick Faldo-designed parkland golf course. Children are specifically catered for with a host of activities.

Prices: B&B from £100 for a double. Various package deals available, e.g. dinner in the Catlina Restaurant plus Thai spa treatment.

Killyhevlin Hotel & Health Club

Dublin Road, Enniskillen BT74 6RW
☎ **028 6632 3481**
www.killyhevlin.com

This four-star luxury hotel on the shores of Lough Erne offers spa treatments, private grounds and lakeside gardens. Rooms are stylishly furnished, and the restaurant has a terrific reputation.

Price: B&B and evening meal from £55 per person sharing.

Belmore Court Motel

Tempo Road, Enniskillen BT74 6HX
☎ **028 6632 6362**
www.motel.co.uk

A distinctive sweep of terraced houses decorated to a very high and comfortable standard, this hotel has long been a popular stopping off point for travellers heading for the west. But it's equally ideal for exploring Enniskillen.

Price: B&B from £59 per person sharing for two nights.

SELF-CATERING

Enniskillen Townhouses & Apartments

8 Tulleevin Park, Drumclay BT74 6NH
☎ **028 6632 6026**
**www.nireland.com/enniskillen.
accommodation**

Three-star and four-star townhouses overlooking Enniskillen town centre – perfect if you want to avail yourself of both Enniskillen's attractions and explore the surrounding countryside. The apartments are furnished to a very high standard, and are comfortable and well equipped.

Price: low season £250, high season £400 for a week.

Devenish Villa Holiday Homes

Garrison BT93 4AE
☎ **028 6865 8743**
www.devenishvillas.com
email: peterandpam78@yahoo.com

Utterly charming accommodation in the west of the county, these two cottages make a perfect base for exploring Fermanagh's attractions. All types of fishing are catered for, as well as boating and canoeing.

Price: low season £200, high season up to £500 for a week.

- **Old Pal's Bar** – 75, Main Street, Derrygonnelly BT93 6HW, ☎ 028 6864 1254
- **Cosy Bar** – 54 Main Street, Derrygonnelly BT93 6HW, ☎ 028 6864 1679

Enniskillen's young, up-for-it population head for the **Crow's Nest Bar & Bistro** – two bars, an up-market night club, live music, late bars and a traditional Irish music session of a Saturday afternoon and Monday night make this one of the liveliest venues in the west of Northern Ireland. In **Garrison** in the very west of the county, two local pubs – the **Melvin Bar** and the **Riverside Bar** – provide music, craic and entertainment.

🛒 Shopping

The **Buttermarket Art, Craft and Design Courtyard** (Down Street, Enniskillen; www.thebuttermarketenniskillen.com) is a centre for pottery, ceramics, hand-made jewellery, textiles and other creations by more than a dozen craftsmen and women. The renovated 19th-century complex includes a coffee shop and gift shop, too. And of course, this being in the middle of Lough Erne country, there's a shop selling fishing tackle.

The best... FOOD AND DRINK

▶ Staying in

Leslie's Bakery (10 Church Street, Enniskillen, ☎ 028 6632 4902) produces superb quality, distinctive regional breads. One of the main tastes of Ireland is soda bread – Irish flour is very soft and doesn't take well to yeast. So bicarbonate of soda combined with buttermilk came to be used as the leavening agent; the result was today's delicious soda bread. Also available are Ulster's other two mainstays – wheaten bread (called brown bread as well) and potato farls. **Flo's** (15 Townhall Street BT74 7BE; ☎ 028 6632 6860) is a friendly, centrally located café in Enniskillen – but it's also a terrific place to load up with local bread, pastries, ready-cooked meals, cooked meats etc. Stock up here and head for the lakes.

    Patrick O'Doherty's Fine Meats (3 Belmore Street, Enniskillen BT74 6AA; ☎ 028 6632 2152) is one of the best butchers in all of Ireland – and they even have awards to prove it. In the business for 40 years, they've won the 'Best Steakburger in Ireland Award' on three occasions. Their black bacon – matured to perfection – has similarly won national and UK awards.

EATING OUT

FINE DINING

Café Merlot
Blake's of the Hollow, 6 Church Street, Enniskillen
☎ **028 6632 0918**

Café Merlot, the below stairs restaurant of the famous old Blake's pub, provides upmarket, imaginative fare – smoked duck is served with bean sprouts and coriander, while a perfect risotto is served with local turbot. Food is presented nicely, the atmosphere is friendly and relaxed. A meal will cost around £15 for two courses.

Silk's
Killyhevlin Hotel, Dublin Road, Enniskillen BT74 6RW
☎ **028 6632 3481**
www.killyhevlin.com

Fine dining, fine views – the cuisine here features a modern twist on traditional Irish dishes. Being so close to the lough – the dining room has panoramic views of Erne – the fish are as fresh as you might imagine. Main courses cost £10–£15.

RESTAURANT

Bilberry Restaurant
Main Street, Garrison BT93 4ER
☎ **028 6865 9999**

The Bilberry is a well-established restaurant in the North West, drawing custom not just from Fermanagh but most of Donegal as well. It has a comfortable setting with reasonable prices and great food. Main courses cost from £7.

CAFÉ

Le Bistro
Erneside Shopping Centre, The Point, Enniskillen BT74 6JQ
☎ **028 6632 6954**

A busy self-service café overlooking Lough Erne. Soups, salads, sandwiches of all kinds are served fresh daily. The Johnson family who run the place pride themselves on their use of local, in-season produce. Closed on Sundays.

Flo's Restaurant
15 Townhall Street BT74 7BE
☎ **028 6632 6860**

Just about the friendliest place in Fermanagh, this town centre restaurant serves huge roast dinners for £7, soups and wheaten bread for £2.50, and all kinds of cakes and buns. And you're certain to pick up whatever local information – or gossip – you require.

🍺 Drinking

Fermanagh is well supplied with pubs, with some of the oldest drinking establishments in Ireland taking pride of place in Enniskillen.

The **Linen Hall**, (13 Townhall Street BT74 7EH), is part of the British Wetherspoon's chain and is excellent for a pint and a meal. The Blakes of County Fermanagh may be the only family to have held two pub licences for well over 100 years. Both of their pubs – one in Enniskillen and one in Derrylin – have been in the family since 1887. **Blakes of the Hollow** (Church Street, Enniskillen; ☎ 028 6632 2143) is renowned for its Guinness and Irish coffees. One of the most famous pubs in Ireland, it has been frequented by writers, poets and ordinary drinkers. The author John McGahern, (The Dark and Amongst Women) said: 'I've been going to Blakes of the Hollow for close to 20 years and think of it as one of the happiest and most beautiful bars in the whole of Ireland.'

Magee's Spirit Store (21 East Bridge Street, Enniskillen; ☎ 028 6632 4996) is the oldest pub on the Island of Fermanagh. Neil Hannon, of the Divine Comedy and the writer of the *Father Ted* theme music, regards it as his favourite pub (see p. 289), and it's not difficult to see why – it's friendly, comfortable, full of locals, and while resolutely traditional, somewhat incongruously offers some superb New York cocktails. The **Horseshoe and Saddlers** (66 Belmore Street, Enniskillen; ☎ 028 6632 6223) has a solid reputation for good Guinness and fine restaurant upstairs.

ℹ️ Visitor Information

Tourist information centre: Fermanagh Tourist Information Centre, Wellington Road, Enniskillen BT74 7EF, ☎ 028 6632 3110, tic@fermanagh.gov.uk, www.fermanagh.gov.uk.

Hospitals: Erne Hospital, Cornagrade Road, Enniskillen, ☎ 028 6638 2000.

Doctors: Out of Hours Medical Centre, Erne Hospital, Cornagrade Road, Enniskillen, ☎ 0870 606 2288.

Police: PSNI Station, Queen Street, Enniskillen, ☎ 028 6632 2823.

Supermarkets: Erneside Shopping Centre, The Point, Enniskillen, ☎ 028 6632 5705, is the biggest complex of shops and supermarkets.

Parking: Enniskillen is the only town where parking is charged for; the town is amply provided with parking facilities.

Internet access: Most hotels now provide Wi-Fi or internet access (prices vary, sometimes free); M3 Connect, Corporation Street, ☎ 028 6632 0302.

Taxis: Minibus and taxi – Charity's, Enniskillen, ☎ 028 6632 2555; County Cabs, Enniskillen, ☎ 028 6632 8888; Lochside Garages ☎ 028 6632 4366.

NORTH FERMANAGH

Great loughs lying between meadows carpeted with wild flowers, quiet, serenely flowing rivers (the most lightly fished waters in Europe) and ethereal, mist-shrouded islands – welcome to Fermanagh's lakeland. This is the most westerly point of the Six Counties, and one of the most westerly parishes in Europe – from here there are only a few miles of the Old World left before it crumbles into the Atlantic; in the summer the twilight lingers till gone midnight. On the loughside it's silent except for the gentle lapping of the waters and the lonely call of the plover – the kind of place where Celtic legends are born; and you may be sure there are plenty of them.

North Fermanagh is very rural, very under-populated (with fewer than 15,000 people) and, it would have to be said, very wet. It rains here two days out of three – it's just a pity you can't tell which days. On the other hand – the land doesn't get that green by accident. 'The forty shades of green', even though it's a song written by Johnny Cash, doesn't even begin to address the situation. It's probably more like 140 shades, particularly in this iridescently green part of Fermanagh. For one set of visitors who have long favoured this westerly outpost for their holidays, the rain makes little difference. Anglers don't mind if it's teeming down – in fact, some even prefer it.

This part of Fermanagh is predominantly Catholic, and during the Troubles it had its fair share of civil unrest. Today it is totally peaceful, but the religious differences still surface in surprising ways. Although Ireland (aside from Dublin) has no postcodes, the Six Counties, under British jurisdiction, now have their own codes. Fermanagh was the last county to fall to this idea, but the population has largely held out against numbers on their houses. This means that large swathes of the county have no means of identifying households except by ancient townland names – which of course is no problem in areas where the postie knows everyone. The row, like most administrative and political squabbles in the Six Counties, eventually took a sectarian turn. If you were Catholic you wanted to keep the old Irish-named townlands; Protestants sided with modern technology, i.e. house numbers. Although the wrangle has been largely settled, house numbers and postcodes can still be elusive.

So what do you do if you want to find a specific location and you're a stranger to the area? Easy, really: if you're a woman you stop and ask someone; if you're a man you just drive around aimlessly for a while and then go home. In that respect, at least, Fermanagh is the same as anywhere else!

WHAT TO SEE AND DO

Lower Lough Erne
Lower Lough Erne and **Upper Lough Erne** – in all some 70km in length – are now linked to the **River Shannon** and its waterways via the **Shannon-Erne Waterway** canal, making the entire system the longest navigable inland waterway in Europe. Both Upper and Lower Lough Erne have a maze of islands – most of which are suitable for landing by boat – and are the very stuff of legends. Just imagine gently floating into a little natural stone jetty, jumping onto the soft turf and hauling your boat ashore. Then the search begins for a good place to have lunch – under that hawthorn bush perhaps? Or maybe the tip of the island – after all it's only 50ft away. And who knows, the last person to have picnicked here might have been a follower of St Patrick. Or some disgruntled Viking intent on stealing his picnic.

Lough Erne – from the Irish *Loch Éirne* meaning 'Lake of Ernai', referring to an ancient tribe of Ireland – is one of the least congested lakelands in all Europe. Overlooked by mysterious castles, stunning stately homes and dark forbidding caves, Lough Erne forces you into using one of travel writing's abiding clichés – this truly is one of Europe's best kept secrets.

Northern Ireland has fewer coastal islands than other parts of Ireland, but its loughs teem with them. In Lower Lough Erne the bigger ones include **Cleenishmeen Island**, **Crevinishaughy Island**, **Cruninish Island**, **Ely Island**, **Goat Island**, **Horse Island**, **Inish Doney**, **Inish Fovar**, **Inish Lougher**, **Inish More**, **Inishmakill**, **Lusty Beg Island**, **Lusty More Island** and **White Island**. The viability of many of Ireland's islands has been enhanced since time immemorial by religious concerns. Lower Lough Erne's **Devenish Island**, although only about 1¼ miles long and two-thirds of a mile wide, comes complete with a Round Tower and High Cross. This is one of the finest monastic sites in the Six Counties. You can climb the 12th-century Round Tower, built to withstand the Danes. But of course, there ain't nothing like a Dane (not the favourite song of the Irish back then) and this site was regularly ravished. You can climb the 30m high Round Tower – albeit in uncomfortably cramped fashion – for a magnificent technicolour view of the lough.

Nearby is **St Mary's Priory**, the Augustinian Abbey, a 15th-century High Cross and the ruins of a monastery founded by St Molaise. He established the monastery in the 6th century specifically on a pilgrim route to Croagh Patrick in County Mayo. It became a centre of scholarship and although raided by Vikings in 837 and burned in 1157 by the Normans, it later flourished as the site of the parish church and St Mary's Priory. A ferry (☎ 028 6821 1588) crosses to the island from Trory Point. Take the lane at the junction of the A32/B82, some 5km north of **Enniskillen**.

Cadaragh Cemetery on nearby **Boa Island** is home to two extraordinary stone statues – the seemingly gloating Boa Man, also known as the Lusty Man (because he came from the island of **Lusty More**), and the Janus Stone. No-one knows if this is a pagan idol or an early Christian statue, although the latest guesstimate for

The Boa Man on Boa Island

DEVENISH ISLAND: ☎ 0208 9054 6518; www.ni-environment.gov.uk/devenish. Entry: adults £3, children and senior citiziens £2, pre-booked school parties £1, this includes a guide; 1 Apr to 30 Sept: Northern Ireland Environment Agency ferry from Trory daily 10am–6pm, with scheduled sailings at 10am, 1pm, 3pm and 5pm; ferry leaves from Trory point, down a short lane at the junction of the B82 to Kesh and the A32 to Ballinamallard 3 miles north of Enniskillen Town Centre; short stop on Devenish is included in the tour of Lower Lough Erne on the *MV Kestrel* from the 'Round O', Enniskillen.

the stones' age is around 2,000 years. So if they are Christian, somebody must have been very quick with the news from the Middle East. Pop along and see if you can throw some light on it yourself. Several other islands, such as **White Island** (12th century abbey, pre-Christian artefacts) or **Inishmacsaint Island**, the site of 6th century **St Ninniad's Abbey**, are also essential visits if you want to try to make some sense of what makes this land tick. (Call **Erne Tours** on 028 6632 2882 for full itinerary.)

Bird-watching

The now universal procedure of ringing birds to map their distribution and habits was devised by Fermanagh man James Burkitt back in 1920. Probably the extravagance of the local avian population inspired him – the loughs and rivers here are home to thousands of waders, ducks, geese and sea-birds. The Lower Lough Erne Islands are one of the RSPB's reserves, with 39 islands constituting the bird sanctuary. Although most of them can't be visited, several viewpoints are available right round the lough's shoreline. Only two islands – **Lusty More** and **White Island North** – are can be accessed by the public and everything from swans to scoters are resident.

The woodlands round Fermanagh are the ideal habitat to spot one of Ireland's three unique indigenous birds – the Irish jay. This member of the crow family, glorying in the scientific name of *Garrulus glandarius hibernicus*, can be seen flitting from tree to tree, its blue feathers an unmistakable identification guide. As well as waders, fowl and jays, this area of Fermanagh is one of the last European redoubts of the corncrake. This is a bird that causes much excitement in the twitching world despite a dull appearance. That's because its cry – its booming two tones – is the very sound of our rural past. However the evocative call doesn't pleased everyone – one zoologist described it thus: 'Unfortunate birds, corncrakes. God only gave them two notes – and one of them is flat.'

But, *Crex crex*, as the corncrake is pleased to call itself on formal occasions, stirred the muse in Shane MacGowan:

As I walked down by the riverside
One evening in the spring
Heard a long gone song
From days gone by
Blown in on the great North wind
The lonesome corncrake's cry
Of sorrow and delight.

Sinn Féin's Gerry Adams remembers hearing corncrakes at the top of the Falls Road in Belfast when he was a lad. Nowadays, though, you have to travel to the loneliest parts of Europe to hear them – like the under-farmed land of North Fermanagh.

Boating and fishing

A number of companies on Lower Lough Erne hire out day boats. Expect to pay something in the region of £12–£15 per hour for an open rowing boat with outboard motor, or upwards of £50 for a half day on a six-seater cruiser with cabin. Lough Erne provides both coarse and game fishing – so everything from the finest trout to roach and bream are available. Salmon fishing runs from June to the end of September, trout fishing from March to September. Coarse fishing has no closed season. To pluck your succulent salmon from the waters of Erne you will need a licence (issued by the Fisheries Conservancy Board), as well as a permit from the owner of the stretch of water you want to fish. On Lower Lough Erne you can get all the necessary paperwork out of the way at the **Castle Archdale Country Park**, where you can also hire out fishing rods and tackle.

Boating on Lower Lough Erne

For qualified instruction in fly-fishing – for trout, salmon and pike – contact **Michael Shortt** (Sydare, Ballinamallard; ☎ 028 6638 8184/0708 204 401) who is a mine of information about the local piscean population, and has a very user-friendly attitude to instruction. Erne Angling (www.erneangling.com) provides boats, equipment, tuition – the fish you have to find yourself – although they will point you in the right direction.

> ULTIMATE WATERSPORTS: Castle Archdale Marina, Lisnarick; ☎ 07808 736818; www.ultimatewatersports.co.uk. Price: wakeboarding £30 for half an hour, banana boat £10 per person, canoe hire £20 per hour, kayak hire £10 per hour, special rates for longer periods available on request; open Apr to Oct.

Those interested in watersports on Lough Erne should contact **Ultimate Watersports**, which offers a range of activities including kayaking, dinghy sailing, canoeing, water-skiing, as well as the more idiosyncratic sports of banana boating, wake-boarding and inflatable riding.

Cycling in Fermanagh

In the slowly undulating countryside of North Fermanagh, cycling is a rarefied pleasure. The **Kingfisher Trail**, a 230-mile cycle route that also takes you through neighbouring counties (North and South), is a figure-of-eight route meandering along the area's quietest and leafiest roads. And if you don't fancy lugging your luggage round Ireland, Irish Cycling Safaris (☎ 00 353 1 260 0749) will carry it for you.

Castle Archdale Country Park

Red deer, wild fowl, Second World War remnants – these are just a few of the features of Castle Archdale. The country park is situated about 10 miles north-west of Enniskillen and extends 230 acres along the shores of Lower Lough Erne. Boats are available for hire if you wish to explore the nearby islands, some of them National Nature Reserves (the RSPB sites, however, are out of bounds). Pony trekking and bicycle hire are also available.

Within the park are a nature trail, butterfly garden and wildflower meadow. The Archdale Centre, in the corner of the main courtyard, houses various exhibitions that

Castle Archdale Country Park

explain the fascinating natural history of the area, and the Northern Ireland Department of Environment's sterling efforts to preserve it. Evidence of the Second World War can also be found throughout the park in flying-boat docks, ammunition dumps, trenches, etc. Lough Erne played an important role as the most westerly flying-boat station of the Allies. From here aircraft protected the allied convoys from the U-boat threat in the

CASTLE ARCHDALE COUNTRY PARK: Lisnarick, Irvinestown BT94 1PP; ☎ 028 6862 2211; www.ni-environment.gov.uk. Entry: free; park opens daily 8.30am to dusk; museum and countryside centre opens from Easter to end of June, Sat/Sun 10pm–6pm; May bank holiday 10am–6pm; 1 Jul to 30 Aug 10am–6pm; Sept, Sat/Sun 10am–6pm.

North Atlantic. Castle Archdale was the main base from which they flew, highlighted in an exhibition within the Centre, 'Castle Archdale at War'.

The Cliffs of Magho

If somebody asked you in a quiz where you'd find the **Blue Stack Mountains**, you'd probably say something like West Virginia. But despite their unusual name they are, in fact, among Ireland's most northerly mountains, ranging roughly from **Donegal Town** northwards towards **Letterkenny**. And you can get a smashing view of them from the Cliffs of Magho at the western end of Lower Lough Erne. This 250m-high and 9km-long limestone escarpment, rising above the lough and woodland, is some 13km west of **Belleek**. A hike to the top is strenuous enough, but the rewards are ample. As well as the Blue Stacks, one further treat is in store – a view of the highest sea cliffs in Europe. The savage **Slieve League** tumbles almost 2,000ft into the sparkling waters of Donegal Bay. The trail begins in the **Lough Navar Forest Park** (see box), but you can also get to the Magho viewpoint by car through Lough Navar Forest.

LOUGH NAVAR FOREST PARK: Signposted off the A46, 5 miles north-west of Derrygonnelly; ☎ 028 6634 3040; www.forestserviceni.gov.uk. Entry: free; open daily 10am to dusk.

The cliffs of Magho

Castle Caldwell Forest Park

Castle Caldwell, a Norman fortification, today lies in ruins. But at the entrance is a very odd stone shaped like a violin. The inscription on the Fiddle Stone is now too worn to read, but it commemorated a popular local musician who fell out of a boat when drunk. The inscription, written with the benefit of 20–20 hindsight, reads:

On firm land only exercise your skill; there you may play and safely drink your fill. To the memory of Denis McCabe, Fiddler, who fell out of the St Patrick Barge belonging to Sir James Caldwell Bart and Count of Milan and was drowned of this point August ye 13 1770.

> **CASTLE CALDWELL FOREST PARK:** About halfway between Boa Island and Belleek on the A47. Entry: free; open 24 hours.

After reading this melancholy advice, head for the nature reserve within the forest to uplift your spirits. Teeming with birdlife, the woodland is a major breeding ground for the common scoter. Denis McCabe would have been better off observing them from a lakeside hide rather than getting blootered on the barge.

Killadeas

If you only visit one ancient graveyard this year, then this should be high on your list of candidates. The churchyard at Killadeas (11km north of Enniskillen on the B82) has everything any self-respecting Irish graveyard should be able to lay claim to – a Bishop's Stone, dating from between the 7th and 9th centuries, a Celtic statue almost worn smooth by 1,500 years of 'fine soft weather', various ancient tombstones, lots of wrought iron Celtic crosses. Go as the sun is setting for maximum atmosphere.

Wet weather

Belleek

Belleek is the most westerly town in the Six Counties. But being the final westerly outpost of British rule in Ireland is not its main claim to fame. Established over 140 years ago, Belleek is to pottery what Wagner is to Bayreuth, Waterford is to crystal, or Cornwall is to pasties. The village (with a population of 505 according to the 2001 census) is smack bang on the border – the other side of the bridge across the River Erne is the Republic of Ireland. The pretty street leads to the imposing Georgian-style building which houses the internationally famous **Belleek Pottery**.

Guided tours are conducted at the factory, and you can watch pottery being made and delicately painted, and visit the

> **BELLEEK POTTERY:** Belleek BT93 3FY; ☎ 00 44 28 6865 9300; www.belleek. ie. Entry: free; times vary widely during the year; summer opening is 7 days a week, winter 5 days.

Belleek Pottery

museum – where some of the oldest examples of Belleek china are on show. Pottery wares are available in the shop at prices considerably less than you might expect in Dublin or London.

Belleek is also the home of **Fermanagh Crystal** (29 Main Street, Belleek BT93 3FY; ☎ 028 6865 8631). You can visit the factory and showroom to see the crystal being made and engraved. Here too, you'll find plenty of opportunity to buy the finished product.

What to do with children...

The maze of islands in Lower Lough Erne – apparently there are 369 islands so one for each day of the year plus four spare ones, or so the locals will tell you – make this a canoeist's paradise. A boating trip here with a company such as the **Lough Erne Canoe Trail** offers intriguing opportunities for children and teenagers to sample the abundant wildlife hereabouts (otters in the water, pine martens on the shore) natural history and aquatic sports. If the children are feeling very adventurous, easily accessible campsites are within reach. The Lough Erne Canoe Trail (www.canoeing.com) provides maps, guides and advice, while the Lakeland Canoe Centre, Castle Island (☎ 028 6632 4250; www.arkoutdooradventure.com), can provide all types of canoe; for further information on kayaks, canoes and umiaks check out www.canoeni.co/www.nisurfkayak.com.

✕ ... and how to avoid children

If you really want to get away from it all, you can have your timbers suitably shivered aboard your own motor cruiser in the middle of Lough Erne. In the olden days on the open sea the captains of the old sailing ships would be careful never to let the crew have a glimpse of the charts or an inkling of the boat's position, for fear the crew would mutiny and force the ship ashore. No danger of this on the Erne – you're never far from dry land; even better,

AGHINVER BOAT COMPANY: Lisnarick, Lower Lough Erne; ☎ 028 6863 1400; www.abcboats.com.

CARRICK CRAFT: Tully Bay, Lower Lough Erne; ☎ 028 3834 4993; www.cruise-ireland.com. Weekly rates range from about £500 for a week depending on season/size of boat; 2/4/8 berths available.

you're never more than a few miles from a cosy little pub. But you'll be wondrously removed from the general hubbub of modern life – with not a child in sight.

You can explore Lough Erne by boat without any previous experience or qualification – you'll get a swift course in boatcraft and navigation at the start of your voyage. Recommended cruise hire companies include **Aghinver Boat Company** and **Carrick Craft**.

Entertainment

Irvinestown, the hub of North Fermanagh, hosts a 10-day summer festival and carnival, **The Lady of the Lake Festival**, every July. The name alludes to the fact that through the mists of May a graceful woman glides across Lower Lough Erne carrying a garland of wild flowers. Her appearance (if you're lucky) is an omen of good times to come.

Moohan's Fiddlestone Pub (15–17 Main Street, Belleek) is named after the Castle Caldwell Fiddle Stone (see elsewhere), and eponymously lives up to its name. Fermanagh fiddling is heavily influenced by the next county along, Sligo, which is revered as the very home of the style of fiddling we now describe as the specific and generic Irish traditional style. But you don't need to be get all ethno-musicological to appreciate the sessions in the Moonstone. The **Black Cat Cove, Belleek** (28 Main Street; ☎ 028 6865 8181) is a friendly local with a music programme during the summer months that includes traditional music, ballads and that odd hybrid country & Irish.

LOCAL KNOWLEDGE

Martin Preshaw is a manufacturer of Uillean pipes, the exclusively Irish version of the bagpipes. He lives on a farm on the county border with Donegal in the townland of Mullanmeen Under.

Favourite pub – my local, the Crosses. It's a meeting place for neighbours to discuss stuff agricultural, and justly renowned for its Guinness (a very modest £2.50 a pint).

Favourite activity – without a doubt, visiting the Marble Arch Caves. Some of the stalactites are over 15ft long and, given that they grow at approximately 25 ft every millennium, gently remind me that my time is nothing but a 'blip' on this earth.

Best view – from my neighbour's farm - truly breathtaking. The checkered fields of Counties Fermanagh, Donegal and Tyrone all blend into one another.

Quirkiest attraction – Drumskinney Stone Circle, which is a miniature Stonehenge. Although it's pagan, I often think of the 'Holy Stone of Clonrickard' from *Father Ted*.

Best kept secret – to our shame, it's local historian and folklorist Mr Johnnie McKeagney. A collector of local history, his museum in the Diamond in Tempo is bursting to the seams with artefacts from Fermanagh and surrounding counties.

Favourite treat – one which unfortunately further enhances my increasing girth, is a post-Sunday lunch drive to the now world renowned, Tickety Moo ice cream parlour in Kiladeas – the product is handmade from the cream of free range Jersey cows.

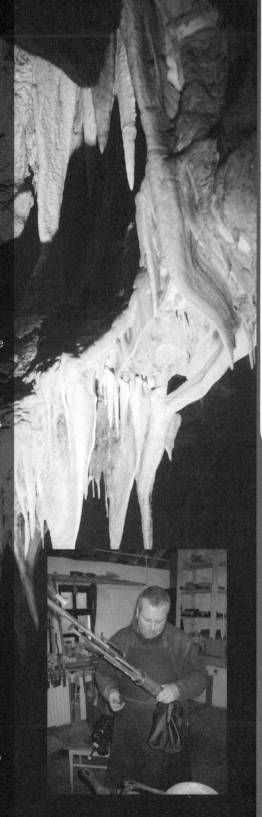

The best... PLACES TO STAY

HOTEL

Manor House Resort Hotel

Killadeas BT94 1NY
☎ **028 6862 2211**
www.manor-house-hotel.com

An impressive loughside period house, this is probably North Fermanagh's most luxurious stay. Even if you aren't an angler you will still enjoy the view of the lough from your bedroom – be sure to ask for a front room.

Price: from £125 for a double.

INN

Drumrush Lodge

Boa Island Road, Kesh BT93 1AD
☎ **028 6632 3481**
www.drumrushlodge.co.uk

Overlooking Lower Lough Erne, Drumrush is right beside the marina. The lodge has beach and bathing facilities, as well as tennis court and facilities for all watersports. Straightforward, big-fisted bar food – with the added ingredient of wonderful views of Lough Erne. Main courses cost from around the £10 mark. The bar also features live music regularly.

Price: doubles from £75.

SELF-CATERING

Fermanagh Lakeland Lodges

Letter, near Boa Island BT93 2BF
☎ **028 6863 1957**
www.fermanaghlakelandlodges.com

Four star luxury by the lough. On an 85 acre woodland site, there's a marina with sailing boats, fishing licences available, angling tuition, barbecue area, canoes and outboard motor boats.

Price: from £500 for a week.

Coole Cottage

Belleek BT93 3FX
www.coolecottage.com

Nestling on the banks of Lough Erne in the naturally charming village of Belleek, this is an ideal base for exploring the Erne waterway, or merely chilling out in tranquil, pastoral landscape. And even if the clouds do descend to shoulder height on the odd occasion, it's a mere 250 yard stagger to the village's pubs and restaurants.

Price: from £400 for a week for two people in the low season.

UNUSUAL

Lusty Beg Island

Boa Island, Kesh BT93 8AD
☎ **028 6863 3300**
www.lustybeg.co.uk

You can stay on this private island retreat in a self-catering chalet, or B&B in the rustic, but unrustically named Courtyard Motel, a misnomer if there ever was one. Tennis court, nature trail and canoeing on the lough are all available for residents.

Price: from £500 for a week; various specials available throughout the year.

The best... FOOD AND DRINK

▶ Staying in

At the **Apple-box Barn** (68 Main Street, Ballinamallard; ☎ 028 6638 8086) you can stock up on local farm produce as well as gifts and crafts from local artisans. The **Kesh Home Bakery** (27 Main Street, Kesh BT93 1TF; ☎ 028 6863 1698)) does exactly what is says on the sign – everything is baked here on the premises: soda bread, potato farls, pancakes, pastries etc. The Kesh Bakery supplies supermarkets across Fermanagh and Tyrone. For cakes, head for Viola's **Contemporary Cakes and Cookies** (46 Ardgart Road, Mullaghmeen BT94 2HE; ☎ 07592 744879). Viola specialises in handmade Irish boiled fruitcake. And don't leave without buying the oaten black treacle bread.

🍸 Drinking

This drinking section starts rather idiosyncratically with a pub which isn't even in the right country. But with good reason. The **Pettigo Inn** Main Street, Pettigo, County Donegal/Fermanagh (☎ 00 353 7198 61720) is worthy of your attention from several points of view. **Pettigo** itself is a picturesque little village that straddles the international border. There are pubs here where you can drink your pint in the Republic and then go for a pee in the United Kingdom – the High Street, you see, is in the UK, while the Main Street is in the Republic of Ireland. The Pettigo Inn, however, is firmly in the Republic, on Main Street. However it's worth the 10 yard walk across the frontier to visit this establishment, locally favoured for its craic, cuisine, Guinness and excellent choice of music – mostly traditional, and featuring heavily the energetic Donegal style of fiddling.

If you get chatting to locals about Pettigo's anomalous geographical position (they don't mind talking about it) you'll likely get the whole story about the Irish War of Independence in 1922. Apparently matters in Pettigo became very confused between the IRA and the British Army which resulted in the somewhat baroque carve-up of territory. Show an interest at the Pettigo Inn and you'll get chapter and verse. Then again you might just prefer to talk about fishing. Everybody else probably will be.

The **Central Bar** in **Irvinestown** is a traditional old pub full of character. Distinctive high windows, open turf fire and oak spirit-barrels for dispensing whiskey all add to the atmosphere. The Central was popular with Canadian Airforce men stationed nearby during the Second World War and is still visited by relatives of those men – and indeed the occasional surviving veteran. But mainly the Central Bar is a home from home

EATING OUT

RESTAURANT

Belleek Restaurant
Manor House Country Hotel, Killadeas BT94 1NY
☎ **028 6862 2211**
www.fermanaghlive.com/ ManorHouseCountryHotel

A striking restaurant on the shores of Lough Erne, famous throughout the local area as one of Fermanagh's top tables. The view across the lough itself is worth booking a table for. The emphasis is on local produce, and as the establishment is on the shores of Lough Erne, that means fresh fish – try the salmon sushi, by the way, once you've had your fill of the signature dish, oysters. There's also a reasonable vegetarian menu. Allow around £10 for starters, £20 for main courses.

Encore Steak House
66 Main Street, Ballinamallard
☎ **028 6638 8606**

Naturally enough steak is the speciality here, and goodness knows there are enough fine plump heifers in the green fields around Ballinamallard to guarantee succulence. Lamb steaks are on offer too, if you want a bit of variety. Open Wednesday to Sunday, evening only, expect to pay around £20 per head.

The Oaks Restaurant
Drumarky, Lisnarick
☎ **028 6862 1493**

A fine rural hostelry, but the sort of place where 'haute cuisine' means hot food. However, there's plenty of good standard fare – escarpments of mashed potato (called 'champ') served with local meat and fish, all tastefully done. Moderately priced, from around £10 per head.

Ederney Country House
9 Castlederg Road, Ederney BT93 0AL
☎ **028 6863 2777**

Set in an idyllic rural setting – and really, they don't come much more rural than this neck of the woods – the Ederney caters for a reasonably eclectic taste. Local produce is served with flair, fish is, of course, a staple. Main courses range from about £10 to £20.

GASTRO PUB

Island Lodge Restaurant
Lusty Beg Island, Boa Island, Kesh BT93 8AD
☎ **028 6863 3300**
www.lustybeg.co.uk

Fine dining and extravagant views – you get there by ferry from Kesh jetty, summoned by phoning the number above. Bar meals cost £6–£12, four-course meals from £25.

CAFÉ

Thatch Coffee Shop
20 Main Street, Belleek
☎ **028 6865 8181**

This listed historic building is the only original thatched cottage in any town or village in County Fermanagh. The full panoply of local bakery is available – soda farls, wheaten bread, potato cakes, scones. Soups, sandwiches and coffee are also available, and, unlike most coffee shops, it has its own fishing tackle shop, the Belleek Angling Centre.

for the many time-worn locals who add to the bar's character. A gem of a place where you'll be treated like a local yourself – and a traveller can ask for no more than that.

Mahon's (Mill Street, Irvinestown; ☎ 028 6862 1656) is something of an institution in the Fermanagh/West Tyrone area. Established in 1883, the Guinness here is reckoned to be among the best in the area. This is a recommendation which is taken very seriously in these parts. The **Mallard Bar**, Ballinamallard, is a friendly place with food, live music and craic. It caters for more of a younger crowd at the weekend. The **Poachers' Inn**, Ballinamallard, caters for an older crowd, but things fairly buzz at the weekend. The **Mayfly Inn Bar, Kesh** (Main Street; ☎ 028 6863 1281) is renowned for its great sessions at the weekend, and is a terrific place to sit with a pint and ruminate that here, at least, Ireland has not changed very much.

ⓘ Visitor Information

Tourist information centres: Fermanagh Tourist Information Centre, Wellington Road, Enniskillen, Fermanagh BT74 7EF; Fermanagh Tourism ☎ 028 6632 3110/028 9032 3110.

Hospital: Erne Hospital, Cornagrade Road, Enniskillen, County Fermanagh BT74 6AY, ☎ 028 6638 2000.

Doctors: Roslea Medical Practice, 20 Upper Main Street, Roslea, Enniskillen, County Fermanagh BT92 7LT, ☎ 028 6775 1496; Dr RT Leary, Lisnaskea Health Centre, Drumhaw, Lisnaskea, Enniskillen, County Fermanagh BT92 0FP, ☎ 028 6772 2913.

Pharmacies: Gordans Chemists, 2–4 Main Street, Irvinestown, Enniskillen, County Fermanagh BT94 1GJ, ☎ 028 6862 1221; MT McGuinness, 4 Main Street, Belleek, Enniskillen, County Fermanagh BT93 3FX, ☎ 028 6865 8218.

Police: 12 Cliff Road, Belleek, Enniskillen, Fermanagh BT93 3FJ; ☎ 028 6865 8212.

Supermarket: Spar Supermarket, 49 Main Street, Belleek, Enniskillen, County Fermanagh BT93 3FY, ☎ 028 6865 8395.

Cash point: Bank of Ireland, Main Street, Belleek, Enniskillen, County Fermanagh BT93 3FX, ☎ 028 6865 8340; First Trust Bank, 8 Main Street, Belleek, Enniskillen, County Fermanagh BT93 3FX, ☎ 0845 600 5925.

Taxis: A O'Connor, Station House, Legg, Belleek, Enniskillen, County Fermanagh BT93 3BP, ☎ 028 6865 8552; Speedie Cabs, Cornagrade Road, Enniskillen, County Fermanagh BT74 6AX, ☎ 028 6632 7327.

SOUTH FERMANAGH

Gaelic games – that is Gaelic football, hurling, camogie (women's hurling) and court handball – are almost exclusively played in Northern Ireland by Catholics. The GAA is one of the most powerful amateur sporting bodies in the world and the very backbone of rural Irish society, a situation that carries over into the nationalist areas of the Six Counties. Croke Park in Dublin, built entirely for amateur games, is the fifth largest sporting stadium in Europe – with only the likes of Real Madrid's home ground, or AC Milan's stadium edging ahead of it. Fermanagh is alone in Ulster in never having had any national success in the All Ireland GAA championships. When asked why, the manager of the Fermanagh hurling team could only reply, 'Sure, we're half bogland, half Protestants.' He was certainly right about the bogland bit. Blanket bogs, raised bogs, water meadows, marshland, all alive in spring and summer with a riot of wild flowers, many of which have disappeared elsewhere in Europe. The streams, rivers and loughs which abut these meadows are all rich, rich fishing grounds. At almost every road junction, signs will guide you to the best angling sites. The symbol of a white fish against a brown background has to be the commonest sign in the area.

Fermanagh is the least populated county in the whole of Ulster, with only 57,000 inhabitants – a large number of them living in Enniskillen. South Fermanagh remains one of the least populated areas in the EU, so if you're looking for a quiet, unhurried, untroubled holiday this is an ideal destination. Visit **Crom Castle** mid-week in October and you will have the place to yourself; climb **Cuilcagh Mountain** any time of the year and you will be lucky if you meet half a dozen other climbers.

Like the rest of Fermanagh, the southern part of the county is dominated by **Lough Erne**. It was on an island in Upper Lough Erne that the *Annals of Ulster* (*Annála Uladh*) were written, on **Belle Isle**. The *Annals* are an invaluable chronicle of medieval Ireland, spanning the years between AD431 and AD1540. Should you wish to check the area out before you come, the Bodleian Library in Oxford holds a contemporaneous copy – you will just have to brush up on your Old Irish and Latin as it's all written in those two languages.

Although going into some detail about life in Fermanagh, the *Annals* are unlikely to have contained any recipes such as deep fried breaded brie with rosemary and garlic brioche topped with rhubarb chutney – which is what you can find on Belle Isle nearly 500 years after the writers of the *Annals* shut up shop. **Belle Isle School of Cookery** is one of the top cuisine colleges in Ireland, set in some of the most beautiful surroundings. A historic place then, but **Upper Lough Erne** also provides angling, boating, canoeing and aquatic sports of just about every description.

WHAT TO SEE AND DO

Upper Lough Erne

Upper Lough Erne is less populated and more remote than the Lower Lough. Look at a map of the area and its dozens of islands give the appearance of a jigsaw puzzle that isn't going to be sorted out anytime soon. Between Enniskillen and Galloon Bridge 57 islands form a maze impossible to navigate without a chart. Exploring this wanton promiscuity of space is truly a voyage of discovery.

The islands include **Bleanish Island**, **Dernish Island**, **Inishcorkish**, **Inishcrevan**, **Inishfendra**, **Inishleague**, **Inishlught**, **Inishturk**, **Killygowan Island**, **Naan Island** and **Trannish**. A few islands are inhabited (by humans), some by wild goats. Several are privately owned, and occasionally come onto the open market. In 2007 **Inishturk** reportedly fetched a price of £695,000.

Fishing and cruising are available throughout the area – you will see lots of men behaving nautically; indeed, whole families behaving nautically. For guided cruises in the Upper Lough, the **Inishcruiser** in **Lisnaskea** will both conduct you through this watery wonderland.

> **THE INISHCRUISER:** Share Holiday Village, Smith's Stand, Lisnaskea BT92 0EQ; ☎ 028 6772 2122; www.sharevillage.org. Entry: adults £7.50, family £21; public cruises every Sun and bank holidays, Easter to Sep.

If you want to go independent and crew your own boat on the Upper Lough, **Knockninny Marina** in **Derrylin** provides boats with front cabin (Knockninny Quay, Derrylin BT92 9JU; ☎ 028 6774 8590).

The Upper Lough, with its peninsulas, jetties and wooded banks provides superb angling. There is no close season for the coarse fisher person – bream, roach, perch and tench can be pursued the whole year round. The pike fishing here is regarded as second to none. The game angler can fish for salmon and wild brown trout as well as rainbow trout, sonaghan, gillaroo and ferox, three unusual local species of trout. The latter, the ferox, a heavyweight with very strong jaws, is particularly sought after for sport.

The **Erne & Melvin Enhancement Co** is a local community-led non-profit organisation which has recently developed some great fishing sites on several stillwater loughs which drain into Upper Lough Erne. **Lyon's Lough**, **Drumacrittan Lough** and **Inver Lough** are all available for pike fishing and coarse fishing (roach, rudd, tench etc). Day tickets are not required, although you will need a fishing licence from the Fermanagh Tourist Information Centre (Wellington Road, Enniskillen BT74 7EF; ☎ 028 6632 3110; www.dcal-fishingni.gov.uk). Lyon's Lough has two designated disabled stands available. Keen anglers rarely miss **Lisnaskea** – not just because of its proximity to the Upper Lough, but also the **Colebrooke River**, **Moorlough**, **Kilmacbrack Lough** and **Lough Doo**. For licences, day tickets, information on seasons, again contact the Fermanagh Tourist Information Centre.

Cuilcagh mountain

Hill walking

The **Ulster Way** wends through County Fermanagh, and crosses a modest peak called **Benaughlin**, some 1000ft in height. You won't need crampons, harnesses and altitude sickness pills, but you will need good hiking equipment. It's steep enough in places, and underfoot is quite rough. But at the top you're rewarded with a view that is remarkably extensive for a hill of modest height.

To one side are the hills of **Moher** and **Erveny**, and across to Fermanagh's highest peak **Cuilcagh**. To the north and north-west is the **Florence Court** estate, to the east the silvery waters of **Upper Lough Erne**.

Cuilcagh Mountain Park

With 8% of the world's blanket bog, Ireland is the most important country in Europe for this specific type of habitat. Cuilcagh Mountain Park lays claim to one of Ireland's most extensive boglands, and together with the **Marble Arch Cave System** makes up a UNESCO-designated European Geopark. The habitat is a haven for golden plovers, red grouse, hen harriers and merlins – this is the RSPB's only upland reserve in Ireland (jointly managed with Fermanagh District Council). Take care, though, if you're bird-spotting and have your eyes trained upwards. The blanket bog is dotted with concealed swallow holes and caves. Just remember the old Irish saying, 'Where every hill has its heroes, and every bog its bones.' At 2,188ft **Cuilcagh Mountain** itself is a reasonable climb. The route is waymarked by yellow painted posts, and begins in leafy lanes just beyond **Florence Court**.

By the way, don't worry about the oil pollution you might spot in the bog pools. No need to alert the authorities. Plants in these damper regions are paranoid about drought (a somewhat pessimistic outlook given the rainfall here) and when water levels drop even slightly they extrude an oily substance over the surface to prevent evaporation. This cunning plan is used by one of our favourite carnivorous plants, the sundew. In a year, one plant can account for 2,000 insects.

Florence Court

Florence Court is the former demesne of the Earls of Enniskillen, now owned by the National Trust. The main attractions of the Palladian Mansion, completed in 1764 for Lord Mount Florence, include two travelling chests of Queen Mary and King William III (King Billy himself), excellent rococo plasterwork and a painting attributed to Poussin.

Florence Court

However, keen horticulturalists will want to rush past the fine antique Irish furniture holding some outstanding **Belleek china** and head for the gardens. As well as more trees than you could shake a very long stick at, the park also can lay claim to one VIT (Very Important Tree). This is the Florence Court Yew, from which the strain known as the Irish yew – familiar in graveyards throughout the world – was propagated. Every Irish

yew tree in the world – no matter where you see it – came from this original plant. The original tree, grown from a seedling in around 1750, can be found lurking unassumingly near the main house.

The Irish yew, *Taxus baccata fastigiata* is simply a narrow sport of the common yew of Eurasia, but its shape, perfect for formal designs and tight places, led to it being planted throughout the world, particularly graveyards. The estate includes a walled garden with displays of both temperate and semi-tropical plants enough to bewitch any botanist, a working water-powered sawmill, an ice house, and a natural spring well. The **Larganess River** flows through the pasturelands and forestry which make up most of the demesne.

The kingfisher trail

This 230-mile cycle route, which meanders through Fermanagh and four neighbouring counties, is a figure of eight route utilising roads that won't be facing congestion charges any time soon. For more local cycling round South Fermanagh, **Sliabh**

Beagh Cycling (Unit 7, Roslea Enterprise Centre, Liskilly, Roslea BT92 7FH) has five cycling routes on minor country roads from 18 miles to 37 miles. Fully signposted, the routes take in the counties of **Monaghan**, **Fermanagh** and **Tyrone**. Several companies, such as the Greenbox, can source accommodation throughout the route. The North

Crom Castle on the Crom Estate

West Cycle Tour is a 200 mile route through the counties of **Fermanagh**, **Donegal**, **Tyrone**, **Leitrim** and **Sligo** – the trail takes you from the islands of Upper Lough Erne to the shores of the **Atlantic Ocean** (www.northwest-trail.com).

Crom Estate

Crom Estate is the largest area of natural woodland in Northern Ireland, a haven for pine martens, rare bats and many species of bird. Herons (and several other waders) can be spotted in the extensive wetlands, while the bogland is home to a profusion of flowers, plants and mosses. The wooded islands and peninsulas are often cited as the loveliest in all Ireland. Boardwalks lead around the loughside and over the bog, leading eventually to the old ruined **Crom Castle**. Built as a Plantation stronghold in 1611 (last weekend in Northern Ireland terms), it was garrisoned by settlers. The forces of James II attacked in 1689, but the settlers scored a decisive victory, killing some 2,000 of James's troops. Today the castle sits in derelict beauty beside a newer castle built by the Earl of Erne. The fine grounds of this building are home to a yew tree that is claimed to be the largest in Ireland.

CROM ESTATE: Newtownbutler; ☎ 028 6773 8118; www.nationaltrust.org.uk/www.ntni.org.uk. Entry: cars £5.50, pedestrians free; open 10am–7pm Jun to Aug, to 6pm rest of the year.

The best way of exploring the riverbanks and islands is by boat rented in Crom Estate. 17ft open boats are available for hire at the visitor centre. They come with outboard motor, oars and buoyancy aids. Loughside stops include **Crichton Tower** on **Gad Island**; **Derryvore Trinity Church**, a beautiful Victorian church situated atop a hill on Derryvore Peninsula. Surrounded by mature parkland trees and a glorious native hay meadow, this is one of the last great and unchanging landscapes left in Europe.

Belcoo (Fermanagh) and Blacklion (Cavan)

It's worth visiting these two places purely to speculate on what life in a border town must have been like just a short decade ago. Today there are few manifestations of the frontier between the two jurisdictions, the British and the Irish. If you travel from, let's say, County Armagh to County Louth you will pick up few clues to the fact that you've left one country and entered another. There's more of a border between Wales and England, or even between Surrey and Sussex. But between Belcoo and Blacklion, although there's no formal border, there are many subtle differences. Like different currencies (although the red telephone box in the North does take euros), different speed limits, different armies, different coloured post offices, different police forces and different war memorials.

Roslea

Like any self-respecting Irish county, Fermanagh can lay claim to links with at least one US president – Bill Clinton. His mother's maiden name was Cassidy, which along with Maguire is a common name. During a 1995 visit President Clinton visited his ancestral home, a Cassidy farm in the village of Rosslea.

Should you wish to trace your own Fermanagh roots – pop into the **Roslea Heritage Centre**. The restored cut stone building has a genealogical searching service. It also features traditional tools including turf-cutting implements. Turf-cutting is relatively simple – as long as you have turbary rights. Basically you go along the togher with your flachter, remove the scraw, cut your turf by slane, and head back up the togher with your slipe full of turf. Learn all about it at the Heritage Centre.

> **ROSLEA HERITAGE CENTRE:** Monaghan Road, Roslea BT92 7DD; ☎ 028 6775 1750. Entry: adults £2, children 50p, concessions £1; Apr to Sept, Mon–Fri 10pm–3pm; out of hours by appointment.

Wet weather

Marble Arch Caves

The Marble Arch Caves and **Cuilcagh Mountain Park** are in an elite of 12 sites across Europe in that they have been designated by UNESCO as a European Geopark. This mesmerising world of rivers, waterfalls, winding underground passages and lofty subterranean chambers houses one of Europe's finest and most accessible collections of stalagmites and stalactites. And from the visitor's point of view it doesn't matter if the weather is a little inclement – an important consideration in Fermanagh. (Note however, the Caves are occasionally closed if the water table has risen too much, so best check ahead). Spectacular walkways allow access to

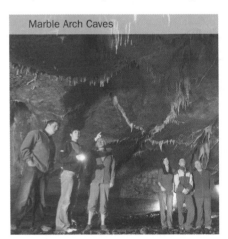
Marble Arch Caves

MARBLE ARCH CAVES: Marlbank Scenic Loop, Florence Court BT92 1EW; ☎ 028 6634 8855; www.marblearchcaves.net. Entry: adults £8, children £5; open 10am–5pm Jul/Aug, 10am–4.30pm Easter/Jun to Sep.

the caves where seeping acid water, lime and carbon dioxide have interacted since the Ice Age to produce chambers of silent beauty. Powerful, brilliant lighting reveals huge caverns and shimmering white terraces in all their undisturbed splendour. Tours on board quiet electric boats take you round this remarkable limestone cave system.

Sliabh Beagh Arts

Alternatively, you could explore your artistic side at Sliabh Beagh Arts (Unit 7, Roslea Enterprise Centre, Liskilly, Roslea BT92 7FH; ☎ 028 6775 1918; www.sliabhbeagh. org). A wide range of arts activities are available here, from pottery to painting. You can have your own creativity inspired alongside professional artisans. Other activities available to both residents and visitors include video production, circus skills, costume/puppet design, environmental art, music technology and much more.

What to do with children...

Several aquatic recreational centres provide excellent boating and fishing facilities, but

Water activities at the Corralea Activity Centre

Corralea Activity Centre (Upper Lough McNean, Belcoo; ☎ 028 6638 6123; www.activityireland.com) concentrates on showing children and teenagers the secrets of watercraft. Water trampolining, windsurfing, dinghy sailing, canoeing, kayaking, banana skiing etc. It's suitable for families, and accommodation is available.

... and how to avoid children

Belle Isle School of Cookery

Belle Isle Castle sounds as if it should be in the Mediterranean, but is in fact a 17th century Anglo-Irish pile complete with its own island, lough and 450 acres of private land to wander through. But what marks it out as child-free is its School of Cookery (☎ 028 6638 7231; www.irish-cookery-school.com). This is one of the top colleges of cuisine in Ireland where, in a relaxed atmosphere, with expert tuition, you can learn all about blanching, sautéeing, flambéeing etc in one of the most beautiful settings in Ireland. Sessions range from one-day vegetable courses to outdoor cuisine, Christmas cookery and seasonal menus.

If, however, your significant other wants to take a course, but your idea of cooking is waiting till the smoke alarm goes off and then it's done, never fear. Belle Isle offers lots of sporty stuff too – an all-weather tennis court, fishing, hiking, canoeing.

Entertainment

Lisnaskea is the second town in Fermanagh after Enniskillen, with a population of just over 2,000. As such, it's the main centre for pubs, clubs and traditional sessions. It is also the birthplace of Johnny Patterson a circus showman who wrote the songs 'The stone outside Dan Murphy's door' and 'The garden where the praties grow' – both staple fare in Ireland's immense, and variable, song canon.

Have you ever been in love, me boys?
Oh! have you felt the pain?
I'd rather be in jail, me boys,
Than be in love again.
For the girl I loved was beautiful,
I'd have you all to know,
And I met her in the garden
Where the praties grow.

Praties, by the way, are potatoes – derived from the Irish *prátai*. Songs such as these fall into a category of the canon now largely ignored by most Irish musicians and performers. They are seen as hangovers from the same vaudevillian tradition that produced 'When Irish eyes are smiling', 'A little bit of heaven fell out of the sky and they called it Ireland' and 'Did your mother come from Ireland?' Charming though some of these songs are, don't expect to hear any of them at the **White Thorn** in Lisnaskea (175 Main Street, Lisnaskea, Enniskillen BT92 0JB; ☎ 028 6772 3225) which features everything from cover bands to ballad groups.

Melarkey's in Newtownbutler has full-on traditional sessions of a Wednesday night, with the added bonus of the pub being famous for serving a good pint of Guinness. **Blake's** of Derrylin (Main Street, Derrylin BT92 9LA; ☎ 028 6774 8203) is a friendly, garrulous pub in the middle of Derrylin. Three generations of the Blake family have tended to the needs of Fermanagh's thirsty folk – it's probable that the Blake family is the only one in Ireland to have held two pub licences for over 100 years; their Enniskillen pub is regarded as one of the top in the Six Counties. Blake's of Derrylin is a high quality place – with awards to prove it, including Winner of British Airways Tourism Award and Bushmills Pub of the Year. Music ranges from jazz to traditional sessions; the Blake's nightclub is where Fermanagh's young up-for-it people congregate.

Blake's also features that peculiar hybrid of music known as country & Irish. Now this should be an electrifying mix of music, coming from two terrific parents, American country music on one side and Irish traditional on the other. But, the reality is not to everyone's taste, sometimes being accused of bordering on the maudlin. However, it can be strangely riveting at 3am on a Fermanagh morning, when the requisite number of Guinnesses have been drunk. Whatever the reasons, country & Irish is enormously popular in Fermanagh and neighbouring Tyrone, and Blake's regularly presents the best of the genre. See what you think yourself – brand leaders at the minute are the likes of Mick Flavin, Dominic Kirwan and Philomena Begley.

🛒 Shopping

One of the garments on show at the Sheelin Lace Museum

All the lace on show at the **Sheelin Antique Irish Lace Museum** (Bellaneleck BT92 2BA; ☎ 028 6634 8052; www.irishlacemuseum.com) dates from between 1850 and 1900. More than 400 exhibits – including crochet, wedding dresses, veils, shawls, parasols – trace the history of lacemaking in Ireland. The museum also highlights the one-time economic importance of the industry to the local economy. The museum shop sells an impressive range of lace and linen.

The best... PLACES TO STAY

B&B

Abbocurragh

Letterbreen BT74 9AG
☎ **028 6634 8484**
www.abocurragh.com

A farm B&B with three rooms, breakfast is in the conservatory overlooking the pastures. The rooms are comfy, quiet and restful – and there's a cosy sitting room if you want to be sociable (most people tend to that position in these parts). Dinner is available for £18, but remember to bring your own wine.

Price: from £30 for a single; from £50 for a double.

CAMPSITE

Lough Melvin Holiday Centre

Garrison, Enniskillen, County Fermanagh BT93 4ET
☎ **028 6865 8142**
www.melvinholidaycentre.com

Camping, caravan sites, dormitory accommodation and en suite rooms are all available here, as well as restaurant and coffee shop. But it's not really for the accommodation you will be staying here – you're more likely to be up early and off canoeing, boating, fishing, caving. All can be organised here.

Price: campsites from £9, rooms from £30.

SELF-CATERING

Corradillar Cottages

208 Newbridge Road, Lisnaskea BT92 0JW
☎ **028 6772 2240/077790 039524**
www.fermanaghlodges.com

Ten cottages set in 16 acres of woodland on the banks of Upper Lough Erne. Comfortable and traditional – the fires can be stacked up with turf from the bogs of Fermanagh delivered daily.

Price: From £350 to £600 per week.

Sophie's Cottage

Glassmullagh, Derrylin
☎ **028 6774 8551/07837 888250**
www.irishthatchedcottage.co.uk

A beautiful five-star holiday cottage – something of a style statement deep in Fermanagh – in a listed building, situated near Crom Church. Woodburner stove, DVD player, Wi-Fi, stereo, etc. A welcome pack includes local and organic products.

Price: from £200, low season.

The best... FOOD AND DRINK

▶ Staying in

If you are suspicious of anything which advertises itself as 'famous', you can make an exception in the case of 'the famous Fermanagh Black Bacon'. Fresh pork is selected from the black pigs on the island of **Inishcorkish**, **Upper Lough Erne**. The pigs live wild on the island, and don't rely on artificial food additives to survive. The bacon is then cured for three months – and brought to Enniskillen. It's available at **O'Doherty's** (Belmore Street, Enniskillen; ☎ 028 6632 2152; www.blackbacon.com). The island can be visited by arrangement.

For a master-class in farm shops head for **Arch House Farm** (Tullyhona, Florence Court BT92 1DE; ☎ 028 6634 8452; www.archhouse.com). Daily farm life continues round shoppers, B&B residents and dinner guests. Produce in the shop could scarcely be fresher, coming straight from the farm or the lough. Bakery is a speciality and big here – you can even learn how to make scones or soda farls – and the smoked salmon is melt-in-your-mouth tender. The place to pick up a few wheaten loafs or soda farls stuffed with bacon and tomatoes is the **Kissin' Crust** (125 Main Street, Lisnaskea BT92 0JE; ☎ 028 6772 2678). Homemade soups, scones, sausage rolls, cakes are all available – but if it suddenly occurs to you that Northern Ireland has a bit of an iffy reputation as regards cardiac health (it has one of the worst rates in the world), you could always just get a coffee.

For all things sweet, **Graydon's Sweet Temptations** (20 Boyhill Road, Maguiresbridge BT94 4LL; ☎ 028 8953 1772) should be able to satisfy all your requirements – as well as providing excellent bread.

EATING OUT

FINE DINING

McNean Bistro
Main Street, Blacklion, County Cavan
☎ **00 353 71 9853022**

McNean's is worth crossing the international boundary down Main Street in Belcoo. This restaurant has picked up various accolades and awards for its cuisine – which includes dishes such as saddle of rabbit stuffed with smoked bacon and honey and parsnip soup. And Neven Maguire makes some of the best desserts this side of Vienna – try the chocolate fondants with ginger ice cream, followed perhaps by a hazelnut nougat with passion-fruit flavoured whole cream. Cakes come in cliff-sized wedges. Starters cost from €10 and mains from €15.

RESTAURANT

The Customs House
25–27, Main Street, Belcoo BT93 5FB
☎ **028 6638 6936**
www.customshouseinn.com

Decked out in oak and pine, you can't help feeling as soon as enter you will be treated to good local food without too many frills. And so it is – fresh fish from the lough, steaks from the cattle reared on Fermanagh's green, green grass. Main courses cost from around £12.

The Inishmore Restaurant
Carrybridge Hotel & Marina, 171 Inishmore Road, Carry, Enniskillen, County Fermanagh BT94 5NF
☎ **028 6638 7148**

Sunday lunches are something of an institution in this well-established, family-run restaurant. Portions are gigantic – they say you should never eat anything bigger than your head but the Inishmore puts this sorely to the test. Main courses cost £8–£15 and a three-course Sunday lunch £13.95.

Fusion Brasserie
The Donn Carragh, 95–97 Main Street, Lisnaskea BT92 0JD
☎ **028 6772 1206**
www.discovernorthernireland.com/ donncarragh/

The Donn Carragh is located in the centre of Lisnaskea, its name coming from Don Carrach Maguire the first king of his tribe. The food in the Don is hearty and hefty, but has a nod in the direction of 'new Irish cuisine' – the best seasonal ingredients produced locally. A three-course set dinner menu costs £23.

🍺 Drinking

Rural Fermanagh has more than its fair share of drinking establishments. The old historic town of **Lisnaskea** has several pubs, but for a quiet drink **Frank's Bar** (Main Street, Lisnaskea BT92 0JE; ☎ 028 6772 1381) is the place. A traditional pub, it will be full of locals checking the day's sporting results, or discussing the latest ructions in Stormont in the most erudite terms. The **Corner House** is a traditional, snug little bar.

The **Halfway House** (Letterbreen BT74 9FH; ☎ 028 6634 1367), is an old coaching inn, on the go since the late 1760s. Originally servicing the Enniskillen-Sligo-Galway coach, today the pub remains a welcome stopping off point. Designate a driver and tuck into a beautifully poured pint of stout, and if it's summer time it's sit back and cheer on the local cricket team, the Islanders MCC. Players from this team proudly appeared for the national side in 1969 at Sion Mills in County Tyrone – when the Northern Ireland team almost unbelievably beat the West Indies. (It would be fair to point out that the West Indies players had spent most of the previous day having a tour of the Bushmills Distillery.)

ℹ️ Visitor Information

Tourist information centre: Fermanagh Tourist Information Centre, Wellington Road, Enniskillen BT74 7EF, ☎ 028 6632 3110, tic@fermanagh.gov.uk, www.fermanagh.gov.uk.

Hospital: Erne Hospital, Cornagrade Road, Enniskillen, ☎ 028 6638 2000.

Doctor: Out of Hours Medical Centre, Erne Hospital, Cornagrade Road, Enniskillen, ☎ 0870 606 2288.

Police: Enniskillen Police Station, 48 Queen Street, Enniskillen, County Fermanagh BT74 7JR, non-emergency ☎ 0845 600 8000.

Supermarket: There are no major supermarkets in South Fermanagh.

Parking: there are no parking meters in any part of South Fermanagh.

Internet access: most hotels now provide Wi-Fi or internet access (prices vary, sometimes free).

Taxis: Charity's, Enniskillen, ☎ 028 6632 2555; County Cabs, Enniskillen, ☎ 028 6632 8888; Lochside Garages ☎ 028 6632 4366.

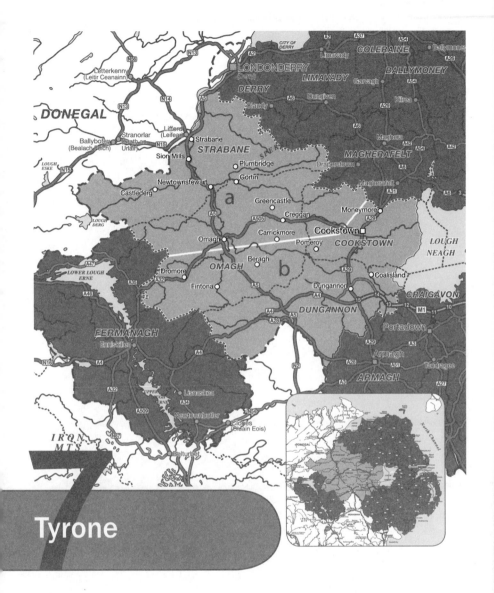

Tyrone

a. North and Mid Tyrone
b. South Tyrone

Unmissable highlights

01 Stare in wonder. Some 44 monuments 'of prehistoric significance' within a 5 mile radius of the Burren Centre, p. 329

02 Contemplate the 10th-century Ardboe Cross on the shores of Lough Neagh, p. 346

03 Learn about emigration to the New World at the Ulster American Folk Park – from Omagh to Omaha, as it were, p. 332

04 Enjoy huge views across the once terribly troubled lands of mid Ulster from the Dun Ruadh neolithic tombs and stone circle, p. 330

05 Fancy a new tablecloth? Wellbrook Beetling Mill, Cookstown carries on the famous Northern Ireland linen tradition, p. 334

06 Go to a green hill far away, in the Sperrin Mountains – the inspiration for the eponymous hymn written by Mrs Cecil Frances Alexander, p. 211

07 Visit the Black Bog, very old and very deep. But beware, in these parts, 'every hill has its heroes, and every bog its bones', p. 348

08 Climb Sawel Mountain (2240ft) for hypnotic views of the biggest lake in the British Isles, Lough Neagh, p. 328

09 Pay your respects to Davy Crockett – or at least to his people, who came from Castlederg. A model of the Alamo adorns the Castlederg Visitor Centre, p. 336

10 Visit Omagh, some of the scars have healed, but a cloak of melancholy still hangs over this lovely old town, p. 332

TYRONE

As you stand in the quiet bogland in the heart of old Tyrone, it's not difficult to believe that some of the oldest known manmade structures in Europe were built here. The Megalithic culture of Tyrone was long underway by the time the Celtic culture began to spread throughout the island. This landscape, richly strewn with stone circles, dolmens and burial chambers, has its spiritual past inscribed on the land. Tyrone has more than stone monuments, however, and could reasonably call itself the most under-rated holiday destination in Ireland, if not Europe.

Walking, fishing, golfing, poetry, literature, dance and song are all on the county's checklist – and all set against a backdrop of history which is both lengthy and terrible, even up to recent times. Irish history, even from the earliest times, has been described as current affairs, and nowhere is that truer than here.

Any tour of Tyrone eventually leads to the north of the county and the very heart of the Sperrins, which straddle the Tyrone-Derry border, stretching some 35 miles from north-west to south-east – a truly unspoilt paradise of gentle ridges and winding valleys. This is not exactly the end of the known world – but you suspect you might be able to see it from here. Mrs Cecil Frances Alexander would wander the, quiet, empty, primrose-dotted paths that criss-cross the **Sperrins**. It's said that this was her inspiration to write 'There is a green hill far away'. Mrs Alexander also wrote 'Once in royal David's city' – but then the verdant countryside round here would awaken the lyrical muse in anyone.

NORTH AND MID TYRONE

North Tyrone has produced a remarkable range of famous people and famous songs: humourist Flann O'Brien, 'There is a green hill far way', 'Once in royal David's city', the 'Teddy bears' picnic', singer Paul Brady (Planxty), writer Benedict Kiely, playwright Brian Friel. And also William Burke, grave robber and murderer who plied his trade alongside fellow Irishman William Hare in Edinburgh.

This exceptionally sparsely populated area of Tyrone has produced an astonishing amount of art, music, literature and poetry. They either put something into the porridge here, or – more likely – the scenery, the tranquillity, the emptiness, is enough to inspire any artist. This part of Tyrone is also a quiet place, a gentle place. The weather won't batter you to the ground with an unexpected Atlantic squall, while on the other hand you're unlikely to need your sunblock (although you never know). But if you want a restful, contemplative and truly Irish holiday, far away from noisy tourists and rampant commercialism, this place is worthy of your attention.

WHAT TO SEE AND DO

Strabane

Strabane has some of the best fishing in the world. So good, it has attracted its fair share of high profile visitors over the years including Tiger Woods, the late British Queen Mother, Chris Tarrant, Jackie Charlton and Deputy First Minister Martin McGuinness. The River Mourne flows through the centre of the town, and meets with the River Finn to form the River Foyle, and this serendipitous confluence of the waters has produced what is reckoned to be the finest salmon river in Ireland. People come from all over the world to fish in the beautiful waters as they babble through meadows and woodland. Hint – the area between **Victoria Bridge** and Strabane is reckoned to be one of the most fecund stretches.

Apart from the fishing, these days with peace having come and the economy on the up, Strabane has a certain recherché charm – as well as being the hometown of the families of both Davy Crockett and US President Woodrow Wilson. *An Srath Bán*, as it was originally called, has long been a garrison town, taken by Phelim O'Neill in 1641. It straddles the international border – just across the river in County Donegal is the town of **Lifford**. There are half a dozen such towns in Ireland, and it's always interesting to see how the folk get round such an elephant in the front room.

Strabane is British, but not in the way that Tunbridge Wells or Finchley is. For a start there's the monster barracks of a building overlooking the river, once an RUC

Civic Sculpture

base, now a PSNI station. Even though the country is at peace, the station is buried under a ton of concrete with surveillance cameras and electronic equipment bristling from every rooftop – it makes Colditz look positively friendly.

With the peace process and the subsequent de-commissioning of British army posts Strabane has managed to regain an air of normality, but a sense of siege mentality still somewhat pervades the town. Despite the years of the Troubles and economic stagnation, Strabane is quite a handsome place, especially approached from the Donegal side. Crossing the river from **Lifford** the five spires of Strabane's churches rise up towards the gorse covered hills. Novelist Anthony Trollope was quite taken with the place. In his 'letter from Strabane' to a friend in England in 1854, he wrote: 'The North of Ireland has some charms for the tourist – & should you take my advice & visit there I beg to offer myself as your host and guide.'

One thing Trollope – who lived in Ireland – wouldn't have seen back in the 19th century is a truly remarkable sculpture just outside the town. Entitled '**Let The Dance Begin**', it was built to celebrate the Millennium. Five semi-abstract stainless steel and bronze figures – approximately 18ft in height – play fiddle, fife, drum etc, in a representation of Music and Dance. Designed by Maurice Harron, they were placed at the former British army base at the Donegal border. They are affectionately known locally as The Tinneys.

Strabane Glen, just over a mile outside town, is a narrow gully with steep rock faces and views over the **River Foyle**. **Lundy's Cave** is said to have been a hiding place of the military governor of Derry, who defected to the besiegers when the apprentices closed the city gates against the Jacobites. 'Lundy' is still an insult hurled by Loyalists, in an area where the events of four hundred years ago are still fresh in the mind.

The Sperrins

The Sperrins are a truly unspoilt paradise of gentle ridges and winding valleys. As English poet Kit Wright wrote: 'When I think of peacefulness I think of the Sperrins, Bonventura the nun, and me.' It's not clear what the business with the nun is about, but certainly in terms of peacefulness, Kit was spot on. And he's officially backed up too – the Sperrins are designated as an Area of Outstanding Natural Beauty. Not everyone, however, has been taken with the view. When representatives of the London guilds visited Ulster in 1609 – the people who gave Derry its prefix – the Lord Deputy of Ireland made it his business to keep them well away from the Sperrins, fearing that their remote bleakness might put settlers off.

Literary and musical connections in Strabane

Mrs Cecil Frances Alexander, who was born in Dublin but brought up in Strabane, wrote the hymn 'There is a green hill far away'. It is generally believed that Mrs Alexander (née Fanny Humphreys), who also wrote 'Once in royal David's city' and 'All things bright and beautiful', was also alluding to the nearby **Sperrins** when she wrote of 'the green hill, far away', and not just Calvary.

Flann O'Brien was born Brian O'Nolan at 17 Bowling Green Square, Strabane. Today it is a locked, downcast, three-storey terraced house, dour and unkempt. Little attention is paid to Flann in Strabane; perhaps his satirical humour and biting wit were at odds with the parochial nature of the town back then – and the reason he had to head to Dublin to make his name. Nonetheless, his memorable lines on the recuperative effects of alcohol during hard times are probably among the most quoted in the whole canon of Irish poetry:

> When money's tight and hard to get,
> And your horse is also ran
> And all you have is a heap of debt
> A pint of plain is your only man.

Strabane has given rise to an extraordinary amount of poetry and song. 'The flower of sweet Strabane' is one of Ireland's favourite love ballads:

> If I were King of Ireland's Isle, and had all things at my will
> I'd roam for recreation, and I'd seek for comfort still.
> The comfort I would ask for, so that you may understand
> Is to win the heart of Martha, the Flower of Sweet Strabane.

The highest peak is **Sawel** (678m), rising above the B47 road from **Plumbridge** to **Draperstown** in County Derry. Your effort in climbing it (it's not that difficult) will be well rewarded with fine views. **Plumbridge**, a picturesque mountain village astride the **Glenelly River**, lies at the junction of five roads leading through the hills. This is an ideal base for exploring the mountains – and indulging in the wealth of activities on offer. The Sperrin rivers and loughs are renowned for their angling, and the quiet leafy boreens are tailor-made for horse riding, hiking and cycling.

Cycling in the Sperrins

The Gold Cycle Route (31 miles in length) begins in **Gortin** and is marked with brown Route 1 signs. The first part of the route takes you into the **Glenelly Valley** and through the **Barnes Gap**, a dramatic U-shaped glacial channel. Speed your way up to the wilds of **Sawelabeg** and **Doraville**, past a gold mine opposite the bridge at **Glenlark**, and finally follow the **Owenkillew Valley** back into **Gortin**. En route you pass the **Sperrin Heritage Centre** where you can find out all about the geology of this stunning region and pick up maps with suggested hiking routes, nature trails and bridle paths.

Walking in the Sperrins

SPERRIN HERITAGE CENTRE: 274 Glenelly Road, Plumbridge, Omagh; ☎ 028 8164 8142; www.strabanedc.com. Open Easter to Oct, Mon–Fri 11:30am–5:30pm, Sat 4pm; Sun 2pm–6pm.

You might even meet Murphy, the centre's resident ghost. Admission to the centre is £2.75, and for an extra quid you can pan for gold in a nearby stream.

In the rural vastness of the mountains look out for buzzards soaring, otters and kingfishers in and around the rivers, and deer in the forest before **Doraville**.

The heritage centre's Glenelly Kitchen does homemade cuisine.

An Creagán

Set in an area of great historical importance among the foothills of the Sperrin Mountains, the **An Creagán Heritage Centre** (Creggan, Omagh BT79 9AF; ☎ 028 8076 1112; www.an-creagan.com) is built in a vernacular style using indigenous stone so that it blends in beautifully with the surroundings. The words of the area's most famous song, 'The Creggan White Hare', are inscribed round the walls of the reception area. Stick around for any length of time and somebody is sure to sing it. Stick around even longer and you might actually see the hare – although, as it's magical, unpredictability is an integral part of its nature.

A short film in the Heritage Centre will tell you that within a 5 mile radius are some 44 prehistoric monuments, some of which date back 5,000 years. An Creagán has maps and suggested walks to these ancient stones, the most intriguing rock groups you will ever see. Exhibits also graphically display the natural history of the area – the hare, of course, takes a starring role. The Irish hare is a separate sub-species on its own – *Lepus timidus hibernicus* – although differences with the European hare are so striking that some authorities believe it should be a species in its own right, the *Lepus hibernicus*.

An Creagán has a restaurant, bar, concert area – it's a well known centre for traditional music and dance – as well as accommodation.

An Creagán Visitor Centre

Megalithic Tyrone

Homo sapiens hibernicus was alive and well in this part of Ireland just after the Ice Age, probably the first settled area of the entire island. By BC4,000 a vibrant culture had begun, already ancient by the time the Celts arrived (or evolved – opinion is divided). Not only were the Neolithic colonisers of Ireland building places to live, but also tombs for their dead.

An Creagán Centre will provide you with guides and maps to some of the more accessible ancient Megalithic constructions. The **Dun Ruadh** tombs and stone circle, situated on the sweeping curve of **Crockyneill** roughly between **Cookstown** and **Omagh**, is what is known in archaeological terms as a multiple cist cairn, a complex series of structures. Situated in the **Broughderg** area, this is a remote and peaceful landscape renowned for its unique archeological remains. The scenery includes the **Coneyglen** valley and **Darvagh Forest**, with walks over extensive blanket bog – startlingly beautiful in the springtime when lit up by wild flowers (7km north of An Creagán).

Beyond the Dun Ruadh graves, further up the hill, another monument lies well hidden from view. This is a **Mass Stone** built sometime in the 19th century so that the oppressed Catholic faithful could worship in safety. An evocative walk gives you both huge views across the once troubled lands of mid Ulster, and much food for thought. **Balix Lower Court Grave**, about 3 miles north of **Plumbridge**, high on a hillside overlooking **Butterlope Glen**, is situated in a magnificent position, above one of the ancient thoroughfares through the Sperrins. The spectacular panorama from this point demonstrates one thing – evidently prehistoric man enjoyed a view as much as we do. **Creggandeveskey** is a well-preserved court tomb just over 2 miles north-east of **Carrickmore** – itself a town worth a visit just to see the impressive Republican memorial – and sign-posted south of An Creagán.

The stone circles of Beaghmore

Many of the prehistoric graves found in Ireland, such as Creggandeveskey, indicate they were built to accommodate ritual alongside, or perhaps inside, the graves. The actual nature of these rituals is obscure but they may not have been universally benign. It seems that when any structure was built a sacrifice was made, possibly to compensate the gods for any interference caused in the unity of the earth. A wide range of victims seem to have been pressed into service, including sheep, hares – and humans. The humans are usually what we would call middle-aged men (40 plus) but of course back in Ancient Ireland this may have been regarded as a ripe old age.

Loughmacrory Wedge, dating back to 2000BC, is a many-chambered construction – a burial chamber where evidence of sacrifices have been found – some 3km southwest of Creagán. **Aghascrebagh** (sign-posted north from Greencastle) is a standing stone only going back as far as 500BC. Being modern, it has the new-fangled Ogham writing decorating one side of the structure – using a linear style of writing. Nearby, the **stone circles of Beaghmore** date back to the Bronze Age – and may have served as a prehistoric temple. These are just to the west of **Lough Fea**, in a remote, spellbinding area. It was originally believed that these stones had something to do with astronomy (or astrology) but the thinking now is that the structure served some function in fertility rites.

Collow Quarry Shoot

Situated on the glorious setting of the historic Haughey Farm on the An Creagán estate, this is a great day out. Clay pigeon shooting in such terrific surroundings is a true adventure. No experience is needed. A variety of traps are tailored to simulate a whole range of quarry types; it'll awaken the primordial hunting instinct in you without having to hurt anything.

COLLOW QUARRY SHOOT: 44 Bradan Road, Collow, Drumquin BT78 4QQ; www. GQSshootingground.com. Entry: cost depends on whether you link your day with a range of other activities etc.

Gortin Glen Forest Park, Omagh

Gortin Glen Forest Park, 6 miles north of **Omagh**, is the western gateway to the **Sperrin Mountains**. Traces of the ancient oak forest which once covered Ireland are still visible, but today the woodland is mainly coniferous, planted originally for timber production. But there's enough open heathland to make this a very attractive estate – and give great views of the Blue Stack Mountains in Donegal, away to the west. In the spring and early summer the air rings with the sound of the cuckoo – this is prime birdwatching territory. The forest has a 5-mile-long drive with breathtaking views across the Tyrone landscape. A number of vista parks do the job perfectly.

The park also has hiking routes, horse-riding trails and three mountain-biking routes threading through the northern section of the forest above the **Glenpark Road**. The bike trails are graded basic, moderate and off-road (the latter suitable only for experienced cyclists). All trails provide excellent views of the **Plain of Omagh**,

GORTIN GLEN FOREST PARK: On the B48 Omagh to Gortin; bike hire available at the Glens Centre in the park; ☎ 028 8164 799. Entry: free; car parking £4; open daily from 10am until sunset.

Mullaghcarn Mountain and **Bessy Bell Mountain**. En route you will see red squirrels, deer, and buzzards and other raptors. On the last Sunday of July (called Cairn Sunday), hundreds of people make a pilgrimage to the top of Mullaghcarn as part of an ancient tradition.

Ulster American Folk Park

Although Britain and Ireland both have what is called a 'special relationship' with America, there is a difference – while the British on the whole merely suffer the Americans, the Irish actually like them. One reason for this is the whole emigration business. There can be few families in Northern Ireland – Protestant or Catholic – who don't have near relatives in America. The **Ulster American Folk Park** tells the story of emigration to the New World. The park is centred round the restored farmhouse of Thomas Mellon who left Tyrone in 1818 and eventually founded the Mellon Bank of Pittsburgh. Even by Tyrone standards that's going some.

The folk park boasts, among many other exhibits, a beautifully restored weaver's cottage, a local schoolhouse and a blacksmith's forge. The New World area consists of several types of log cabins, a Conestoga wagon (a 'prairie schooner'), and of course a complete list of the US presidents who had connections with the North (over a dozen of 'em). Costumed demonstrators go about their everyday tasks including spinning, open hearth cookery, printing and blacksmithing.

The Ulster American Folk Park

ULSTER AMERICAN FOLK PARK: 2 Mellon Road, Castletown, Omagh BT78 5QY; ☎ 028 8224 3292; www.folkpark.com. Entry: adults £5.50, children £3.50; Nov to Mar, Mon–Fri 10.30am–5pm; Apr to Oct, Mon–Sat 10.30am–6pm, Sun 11am–6.30pm.

The centre also has the restored cottage of John Joseph Hughes from Augher, who became the first Catholic Archbishop of New York, responsible for building St Patrick's Cathedral in the city. Around this simple cottage, a 200-year-old village has been meticulously reconstructed. An antiquated shopping street leads to an emigrant sailing ship, and on to a New World homestead – a cluster of log cabins, surrounded by fields of maize. It's a dramatic recreation of the life these emigrants made when they reached America, and the life they left behind.

Omagh

The name Omagh became etched on the blood-stained history of Ireland in 1998

Omagh

when a bomb exploded killing 29 people. Numbered among the dead were three Spanish students – the only tourists killed in the Troubles. Two hundred people were injured in the blast – the single worst atrocity in the whole of the Troubles. Today in Omagh the scars of that dreadful day remain, but the handsome town has recovered some of its poise. A memorial garden on **Drumragh Avenue** commemorates the dead.

To get a good grasp of Omagh, or *An Óghmagh* in Irish, make your way up the steep, wide High Street to the classical-style **courthouse**, behind which stands the **Catholic Church**. The Gothic style spires have caused it to be likened to Chartres Cathedral, and inside is no less impressive – make sure you see the 9th-century Black Bell of Drumragh and some fine marble carvings. A stroll through the town will give you glimpses of the **Strule River**, the finest salmon river in Ireland, you won't be surprised to hear (see also Mourne River, Strabane). As it says in the song:

I've tramped through Derry,
And to Portaferry in the County Down
But with all my achings and undertakings
My heart was aching for Sweet Omagh Town.

No wonder the writer of 'Philadelphia here I come', Brian Friel, born in the town, found artistic inspiration here, or novelist Benedict Kiely for that matter, also from the townland.

Omagh with a population of 22,182, is the county town of Tyrone and also the largest town of the county. Although its roots probably stretch back to the 8th century, modern-day Omagh was founded in 1610, nearly 150 years after the **Franciscan Friary** set up business in town – you can still see remnants of it near the bridge. It served as a refuge for fugitives from the east of Tyrone during the 1641 Rebellion. In 1689, the same year as the Battle of the Boyne, James II arrived at Omagh, en route to Derry. Supporters of William III, Prince of Orange, duly burnt the town to the ground.

The Church of the Good Shepherd, Sion Mills

Sion Mills

A lovely little village south of Strabane, Sion Mills was at one time synonymous with linen production. The millworkers' old cottages are still there and give the town great charm, as does the **Parish Church of the Good Shepherd**, the most striking Italian-style church in Northern Ireland, modelled on a church at Pistoia near Florence. The most remarkable sight, however, is **St Teresa's Catholic Church** which has a large stylistic representation on slate of the Last Supper. The church, built in 1963, is decorated inside with several works of modern art, including a window representing Our Lady engaged in the town's main industry, spinning.

Wet weather

Gray's Printing Museum, Strabane

John Dunlap emigrated from Strabane to America, and in 1776 published the American Declaration of Independence as well as the *Pennsylvanian Packet*, America's first daily paper. At Gray's Printing Press (49 Main Street, Strabane; ☎ 028 7188 4094) you can take a tour of the 18th-century printing press – where James Wilson, grandfather of President Woodrow Wilson, learned his trade. A collection of 19th-century machines as well as other printing paraphernalia are on show.

The museum also contains a huge treasure trove of other exhibits, many of them courtesy of a local historian Billy Dunbar. Highlights include a threepenny bit engraved with the Lord's Prayer, a 1906 Edison light bulb, a hand grenade, a sword used by an executioner, a clockwork dancing lady, a Long Way to Tipperary Bowl... and so on. In all there are several thousand exhibits in store; the museum has only room to exhibit a hundred or so items at a time. Truly an Aladdin's Cave of curios.

Wellbrook Beetling Mill

South Tyrone is rich in sheep pastureland, but there was a time when the landscape was blue with flax flowers, the basis of the wealthy linen industry. The Wellbrook

CELEBRITY CONNECTIONS

In America, when 'Red Sails in the Sunset' is performed, people assume it is set on some sunswept beach in Hawaii; in Britain it is assumed to be the Mediterranean. But in fact it was inspired by a scene from Portrush, on the north coast of Ireland. The writers of the song were Jimmy Kennedy and Will Gorsz.

Jimmy Kennedy, born in Omagh in 1902, also wrote the lyrics of the 'Teddy Bears' Picnic' and the beautifully romantic 'Isle of Capri'. With the latter, the Tyrone man managed to single-handedly change the English language. Kennedy, who could conjure a lyric out of anything, couldn't get the word Capri to scan in the way it was pronounced in those days (as in the Italian *capry*). So the wily songsmith simply wrote the word into the song to suit his own metre, and to this day we refer to the place as the Isle of Cap-reee. Jimmy also wrote 'South of the Border' (Down Mexico way), and should you have occasion to buy the sheet music of 'The Hokey Cokey', you will see the Omagh man is credited with the lyrics, although this remains the subject of some dispute. Jimmy Kennedy died in 1984 – Denis Thatcher, husband of the former prime minister Margaret Thatcher, gave the eulogy at his funeral.

Beetling Mill near Cookstown is one of the very few places where the crop is still grown and is the last beetling mill left on the island. Beetling is the process of pounding the linen to give a lustrous finish to the material. After this lengthy process, the cloth was so precious that it had to be put under armed guard.

Beth Black, the mill's curator, herself descended from a long line of linen workers, demonstrates the process, as well as bleaching, spinning and weaving. Outside are fine walks and picnic opportunities by the Ballinderry River.

WELLBROOK BEETLING MILL: 20 Wellbrook Road, Corkhill, Cookstown BT80 9RY; ☎ 028 8675 1735; www.nationaltrust.org. uk/main/w-vh/w-visits/w-findaplace/w-wellbrookbeetlingmill. Prices for tour: adults £4 (£3.63), child £2.30 (£2.09), family £10.30 (£9.36), groups (£3.20); opening hours Mar to Jun, Sat/Sun only 2–6pm, Jul to Aug 2–6pm Mon–Sun (closed Fri), Sept 2–6pm Sat/Sun.

What to do with children...

The **Ash Lee Riding Centre** is particularly geared towards beginners. By the time the children have finished here they'll be able to tell their pommel from their tingles.

They'll hack up gorse clad slopes, learn how to jump 3ft hedges astride a fine bay stallion (they'll soon learn that it's easier to ride a big horse than a pony), and find out what a tack-room is.

The **Melvin Sports Complex** (Melvin Park, Strabane BT82 9AE; ☎ 028 7138 2660) in Strabane has all the major sports facilities – but also provides an extensive children's play area, as well as table tennis for children, and half size snooker tables.

BARRONTOP FUN FARM: Donemana, Strabane BT82 0JD; ☎ 028 7139 8649; www.barrontop.co.uk. Entry: £4, children under-2s free, family £20. open April to June, Mon–Fri 10am–2.30pm, Sat 10am–5pm, Sun 2pm–5pm; June to August, Mon–Sat 10am–5pm, Sun 2pm–5pm; Sept to Nov, Sat 1pm–5pm, Sun 2pm–5pm; Nov to Dec, Mon–Fri 10am–2.30pm, Sat 10am–5pm, Sun 2pm–5pm.

The **Barrontop Fun Farm** provides a terrific opportunity for children to feed, handle, and make friends with many animals in a farm environment. They can bottle-feed a lamb, stroke a calf, cuddle a rabbit or puppy, or hold a newly hatched chick. They can also get up close to ostriches, emus, pot-bellied pigs, deer and rare breeds of poultry. A bouncy castle and adventure playground are also on-site – but the younger children might prefer a leisurely ride on a novelty cart pulled by Rollo the carthorse.

THE WOODVIEW LAND OF LITTLE ANIMALS: 31 Rash Road, Omagh BT78 5NJ; ☎ 028 8224 2937; www.woodviewlandscapes. co.uk. Entry: £4, under-2s free; open Mon–Sat 11am–4pm, Sun 2pm–5pm.

The **Omagh Leisure Complex** (Old Mountfield Road, Omagh BT79 7EG) has swimming pool, giant water slides, and not forgetting Dr Gurgley's House of Fun indoor adventure play area. The **Woodview Land of Little Animals** features a range of animals and birds which the children can get right neighbourly with. A particularly fine collection of owls is sure to have the youngsters enthralled.

... and how to avoid children

For escaping the stresses of modern life, the rolling county of Tyrone is halfway there – open countryside, spiritual history, and a marked lack of madding crowds; all a tonic on their own. The other half of a recovery programme can be provided by the **Angel Sanctuary Healing Centre** (42 Cashel Road, Greencastle, Omagh BT79 7QJ; ☎ 028 8077 14575; www.angelsanctuary.co.uk). A wide range of complementary therapies are available: reflexology, aromatherapy, colonic hydrotherapy – and general pampering.

The **Wellbeing Spa Health and Beauty Spa** provides much of the same sort of treatment (11 Peacock Road, Sion Mills, Strabane BT82 9NN; ☎ 028 8165 9871; www.wellbeingspa.co.uk). This luxury retreat stands in its own (very private) grounds outside the small village of **Sion Mills**. Wellness treatments as well as straightforward beauty treatments are dispensed with utmost luxury and in utter tranquillity. Should you feel you're in the need of some serious pampering, this is the place.

Entertainment

The **Dun Uladh Centre**, 'Fort of Ulster', is the Ulster headquarters of the *Comhaltas Ceoltorí Éireann*, the body that promotes and looks after traditional music throughout Ireland, Britain and the USA (Ballinamullan, Carrickmore Road, Omagh; ☎ 028 8224 2777; www.comhaltas.com). As such, the centre is used as a cultural base for locals, visiting musicians and interested visitors. Sessions, workshops, concerts, ceili dancing, set dancing and *sean nós* (old style) dancing are all given an outing. **An Creagán Visitor Centre** (see above) presents a full programme of cultural events – traditional music, story telling, Irish dance. **Strule Arts Centre** (Townhall Square, Omagh BT78 1BL; ☎ 028 8224 7831, www.struleartscentre.co.uk) presents everything from plays to pantomime. If you're a country and western fan, consult the programme here regularly – Tyrone is a big country & Irish area, with the likes of Daniel O'Donnell and Philomena Begley ('The queen of country' and mentioned in the Pogues' *A Fairytale of New York*) regularly making appearances.

The premises of **Molly Sweeney's** (28 Gortin Road, Omagh BT79 7HX; ☎ 028 8225 2595) is an entertainment itself: cobbled stones, intricate wood carvings, original mirrors, priceless artefacts, tree rings, delicate ironwork, gothic doorways, Celtic tapestries, hand painted tiles, snugs and historic oaken tables. For more active entertainment, the pub has a nightclub with music, dancing and *craic agus ceol* (basically rock n roll) Wednesdays to Sundays.

Omagh Agricultural Show is a two-day event which takes place in and around Omagh in the first week in July. Traditional music sessions are held every first Thursday of each month in **Felix's Bar**, **Strabane**, on second Fridays in **Christy's Bar**, **Strabane** and on last Tuesdays for learners in **Ballycolman Community Centre**, **Strabane**.

Some of Ireland's best Irish dancers (including several Riverdancers) come from Tyrone. You could try your luck, and footsteps, at the **Melmount Centre** (37 Melmount Road, Strabane BT82 9EF).

Shopping

The **Cavanacaw Gold Mine**, located on a peat bog in the west of the county, is believed to be sitting on top of 14 tonnes of gold. A company called Galantas runs the enterprise, the only gold mine in Ireland. To date, you can't visit the mine – but you can buy beautifully crafted jewellery made from the gold: Hazel Allen Jewellers, 4 Scarffes Entry, Omagh BT78 1JH; ☎ 028 28 8224 2270.

The best... **PLACES TO STAY**

HOTEL

The Hunting Lodge Hotel

1 Letterbin Road, Newtownstewart BT78 4HR
☎ **028 8166 2888**
www.thehuntinglodge.co.uk

This converted 19th-century school house is situated in the heart of the Baronscourt Estate (now part of Northern Ireland Forestry) looking out at Bessy Bell and Mary Gray – no, not two local ladies, but two mountains. Comfortable rooms and great restaurant.

Price: from £70 for a double.

Fir Trees Hotel

Dublin Road, Strabane BT82 9EA
☎ **028 7138 2382**
www.firtreeshotel.net

Standing in its own grounds at the foot of the Sperrins, the Fir Trees has a relaxed and friendly atmosphere. The hotel also has a lively bar and bistro.

Price: Double rooms (inc breakfast) £120.

B&B

Golden Hill Guest House

32 Tattykeel Road, Omagh BT78 5DA
☎ **028 8225 1257**

With panoramic views over four counties, this luxurious family run guest house with five spacious ensuite bedrooms offers all modern facilities.

Price: B&B from £20 per person sharing.

Tattykeel House

115 Doogary Road, Omagh BT79 0BN
☎ **028 8224 9801**

In deepest country, this Georgian-style mansion, is a luxury B&B. Surrounded by two acres of gardens, the atmosphere is rural and restful.

Price: £60 for a double.

SELF-CATERING

Ballinasollus

7 Ballinasollus Road, Plumbridge BT79 8DT
☎ **028 8164 7618**
www.tyrone-cottages.com

Originally built in 1871 in local red sandstone, this cottage has been fully restored and modernised, while retaining its original features. Set in 130 acres of privately owned moorland and heath, with its own river and woods.

Price: from £150 to £200 for a weekend depending on season; £320–£400 for a week.

Grange Court

22–27 Moyle Road, Newtownstewart BT78 4AP
☎ **028 8166 1877**
www.grangecourt.co.uk

A modern, four-star purpose built complex overlooking the Mourne River with 12 spacious, well-furnished apartments.

Price: from £55 to £70 for an apartment per night, £290–£390 for a week; B&B from £25 per person sharing.

The best... PLACES TO STAY

Baronscourt Cottages

The Ferns, Golf Course Road, Newtownstewart BT78 4HU
☎ 028 8166 2360
www.baronscourtcottages.com

An ideal place for the outdoor activities enthusiast – particularly if golf is one of them. These cottages border the Newtownstewart Golf Club and the stunning Baronscourt Estate. The cottages are three star standard, and golf and fishing packages are available.

Price: £200 (low season), £300 (high season) for a week.

An Creagán

Creggan, Omagh BT79 9AF
☎ 028 8076 1112
www.ancreagan.com

Tyrone isn't the most visited area even of the Six Counties, let alone Ireland in general. Yet it is superbly equipped for visitors – Rural Cottages Ireland offer exceptional accommodation at very keen prices, the precious heritage of the county is sensitively handled, and the countryside is pastoral scenery at its very finest. Walking is available from your front door. At An Creagán several cottages are available, and can be booked through Rural Cottage Holidays (☎ 028 9024 1100; www.cottagesinireland.com).

Price: from £180 per cottage for a weekend.

Gortin Accommodation Suite & Activity Centre

62 Main Street, Gortin, Omagh
☎ 028 8164 8346
www.gortin.net

Four star self-catering cottages as well as family rooms and hostel facilities, with many activities onsite – from badminton to bouldering, and from canoeing to abseiling. Other esoteric sports include body boarding, mountain-biking and orienteering.

Price: from £240 to £400 for a week.

HOSTEL

Omagh Hostel at Glenhordial Ecofarm

9a Waterworks Road, Omagh BT79 7JS
☎ 028 8224 1973
www.omaghhostel.co.uk

Family-friendly, self-catering accommodation on a small farm on the edge of the Sperrin Mountains. Omagh Hostel is the first hostel in Northern Ireland to be awarded the EU flower, the European eco-label in the accommodation category.

Price: £12.50 per person per night; £25 for a private single room.

The best... FOOD AND DRINK

▶ Staying in

The **Erganagh Dairy**, Castlederg, is one of the best places to stock up with cheeses, butter, buttermilk, bottled sheep's and goat's milk, and yoghurts (29 Erganagh Road Castlederg; ☎ 028 8167 0626). For first-class victualling, **Mr Eatwell's** (16 Campsie Road, Omagh; ☎ 028 8224 1104) is an amazing complex of fresh produce and cooked foods. Joe McMahon's row of wee shops includes a butcher's shop specialising in local meat of course – especially Aberdeen Angus; it's also hugely popular for sausages, with more than 20 varieties. A small bakery provides your daily soda farls (and wheaten bread and soda scones) and there's a hot food bar and a chip shop.

Camowen Green Organic Farm (42 Camowen Road, Omagh BT79 0HA; ☎ 028 8224 2171) specialises in organic potatoes, seasonal vegetables and beef from prime Aberdeen Angus specimens. The farm has been winner of the Soil Association 'Loraine Award' and in 2008 won first prize in the 'Nature for Farming Award' by the RSPB/Northern Ireland.

EATING OUT

RESTAURANT

The Mellon Country Hotel
134 Beltany Road, Omagh BT79 7BL
☎ 028 8224 5321
www.melloncountryhotel.com

The Mellon Country Hotel is situated on the main A5 road, between Omagh and Newtownstewart. It nestles between Mary Gray and Bessie Bell Mountains, overlooking the Strule River, offering outstanding scenery and views of the Sperrins. The restaurant has won numerous awards for its cuisine, which includes the likes of oven baked Irish salmon, served with orange and crispy bacon salad. Main courses start at around £10.

Oysters
37 Patrick Street, Strabane BT82 8DQ
☎ 028 7138 2690

An intimate, warm restaurant with a menu which uses the best local food. Irish steak from local cattle and a great selection of fish dishes have made Oysters one of the most popular restaurants around.

The Foothills Bar & Restaurant
16 Main Street, Gortin BT79 8PH
☎ 028 8164 8157

Peter Doherty's wine list at the Foothills is both comprehensive and imaginative. Wines from the New World are particularly well represented, and go well with the chef-proprietor's creations. The signature dish is tian of baby prawn and warm garlic crab claws. Glenarm organic salmon with langoustines and spiced risotto will set you back some £15.

GASTRO PUB

The Smugglers Inn Bar & Restaurant
157 Urney Road, Clady BT82 9RP
☎ 028 7188 5004

About 3 miles from Strabane, and situated right on the international border with Donegal, the Smugglers specialises in fresh seafood from nearby (sea) Lough Foyle. A warm and friendly atmosphere, children are specially catered for. For adults, a very good wine list is a feature of the establishment. Mains cost from £11.85 to £15.95.

The Derg Arms
43 Main Street, Castlederg BT81 7AS
☎ 028 8167 1644
www.dergarms.com

A long established family business in one of Northern Ireland's most westerly towns. The cuisine is almost exclusively local produce (the avocados and swordfish have to be brought in) but the beef, salmon and duck are (were) all Tyrone residents. During the summer months – and dusk doesn't arrive here till gone 11 – round the barbecue is a great place to meet the locals. Allow about £15 per head.

CAFÉ

An Creagán
Creggan, Omagh BT79 9AF
☎ 028 8076 1112
www.ancreagan.com

A licensed restaurant in the heart of the Tyrone countryside, An Creagán is an atmospheric place to have lunch or evening dinner. Local produce, good cooking, reasonable prices. Lunch around the £5 mark; main courses in the evening start about £10.

⛏ Drinking

The **Gateway Inn** (1 Glenpark Road, Gortnagarn, Omagh BT79 7SP; www.thegatewayinn. com) is a snug pub in the middle of the village. Renowned for a good pint and great craic. **Farley's** (65 Main Street, Beragh, Omagh; ☎ 028 8075 8227) is a traditional pub with strong GAA links. Tyrone is one of the strongest Gaelic footballing counties, winning the All-Ireland title in 2008. You'll hear plenty of stories about the footballing exploits from Colm the barman. Like the time Tyrone played Armagh in the All-Ireland final in the iconic Croke Park stadium in Dublin – where all All-Ireland finals take place. When roughly 75,000 supporters crossed the border and headed for north Dublin, they were claimed as 'visiting tourists' in Tourism Ireland figures. As you savour your pint you can ponder on this – or prepare for an impromptu traditional music session. One is always liable to break out here.

The **Coach Inn** (1 Railway Terrace, Omagh BT78 5AJ; ☎ 028 8224 3330) has been servicing the thirsty travellers of Ireland for 150 years and more. Its location on the main route from Omagh to Fermanagh has meant that it has always attracted tourists visiting the Lakes of Fermanagh and Donegal. But it's a worthwhile destination in its own right with an inviting bar, good food, and exemplary hospitality. **Harry's Bar** (3 Main Street, Castlederg; ☎ 028 81670946) is a popular place for an afternoon drink or lively night out right in the middle of the town, and often the fulcrum of activities in the surrounding area.

The **Village Inn**, situated 1 mile from Omagh on the Cookstown Road, is now one of the most modern and comfortable lounges in Tyrone. It functions as something of a community centre with everything from music to various types of shows. There is a traditional thatched Irish cottage beside the beer garden that is fully furnished and the only thatched cottage in Northern Ireland with free entry to the public. Perhaps of even more interest to some people – the Village Inn has a late night licence. If you're trekking through the Sperrins, try one of the pubs scattered along the trail – notably **McCrea's** in Glenhull and the **Peddler's Rest** in Gortin.

ℹ️ Visitor Information

Tourist information centre: Omagh Tourist Information Centre, Strule Arts Centre, Townhall Square, Omagh BT78 1BL, ☎ 028 8224 7831.

Hospital: Tyrone County Hospital, Hospital Road, Omagh BT79 0AP, ☎ 028 8283 3100.

Doctor: Gorton Medical Centre, 86 Main St, Gortin, Omagh BT79 8NH, ☎ 028 8164 8216.

Pharmacy: Boots The Chemist, 60–62 Main St, Strabane BT82 8AX, ☎ 028 7138 2916.

Police: Omagh Police Station, 33 Mountjoy Road, Omagh BT79 7BE, ☎ 0845 600 8000.

Supermarkets: Hamilton's Spar, 15 Strabane Road, Newtownstewart, Omagh BT78 4AZ, ☎ 028 8166 1468; Spa, 20 Main Street, Caledon BT68 4TZ, ☎ 028 3756 9792.

Cash points: Abbey, 59 High Street, Omagh BT78 1BA, ☎ 0845 7654321; Halifax, 22 High Street, Omagh BT78 1BQ, ☎ 028 8287 0609.

Taxis: P & L Taxis, 7 Georges Street, Omagh BT78 1DE, ☎ 028 8224 1010.

SOUTH TYRONE

On 5 May 1981, the Speaker of the House of Commons, Mr George Thomas, announced: 'I regret to have to inform the House of the death of Robert Sands Esquire, the member for Fermanagh and South Tyrone.' The Speaker offered no condolences to the family – something traditionally done on the death of a member. Bobby Sands had died on the 66th day of his hunger strike. The South Tyrone and Fermanagh MP had become an honourable member after one of the strangest elections ever to be held in Europe. Sands, then a 27-year-old prisoner, stood against a wealthy Protestant farmer. After a highly polarised campaign, Sands narrowly won the seat on 9 April 1981, with 30,493 votes to 29,046. His subsequent death turned him into a Republican icon.

South Tyrone has always been one of the most strongly nationalist areas in Northern Ireland – its MP today is Sinn Féin representative Michelle Gildernew, although like all Sinn Féin MPs she doesn't take her seat in parliament as that would mean taking an oath to the British Queen. But like the rest of Northern Ireland, there has been peace here for more than 10 years, and without doubt the area's reputation for being the friendliest part of Northern Ireland is well-founded. Likewise its name as one of the most rurally beguiling could hardly be argued with. Bogland and glens, woods and rivers mark out the ancient landscape of South Tyrone. Angling, horse-riding, boating and hiking are the big draws, but cosy villages with even cosier pubs are almost as big a draw.

Driving through southern Tyrone is a relaxing experience, – either to the shores of **Lough Neagh**, the **High Cross of Ardboe**, or through endless soothing drumlin country. As the wind soughs across the great bogland, the remote landscape casts a spell. Richly strewn with stone circles, dolmens and burial chambers, there's probably more history here per square mile than anywhere outside the Middle East.

WHAT TO SEE AND DO

Dungannon

Dungannon, or *Dún Geanainn* (Geann's or Ceanann's Fort), stands on the site of an ancient fortress of the O'Neill's, the Kings of Tir-Owen. Some of the ancient town is left, but the real glory is the remaining 18th-century architecture such as the Royal School (built during the reign of James I) and the buildings round Market Square. Dungannon is famous throughout the golfing world as the home of Darren Clarke – and indeed the home to half a dozen excellent golf courses. Prior to Clarke's rise to prominence, the town's last brush with fame was in 1905 when Bulmer Hobson – a Quaker – founded the Dungannon Cub, a forerunner of Sinn Féin.

Before that, Brigadier General John Nicholson, a pupil at **Dungannon Royal School**, was killed during the Indian Mutiny in 1841. His statue in New Delhi was moved to the town in 1960 – which may have given rise to one of Dungannon's abiding urban legends, concerning one of the town's most notable architectural features – the former

RUC barracks, now a PSNI station. **Dungannon Police Station** is the most curious architectural folly – with turrets, battlements and towers. The reason for this is quite simple – or so the story goes. At the turn of the century, before the British left India, a department of the civil service was employed to furnish plans for municipal buildings throughout the Empire. At one point the department was simultaneously working on plans for both a fort for the Khyber Pass and a police station for Dungannon. Somehow the plans got mixed up, and the Indian fort ended up in County Tyrone, where it stands to this day. Moreover, somewhere in the vast expanse of the frontier between Afghanistan and Pakistan there sits a lonely RUC barracks. It would also be fair to point out that versions of this urban legend exist elsewhere in Ireland and beyond.

Pomeroy
Pomeroy is the highest village in County Tyrone. Its prominent site dominates the surrounding countryside, and is marked out by several church spires. From the **Cookstown** end, the road through the village gradually climbs a gradient up to the middle of the square, The **Diamond**. Here the **Altedesert Church of Ireland** and the Central Bar face each other across the square, where a Market Day (livestock, produce) is held every Tuesday.

The **Central Bar** has a well-documented ghost – not uncommon round these parts. This particularly noisy spirit haunted the attic of the pub some time at the beginning of the 19th century, until the local priest was called in. He duly exorcised the ghost, trapping it in a bottle. The bottle was promptly corked and bricked into a wall in the backyard.

The **Mountains of Pomeroy** are a small range of hills that run west of the town. The mountains have remained in local folk memory because of the famous ballad 'The Mountains of Pomeroy' by Dr George Sigerson, a Strabane man.

I'm an outlawed man in a land forlorn
Who'd rather fight than die
And who's kept the cause of freedom bright
On the Mountains of Pomeroy.

Climbing the Pomeroy Mountains couldn't really be easier. Basically you drive west from the town, park the car wherever you want, and start walking upwards. There are no marked trails, but several well-tramped paths lead up into the mountain – previously used by farmers, sheep, rebels and the odd outlaw.

Cookstown
Cookstown is reckoned to be in the exact geographical centre of Northern Ireland. It's a market town, and still has a good number of old-fashioned pubs, usually full to overflowing on livestock market days in the town.

Through most of its history relatively good relations between Protestants and Catholics have been maintained – the town is just about 50: 50. But during the Troubles (1969–96), Cookstown suffered from several bomb and other attacks, robbing the town centre of most of its Victorian buildings including the sandstone façade of the Hibernian Bank as well as the Adair's former Italianate residence at Glenavon (which had been converted to a hotel).

In 1989, two permanent armed checkpoints were erected at either side of the town centre and an army base was established at Church Street. Barriers were also erected around the town so that the Main Street could be cordoned off in the evening. The 61m spire of the Gothic-style Catholic church on a hill in the middle of the town acts as a wonderful orientation mark, both in the town, and for miles around.

The main street of Cookstown is some 2km long and 50 metres wide with a hump in the middle. This almost ludicrously wide thoroughfare was part of an ambitious plan by William Stewart of Killymoon, an 18th-century Tyrone landlord, to make Cookstown into a major hub of commerce. However, neither he nor his descendants, nor anyone since, got round to developing the town beyond this remarkable central avenue. But none of his descendants could have foreseen the benefit this would have for 21st century Tyrone people – ease of parking in a busy market town. And by the way, don't be fooled by the number of names of streets in the town – they're mostly the main street, which in 2km changes its name seven times.

Nearby is **Killymoon Castle,** a Norman revival pile wherein the Stewarts – see William above – resided in some style. It was designed by John Nash (of London's Regent Street and Brighton Pavilion fame).

The Old Cross of Ardboe

Ardboe, on the shores of Lough Neagh, has been an eel-fishing area for the best part of 5,000 years. The small farms round the lough shore were mostly built by eel fishermen. The history and mechanics of eel fishing are gone into in some detail at the **Kinturk Cultural Centre**.

Nearby, in an old graveyard some dozen miles east of Cookstown stands the best preserved High Cross in the North. The 10th century cross is over 18ft tall with 22 sculptured panels, many of whose Biblical subjects are recognisable, from Adam and Eve to the Last Judgement. There are remnants of two churches 1,000 years different in age (6th and 16th century). At the corner of the graveyard is the Ardboe Pin Tree,

The Old Cross of Ardboe

hammered full of coins. This beech, a votive tree, can intercede on your behalf – as long as you hammer a coin or pin in the tree. Regrettably it hasn't been able to intercede on its own behalf, as all that metal has poisoned the poor thing.

Fishing in South Tyrone

Ardboe is the scene of the *Lughnasa* (Lammas) Fair in August, attended by country people from all over Tyrone and particularly noted for the quality of traditional music on offer.

Fishing and golf

Most of South Tyrone has facilities for fishing. The **Ballinderry River** flows east through Cookstown and into Lough Neagh, and is regarded by anglers as one of the best trout rivers in Ulster as well as being good for salmon and dollaghan. Anglers can also enjoy **Lough Fea**, a lake covering some 180 acres, and particularly renowned for brown trout and rainbow trout; **Lough Bracken** is good for pike and perch, and **Camlough** for wild brown trout. **Lough Neagh**, the largest lake in the British Isles, covers an area of 153sq miles.

Newport Trench, some 2km north of Ardboe is a good place to catch pollan, a delicious fish peculiar to Lough Neagh and Lough Erne. The little quay is an excellent place for a picnic or swim. **Stewartstown Lough**, between Dungannon and Cookstown, has yielded perch of a size to equal the British record. To fish any of the waters in the district you have to have a rod licence. For club waters a permit will also be required – you can get that from the specific club (see list below for clubs in the area that welcome visitors).

- Cookstown Tourist Information Centre – Burn Road, Cookstown BT80 8DN; ☎ 028 8676 9949; www.cookstown.gov.uk
- Fisheries Conservancy Board Northern Ireland ☎ 028 3833 4666; www.fcbni.com; further information on fishing in Northern Ireland, Ballinderry Bridge Angling Club – ☎ 028 7941 8779
- Coagh Angling Club – ☎ 028 8673 7085
- Mace Shop, Coagh – ☎ 028 8673 6824
- Kings Bridge Angling Club – ☎ 028 8676 5905

- Kildress Angling Club – ☎ 028 8676 3809
- Mid Ulster Angling Club – ☎ 028 8673 6558
- Tullylagan Angling Club – Tullylagan Filling Station; ☎ 028 8676 5021
- Tullylagan Hotel – ☎ 028 8676 5100

KILLYMOON GOLF CLUB: Cookstown; ☎ 028 8676 3762; www.killymoongolfclub.com. Contact resident professional Gary Chambers on 028 8676 3460; or try **SLATE GOLF CLUB:** ☎ 028 8775 8747; www.slategolfclub.com. Privately-owned; nine-hole, takes bookings for groups.

Darren Clarke learnt his trade in the parkland courses of South Tyrone, and Denis Taylor – from Coalisland and former Snooker World Champion enjoys a round of golf here. **Killymoon Golf Club**, Cookstown, founded in 1889, is set on high ground skirting the woods of Killymoon Castle. Visitors are welcome although days to avoid are Saturday until after 4.00pm and Thursdays (Ladies' Day).

Walking

The **Lough Fea walk** starts from the main car park on the B162 Cookstown to Draperstown Road. The circular route follows the shores of the Lough, finishing back at the car park. The route can be followed either way around the shores and is clearly marked. The **Ballinderry River** walk – look out for kingfishers – starts at Killucan Picnic Site car park cross the footbridge over the Ballinderry River and turn left following the riverside path. This is a beautiful, peaceful stroll along this famous fishing river. Nearby, the stone circles of **Beaghmore** date back to the Bronze Age – and may have served as a prehistoric temple. These are just to the west of **Lough Fea**, in a remote, spellbinding area. It was originally believed that these stones had something to do with astronomy (or astrology) but the thinking now is that the structure served some function in fertility rites.

Knockmany Passage Grave, or **Annia's Cove**, is about a mile north-west of Augher and on the summit of Knockmany at the top of the Forest Park – another good walk. The Cairn at the top gives you a spectacular view across the Clogher valley. Funny thing about those ancient Irish farmers – they obviously valued a good view as much as we do. A wonderful place to see the unique boglands of mid-Ulster is **Peatlands Country Park**. Boardwalks are provided for walking across the bogs so you can see the wild flowers up close. A narrow gauge railway trundles across the bog, giving superb views of this strange, black landscape.

PEATLANDS COUNTRY PARK: 33 Derryhubbert Road, Dungannon BT71 6NW; ☎ 028 3885 1102. Entry: free; trip on the narrow gauge railway: adults £1, children 50p.

Charles Wolfe's Memorial

Outside the graveyard of the 17th-century **Parish Church in Castlecaulfield** a blue plaque commemorates the poet Charles Wolfe (1791–1823), who was curate here

LOCAL KNOWLEDGE

Dr Martin Clancy, originally from Tipperary, now splits his time between County Louth and County Tyrone. And for a very specific reason. Dr Clancy, who originally qualified in agriculture, has taken part in various archeological digs throughout Ireland, and is intrigued by the megalithic culture and artefacts to be found in Tyrone.

Favourite restaurant – Hard to say – if I had time I'd drive over to McNean's in Blacklion. It's not just the best restaurant in County Cavan, it's the best restaurant in Ireland. And for a nice Sunday lunch the Royal Hotel in Cookstown is a great place.

Secret tip for lunch – Sally's Restaurant in Aughnacloy. A friendly, family restaurant-cum-deli.

Favourite activity – Walking with my friends in the boglands or the hills on a Sunday afternoon, then stopping off at some wee pub along the way for a feed of pints.

Best view – The Old Cross of Ardboe, and Lough Neagh. There are probably more spectacular views but they'd be hard put to be more atmospheric.

Favourite shop – I don't really like shopping at all. I can even need something in a shop and not be able to go in. I suppose any second hand bookshop might be an exception.

Quirkiest attraction – What used to be the RUC barracks in Dungannon, now the PSNI station. They reckon whoever designed it also designed a fort in India, and the plans got mixed up. Which is why it looks so outré.

and of Donaghmore between 1818 and 1821. His famous lines on 'The Burial of Sir John Moore after Corunna' were published in the *Newry Telegraph* in 1817.

> *Not a drum was heard, not a funeral note*
> *As his corse to the rampart hurried.*

In the south transept of the church is the grave of the Rev George Walker, Rector of Donaghmore from 1674. Better known as the Governor of Londonderry during the Great Siege, he was eventually killed at the Battle of the Boyne.

☂ Wet weather

The Argory, a neo-classical Irish gentry house virtually unchanged since 1900, overlooks the Blackwater River. The former home of the MacGeough-Bond family, the house contains its original furniture and a fabulous cabinet barrel organ. The splendid stable yard is still lit by an original 1906 acetylene gas plant. Outside, 320 acres of formal gardens and lime and yew walks lead down to the lazily-flowing Blackwater. No wonder our old friend Anon felt moved to write the poignant love song 'It was down by Blackwaterside':

> *One evening fair I took the air*
> *Down by Blackwaterside*
> *'Twas gazing all around me*
> *When the Irish lad I spied*
> *All through the first part of that night*
> *We did lie in sport and play,*
> *When this young man arose and he*
> *gathered his clothes,*
> *Saying, 'fare thee well today.'*

The Argory

THE ARGORY: Derrycaw, 144 Derrycaw Road, Moy, Dungannon, BT71 6NA, 028 8778 4753, www.nationaltrust.org.uk/theargory. Entry: adults £5.50, children £2.80; open daily all year round.

⚄ What to do with children

Toddsleap is a purpose-built off-road activity set among 100 acres of picturesque countryside in Ballygawley that offers a range of activities including quad biking and paintballing; the older children can even have a go at archery. Log cabins on site provide a nice place for the adults to escape to with the paper; snacks, breakfast and lunch are included in package deals.

> **TODDSLEAP:** 30 Todds Leap Road, Ballygawley BT70 2BW; ☎ 028 8556 7435; www.toddsleap.com. Entry: family package with lunch and off-road driving, climbing wall and archery is £250.

⚄ Entertainment

South Tyrone is renowned for its traditional music. Sessions take place in:

* **JT's Place** – Coalisland; Mondays from 10.30pm-ish
* The **Belfast House** – Cookstown; on Mondays
* **Kelly's** – Cookstown; Sunday evenings
* The **Lark's Bar** – Dungannon; Thursday and Sunday
* **Roper's** – Dungannon; Tuesdays
* **Tomney's** – The Square, The Moy; Fridays
* **McLoughlin's Bar** – The Moy; Saturday evenings
* The **Auction Rooms** – The Moy; Thursdays
* **The Central Bar** – Coalisland; Sundays 6–9pm
* **The Fort Inn** – Scotch Street, Dungannon; Sundays 6–9pm
* **Bank House** – Irish Street, Dungannon; Sundays 2–5pm.
* **Kelly's Inn** – 232 Omagh Road, Garvaghy, Ballygawley; ☎ 028 8556 8218; Fridays and Saturdays
* **Quinn's Corner** – Edencrannon; ☎ 028 8776 7529; live rock music at the weekend, traditional music during the week

The Burnavon Arts & Cultural Centre

The **Burnavon Arts and Cultural Centre** (Burn Road, Cookstown BT80 8DN; ☎ 028 8676 7994; www.burnavon.com) presents a wide range of entertainment throughout the year including concerts (local and national artistes), comedy, children's performances, dance, drama, community and visual arts.

🛒 Shopping

The art of crystal making in the county can trace its beginnings back 200 years to a site near Dungannon. **Tyrone Crystal** was set up by Father Austin Eustace to provide employment for young people in the local community. With a couple of old cutting wheels and a pile of empty whiskey bottles and jam jars to practise on, a small group of trainees began learning their new trade. A factory was built, furnaces were installed and a master blower was brought from Austria to train the young workforce. Commercial production began and Tyrone Crystal soon arrived in the premier league of crystal manufacture. Today, it's situated in Kilbrackey just outside the town, only 2 miles from the original glasshouse, founded in 1771. Conducted tours are available, and of course opportunities to buy the wares. An Antrim Tyrone wine glass will set-back about £32, while a top-of-the-range wine decanter is round the £190 mark.

TYRONE CRYSTAL VISITOR CENTRE:
Killbrackey, Dungannon; ☎ 028 8772 5335; www.tyronecrystal.com. Tours: £5, concessions £2.50; open Mon–Sat 9–5pm.

Tyrone Crystal

The best... **PLACES TO STAY**

HOTEL

The Valley Hotel

60 Main Street BT75 0PW; Fivemiletown BT75 0PW
☎ **028 8952 1505**
www.thevalleyhotel.com

This small, family-run, three-star hotel offers excellent service, award-winning cuisine and comfortable, attractive accommodation. Every room is triple-glazed, with broadband wireless internet access. The traditional cooked Irish breakfast is famous throughout the locality.

Price: from £90 for a double.

Glenavon House Hotel

52 Drum Road, Cookstown BT80 8JQ
☎ **028 8676 4949**

Situated on the banks of the Ballinderry River this three-star hotel is friendly, comfortable and ideally situated for exploring South Tyrone.

Price: from £70 for a double.

Bank House Hotel

68 Irish Street, Dungannon BT70 1DQ
☎ **028 8772 8080**

This three-star boutique-style hotel occupies Bank House, originally a private residence before becoming home to three different banks. Today the hotel is an elegant characterful hostelry.

Price: £99 for a double.

Corick House

20 Corick Road, Clogher BT76 0BZ
☎ **028 8554 8216**
www.corickcountryhouse.com

Nineteen luxury rooms, a bar, restaurant and lounge in a 17th-century country house, and outside the peaceful unspoilt countryside of south Tyrone. The cuisine in the Carleton Restaurant is renowned for its imaginative treatment of local produce.

Price: from £50 per person for a double.

The Tullylagan Country House Hotel

40B Tullylagan Road, Cookstown BT80 8UP
☎ **028 8676 5100**
www.tullylagan.co.uk

A hotel set in truly beautiful surroundings, this is as relaxing a place as you could hope to find. The cuisine is justifiably renowned.

Price: from £90 for a double.

UNUSUAL

Grange Lodge

Grange Road, Dungannon BT71 7EJ
☎ **028 8778 4212**
www.grangelodgecountryhouse.com

Norah Brown runs cookery courses teaching people how to cook using seasonal produce. A non-residential half-day session costs about £75 – with accommodation, £199 per person based on two sharing. The 18th-century house has five bedrooms, all individual, with lots of little extras. Grange Lodge is full of character, set in beautiful surroundings.

Price: from £60 for a single; from £89 for a double.

The best... FOOD AND DRINK

▶ Staying in

Tyrone farmers' market takes place on the first Saturday of every month in Tesco's car park, Dungannon, and on the third Saturday of every month at Market Square, Dungannon. The market offers excellent produce ranging from home-baked Ulster breads to local cheeses and meats – and not forgetting apple juice from neighbouring Armagh. Farmers and shops that supply produce at the markets include:

- **Cloughbane Farm Shop** – 160 Tanderagee Road, Dungannon BT70 3HS; ☎ 028 8775 8246; supplies beef and lamb from their own farm, and locally produced pork and chicken
- **Good Things Farm Kilnageer** – Emyvale, Co. Monaghan; ☎ 00353 4787865; fresh fruit and vegetables organically produced using horticultural farming methods
- **Linda's Bakery** – 53 Tartlaghan Road, Bush, Dungannon BT71 6QR; ☎ 028 8772 5251; some of the best homebaking in the vicinity
- **Farm Vegetables** – 141 Collegeland Road, Moy, Dungannon BT71 6SW; ☎ 028 8778 4786; fruit and vegetables fresh from the farm
- **Kiltermon Country Bakes** – 93 Ballagh Road, Kiltermon, Fivemiletown BT75 0LD; devilishly tempting homemade breads, pastries and cakes

Fivemiletown, as it happens, isn't 5 miles from anywhere. But it used to be. In days gone by an Irish mile was 2,240 yards, as opposed to the more modest 1,760 yards of the British mile. The 5 miles in question were from Fivemiletown to Clogher, Brookeborough and Tempo. The town is most famous today for the **Fivemiletown Creamery** (14 Ballylurgan Road, Fivemiletown BT75 0RX; ☎ 028 8952 1209) a small, farmer-owned cooperative (established in 1898) that has a long tradition of producing exceptional dairy products (their herds roam the lush pastures of the Clogher Valley), with distinctive cheeses being a speciality. Particularly recommended is the Ballyoak cheese, slowly smoked in a kiln using sustainably foraged oakwood from the local and enchanting Forest of Caledon. Other signature cheeses include the blue-veined Ballyblue or the goat's milk brie.

EATING OUT

RESTAURANT

Stangmore Town House
24 Killyman Road, Dungannon BT71 6DH
☎ **028 8772 5600**
www.stangmoretownhouse.com

Chef-proprietor Andy Brace uses top-quality local produce to create breakfast, lunch and dinner of exquisite standard. The restaurant is a member of the Tyrone Good Food Circle, and its use of produce from local farm shops means you will be tucking into the likes of Cloughbane Farm lamb with sweet and sour aubergine or Sperrin Valley ice cream, with homemade shortbread. Around £11 for a main course.

Viscount's Restaurant
10 Northland Row, Dungannon BT7 16AP
☎ **028 8775 3800**
www.viscountsrestaurant.co.uk

Situated in a listed building – in the former Drumglass Parish Hall – the foundation stone of which was laid by the eponymous Viscount Lord Northland. The décor gives maximum impact as well – warm maroon drapes, banners embossed with gold heraldic design, and beautiful old furniture all add to the medieval setting. The restaurant enjoys a terrific reputation locally, partly because prices are reasonable – the two-course early evening meal (Mon–Fri 5pm–6.30) is £11.95.

The Otter Lodge
26 Dungannon Road, Cookstown BT80 8TL
☎ **028 8676 5472**
www.otterlodge.com

One of the best eateries in the area, Harold Moffen's award-winning bistro specialises in local food prepared imaginatively. Fish take a starring role. Main dishes cost around £9.

Salley's Restaurant
90 Moore Street, Aughnacloy BT69 6AA
☎ **028 8555 7064**

In the quaint village of Aughnacloy, this family-run eatery has been feeding the hungry folk of South Tyrone for more than 30 years. Home-cooked dishes are served from 10am to 10pm. Dishes cost from £5.

CAFÉ

The Courtyard Restaurant
56a William Street, Cookstown BT80 8NB
☎ **028 8676 5070**

This award winning café/restaurant in Cookstown town centre specialises in home cooking and baking. Run by two sisters, the Courtyard is a wonderful stopping off place during the day. Try the vegetable soup and wheaten bread for a lunch that'll set you up until dinner-time. Only open 8am–5.15pm, the salad bar uses entirely local produce from the local market. Full meals from £5.

🍺 Drinking

For a quiet pint, a snack or a full meal, **Quinn's Corner** (175 Ballygawley Road, Donaghmore, Dungannon BT70 1RX; ☎ 028 8776 1158) is an ideal stopping off place in the middle of Dungannon. **Askin's** (50–56 Main Street, Ballygawley BT70 2HL; ☎ 028 8556 8910, www.eatdrinksfortywinks.com) is a lively bar, restaurant and hotel. Eddie Quinn, proprietor and third generation of the family to run the establishment ensures that good service comes with craic and value. President Bill Clinton has been in here for a pint.

The **Royal Hotel** in the centre of Cookstown (64–72 Coagh Street; ☎ 028 8676 2224; www.theroyal-hotel.com) is something of an institution – the place to meet friends, have a business meeting, or just while away the morning with a copy of the day's newspaper. **Murphy's Bar** (64–66 Main Street, Pomeroy, Dungannon BT70 2QH; ☎ 028 8775 9766) is a family run pub on the main street, Pomeroy. A traditional public bar at the front is just the place for a contemplative pint. Great Guinness, good craic, and the perfect place to catch up on sports results (when they talk about 'football' in these parts, they mean Gaelic football).

ℹ️ Visitor Information

Tourist information centres: Omagh Tourist Information Centre, Strule Arts Centre, Townhall Square, Omagh BT78 1BL, ☎ 028 8224 7831 (same as North Tyrone), this is the main tourist office in the county.

Hospital: South Tyrone Hospital, Carland Road, Dungannon BT71 4AU; ☎ 028 8772 2821.

Doctor: Parkview Surgery, South Tyrone Hospital Site, Carland Road, Dungannon BT71 4AU, ☎ 028 8772 2019.

Pharmacies: Baird's, 2–4 Market Square, Dungannon BT70 1AB; ☎ 028 8772 2761.

Police: Dungannon Police Station, 1 Quarry Lane, Dungannon BT70 1HX; ☎ 028 8775 2525; Clogher Police Station, 13 Main Street, Clogher BT76 0AA, ☎ 028 8554 8567.

Supermarkets: Curly's Supermarket, The Oak Centre, Dungannon BT71 4NA, ☎ 028 8772 1933.

Parking: Dungannon is the only town in South Tyrone where you will need to pay to park; charges run from 50p an hour in most areas.

ATMs: There are three cash points in the Oak Centre, Dungannon.

Bike rental: Clogher Valley Cycles, 29 Main Street, Augher BT77 0BD, ☎ 028 8554 9802.

Taxis: Seamus McElroy, Clogher, ☎ 028 8554 8597; Desi's Taxis, 27 Cookstown Road BT1 4BG, ☎ 028 8772 7828; PJ Fox, 30 Drumlee Road, Dungannon BT71 7QD.

INDEX